Frommer's

P9-ELT-491

Prague & the Best of the Czech Republic

6th Edition

by Hana Mastrini

Here's what the critics say about Frommer's:

"Amazingly easy to use. Very portable, very complete."

—*Booklist*

"Detailed, accurate, and easy-to-read information for all price ranges."
—*Glamour Magazine*

"Hotel information is close to encyclopedic."

—*Des Moines Sunday Register*

"Frommer's Guides have a way of giving you a real feel for a place."
—*Knight Ridder Newspapers*

WILEY

Wiley Publishing, Inc.

About the Author

Hana Mastrini is a native of the western Czech spa town of Karlovy Vary who became a veteran of the "Velvet Revolution" as a student in Prague in 1989. She is a co-author of *Frommer's Europe* and *Frommer's Europe by Rail*.

Published by:

Wiley Publishing, Inc.

111 River St.
Hoboken, NJ 07030

ISBN-13: 978-0-471-77266-8
ISBN-10: 0-471-77266-6

Editor: Lesley S. King
Production Editor: Jana M. Stefanciosa
Cartographer: Tim Lohnes
Photo Editor: Richard Fox
Production by Wiley Indianapolis Composition Services

Front cover photo: Close-up of face of astronomical clock.
Back cover photo: St. Vitus Cathedral: Stained glass windows with Art Nouveau Mucha designs.

For information on our other products and services or to obtain technical support, please contact our Customer Care Department within the U.S. at 800/762-2974, outside the U.S. at 317/572-3993 or fax 317/572-4002.

Wiley also publishes its books in a variety of electronic formats. Some content that appears in print may not be available in electronic formats.

Manufactured in the United States of America

5 4 3 2 1

Contents

9   Prague Shopping   165

10   Prague After Dark   177

11   Day Trips from Prague   194

12   The Best of Bohemia   214

List of Maps

An Invitation to the Reader

In researching this book, we discovered many wonderful places—hotels, restaurants, shops, and more. We're sure you'll find others. Please tell us about them, so we can share the information with your fellow travelers in upcoming editions. If you were disappointed with a recommendation, we'd love to know that, too. Please write to:

Frommer's Prague & the Best of the Czech Republic, 6th Edition
Wiley Publishing, Inc. • 111 River St. • Hoboken, NJ 07030

An Additional Note

Please be advised that travel information is subject to change at any time—and this is especially true of prices. We therefore suggest that you write or call ahead for confirmation when making your travel plans. The authors, editors, and publisher cannot be held responsible for the experiences of readers while traveling. Your safety is important to us, however, so we encourage you to stay alert and be aware of your surroundings. Keep a close eye on cameras, purses, and wallets, all favorite targets of thieves and pickpockets.

Other Great Guides for Your Trip:

Frommer's Europe

Frommer's Europe from $70 a Day

Frommer's Gay & Lesbian Europe

Europe For Dummies

Hanging Out in Europe

Frommer's Budapest & the Best of Hungary

Frommer's Star Ratings, Icons & Abbreviations

Every hotel, restaurant, and attraction listing in this guide has been ranked for quality, value, service, amenities, and special features using a **star-rating system.** In country, state, and regional guides, we also rate towns and regions to help you narrow down your choices and budget your time accordingly. Hotels and restaurants are rated on a scale of zero (recommended) to three stars (exceptional). Attractions, shopping, nightlife, towns, and regions are rated according to the following scale: zero stars (recommended), one star (highly recommended), two stars (very highly recommended), and three stars (must-see).

In addition to the star-rating system, we also use **seven feature icons** that point you to the great deals, in-the-know advice, and unique experiences that separate travelers from tourists. Throughout the book, look for:

Finds	Special finds—those places only insiders know about
Fun Fact	Fun facts—details that make travelers more informed and their trips more fun
Kids	Best bets for kids and advice for the whole family
Moments	Special moments—those experiences that memories are made of
Overrated	Places or experiences not worth your time or money
Tips	Insider tips—great ways to save time and money
Value	Great values—where to get the best deals

The following **abbreviations** are used for credit cards:

AE	American Express	DISC	Discover	V	Visa
DC	Diners Club	MC	MasterCard		

Frommers.com

Now that you have the guidebook to a great trip, visit our website at **www.frommers.com** for travel information on more than 3,000 destinations. With features updated regularly, we give you instant access to the most current trip-planning information available. At Frommers.com, you'll also find the best prices on airfares, accommodations, and car rentals—and you can even book travel online through our travel booking partners. At Frommers.com, you'll also find the following:

- Online updates to our most popular guidebooks
- Vacation sweepstakes and contest giveaways
- Newsletter highlighting the hottest travel trends
- Online travel message boards with featured travel discussions

What's New in Prague & the Czech Republic

The best parts of Prague have remained unchanged for hundreds of years, but fortunately for visitors, what have improved steadily since the 1989 revolution are the quality and the number of available services. The Internet age has also made the city more accessible. Below are some of the best new ways to plug into Prague, as well as other notable changes of interest to visitors.

PLANNING A TRIP TO PRAGUE The Prague-based firm **E-Travel** has developed a website, **www.travel.cz**, for general Czech tourist information and accommodations. They've also developed **www.apartments.cz** for booking private apartments online. Start any trip planning here. Helpful information can also be found on the official site of the Czech Republic at **www.czech.cz** or the Czech Foreign Ministry site at **www.mzv.cz**. For general tips, check out the Prague Information Service at **www.pis.cz** or **www.prague-info.cz**.

Documents: Citizens of the U.S., Canada, Australia, and New Zealand need no visa for stays less than 90 days. Their passports must be valid for a period of at least 90 days beyond the expected length of stay in the Czech Republic. Nationals from the United Kingdom and Ireland (and all European Union countries) can travel to the Czech Republic with passports (validity is not limited) and they are allowed to stay for an unlimited period of time.

Children inscribed in their parents' passports can travel with their parents up to the age of 15. Once the child has reached the age of 15, a separate passport is necessary.

After 40 years the city's **Prague Information Service (PIS)** has just recently closed its location at Na Příkopě 20, Praha 1. The new one will welcome tourists and visitors at Vodičkova 36, Praha 1 (the Lucerna Passage) ((*C* 12 444; www.pis.cz), and will offer travel advice, tickets, souvenirs, and maps.

WHERE TO STAY & DINE   Accommodations The latest addition to Prague's list of luxury hotels is the Hotel Aria, Tržiště 9, Praha 1 ((*C* 225-334-111). Situated right in the middle of Malá Strana, this hotel will be appreciated especially by those who love music. Modern trends in interior decorations are sensitively combined in this historic building with a musical theme in each room. Don't miss a meal or drink in its roof terrace bar and restaurant, which offers magnificent views of this picturesque neighborhood.

Dining Střelecký Ostrov, Střelecký ostrov 336, Praha 1 ((*C* 224-934-026), a new addition to Prague's fine dining, offers Czech and international cuisine in a great location on an island of the Vltava River under the Legií Bridge. This island was flooded in summer of 2002 and the original popular Ostroff restaurant here has been destroyed. Now it is back with a new management, its brick-cellar dining room with a cozy atmosphere as well as a riverside terrace bar with magnificent views of the river and the National Theater.

On the bank of the Vltava, at Masarykovo nábřeží 2, Praha 2, **Don Pedro** (© **224-923-505**) offers quesadillas, chimichangas, and fried yucca, among other exotic meals on its menu. If you are looking for a purely Czech pub experience, visit the remodeled **U Vejvodů** Restaurant at Jilská 4, Praha 1 (© **224-219-999**). In this Old Town building dating from the 15th century comes traditional Czech roasted pork with cabbage and bread dumplings, or homemade goulash, probably the best in town. All is accompanied with the world-known Pilsner Urquell beer.

EXPLORING PRAGUE Before you start strolling around the city, consider buying an all-inclusive ticket, the Prague Card, to save money on entrance fees. It is valid for 3 days and allows you to visit up to 40 attractions, including Prague Castle. You'll find a full list of sights and more information at www.praguecard.biz. The Prague Card is available at the Čedok office, Na Příkopě 18, Praha 1, or at the PIS office, at the City Hall, Staroměstskénáměstí. 1, Praha 1, and from many travel agents and hotels as well.

On the embankment of the Vltava, in the recently reconstructed Hergetova Cihelna building, the **Franz Kafka Museum,** Cihelná 2b, Praha 1 (© **257-535-507**), shows manuscripts, photographs, and letters of this enigmatic author of the 20th century. The exhibition focuses mainly on the enormous influence of Prague on Kafka's life and work.

ESPECIALLY FOR KIDS Check out the **Mořský svět (Sea World),** Výstaviště, Praha 7 (© **220-103-275**), and escape into a unique world of the tropical sea and its fish. This family-friendly exhibition, which houses the largest aquarium in the country, has become a popular spot.

SHOPPING & AFTER DARK The new shopping mall **Obchodní Centrum Nový Smíchov,** Plzeňská 8, Praha 5 (© **251-511-151**), houses several shops and boutiques as well as an entertainment center. Names such as Benetton, Guess, Zara, Next, and Swatch now welcome you at this site, where thousands of Praguers used to toil at the Tatra Smíchov heavy machine factory. The fourth floor offers entertainment in a bowling center, Equinoxe, along with a modern complex of cinemas and dining in several restaurants, pizzerias, and a sports bar.

BOHEMIA Where to Dine in Karlovy Vary Strolling around a spa town can be a bit tiring. The **XXX long** restaurant, at Vřídelní 23 (© **353-224-232**), is a place for a break. Italian and international cuisine, including pizza, is served in this fresh addition to the town's dining spots.

Where to Dine in České Budějovice The chain of restaurants owned by the Prague brewery Staropramen has spread to southern Bohemia. Its **Potrefeń husa** can be now found also at Česká 29 (© **387-420-560**). And as in Prague, no one will be disappointed here since there is always a wide selection at reasonable prices.

Where to in Stay Tábor What used to be a brewery in the Kotnov Castle complex in Tábor is now a new **Hotel Dvořák** at Hradební 3037 (© **381-251-290**). This historical building has been carefully reconstructed to keep its exterior and architectural character, including a towering memorial to beer making, a huge brick chimney. A colorful modern interior and pleasant staff make this hotel an inviting base for the exploration of southern Bohemia.

MORAVIA Visitor Information in Brno The new **Turistické Informační Centrum (TIC)** at Radnická 8 (© **542-211-090**) provides advice to visitors, maps, souvenirs, and tickets, as well as accommodations and travel service. Its second branch is open at Nádražní 8 (© 542-214-450), just across the street from the train station.

Strolling around Brno You can now visit a permanent exhibition at the **Brno City Museum,** Špilberk 1 (© 542-123-611) called "Jail of Nations," which pays tribute to those who once stood against the Habsburg monarchy or the Nazi occupation.

1

The Best of Prague

Prague has survived many crises, but the floods of August 2002 threatened to ruin centuries of culture and history forever. Happily, the waters were no match for the robust landmarks and iron will of the people of this ancient kingdom, and the city is back, better than ever.

Here, the last 1,000 years of triumphs in art and architecture have collided, often violently, with power politics and religious conflicts. While Bohemia has been the fulcrum of wars over the centuries, it has settled into a post–Cold War peace, spiked with a rough transition to a capitalist economy.

While Prague's rich collection of Gothic, baroque, and Renaissance buildings has stood stoically through all the strife, the streets and squares fronting the grand halls have often been the stages for tragedy. The well-worn cobblestones have felt the hooves of kings' horses, the jackboots of Hitler's armies, the heaving wheels of Soviet tanks, and the shuffling feet of students in passive revolt. Today they're jammed with armies of visitors jostling for space to experience the aura of "Golden Prague" only to be bombarded with peddlers trying to make a quick buck or mark (or crown when the home currency is stable).

The spaghetti-strand alleys winding through Old Town have become so inundated with visitors during high season that they now resemble an intricate network of trails for scurrying ants. This town wasn't built for mass tourism.

The lifting of the iron curtain after 1989's bloodless "Velvet Revolution," one of a flurry of citizens' revolts ending Communist rule in Eastern Europe, has attracted many Westerners, who can finally come search for the secrets of the other side. But the city sees itself as the westernmost of former East Bloc capitals, and Praguers wince when they hear the term "Eastern Europe" used to describe their home.

Conflicts past and present give the city an eclectic energy. The atmosphere continually reminds us that monarchs and dictators have tried to possess this city for much of the past millennium.

THE CITY OF A THOUSAND SPIRES

Viewed from high atop Vyšehrad, the 10-centuries-old citadel at the city's south end, the ancient city of Prague hugs the hills rising from the river Vltava (Moldau, as it is commonly known from the German). Rows of steeples stacked on onion domes pierce the sky, earning Prague the moniker "The City of a Thousand Spires"—an inaccurate title. I've counted many more.

Sadly, in the 4 decades of vacuous Communist rule, the city's classical heart was infected by faceless architecture and neglect. Now, while new owners clean up the grime on decaying masterpieces and rebuild facades on many forgettable follies, the city is recapturing its more avant-garde tastes. Regrettably, a new army of self-commissioned "artists" has laid siege with another weapon: graffiti. The *sprejer* (sprayer) problem is the latest chapter in Prague's cyclical battle of moderating freedom against repression—a conundrum Czech expatriate author Milan Kundera recounted in *The Unbearable Lightness of Being* (see "Recommended Films & Books," in appendix A).

The Czech Republic was branded an economic miracle in the early years of the transformation to a free-market economy, but an experiment in rapid privatization of Communist-era companies led to a massive wave of corruption, turning the dream into a nightmare for many.

Thanks in part to tourism, Prague has been spared the worst impact of a deep recession in the late 1990s, although you should be forewarned that the Czech currency, the crown, remains very volatile, and its value fluctuation can significantly affect the price of your stay (see "The Czech Koruna," in chapter 2).

But while Prague's rebirth has come with labor pains of inflation, traffic jams (with new Western cars), and the ever-present pounding of construction crews, the stately spires of this living baroque and medieval museum rise above it all. Despite the furious development and reconstruction popping up all over, the classical monuments remain the city's bedrock. Prague Castle's reflection in the Vltava or the mellow nighttime glow of the lanterns around the 18th-century Stavovské Divadlo (Estates' Theater) gives the city a Mozart-really-was-here feel.

1 The Most Unforgettable Travel Experiences

- **Strolling Across Charles Bridge at Dawn or Dusk:** The silhouettes of the statues lining the 6-centuries-old crown jewel of Czech heritage hover like ghosts in the still of the sunrise skyline. Early in the morning you can stroll across the bridge without encountering the crowds that appear by midday. With the changing light of dusk, the statues, the bridge, and the city panorama take on a whole different character. See "Walking Tour 1: Charles Bridge & Malá Strana (Lesser Town)" in chapter 8.

- **Making Your Own Procession Down the Royal Route:** The downhill jaunt from Prague Castle, through Malá Strana (Lesser Town), and across Charles Bridge to Old Town Square, is a day in itself. The trip recalls the route taken by the carriages of the Bohemian kings; today it's lined with quirky galleries, shops, and cafes. See chapter 4.

- **Taking a Slow Boat Down the Vltava:** You can see many of the most striking architectural landmarks from the low-angle and low-stress vantage point of a rowboat you pilot yourself. At night, you can rent a dinghy with lanterns for a very romantic ride. See "Sightseeing Options" in chapter 7.

- **Stepping into History at Karlštejn Castle:** A 30-minute train ride south of Prague puts you in the most visited Czech landmark in the environs,

---

Impressions

Your struggle to preserve what you have inherited, and to reintegrate it into the values and character of the society you are rebuilding, is a struggle you must win, or there will not be much hope for any of us.
          —Prince Charles to Prague's leaders (May 1991)

The Czech and Slovak Republics

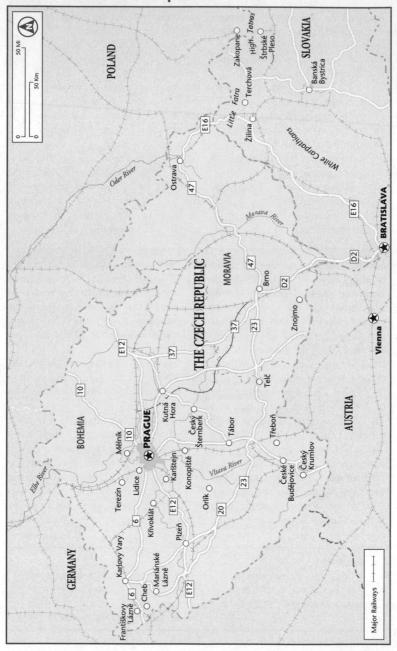

built by Charles IV (Karel IV in Czech—the namesake of Charles Bridge) in the 14th century to protect the Holy Roman Empire's crown

jewels. This Romanesque hilltop bastion fits the image of the castles of medieval lore. See chapter 11.

2 The Best Splurge Hotels

- **Four Seasons Hotel** (Veleslavínova 2a, Praha 1; ℂ 221-427-000): The best luxury Old Town hotel with the best view of Prague Castle and Charles Bridge. If price isn't a concern, choose a room at this new addition to the luxury-hotel list with its unbeatable location. See p. 69.

- **Hotel Savoy** (Keplerova 6, Praha 1; ℂ 224-302-430): An opulent but tasteful small hotel that suggests London more than Prague. Enjoy afternoon tea and a library where you can read by a crackling fire when it's cold outside. See p. 63. The Savoy also houses the **Best Hotel Restaurant,** the **Hradčany,** with exceptionally delicate and innovative Continental cuisine. See p. 84.

- **Hotel Paříž** (U Obecního domu 1, Praha 1; ℂ 222-195-195): This

restored Art Nouveau hotel recalls 1920s Prague, one of the wealthiest cities on earth at that time. It's across from another newly remodeled gem, the Municipal House (Obecní dům). See p. 70.

- **Hotel Aria** (Tržiště 9, Praha 1; ℂ 225-334-111): A new luxurious hotel opened in the heart of Malá Strana just around the corner from the St. Nicholas Cathedral. Its melodious theme will especially please music lovers. See p. 67.

- **Hotel Josef** (Rybná 20, Praha 1; ℂ 221-700-111): The Josef stands out as the new minimalist hotel in Prague and in the new Bohemia. Fully modern, its clean lines welcome you the moment you enter. See p. 75.

3 The Best Moderately Priced Hotels

- **Hotel Cloister Inn** (Konviktská 4, Praha 1; ℂ 224-211-020): This freshly restored hotel in a former convent offers a comfortable room at a fair price in Old Town near Jan Hus's 15th-century Bethlehem Chapel. See p. 72.

- **Pension Větrník** (U Větrníku 40, Praha 6; ℂ 220-612-404): This family-run romantic hideaway is reachable in about 20 minutes by tram from the city center. Its atmosphere and price are unbeatable. See p. 77.

- **Pension Unitas/Art Prison Hostel** (Bartolomějská 9, Praha 1; ℂ 224-221-802): An ideal place for budget

travelers who want to take advantage of staying in the very center of Prague. See p. 73.

- Staying in **Vinohrady,** a gentrified quarter above Wenceslas Square, will put you a bit off the Royal Route, but you can find no better price and selection in central Prague, especially if you arrive without reservations. One example is the **Flathotel Orion** (Americká 9, Praha 2; ℂ 353-232-100). This neighborhood teems with cafes and has easy metro access to the older quarters. See "Vinohrady" in chapter 5.

4 The Most Unforgettable Dining Experiences

- **Kampa Park** (Na Kampě 8b, Praha 1; ⓒ 296-826-102): This is the best bet for summer outdoor dining in Prague. The restaurant has a riverside view, where you can dine in the shadow of Prague's most famous bridge during the high season. See p. 88.
- **U Malířů** (Maltézské nám. 11, Praha 1; ⓒ 257-530-000): Though for years it took heat for its sky-high prices, the now more-affordable menu of this gourmet haunt brings its haute cuisine a little closer to earth. See p. 85.
- **Nebozízek** (Petřínské sady 411, Praha 1; ⓒ 257-315-329):The food may not be anything to write home about, but you can't beat the best bird's-eye view of Prague offered on Petřín Hill. See p. 88.
- **Kavárna Obecní dům** (náměstí Republiky 5, Praha 1; ⓒ 222-002-763): This reinvigorated Art Nouveau cafe at the **Municipal House** has re-created the grandeur of Jazz Age afternoons. See p. 101.
- **Bellevue** (Smetanovo nábřeží 18, Praha 1; ⓒ 222-221-443): This best spot for an important lunch or dinner has artful Continental fare and impeccable business-friendly service with a cozy atmosphere and super views near Charles Bridge. See p. 90.
- **Restaurant U Čížků** (Karlovo nám. 34, Praha 2 ⓒ 222-232-257): With huge portions of hearty Czech food perfectly accompanied by a Pilsner lager, this spot feels like a festive Bohemian hunting lodge. See p. 96.

5 The Best Museums

- **Šternberk Palace** (Hradčanské nám. 15, Praha 1; ⓒ 233-090-570): A permanent exhibition, "European Art from the Classical Era to the Close of the Baroque," has been installed at this newly restored baroque palace adjacent to the main gate of Prague Castle. As part of the National Gallery, it's become a venue with the widest art collection in the country. See p. 118.
- **Alfons Mucha Museum** (Panská 7, Praha 1; ⓒ 224-216-415): Posters, decorative panels, objects, and excerpts from sketchbooks, as well as oil paintings from this well-known Art Nouveau master are displayed at the baroque Kaunick´ý Palace near Václavské náměstí. See p. 120.

6 The Best Things to Do for Free (or Almost)

- **Having a Cup and a Debate at the Kavárna Slavia:** (Národní at Smetanovo nábřeží, Praha 1; ⓒ 224-218-493). The reincarnation of Prague's favorite dissident cafe—reopened in the late 1990s after being closed since 1993 in a real estate dispute—retains its former Art Deco glory. The cloak-and-dagger interactions of secret police eavesdropping on political conversations may be gone, but there's still an energy that flows with the talk and java at the Slavia—and it comes with a great view. See p. 101.
- **Romping Late at Night on Charles Bridge:** "Peace, Love, Spare Change" describes the scene, as musicians, street performers, and flower people come out late at night to become one with the bridge. Why not join them? See chapter 10 for more nightlife options.

- **Enjoying New Year's Eve in Český Krumlov:** At midnight in Bohemia's Český Krumlov, the Na plášti Bridge at the castle overlooking the town turns into a mini–United Nations, as revelers from all over gather to watch and light fireworks, see who can uncork the champagne the fastest, and just plain celebrate. See "Český Krumlov" in chapter 12, p. 242.

- **Exploring Antiques Shops:** If you like old stuff, you'll enjoy finding something "out of this world" in many of Prague's antiques shops *(starozitnosti)* or bookstores selling more-or-less-old publications *(antikvariáts)*. See chapter 9 for shopping suggestions.

7 The Best Activities for Families

- **Riding a Faster Boat Down the Vltava:** For those not willing to test their navigational skills or rowing strength in their own boat, large tour boats offer similar floating views, many with meals. Be sure to check the direction of your voyage to be certain it travels past the castles and palaces. See "Sightseeing Options" in chapter 7.

- **Picnicking on Vyšehrad:** Of all the parks where you can picnic, the citadel above the Vltava standing guard over the south end of the Old Town is the calmest and most interesting spot close to the center. Its more remote location means less tourist traffic, and the gardens, city panoramas, and national cemetery provide pleasant walks and poignant history. See "Other Top Sights" in chapter 7.

8 The Best Neighborhoods for Getting Lost

- **Losing Your Way in Old Town:** Every week a new cafe or gallery seems to pop up along the narrow winding streets of Staré Město (Old Town). Prague is best discovered by those who easily get lost on foot, and Old Town's impossible-to-navigate streets are made for such wanderings. See chapter 7.

- **Relaxing in Třeboň:** If you're looking for a small Czech town not overrun with tourists, travel to Třeboň in Bohemia. This serene place, surrounded by forests and ponds, is a diamond in the rough, a walled city that time, war, and disaster have failed to destroy. See "Třeboň" in chapter 12.

9 The Most Romantic Moment

- **Český Krumlov:** If you have time for only one excursion from Prague, make it Český Krumlov. This living gallery of Renaissance-era buildings housing many galleries, shops, and restaurants is 167km (104 miles) south of Prague. Above it towers the second-largest castle complex in the country, with the Vltava River running underneath. No wonder UNESCO named this town a World Heritage Site. See "Český Krumlov" in chapter 12.

10 The Best Offbeat Experiences

• **Sharing a Moment with the Children of Terezín:** On display at the Ceremonial Hall of the Old Jewish Cemetery are sketches drawn by children held at the Terezín concentration camp, northwest of Prague. These drawings present a touching memoir of the Nazi occupation of Bohemia and Moravia. See p. 114.

• **Jumping into "4-D" at Orlík:** After exploring Orlík Castle, south of Prague, and taking a relaxing stroll through the gardens, you can jump into the fourth dimension, in a variation of bungee jumping. It's quite a pick-me-up. See "Jumping into the Fourth Dimension" in chapter 11.

• **Walking Through the Šatov Wine Cellar:** Some of the finest Moravian wine is produced at the Šatov vineyard, and at this wine cellar you'll find more than the local product. The cellar's walls are carved and painted in intricate detail with scenes from Prague Castle and *Snow White.* See "The Painted Cellar of the Šatov Vineyard" in chapter 13.

• **Visiting a Large Communist-Era Housing Estate:** Anyone wondering how most latter-day Praguers live should see the mammoth housing blocks called *paneláky.* The size astounds, and piques debate over form vs. function and living vs. surviving. See "The Art of Prague's Architecture" in chapter 7.

2

Planning Your Trip to Prague & the Czech Republic

This chapter will help you plan your trip to Prague and the Czech Republic. To get the most out of your stay, find out what events will take place during your visit (see the "Czech Republic Calendar of Events," p. 18).

1 Visitor Information

INFORMATION OFFICES   E-Travel, a private Prague-based firm, has developed a fantastic set of websites, including **www.travel.cz** for general Czech tourist and accommodations information and **www.apartments.cz** for booking private apartments online. Start any trip planning here.

The former Communist-era state travel agency, **Čedok,** is now privatized so its only U.S. office has long since closed its doors, but you can contact English-speaking staff through its London or Prague offices or via the Internet. In the United Kingdom, the address is 314–22 Regent St., London W1B 3BG (*©* **020/7580-3778;** www.cedok.co.uk). You can call the Prague main office for advance bookings at Na Příkopě 18, Praha 1 (*©* **224-197-632;** www.cedok.cz).

Once in the country, you'll find an **information desk** at Prague's newly remodeled Ruzyně Airport. It offers basic help but isn't yet at a standard to match most Western convention and visitors' bureaus. Accommodations information can be found through the private firm **AVE Ltd.,** now at the airport and at two primary rail stations, or on the Internet at **www.avetravel.cz**.

For a comprehensive list of information sources once you get to Prague, see "Visitor Information" in chapter 3.

INTERNET INFORMATION   Those hooked up to the Web can find updated information in English on the official Czech Foreign Ministry site at **www.czech.cz**. See above for the **Čedok, AVE,** and **E-Travel** websites. For general tips, check out the Prague Information Service at **www.pis.cz** or **www.prague-info.cz**. And for the latest city lights and sights, try the weekly *Prague Post* website at **www.praguepost.com**.

2 Entry Requirements & Customs

ENTRY REQUIREMENTS

For an up-to-date, country-by-country listing of passport requirements around the world, go to the "Foreign Entry Requirement" Web page of the U.S. State Department at **http://travel.state.gov**.

DOCUMENTS   American, Canadian, Australian, and New Zealand citizens need only passports and no visa for stays less than 90 days. Their passports must be valid for a period of at least 90 days

---

Tips A Warning About Walking

Unless you're in great shape or are a devoted walker, you should gradually prepare for your trip with a walking program to build up the muscles in your legs and feet for the inevitable pounding they'll take. And make sure to do this while wearing the comfortable shoes you plan to bring. Prague is a city of hills, steep staircases, and cobblestone streets that require strong legs and shock-absorbing shoes. Take your time and go at your own pace.

---

beyond the expected length of stay in the Czech Republic.

Nationals from the European Union (United Kingdom, Ireland) can travel to the Czech Republic with passports (validity is not limited) and they are allowed to stay for an unlimited period of time.

Children inscribed in their parents' passports can travel with their parents up to the age of 15. Once the child has reached the age of 15, a separate passport is necessary.

For more information, go to **www. czech.cz**. A full list of the Czech embassies and consulates abroad is available on **www.mzv.cz**.

CUSTOMS
WHAT YOU CAN BRING INTO THE CZECH REPUBLIC

Czech Customs laws are usually lax, but official allowances for importing duty-free goods are 200 cigarettes (or 250g of tobacco), 1 liter of alcohol (or 2 liters of wine), and 50 grams of perfume (or .25 liters of toilet water). Most items brought for personal use during a visit aren't liable to import duty. Gifts are taxable if the quantity and value aren't in keeping with the "reasonable needs" of the recipient.

There are no longer any currency restrictions at borders, but transactions over 500,000Kč ($20,800) must be declared by financial institutions. Live farm animals, plants, produce, coffee, and tea may not be imported, but household pets can enter with an international health certificate.

WHAT YOU CAN TAKE HOME FROM THE CZECH REPUBLIC

Returning **U.S. citizens** who have been away for at least 48 hours are allowed to bring back, once every 30 days, $800 worth of merchandise duty-free. You'll pay a flat rate of duty on the next $1,000 worth of purchases. Any dollar amount beyond that is subject to duties at whatever rates apply. On mailed gifts, the duty-free limit is $200. Be sure to keep your receipts or purchases accessible to expedite the declaration process. *Note:* If you owe duty, you are required to pay on your arrival in the United States—either by cash, personal check, government or traveler's check, or money order (and, in some locations, a Visa or MasterCard).

To avoid paying duty on foreign-made personal items you owned before your trip, bring along a bill of sale, insurance policy, jeweler's appraisal, or receipts of purchase. Or you can register items that can be readily identified by a permanently affixed serial number or marking—think laptop computers, cameras, and CD players—with Customs before you leave. Take the items to the nearest Customs office or register them with Customs at the airport from which you're departing. You'll receive, at no cost, a Certificate of Registration, which allows duty-free entry for the life of the item.

With some exceptions, you cannot bring fresh fruits and vegetables into the United States. For specifics on what you can bring back, download the invaluable free pamphlet *Know Before You Go* online at **www.cbp.gov**. (Click on "Travel," and then click on "Know Before You Go! Online Brochure") Or contact the **U.S. Customs & Border Protection (CBP)**, 1300 Pennsylvania Ave., NW, Washington, DC 20229 (© **877/287-8667**) and request the pamphlet.

For a clear summary of **Canadian** rules, write for the booklet *I Declare,* issued by the **Canada Border Services Agency** (© **800/461-9999** in Canada, or 204/983-3500; www.cbsa-asfc.gc.ca). Canada allows its citizens a C$750 exemption, and you're allowed to bring back duty-free one carton of cigarettes, one can of tobacco, 40 imperial ounces of liquor, and 50 cigars. In addition, you're allowed to mail gifts to Canada valued at less than C$60 a day, provided they're unsolicited and don't contain alcohol or tobacco (write on the package "Unsolicited gift, under $60 value"). All valuables should be declared on the Y-38 form before departure from Canada, including serial numbers of valuables you already own, such as expensive foreign cameras. *Note:* The $750 exemption can only be used once a year and only after an absence of 7 days.

Citizens of the U.K. who are **returning from a European Union (E.U.) country** will go through a separate Customs Exit (called the "Blue Exit") especially for E.U. travelers. In essence, there is no limit on what you can bring back from an E.U. country, provided the items are for personal use (this includes gifts), and you have already paid the necessary duty and tax. Customs law, however, sets out guidance levels. If you bring in more than these levels, you may be asked to prove that the goods are for your own use. Guidance levels on goods bought in the E.U. for personal use are 3,200 cigarettes, 200 cigars, 400 cigarillos, 3 kilograms of smoking tobacco, 10 liters of spirits, 90 liters of wine, 20 liters of fortified wine (such as port or sherry), and 110 liters of beer.

The duty-free allowance in **Australia** is A$400 or, for those under 18, A$200. Citizens can bring in 250 cigarettes or 250 grams of loose tobacco, and 1,125 milliliters of alcohol. If you're returning with valuables you already own, such as foreign-made cameras, you should file form B263. A helpful brochure available from Australian consulates or Customs offices is *Know Before You Go.* For more information, call the **Australian Customs Service** at © **1300/363-263,** or log on to www.customs.gov.au.

The duty-free allowance for **New Zealand** is NZ$700. Citizens over 17 can bring in 200 cigarettes, 50 cigars, or 250 grams of tobacco (or a mixture of all three if their combined weight doesn't exceed 250g); plus 4.5 liters of wine and beer, or 1.125 liters of liquor. New Zealand currency does not carry import or export restrictions. Fill out a certificate of export, listing the valuables you are taking out of the country; that way, you can

---

ⓘ *Tips* **Passport Savvy**

Allow plenty of time before your trip to apply for a passport; processing normally takes 3 weeks but can take longer during busy periods (especially spring). And keep in mind that if you need a passport in a hurry, you'll pay a higher processing fee. When traveling, safeguard your passport in an inconspicuous, inaccessible place like a money belt and keep a copy of the critical pages with your passport number in a separate place. If you lose your passport, visit the nearest consulate or embassy of your native country as soon as possible for a replacement.

bring them back without paying duty. Most questions are answered in a free pamphlet available at New Zealand consulates and Customs offices: *New Zealand Customs Guide for Travellers,* *Notice no. 4.* For more information, contact **New Zealand Customs,** The Customhouse, 17–21 Whitmore St., Box 2218, Wellington (© **04/473-6099** or 0800/428-786; www.customs.govt.nz).

3 Money

CURRENCY

The basic unit of currency is the **koruna** (plural, **koruny**) or crown, abbreviated **Kč.** Each koruna is divided into 100 **haléřů** or hellers. At this writing, the koruna remains volatile after speculation in the currency forced the central bank to let it float in May 1997. In this guide, I quote the koruna at about $0.0416 in U.S. dollars: US$1 buys 24Kč, and UK£1 buys 43Kč. Even though the Czech Republic is now a member state of the European Union, it has not accepted the euro as its currency—yet. That will be a long political process of negotiations, which may last another 5 to 10 years. You will see in Prague's hotels and restaurants prices listed in euros anyway, so European visitors can easily and quickly compare. At this writing, 1 euro buys 30Kč. These rates may vary substantially when you arrive, as the koruna often gyrates wildly in the open economy.

For up-to-the-minute currency conversion go to **www.xe.com/ucc.**

CHANGING MONEY

You'll avoid lines at airport ATMs (automated teller machines) by exchanging at least some money—just enough to cover airport incidentals and transportation to your hotel—before you leave home (though don't expect the exchange rate to be ideal). You can exchange money at your local American Express or Thomas Cook office or at your bank. American Express also dispenses traveler's checks and foreign currency via www.american express.com or © **800/807-6233,** but they'll charge a $15 order fee and additional shipping costs.

In the Czech Republic, hundreds of new storefront shops provide exchange services but, if possible, use credit cards or bank cards at ATMs (don't forget your PIN). In both cases, rates are better and the commissions are lower. If you must exchange at a storefront shop, beware of fees, which can go as high as 10% of the transaction.

Chequepoint has outlets in heavily touristed areas and keeps long hours, sometimes all night, but their business practices are sometimes questionable. Central Prague locations are 28 října 13 and Staroměstské nám. 21 (both open 24 hr.); Staroměstské nám. 27 (daily 8am–11:30pm); and Václavské nám. 32 (daily 8am–11pm).

If you can't use your credit card at an ATM, stick to larger banks to make your trades; there's usually a 1% to 3% commission. **Komerční banka** is the largest

---

(Tips **A Warning About Currency Trading**

Black-marketers who thrived during Communism by trading the once-fixed soft currency on the street have all but vanished. Still, during violent rate fluctuations and shortages of major currencies, the urchins known as *veksláci* may pop up. Don't trade with them. They may rip you off on rates or give you bogus banknotes.

The Czech Koruna

At press time, US$1 equaled approximately 24Kč (or 1Kč = 4.16¢). This was the rate of exchange used to calculate the dollar values given in this book. At the same time, UK£1 equaled about 43Kč.

Note: The rates given here fluctuate and may not be the same when you travel to the Czech Republic.

Kč	US$	UK£	Kč	US$	UK£
1	0.04	0.02	150	6.25	3.48
5	0.21	0.12	200	8.32	4.65
10	0.41	0.23	250	10.40	5.81
15	0.62	0.34	500	20.80	11.62
20	0.83	0.46	750	31.20	17.44
30	1.25	0.69	1,000	41.60	23.25
40	1.66	0.93	1,500	62.40	34.88
50	2.08	1.16	2,000	83.20	46.51
75	3.12	1.74	2,500	104.00	58.13
100	4.16	2.32	3,000	124.80	69.76

The Czech Republic issued new currency in August 1993, and all notes and coins bearing earlier dates became invalid. There are now seven banknotes and nine coins. Notes, each of which bears a forgery-resistant silver strip and a prominent watermark, are issued in 50, 100, 200, 500, 1,000, 2,000, and 5,000 korun denominations. Coins are valued at 50 haléřů and 1, 2, 5, 10, 20, and 50 korun. *Note:* 10- and 20-heller coins, which were in use until November 2003, are not valid any more.

Czech commercial bank, with branches throughout the city and in most towns, and its ATMs are connected to the PLUS and Cirrus systems accepting Visa and MasterCard. Its main office is at Na Příkopě 33, Praha 1 (© **222-432-111**). The branches are usually open Monday to Friday from 8am to 5pm, but the ATMs are accessible 24 hours. **Živnostenská banka,** Na Příkopě 20, Praha 1 (© **224-121-111**), boasts Prague's most beautiful bank lobby and is open Monday to Friday from 9am to 5pm; the change bureau, on the street level, is open Monday to Friday from 10am to 9pm and Saturday from 3 to 7pm. **Komerční banka** has three Praha 1 locations with ATMs: Na Příkopě 33, Na Příkopě 3–5, and Václavské nám. 42. The exchange offices are open Monday to Friday from 8am to 5pm.

ATMS

The easiest and best way to get cash away from home is from an ATM. The **Cirrus** (© **800/424-7787;** www.mastercard.com) and **PLUS** (© **800/843-7587;** www.visa.com) networks span the globe; look at the back of your bank card to see which network you're on, then call or check online for ATM locations at your destination. Be sure you know your personal identification number (PIN) and daily withdrawal limit before you depart. *Note:* Remember that many banks impose a fee every time you use a card at another bank's ATM, and that fee can be higher for international transactions (up to $5 or more) than for domestic ones (where they're rarely more than $2). In addition, the bank from which you withdraw cash may charge its own fee. To compare banks'

What Things Cost in Prague	US$	UK£
Taxi from Ruzyně Airport to city center	29	16
Metro, tram, or public bus to anywhere in Prague	0.83	0.46
Local telephone call	0.16	0.09
Double room at Hotel Paříž (expensive)	193	108
Double room at Hotel Betlem Club (moderate)	137	77
Double room at Hotel Orion (inexpensive)	107	60
Lunch for one at La Provence (moderate)	15	8.37
Lunch for one at most pubs (inexpensive)	3.75	2.09
Dinner for one without wine at Bellevue (expensive)	29	16
Dinner for one without wine at Kogo (moderate)	14	7.81
Dinner for one without wine at Osmička (inexpensive)	4.16	2.32
Half liter of beer in a pub	1.08	0.60
Coca-Cola in a restaurant	1.25	0.69
Cup of coffee	1.25	0.69
Roll of ASA 100 film, 36 exposures	8.33	4.65
Admission to National Museum	4.16	2.32
Movie ticket	7.50	4.18
Ticket to National Theater Opera	16–50	9.30–28

ATM fees within the U.S., use **www.bankrate.com**. For international withdrawal fees, ask your bank.

You can use your credit card to receive cash advances at ATMs. Keep in mind that credit card companies protect themselves from theft by limiting maximum withdrawals outside their home country, so call your credit card company before you leave home. And keep in mind that you'll pay interest from the moment of your withdrawal, even if you pay your monthly bills on time.

Centrally located machines are in Old Town, at the bank **Česká spořitelna;** at the corner of Rytířská and Havelský trh (between Wenceslas Sq. and Old Town Sq.); and at **Komerční banka** at Na Příkopě 33 (as you exit the Můstek metro station) next to the Powder Tower. In Malá Strana, ATMs are on **Mostecká,** the small street linking Charles Bridge with Malostranské náměstí.

TRAVELER'S CHECKS

Traveler's checks are something of an anachronism from the days before the ATM made cash accessible at any time. Given the fees you'll pay for ATM use at banks other than your own, however, you might be better off with traveler's checks if you're withdrawing money often.

You can get traveler's checks at almost any bank. **American Express** offers denominations of $20, $50, $100, $500, and (for cardholders only) $1,000. You'll pay a service charge ranging from 1% to 4%. You can also get American Express traveler's checks over the phone by calling ℂ 800/221-7282; Amex gold and platinum cardholders who use this number are exempt from the 1% fee.

⸮Tips Dear Visa: I'm Off to Bohemia!

Some credit card companies recommend that you notify them of any impending trip abroad so that they don't become suspicious of foreign transactions and block your charges. If you don't call your credit card company in advance, you can still call the card's toll-free emergency number if a charge is refused—provided you remember to carry the phone number with you. Perhaps the most important lesson here is to carry more than one card, so you have a backup.

Visa offers traveler's checks at Citibank locations nationwide, as well as at several other banks. The service charge ranges between 1.5% and 2%; checks come in denominations of $20, $50, $100, $500, and $1,000. Call ⓒ 800/732-1322 for information. AAA members can obtain Visa checks a $9.95 fee (for checks up to $1,500) at most AAA offices or by calling ⓒ 866/339-3378. MasterCard also offers traveler's checks. Call ⓒ 800/223-9920 for a location near you.

Foreign currency traveler's checks are useful if you're traveling to one country, or to the euro zone; they're accepted at locations where dollar checks may not be, such as bed-and-breakfasts, and they minimize the currency conversions you'll have to perform while you're on the go. American Express, Thomas Cook, Visa, and MasterCard offer foreign currency traveler's checks. You'll pay the rate of exchange at the time of your purchase (so it's a good idea to monitor the rate before you buy), and most companies charge a transaction fee per order (and a shipping fee if you order online).

If you do choose to carry traveler's checks, keep a record of their serial numbers separate from your checks in the event that they are stolen or lost. You'll get a refund faster if you know the numbers.

CREDIT CARDS

Credit cards are another safe way to carry money. They also provide a convenient record of all your expenses, and they generally offer relatively good exchange rates.

You can also withdraw cash advances from your credit cards at banks or ATMs, provided you know your PIN. If you don't know yours, call the number on the back of your credit card and ask the bank to send it to you. It usually takes 5 to 7 business days, though some banks will provide the number over the phone if you tell them your mother's maiden name or some other personal information.

Keep in mind that many banks now assess a 1%-to-3% "transaction fee" on **all** charges you incur abroad (whether you're using the local currency or U.S. dollars). But credit cards still may be the smart way to go when you factor in things like exorbitant ATM fees and the higher exchange rates and service fees you'll pay with traveler's checks.

American Express, MasterCard, and Visa are widely accepted in central Prague, but shopkeepers outside the city center still seem mystified by plastic. The credit card companies bill at a favorable rate of exchange and save you money by eliminating commissions. You can get cash advances on your MasterCard, Visa, or American Express card from **Komerční banka,** at its main branch, Na Příkopě 33, Praha 1 (ⓒ 222-432-111); or at most any of its branches, which now have 24-hour ATMs.

The American Express branch at Václavské nám. 56, Praha 1 provides the lost/stolen card service on ⓒ 222-800-237. For more information and facts go to chapter 3, p. 46.

4 When to Go

Spring, which can occasionally bring glorious days, is best known for gray, windy stints with rain. The city and the countryside explode with green around the first of May, so if you're depressed by stark contrasts and cold-weather pollution, plan your trip for between May and October. May is also the month of the renowned **Prague Spring Classical Music Festival,** drawing stars and fans of serious music from around the world. The high summer season brings a constant flow of tour buses, and people-watching (of practically every culture) is at its best. Most Praguers head for their weekend cottages in high season, so if you're looking for local flavor, try another time.

September into October is one of my favorite periods as cool autumn breezes turn trees on the surrounding hills into a multicolored frame for Prague Castle. The crowds are thinner and the prices are better.

A true lover of Prague's mysticism should aim to come in the dead cold of February. It sounds bizarre, but this is when you can best enjoy the monochrome silhouettes, shadows, and solitude that make Prague unique. You'll never forget a gray, snowy February afternoon on Charles Bridge. The only drawback of a winter visit to Prague, if you forget about the cold and occasional snow, is that castles and other attractions in the provinces are closed (though not Prague Castle). During this time, Praguers dress up in their finery to attend dozens of winter balls (some are open to the public; others can be tactfully gate-crashed).

WEATHER

Prague's finicky weather has even rattled a few Brits who live here. The average summer temperature is about 66°F (19°C), but some days can be quite chilly and others uncomfortably sultry. In winter, the temperature remains close to freezing. During an average January, it's sunny and clear for only 50 hours the entire month; in February, the average is 72 hours. Pollution, heaviest in winter, tends to limit snowfall in Prague; however, outlying areas get blanketed. July is rainiest and February is driest.

Monthly Average Temperature

	Jan	Feb	Mar	Apr	May	June	July	Aug	Sept	Oct	Nov	Dec
°C	0.9	0.8	4.6	9.2	14.2	17.5	19.1	18.5	14.7	9.7	4.4	0.9
°F	30	33	40	48	57	63	66	65	58	49	39	33

HOLIDAYS

Official holidays are observed on January 1 (New Year's Day); Easter Monday; May 1 (Labor Day); May 8 (Liberation Day, from Fascism); July 5 (Introduction of Christianity); July 6 (Death of Jan Hus); September 28 (St. Wenceslas Day); October 28 (Foundation of the Republic); November 17 (Day of Student Movements in 1939 and 1989); December 24 and 25 (Christmas); and December 26 (St. Stephen's Day).

Note: The Senate has recently proposed a Good Friday holiday. At this writing, it hasn't been accepted yet.

On these holidays, most businesses and shops (including food shops) are closed, and buses and trams run on Sunday schedules.

CZECH REPUBLIC CALENDAR OF EVENTS

The best way to stay on top of the schedule, which is expected to be revised throughout the year, is to tap into the Prague Information Service (PIS) website at **www.pis.cz** or **www.prague-info.cz**, where all events are updated in English and Czech.

January

Anniversary of Jan Palach's Death. On January 19, 1969, 21-year-old philosophy student Jan Palach set fire to himself on Wenceslas Square as a protest against the Soviet invasion of Czechoslovakia. He died a few days later and became a symbol for dissidents. His death is commemorated annually at a Memorial to the Victims of Communism on Wenceslas Square and at Olšany Cemetery, where he's buried. January 19.

March

Febiofest 2004. This is one of the largest noncompetitive film and video festivals in central Europe. More than 500 movies from 50 countries will be presented in 15 cinemas in Prague. You will find more information on www.febiofest.cz or by calling © **221-101-111**. Late March.

Prague City of Music Festival. Contemporary and classical concerts are performed at this festival. For details, contact Čedok, Na Příkopě 18, Praha 1 (© **224-197-632**); or try almost any information/travel agency in Prague (see "Visitor Information," in chapter 3). Throughout the month.

April

Witches' Night. This annual bucolic ritual is meant to bring luck to the planting season. Bonfires are lit and an effigy of an old hag is thrown on the flames. Prague largely ignores this event, but blazes dot the countryside beginning at twilight. April 30.

May

Karlovy Vary Blessing of the Waters. One of Europe's oldest and most famous spas (the original Carlsbad) kicks off its high season with a traditional blessing of its 12 hot springs, complete with a coronation and a reenactment of the town's founding by Charles IV. The spa zone is filled with medieval sights and sounds. For details, contact the Info Centrum in Karlovy Vary (© **353-224-097**) or go to www.karlovyvary.cz. First weekend in May.

Prague International Marathon. Annual meeting of runners from all over the world. Go to **www.pim.cz** to find out more. Mid- to late May.

Prague Spring Music Festival. This world-famous 3-week series of classical music and dance performances begins with the anniversary of Bedřich Smetana's death on May 12. An exclusive opening night tradition is the performance of Smetana's symphonic poem, *Má Vlast (My Country),* attended by the president. Throughout the fest, symphony, opera, and chamber performances bring some of the world's best talent to Prague. Concert tickets are usually 250Kč to 2,000Kč ($10–$83) and are available in advance (beginning in Jan) from Hellichova 18, Praha 1 (© **257-312-547**; www.festival.cz). Mid-May to early June.

June

Tanec Praha (Dance Prague). This year will be the 18th anniversary of this international festival. In theaters around the city, you can find performances of artistic dance. For more information, go to www.tanecpha.cz or call © **224-817-886**. Throughout the month.

Slavnost Pětilisté Růže (Festival of the Five-Petaled Rose). Held annually to mark the summer solstice, the festival gives residents of Český Krumlov the excuse to dress up in Renaissance costumes and parade through the streets. Afterward, the streets become a stage with plays, chess games with people dressed as pieces, music, and more. For details, contact the town's information center at ℂ **380-704-621** or go to www.ckrumlov.cz. Third weekend in June.

July

Karlovy Vary International Film Festival. This annual 10-day event, being held for the 41st year, predates Communism and has regained its "A" rating from the international body governing film festivals. That puts it in the same league with Cannes and Venice, though much further down the standings since it doesn't yet have the star-drawing power of the more glittery stops. A blanket ticket policy putting 1-day advance-sell seats at a buck each means that screenings are mostly filled with students willing to stand in line the day before. For more information check www.iffkv.cz. Late June to early July.

August

Chopin Festival. Karlovy Vary's younger and smaller sister spa town of Mariánské Lázně (Marienbad) honors one of its past guests, Chopin, with an annual 8- to 10-day festival. Concerts and recitals, mostly for piano, are held throughout the town. For details or tickets, contact **Městské InfoCentrum** at ℂ **354-622-474.** Late August.

September

Prague Autumn International Music Festival. This festival features local orchestras from around the country and some international guests. Most concerts are at the Rudolfinum. You can buy tickets in advance through the **Festival Office** (ℂ **22-540-484;** www.pragueautumn.cz) or call **Ticketpro** at ℂ **296-333-333.** Late September.

Moravian Autumn International Music Festival in Brno. This annual event, now in its 41st year, is dedicated to symphonic and chamber musical works. Tickets are available at the **Informační středisko** ℂ **542-211-090,** or go to www.mhf-brno.cz for more info. Late September, beginning of October.

October

International Jazz Festival. This 30-year-old celebration of jazz music is held in several venues in the town. For more details call Pragokoncert, Peckova 12, Praha 8 (ℂ **224-817-272**), or call the **Ticketpro** office (ℂ **296-333-333**). Last week in October.

Renaissance Days at Křivoklát Castle. Amid the cold winds and blazing fall colors in the Berounka valley, this Gothic relic of famous Czech lore gets decked out in all the trappings of the 14th and 15th centuries. With merchants, minstrels, and merrymakers filling the fortress grounds, this time-warp event can be a lot of fun. For information, call ℂ **313-558-120** or check www.krivoklat.cz. Last weekend in October.

November

Anniversary of the Velvet Revolution. The clash between students and police on Národní Street on November 17, 1989, set off the chain of events that eventually brought down the Communist government (many students were injured but none died). Czechs refer to the period since as the Post-November Era, though few commemorate the event, which was recently declared a national holiday. The president usually lays a wreath at the small bronze "free hands" monument hanging on a wall near Národní třída 20. November 17.

December

Christmas in Prague. This is a festive time in Prague. St. Mikuláš (Nicholas), the Czech version of Santa Claus but dressed in a white bishop's costume, kicks off the season on December 5 by giving sweets to well-behaved children and coal and potatoes to rowdy ones. Just before Christmas, large barrels of live carp are brought into the city, where the fish are clubbed to death and gutted on demand for families to take home for the traditional Christmas meal. 'Tis the season. December 5 to 26.

New Year's Eve. Unless you are looking for trouble or enjoy dodging missiles, you should stay well away from the center of Prague on New Year's Eve.

On the night known as **Silvester,** Old Town Square and Charles Bridge become battle zones with indiscriminately fired bottle rockets and other fireworks causing random and often serious injuries. Each year has gotten worse. Best to stay put at one of the many hotel or restaurant galas being offered on that night. December 31.

5 Travel Insurance

Check your existing insurance policies and credit card coverage before you buy travel insurance. You may already be covered for lost luggage, canceled tickets, or medical expenses.

The cost of travel insurance varies widely, depending on the cost and length of your trip, your age and health, and the type of trip you're taking, but expect to pay between 5% and 8% of the vacation itself. You can get estimates from more than a dozen providers through **Insure MyTrip.com.**

TRIP-CANCELLATION INSURANCE

Trip-cancellation insurance will help retrieve your money if you have to back out of a trip or depart early, or if your travel supplier goes bankrupt. Permissible reasons for trip cancellation can range from sickness to natural disasters to the State Department declaring a destination unsafe for travel. (Insurers usually won't cover vague fears, though, as many travelers discovered when they tried to cancel their trips in October 2001.) In this unstable world, trip-cancellation insurance is a good buy if you're purchasing

tickets well in advance—who knows what the state of the world, or of your airline, will be in 9 months? Insurance policy details vary, so read the fine print—and make sure that your airline or cruise line is on the list of carriers covered in case of bankruptcy. A good resource is **"Travel Guard Alerts,"** a list of companies considered high-risk by Travel Guard International (see website below). Protect yourself further by paying for the insurance with a credit card—by law, consumers can get their money back on goods and services not received if they report the loss within 60 days after the charge is listed on their credit card statement.

Note: Many tour operators, particularly those offering trips to remote or high-risk areas, include insurance in the total trip cost or can arrange insurance policies through a partnering provider, which is a convenient and often cost-effective way for the traveler to obtain insurance. Make sure the tour company is a reputable one, however, and be aware that some experts suggest you avoid buying insurance from the tour or cruise

---

(*Tips* **Quick ID**

Tie a colorful ribbon or piece of yarn around your luggage handle, or slap a distinctive sticker on the side of your bag. This makes it less likely that someone will mistakenly appropriate it. And if your luggage gets lost, it will be easier to find.

company you're traveling with. They contend it's more secure to buy from a "third party" than to put all your money in one place.

For more information, contact one of the following recommended insurers: **Access America** (© 866/807-3982; www.accessamerica.com); **Travel Guard International** (© 800/826-4919; www.travelguard.com); **Travel Insured International** (© 800/243-3174; www.travelinsured.com); and **Travelex Insurance Services** (© 888/457-4602; www.travelex-insurance.com).

MEDICAL INSURANCE For travel overseas, most health plans (including Medicare and Medicaid) do not provide coverage, and the ones that do often require you to pay for services upfront and reimburse you only after you return home. Even if your plan does cover overseas treatment, most out-of-country hospitals make you pay your bills upfront, and send you a refund only after you've returned home and filed the necessary paperwork with your insurance company. As a safety net, you may want to buy travel medical insurance, particularly if you're traveling to a remote or high-risk area where emergency evacuation is a possible scenario. If you require additional medical insurance, try **MEDEX Assistance** (© 410/453-6300; www.medexassist.com) or **Travel Assistance International** (© 800/821-2828; www.travelassistance.com; for general information on services, call the company's Worldwide Assistance Services, Inc., at © 800/777-8710).

LOST-LUGGAGE INSURANCE On domestic flights, checked baggage is covered up to $2,500 per ticketed passenger. On international flights (including U.S. portions of international trips), baggage coverage is limited to approximately $9.07 per pound, up to approximately $635 per checked bag. If you plan to check items more valuable than what's covered by the standard liability, see if your homeowner's policy covers your valuables, get baggage insurance as part of your comprehensive travel-insurance package, or buy Travel Guard's "BagTrak" product. Don't buy insurance at the airport, where it's usually overpriced. Be sure to take any valuables or irreplaceable items with you in your carry-on luggage, because many valuables (including books, money, and electronics) aren't covered by airline policies.

If your luggage is lost, immediately file a lost-luggage claim at the airport, detailing the luggage contents. Most airlines require that you report delayed, damaged, or lost baggage within 4 hours of arrival. The airlines are required to deliver luggage, once found, directly to your house or destination free of charge.

6 Health & Safety

STAYING HEALTHY

In most cases, your existing health plan will provide the coverage you need. But double-check; you may want to buy **travel medical insurance** instead. (See the section on insurance, above.) Bring your insurance ID card with you when you travel.

If you suffer from a chronic illness, consult your doctor before your departure. For conditions like epilepsy, diabetes, or heart problems, wear a **MedicAlert Identification Tag** (© 800/825-3785; www.medicalert.org), which will immediately alert doctors to your condition and give them access to your records through MedicAlert's 24-hour hot line.

Pack **prescription medications** in your carry-on luggage, and carry prescription medications in their original containers, with pharmacy labels—otherwise they won't make it through airport security.

Also bring along copies of your prescriptions in case you lose your pills or run out. Don't forget an extra pair of contact lenses or prescription glasses. Carry the generic name of prescription medicines, in case a local pharmacist is unfamiliar with the brand name.

Contact the **International Association for Medical Assistance to Travelers (IAMAT)** (© 716/754-4883 or, in Canada, 416/652-0137; www.iamat.org) for tips on travel and health concerns in the countries you're visiting, and for lists of local, English-speaking doctors. The United States **Centers for Disease Control and Prevention** (© 800/311-3435; www.cdc.gov) provides up-to-date information on health hazards by region or country and offers tips on food safety. The website **www.tripprep.com**, sponsored by a consortium of travel medicine practitioners, may also offer helpful advice on traveling abroad. You can find listings of reliable clinics overseas at the **International Society of Travel Medicine** (www.istm.org).

VACCINATIONS

Unless you're arriving from an area known to be suffering from an epidemic, no inoculations or vaccinations are required to enter the Czech Republic.

WHAT TO DO IF YOU GET SICK AWAY FROM HOME

Any foreign consulate can provide a list of area doctors who speak English. If you get sick, consider asking your hotel concierge to recommend a local doctor—even his or her own. You can also try the emergency room at a local hospital. Many hospitals also have walk-in clinics for emergency cases that are not life-threatening; you may not get immediate attention, but you won't pay the high price of an emergency room visit. We list hospitals and emergency numbers under "Fast Facts: Prague," in chapter 3.

STAYING SAFE

Citizens are reporting more burglaries and violent assaults, and some visitors have been targeted, though Prague remains safe by Western standards. The best strategy is to use common sense. Women especially should avoid walking alone late at night on dark streets, through parks, and around Wenceslas Square—one of the main areas for prostitution. All visitors should be watchful of pickpockets in heavily touristed areas, especially on Charles Bridge, in Old Town Square, and in front of the main train station. Be especially wary on crowded buses, trams, and trains. Don't keep your wallet in a back pocket and don't flash a lot of cash or jewelry.

7 Specialized Travel Resources

TRAVELERS WITH DISABILITIES

The Czechs have made little effort to accommodate the needs of those with disabilities. There are few elevators or ramps for wheelchairs, and few beeping crosswalks for the visually impaired. TTD phones for the hearing-impaired are rare.

In the cobblestone streets of downtown Prague, wheelchairs are almost unknown. Only a few hotels (like the Renaissance and the Palace) offer barrier-free accommodations, and most stores, public transport, theaters, and restaurants are inaccessible to wheelchairs. The following metro stations in the city center are accessible: Florenc, Hlavní nádraží, Pankrác, Roztyly, Chodov, Karlovo náměstí, Skalka, and Nádraží Holešovice.

For the most part, attractions don't offer discounts to people with disabilities. There are exceptions, however, so always ask before paying full price.

Many travel agencies offer customized tours and itineraries for travelers with disabilities. **Flying Wheels Travel** (© 507/451-5005; www.flyingwheelstravel.com)

offers escorted tours and cruises that emphasize sports and private tours in minivans with lifts. **Access-Able Travel Source** (© 303/232-2979; www.access-able.com) offers extensive access information and advice for traveling around the world with disabilities. **Accessible Journeys** (© 800/846-4537 or 610/521-0339; www.disabilitytravel.com) caters specifically to slow walkers and wheelchair travelers and their families and friends

Organizations that offer assistance to disabled travelers include **MossRehab** (www.mossresourcenet.org), which provides a library of accessible-travel resources online; the **American Foundation for the Blind (AFB)** (© 800/232-5463; www.afb.org), a referral resource for the blind or visually impaired that includes information on traveling with Seeing Eye dogs; and **SATH** (Society for Accessible Travel & Hospitality) (© 212/447-7284; www.sath.org; annual membership fees: $45 adults, $30 seniors and students), which offers a wealth of travel resources for all types of disabilities and informed recommendations on destinations, access guides, travel agents, tour operators, vehicle rentals, and companion services. **AirAmbulanceCard.com** is now partnered with SATH and allows you to preselect top-notch hospitals in case of an emergency for $195 a year ($295 per family), among other benefits.

For more information specifically targeted to travelers with disabilities, the community website **iCan** (www.icanonline.net/channels/travel) has destination guides and several regular columns on accessible travel. Also check out the quarterly magazine *Emerging Horizons* (www.emerging horizons.com; $14.95 per year, $19.95 outside the U.S.); and *Open World* magazine, published by SATH (see above; subscription: $13 per year, $21 outside the U.S.).

GAY & LESBIAN TRAVELERS

During the Communist regime, homosexuality was met with official silence. Individual rights were not recognized, and gay rights were unheard of. However, many Czechs have always had a genuine live-and-let-live attitude. Open hostility toward homosexuals is rare in Prague. Since November 1989, many gays have "come out." Gay sex is legal, with the age of consent at 15. Several bars and nightclubs in Prague cater exclusively to the gay community and are listed in chapter 10.

The **Gay Iniciativa** (formerly known as SOHO) (© 224-223-811; www.gay.iniciativa.cz) was founded in 1991 as an umbrella group uniting several smaller gay organizations. The best information on happenings for gay visitors is on http://prague.gayguide.net. The *Prague Post* prints updated gay and lesbian reviews.

The **International Gay and Lesbian Travel Association (IGLTA)** (© 800/448-8550 or 954/776-2626; www.iglta.org) is the trade association for the gay and lesbian travel industry, and offers an online directory of gay- and lesbian-friendly travel businesses; go to their website and click on "Members."

Many agencies offer tours and travel itineraries specifically for gay and lesbian travelers. **Above and Beyond Tours** (© 800/397-2681; www.abovebeyond tours.com) is the exclusive gay and lesbian tour operator for United Airlines. **Now, Voyager** (© 800/255-6951; www.nowvoyager.com) is a well-known San Francisco–based, gay-owned and -operated travel service. **Olivia Cruises & Resorts** (© 800/631-6277; www.olivia.com) charters entire resorts and ships for exclusive lesbian vacations and offers smaller group experiences for both gay and lesbian travelers. (In 2005, Czech-born tennis great Martina Navrátilová was named Olivia's official spokesperson.)

The following travel guides are available at many bookstores, or you can order

> ## ⓘ Tips Catching Some Decent Z's
>
> Anywhere in the Czech Republic you have the option of staying in hotels or pensions on a town's main square. It's a beautiful sight, but be prepared for the possibility of serious noise, particularly on weekends, as revelers rage on late into the night. Light sleepers may prefer to trade the view for a good night's sleep.
>
> Pensions are less expensive than hotels, and often the best pensions are friendlier, more tasteful, and far more in tune with the surroundings.
>
> You may find that service tends not to be up to Western standards in many places; be warned that desk staff can be surly and unhelpful, and hotels may be woefully understaffed.

them from any online bookseller: *Frommer's Gay & Lesbian Europe* (www.frommers.com), an excellent travel resource to the top European cities and resorts; *Spartacus International Gay Guide* (Bruno Gmünder Verlag; www.spartacusworld.com/gayguide) and *Odysseus: The International Gay Travel Planner* (Odysseus Enterprises Ltd.), both good, annual, English-language guidebooks focused on gay men; and the *Damron* guides (www.damron.com), with separate, annual books for gay men and lesbians.

SENIOR TRAVEL

Because Communist equality meant that seniors were no worse off financially than younger persons, Czechs have little experience offering special discounts to seniors. Several attractions, such as the National Museum, have senior discounts, many times announced only in Czech with the price for *důchodce* (pensioner). Always ask if a markdown applies to you as well, since there's an accepted Czech system of dual pricing for foreigners. When making hotel reservations at major chains, ask about a senior discount (usually 10%).

Members of **AARP** (formerly known as the American Association of Retired Persons), 601 E St. NW, Washington, DC 20049 (ⓒ **888/687-2277**; www.aarp.org), get discounts on hotels, airfares, and car rentals. AARP offers members a wide range

of benefits, including *AARP: The Magazine* and a monthly newsletter. Anyone over 50 can join.

Many reliable agencies and organizations target the 50-plus market. **Elderhostel** (ⓒ **877/426-8056**; www.elderhostel.org) arranges study programs for those ages 55 and over (and a spouse or companion of any age) in the U.S. and in more than 80 countries around the world. Most courses last 5 to 7 days in the U.S. (2–4 weeks abroad), and many include airfare, accommodations in university dormitories or modest inns, meals, and tuition. **ElderTreks** (ⓒ **800/741-7956**; www.eldertreks.com) offers small-group tours to off-the-beaten-path or adventure-travel locations, restricted to travelers 50 and older. **INTRAV** (ⓒ **800/456-8100**; www.intrav.com) is a high-end tour operator that caters to the mature, discerning traveler (not specifically seniors), with trips around the world that include guided safaris, polar expeditions, private-jet adventures, and small-boat cruises down jungle rivers.

Recommended publications offering travel resources and discounts for seniors include: the quarterly magazine *Travel 50 & Beyond* (www.travel50andbeyond.com); *Travel Unlimited: Uncommon Adventures for the Mature Traveler* (Avalon); *101 Tips for Mature Travelers,* available from Grand Circle Travel (© **800/221-2610** or 617/350-7500; www.gct.com); and *Unbelievably Good Deals and Great Adventures That You Absolutely Can't Get Unless You're Over 50* (McGraw-Hill), by Joann Rattner Heilman.

FAMILY TRAVEL

If you have enough trouble getting your kids out of the house in the morning, dragging them thousands of miles away may seem like an insurmountable challenge. But family travel can be immensely rewarding, giving you new ways of seeing the world through the eyes of children.

Prague though isn't the easiest place to explore with kids. Only strollers with large wheels can manage the cobblestone streets, and few restaurants have smoke-free areas or cater to the needs of kids. For a selection of family-friendly accommodations and restaurants, see the "Family-Friendly Accommodations" and "Family-Friendly Restaurants" boxes in chapters 5 and 6 respectively. While you should pack medicines or special foods that your children need, you'll find baby food, diapers (including familiar brands), and other sundries available in food stores and pharmacies around town. For special activities, see "Prague with Kids," in chapter 7.

Familyhostel (© **800/733-9753;** www.learn.unh.edu/familyhostel) takes the whole family, including kids ages 8 to 15, on moderately priced domestic and international learning vacations. Lectures, field trips, and sightseeing are guided by a team of academics.

Recommended family travel Internet sites include **Family Travel Forum** (www.familytravelforum.com), a comprehensive site that offers customized trip planning; **Family Travel Network** (www.familytravelnetwork.com), an award-winning site that offers travel features, deals, and tips; **Traveling Internationally with Your Kids** (www.travelwithyourkids.com), a comprehensive site offering sound advice for long-distance and international travel with children; and **Family Travel Files** (www.thefamilytravelfiles.com), which offers an online magazine and a directory of off-the-beaten-path tours and tour operators for families.

STUDENT TRAVEL

Prague's hostels not only are some of the cheapest places to stay but also are great for meeting other travelers. You don't have to be a card-carrying member of the International Youth Hostel Federation (IYHF) to lodge at most of them.

If you want to make some music or do some magic busking for money, you can do so legally anywhere in the city. If you want to sell something, though, beware that authorities require permits for those who wish to hawk on Charles Bridge and elsewhere.

If you're planning to travel outside the U.S., you'd be wise to arm yourself with an **International Student Identity Card (ISIC),** which offers substantial savings on rail passes, plane tickets, and entrance fees. It also provides you with basic health and life insurance and a 24-hour help line. The card is available for $22 from **STA Travel** (© **800/781-4040** in North America; www.sta.com or www.statravel.com), the biggest student travel agency in the world. If you're no longer a student but are still under 26, you can get an **International Youth Travel Card (IYTC)** for the same price from the same people, which entitles you to some discounts (but not on museum admissions). **Travel CUTS** (© **800/667-2887** or 416/614-2887; www.travelcuts.com) offers similar services for both Canadians and U.S. residents. Irish students may prefer to turn to **USIT** (© **01/602-1600;** www.usitnow.ie), an Ireland-based specialist in student, youth, and independent travel.

8 Planning Your Trip Online

SURFING FOR AIRFARES

The "big three" online travel agencies, **Expedia.com, Travelocity,** and **Orbitz,** sell most of the air tickets bought on the Internet. (Canadian travelers should try expedia.ca and Travelocity.ca; U.K. residents can go for expedia.co.uk and opodo.co.uk.). **Kayak.com** is also gaining popularity and uses a sophisticated search engine (developed at MIT). Each has different business deals with the airlines and may offer different fares on the same flights, so it's wise to shop around. Expedia.com, Kayak, and Travelocity will also send you **e-mail notification** when a cheap fare becomes available to your favorite destination. Of the smaller travel-agency websites, **SideStep** (www.sidestep.com) has gotten the best reviews from Frommer's authors. The website (with optional browser add-on) purports to "search 140 sites at once," but in reality only beats competitors' fares as often as other sites do.

Also remember to check **airline websites,** especially those for low-fare carriers such as Southwest, JetBlue, AirTran, WestJet, or Ryanair, whose fares are often misreported or simply missing from travel agency websites. Even with major airlines, you can often shave a few bucks from a fare by booking directly through the airline and avoiding a travel agency's transaction fee. But you'll get these discounts only by **booking online:** Most airlines now offer online-only fares that even their phone agents know nothing about. For the websites of airlines that fly to and from your destination, go to "Getting There," p. 28.

Great **last-minute deals** are available through free weekly e-mail services provided directly by the airlines. Most of these are announced on Tuesday or Wednesday and must be purchased online. Most are only valid for travel that weekend, but some (such as Southwest's)

can be booked weeks or months in advance. Sign up for weekly e-mail alerts at airline websites or check mega-sites that compile comprehensive lists of last-minute specials, such as **Smarter Travel** (www.smartertravel.com). For last-minute trips, **site59.com** and **lastminutetravel.com** in the U.S. and **lastminute.com** in Europe often have better air-and-hotel package deals than the major-label sites.

SURFING FOR HOTELS

Shopping online for hotels is generally done one of two ways: by booking through the hotel's own website or through an independent booking agency. These Internet hotel agencies have multiplied in mind-boggling numbers of late, competing for the business of millions of consumers surfing for accommodations around the world. This competitiveness can be a boon to consumers who have the patience and time to shop and compare the online sites for good deals—but shop they must, for prices can vary considerably from site to site. And keep in mind that hotels at the top of a site's listing may be there for no other reason than that they paid money to get the placement.

Of the "big three" sites, **Expedia.com** offers a long list of special deals and "virtual tours" or photos of available rooms so you can see what you're paying for (a feature that helps counter the claims that the best rooms are often held back from bargain-booking websites). **Travelocity** posts unvarnished customer reviews and ranks its properties according to the AAA rating system. (**Trip Advisor,** at www.tripadvisor.com, is another excellent source of unbiased user reviews of hotels around the world. While even the finest hotels can inspire a misleadingly poor review from picky or crabby travelers, the body of user opinions, when take as a whole, is usually a reliable indicator.)

Frommers.com: The Complete Travel Resource

For an excellent travel-planning resource, we highly recommend **Frommers.com** (www.frommers.com), voted Best Travel Site by *PC Magazine*. We're a little biased, of course, but we guarantee that you'll find the travel tips, reviews, monthly vacation giveaways, bookstore, and online-booking capabilities thoroughly indispensable. Among the special features are our popular **Destinations** section, where you'll get expert travel tips, hotel and dining recommendations, and advice on the sights to see for more than 3,500 destinations around the globe; the **Frommers.com Newsletter,** with the latest deals, travel trends, and money-saving secrets; our **Community** area featuring **Message Boards,** where Frommer's readers post queries and share advice (sometimes even our authors show up to answer questions); and our **Photo Center,** where you can post and share vacation tips. When your research is finished, the **Online Reservations System** (www.frommers.com/book_a_trip) takes you to Frommer's preferred online partners for booking your vacation at affordable prices.

9 Getting There

BY PLANE
THE MAJOR AIRLINES

About two dozen international airlines offer regularly scheduled service into Prague's **Ruzyně Airport.** The only U.S. carrier flying direct to Prague is Continental via its New York/Newark hub using a code-sharing arrangement with the Czech national carrier **ČSA Czech Airlines** (© 800/223-2365; www.czech-airlines.com). ČSA also flies to Prague from Toronto and Montreal. Germany's **Lufthansa** (© 800/645-3880; www.lufthansa-USA.com) has frequent connections to Prague with flights from New York and San Francisco via their Frankfurt hub.

Other major carriers serving the Czech Republic are **Air France** (© 800/237-2747; www.airfrance.com); **Alitalia** (© 800/223-5730; www.alitaliausa.com); **Austrian Airlines** (© 800/843-0002; www.aua.com/us/eng/); and **British Airways** (© 800/AIRWAYS in the U.S., or 08708-509-850 in the U.K.; www.british-airways.com), as well as economy short-haul service from **easyJet** from London's Stansted, and Gatwick Airports, www.easyjet.com; **KLM Royal Dutch Airlines** (© 800/447-4747; www.klm.com); **SAS** (© 800/221-2350; www.scandinavian.net); and **Swissair** (© 877/359-7947; www.swiss.com).

PRAGUE AIRLINE OFFICES To get flight information in Prague or to make reservations or changes, contact **Air France,** Václavské nám. 57, Praha 1 (© 221-662-662); **Alitalia,** Václavské nám. 11, Praha 1 (© 221-629-150); **Austrian Airlines,** the Ruzyně Airport, Praha 6 (© 220-116-272); **British Airways,** the Ruzyně Airport, Praha 6 (© 239-000-299); or **ČSA Czech Airlines,** V Celnici 5, Praha 1, next to the Renaissance Hotel (© 239-007-007). For **easyJet** information and reservations go to www.easyjet.com; **KLM Royal Dutch Airlines,** Ruzyně Airport, Praha 6 (© 233-090-933); **Lufthansa,** the Ruzyně Airport, Praha 6 (© 234-008-234); **SAS,** Ruzyně Airport, Praha 6 (© 220-116-031); and **Swissair,** Lazarská 8, Praha 2 (© 221-990-444).

Eastern European Rail Routes

GETTING THROUGH THE AIRPORT

With the federalization of airport security, screening procedures at U.S. airports are more stable and consistent than ever. Generally, you'll be fine if you arrive at the airport **1 hour** before a domestic flight and **2 hours** before an international flight; if you show up late, tell an airline employee and he or she will probably whisk you to the front of the line.

Bring a **current, government-issued photo ID** such as a driver's license or passport. Keep your ID at the ready to present at check-in, the security checkpoint, and sometimes even the gate. (Children under 18 do not need government-issued photo IDs for domestic flights, but they do for international flights to most countries.)

In 2003, the TSA phased out **gate check-in** at all U.S. airports. Passengers with e-tickets, which have made paper tickets nearly obsolete, can beat the ticket-counter lines by using airport **electronic kiosks** or even **online check-in** from their home computers. Online check-in involves logging on to your airline's website, accessing your reservation, and printing out your boarding pass—and the airline may even offer you bonus miles to do so! If you're using a kiosk at the airport, bring the credit card you used to book the ticket or your frequent-flier card. Print out your boarding pass from the kiosk and simply proceed to the security checkpoint with your pass and a photo ID. If you're checking bags or looking to snag an exit-row seat, you will be able to do so using most airline kiosks. Even the smaller airlines are employing the kiosk system, but always call your airline to make sure these alternatives are available. **Curbside check-in** is also a good way to avoid lines, although a few airlines still don't allow it; call for your airline's policy before you go.

Security checkpoint lines are getting shorter than they were during 2001 and 2002, but an orange alert, suspicious passenger, or high passenger volume can still make for a long wait. If you have trouble standing for long periods of time, tell an airline employee; the airline will provide a wheelchair. Speed up security by **not wearing metal objects** such as big belt buckles. If you've got metallic body parts, a note from your doctor can prevent a long chat with the security screeners. Keep in mind that only **ticketed passengers** are allowed past security, except for people escorting disabled passengers or children.

Federalization has stabilized **what you can carry on** and **what you can't.** The general rule is that sharp things are out, nail clippers are okay, and food and beverages must pass through the X-ray machine—but security screeners can't make you drink from your coffee cup. Bring food in your carry-on rather than checking it, as explosive-detection machines used on checked luggage have been known to mistake food (especially chocolate, for some reason) for bombs. Travelers in the U.S. are allowed one carry-on bag, plus a "personal item" such as a purse, briefcase, or laptop bag. Carry-on hoarders can stuff all sorts of things into a laptop bag; as long as it has a laptop in it, it's still considered a personal item. The Transportation Security Administration (TSA) has issued a list of restricted items; check its website (www.tsa.gov/public/index.jsp) for details.

Airport screeners may decide that your checked luggage warrants a hand search. You can now purchase luggage locks that allow screeners to open and relock a checked bag if hand searching is necessary. Look for Travel Sentry certified locks at luggage or travel shops and Brookstone stores (you can buy them online at www.brookstone.com). Luggage inspectors can open these TSA-approved locks with a special code or key—rather than having to cut them off the suitcase, as they normally do to conduct a hand search. For more information on the locks, visit www.travelsentry.org.

FLYING FOR LESS: TIPS FOR GETTING THE BEST AIRFARE

Passengers sharing the same airplane cabin rarely pay the same fare. Travelers who need to purchase tickets at the last minute, change their itinerary at a moment's notice, or fly one-way often get stuck paying the premium rate. Here are some ways to keep your airfare costs down.

- Passengers who can book their ticket either **long in advance or at the last minute,** or who **fly midweek** or **at less-trafficked hours** may pay a fraction of the full fare. If your schedule is flexible, say so, and ask if you can secure a cheaper fare by changing your flight plans.
- Search **the Internet** for cheap fares (see "Planning Your Trip Online," above).
- Keep an eye on local newspapers for **promotional specials** or **fare wars,** when airlines lower prices on their most popular routes. You rarely see fare wars offered for peak travel times, but if you can travel in the off-months, you may snag a bargain.
- Try to book a ticket **in its country of origin.** For multileg trips, book in the country of the first leg; for example, book New York–London–Amsterdam–Prague–New York in the

U.S. If you're going straight to Prague, and you want to plan a trip to another European city, try to get one of the low fare tickets online at www.easyjet.com, www.smartwings.net, www.air-lowcost.cz/index.htm, www.dust.cz, www.letuska.cz, or www.intercontact.cz.

- **Consolidators,** also known as bucket shops, are great sources for international tickets, although they usually can't beat Internet fares. For example, in winter from New York, you can buy bucket-shop tickets to Prague on well-known international airlines for as little as $250 each way; the prices rise to about $600 in summer. Start by looking in Sunday newspaper travel sections; U.S. travelers should focus on the *New York Times, Los Angeles Times,* and *Miami Herald.* For less-developed destinations, small travel agents who cater to immigrant communities in large cities often have the best deals. *Beware:* Bucket-shop tickets are usually nonrefundable or rigged with stiff cancellation penalties, often as high as 50% to 75% of the ticket price, and some put you on charter airlines, which may leave at inconvenient times and experience delays. Several reliable consolidators are worldwide and available online. **STA Travel** has been the world's leading consolidator for students since purchasing Council Travel, but its fares are competitive for travelers of all ages. **ELTExpress (Flights.com)** (✆ **800/TRAV-800;** www.eltexpress.com) has excellent fares worldwide, particularly to Europe. It also has

"local" websites in 12 countries. **Fly-Cheap** (✆ **800/FLY-CHEAP;** www.1800flycheap.com) is owned by package-holiday megalith MyTravel and has especially good fares to sunny destinations. **Air Tickets Direct** (✆ **800/778-3447;** www.airticketsdirect.com) is based in Montreal and leverages the currently weak Canadian dollar for low fares; they also book trips to places that U.S. travel agents won't touch, such as Cuba.

- Join **frequent-flier clubs.** Frequent-flier membership doesn't cost a cent, but it does entitle you to better seats, faster response to phone inquiries, and prompter service if your luggage is stolen or your flight is canceled or delayed, or if you want to change your seat. And you don't have to fly to earn points; **frequent-flier credit cards** can earn you thousands of miles for doing your everyday shopping. With more than 70 mileage awards programs on the market, consumers have never had more options, but the system has never been more complicated—what with major airlines folding, new budget carriers emerging, and alliances forming (allowing you to earn points on partner airlines). Investigate the program details of your favorite airlines before you sink points into any one.

BY CAR

You definitely shouldn't rent a car to explore Prague. But if you want to see the countryside, driving can be a fun way to travel. Czechs, who learned to drive in

---

⌐Tips A Taxi Bargain

At the airport, shrewd travelers might get an honest ride from one of the taxi drivers who linger in their *Škodas* (a type of Czech car) after dropping off departing passengers at the other end of the terminal. A ride should cost no more than 700Kč ($29) to Václavské náměstí (Wenceslas Sq.).

low-powered *Škodas,* still run up your tailpipe before passing, even though many now drive beefier BMWs and Opels. The combination of high-speed muscle cars, rickety East Bloc specials, and smoky cargo trucks crawling along can make driving on two-lane highways frustrating. But a car will make it easier to find a budget hotel or a comfortable spot to camp. The destinations outside Prague described in chapters 11, 12, and 13 include detailed driving directions.

Travelers approaching Prague from the west drive through Nürnberg, Germany, before entering the Czech Republic at the Waldhaus/Rozvadov border crossing on a new superhighway that connects to Prague via Plzeň. Drivers from the north-west motor through Chemnitz (formerly Karl-Marx-Stadt), Germany, before entering the Czech Republic at the Reitzenhain/Pohraničí. From the south, Linz, Austria, is a gateway; and from the east, Žilina, Slovakia, is a gateway. Driving distances: from Vienna, 350km (217 miles); from Warsaw, 750km (465 miles); from Munich, 450km (279 miles); and from Berlin, 380km (236 miles).

See "Getting Around" in chapter 3 for information on car-rental firms.

BY TRAIN

Train fares in Europe are lower than those in the United States. Czech tickets are particularly inexpensive but prices are rising. Because European countries are compact, it often takes less time to travel city-to-city by train than by plane. Prague is about 5 hours by train from Munich, Berlin, and Vienna. Direct trains to Prague depart daily from Paris (via Frankfurt) and Berlin (via Dresden).

You should also check the schedule for the ultramodern, high-speed, passenger-only train that travels from London Waterloo International Station to Europe, the **Eurostar,** at www.eurostar.com or by calling © **01777-777-878.**

Trains connect Prague and Vienna five times daily; the 5½-hour trip costs $30 each way. Trains leave Prague to Warsaw two times daily; the 9-hour trip costs $35 each way.

You can also reach Prague from Munich or Frankfurt. The former runs three times daily, with the 7-hour trip costing $65 each way. The latter runs two times daily, with the 7½-hour trip costing $71 each way.

For more information on traveling on České dráhy (Czech Railways) on www.cd.cz, see chapter 11.

TRAIN PASSES *Note:* The Czech Republic is not covered by the Eurailpass though the **European East Pass** and the **Austrian Czech Railpass** are accepted. The Republic does have two country-specific pass options.

CZECH FLEXIPASS This pass entitles you to any 3 days of unlimited train travel in a 15-day period. It costs $74 for first class and $52 for second class.

PRAGUE EXCURSION PASS This pass provides one round-trip excursion on the Czech National Railways from any Czech border to Prague (note that you don't have to return to the same border town on the way out from Prague). It is valid for 7 days, and stops in other places in the Czech Republic are allowed on the way to and from Prague but your entire journey must be completed within 1 calendar day. The pass costs $60 for first class or $45 for second class. Travelers 12 to 25 years old can get a **Prague Excursion Youth Pass,** which costs only $50 for first class and $40 for second class.

All of the passes above must be purchased in North America before you leave on your trip. You can buy them on the phone or online from **Rail Europe** (© **877/257-2887** in the U.S., 800/361-RAIL in Canada; www.raileurope.com).

If you're visiting more countries in Eastern Europe, you might want to get the **European East Pass,** which combines travel in Austria, the Czech Republic, Hungary, Poland, and Slovakia. It costs $225 (first class) or $158 (second class), and you can use it for 5 days of unlimited train travel in a 1-month period.

Many rail passes are available in the United Kingdom for travel in Britain and Europe. However, one of the most widely used of these passes, the InterRail card, isn't valid for travel in the Czech Republic.

BY BUS

Throughout Europe, bus transportation is usually less expensive than rail travel and covers a more extensive area. European buses generally outshine their U.S. counterparts. In the Czech Republic, buses cost significantly less than trains and often offer more direct routes. **Europabus,** c/o DER Tours/German Rail, 11933 Wilshire Blvd., Los Angeles, CA 90025 (© **800/782-2424** or 310/479-4140), provides information on regular coach service. **Busabout London Traveller's Centre,** 258 Vauxhall Bridge Rd., London, SW 1V 1BS (© **0207-950-1661;** www.busabout.com) is a British operator specializing in economical bus tours of Europe. Bookings can be made online.

If you're coming from London, **Eurolines** (© **08705-143-219;** www.eurolines.co.uk), runs regular bus service from London to Prague at about £102 round-trip. Coaches are equipped with toilets and reclining seats, and trips take about 30 hours. By law, drivers are required to stop at regular intervals for rest and refreshment.

Kingscourt Express, Havelská 8, Praha 1 (© **224-234-583;** www.kce.cz), operates the most popular scheduled bus service between London and Prague, which stops in Prague just across from the Florenc station. The nearly 21-hour trip runs six times weekly, and the round-trip costs 3,100Kč ($129).

A daily bus connection between Prague and Vienna with ČSAD (Křižíkova 4–6, Praha 8; © **222-624-440;** www.jizdnirady.cz) leaves from the Florenc Bus Station. The trip takes 4¼ hours and costs 504Kč ($21). There's bus service between Prague and Warsaw twice a week for 720Kč ($30) each way as well as between Prague and Berlin (960Kč/$40 each way).

You should make reservations as far in advance as possible. See chapters 11, 12, and 13 for more information on traveling by bus from Prague to other destinations in the Czech Republic.

BY FERRY, SEACAT, OR CHANNEL TUNNEL FOR U.K. TRAVELERS

If you're traveling from England and don't want to fly, there are several options for getting to continental Europe. If you want to drive, **P&O Ferries** (© 08705-980-333; www.poferries.com) is one of the U.K.'s largest drive-on ferryboat operators, carrying cars, passengers, and freight. The company offers daily crossings of the English Channel from Dover to Calais, France, and from Folkestone to Zeebrugge, Belgium. **Brittany Ferries** (© 08703-665-333; www.brittanyferries.co.uk), P&O's largest competitor, offers regular ferry service from Portsmouth to St-Malo and Caen in France.

Another way to cross the channel is by **SeaCat** (a form of high-speed motorized catamaran), which cuts your journey time from the United Kingdom to the Continent. A SeaCat trip can be a fun adventure, especially for first-timers and children, as the vessel technically "flies" above the surface of the water. A SeaCat crossing from Folkestone to Boulogne, France, is more timesaving for passengers than the Dover-to-Calais route used by conventional ferryboats. For reservations and information, call **HoverSpeed** at © **08702-408-070;** www.hoverspeed.co.uk.

You can also go via the Channel Tunnel. The drive-on/drive-off "Chunnel" train runs between Folkestone and Calais, France. Travel time under the water between England and France is just 40 minutes. For more information go to www.eurotunnel.com. Train passengers can use the tunnel on direct routes to Paris from London's Waterloo Station. For up-to-the-minute information, check BritRail at www.britrail.co.uk.

10 Packages for the Independent Traveler

Several tour operators offer escorted and independent tours to Prague and the Czech Republic and are described below. However, by using this book you can put together your own itinerary for about one-third of the cost.

Most airlines listed above offer both escorted tours and on-your-own packages—for example, combining airfare and hotel packages departing from major U.S. cities. If you can find round-trip airfare from New York/Newark for $850 or less, you won't be saving any money on package tours. Likewise, the half-dozen add-ons, including walking tours, river cruises, and airport transfers, can all be easily purchased individually for less money, once you arrive in Prague.

The largest Czech agency, **Cedok,** has closed its only U.S. office in New York, but English-speaking staff can be contacted through its London or Prague offices or through the Internet. In the United Kingdom, the address is 314–322 Regent St., London W1B 3BG (© 020/7580-3778). The Prague main office offers advance bookings at Na Příkopě 18, Praha 1 (© 224-197-632). The Čedok English-language link on its website is www.cedok.co.uk or www.cedok.cz.

Isram World of Travel, 233 Park Ave. South, New York, NY 10003 (© 800/223-7460; www.isramworld.com), offers packages to your choice of many Eastern European cities. The company will arrange hotels, sightseeing tours, and airport/train station transfers. Its Prague package starts at $350 per person, based on double occupancy.

3

Getting to Know Prague

Prague (Praha in Czech) has long been considered a city of mysterious intrigue, but this chapter should help visitors clarify some of that mystery. It will also show you how to navigate the twisting cobblestone streets and unique neighborhoods of Prague.

1 Orientation

ARRIVING
BY PLANE

Prague's **Ruzyně Airport** (© 220-113-314; www.prg.aero or www.csl.cz) is located 19km (12 miles) west of the city center. Its new, airy, and efficient departures and arrivals terminals have lost the Communist-era feel and have many added amenities. There's a bank for changing money (usually open daily 7am–11pm), car-rental offices (see "Getting Around" below), and information stands that can help you find accommodations if you've arrived without reservations.

GETTING DOWNTOWN   You can make your way from the airport to your hotel by taxi, airport shuttle bus, or city bus.

Official airport taxis are plentiful and line up in front of the arrivals terminal. Alas, the Volkswagen Passats queued directly outside the terminal's main exit all belong to the same cartel sanctioned by the airport authority. (See "Getting Around" below for details.) The drivers are getting more pleasant but are still often arrogant and dishonest. Negotiate the fare in advance and have it written down. Expect to pay about 700Kč to 800Kč ($29–$33) for the 20 or so minutes to the city center, depending on the whims of the syndicate. If you want to save money, find other travelers to share the expense.

CEDAZ (© 220-114-296; www.aas.cz/cedaz) operates an **airport shuttle bus** from the airport to náměstí Republiky in central Prague. It leaves the airport daily every 30 minutes from 5:30am to 9:30pm and stops near the náměstí Republiky metro station. The shuttle costs 90Kč ($3.75) for the 30-minute trip.

Even cheaper is **city bus no. 119,** which takes passengers from the bus stop at the right of the airport exit to the Dejvická metro station (and back). The bus/metro combo costs only 20Kč (85¢), but the bus makes many stops. Travel time is about 40 minutes.

BY TRAIN

Passengers traveling to Prague by train typically pull into one of two central stations: Hlavní nádraží (Main Station) or Nádraží Holešovice (Holešovice Station). Both are on line C of the metro system and offer a number of services, including money exchange, a post office, and a luggage-storage area.

Prague at a Glance

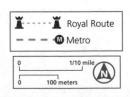

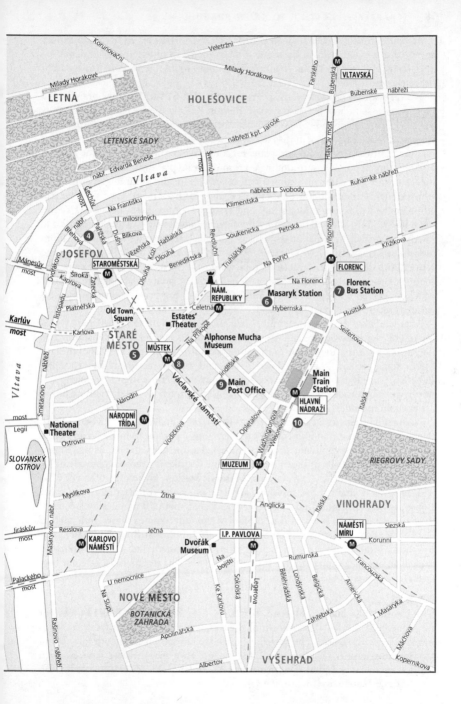

At both terminals you'll find **AVE Ltd.** (© **251-551-011**), an accommodations agency that arranges beds in hostels as well as rooms in hotels and apartments. It's open daily from 6am to 11pm. If you arrive without room reservations, this agency is definitely worth a visit.

Hlavní nádraží, Wilsonova třída, Praha 2 (© **224-614-071**), is the grander and more popular station, but it's also seedier. Built in 1909, this once beautiful four-story Art Nouveau structure was one of the city's beloved architectural gems before it was connected to a darkly modern dispatch hall in the mid-1970s. It has been neglected for years, but the city already has plans for a massive reconstruction of the station's building complex and its surroundings. From the train platform, you'll walk down a flight of stairs and through a tunnel before arriving in the ground-level main hall, which contains ticket windows, a useful **Prague Information Service** office that sells city maps and dispenses information, and restrooms. Also useful is the **ČD center** (© **840-112-113;** www.cd.cz) run by the Czech Railways. It provides domestic and international train information as well as currency exchange and accommodations services. It is open daily 7 to 11am, 11:30am to 2pm, and 2:30 to 5:45pm. Visa and MasterCard are accepted. An information window is open 3:15am to 12:40am (the train station is closed 1–3am). The station's basement holds a left-luggage counter, which is open 24 hours and charges 30Kč ($1.25) per bag per day. The nearby lockers aren't secure and should be avoided.

After you leave the modern terminal hall, a 5-minute walk to the left puts you at the top of Wenceslas Square and 15 minutes by foot from Old Town Square. Metro line C connects the station easily to the other two subway lines and the rest of the city. Metro trains depart from the lower level, and tickets, costing 14Kč to 20Kč (60¢–85¢), are available from the newsstand near the metro entrance. Gouging taxi drivers line up outside the station and are plentiful throughout the day and night but are not recommended.

Nádraží Holešovice, Partyzánská at Vrbenského, Praha 7 (© **224-615-865**), Prague's second train station, is usually the terminus for trains from Berlin and other points north. Although it's not as centrally located as the main station, its more manageable size and location at the end of metro line C make it almost as convenient.

Prague has two smaller train stations. **Masaryk Station,** Hybernská ulice (© **221-111-122**), is primarily for travelers arriving on trains originating from other Bohemian cities or from Brno or Bratislava. Situated about 10 minutes by foot from the main train station, Masaryk is near Staré Město, just a stone's throw from náměstí Republiky metro station. **Smíchov Station,** Nádražní ulice at Rozkošného (© **224-617-686**), is the terminus for commuter trains from western and southern Bohemia, though an occasional international train pulls in here. The station has a 24-hour baggage check and is serviced by metro line B.

BY BUS

The **Central Bus Station–Florenc,** Křižíkova 4–6, Praha 8 (© **900-144-444** for timetable info), is a few blocks north of the main train station. Most local and long-distance buses arrive here. The adjacent Florenc metro station is on both lines B and C. Florenc station is relatively small and doesn't have many visitor services. Even smaller depots are at **Želivského** (metro line A), **Smíchovské nádraží** (metro line B), and **Nádraží Holešovice** (metro line C).

VISITOR INFORMATION

If you want to arrange accommodations before you come, Prague-based **E-travel.cz** offers handy English websites. The general site at www.travel.cz provides booking for hotels and practical touring information, while at www.apartments.cz, you can book a private apartment in a wide range of prices and areas. Once in the city, you can find E-travel.cz near the National Theater at Ostrovní 7; or call their 24-hour call center (✆ **224-990-990;** fax 224-990-999). Especially for those arriving by train or air, **AVE Travel** (✆ **251-091-111;** www.avetravel.cz) can arrange accommodations or transfers inside these terminals. It has outlets at the airport, open daily from 7am to 10pm; at the main train station, Hlavní nádraží, open daily from 6am to 11pm; and at the north train station, Nádraží Holešovice, open daily from 7am to 9pm.

The **Prague Information Service** (PIS), Na Příkopě 20, Praha 1 (✆ **12-444;** fax 222-221-721; www.pis.cz), near Wenceslas Square, provides tips and tickets for upcoming cultural events and tours. It can also help you find a room. From April to October, it's open Monday to Friday from 9am to 7pm and Saturday and Sunday from 9am to 5pm. During the rest of the year, it's open Monday to Friday from 9am to 6pm and Saturday from 9am to 3pm; it's closed on Sunday. There are also PIS offices inside Old Town Hall and the main train station.

The weekly newspaper the ***Prague Post*** (www.praguepost.com) has a fairly beefy culture section and a special supplement to help visitors. It can be found at most central newsstands.

Čedok, at Na Příkopě 18, Praha 1 (✆ **800-112-112** or 224-197-111; fax 224-216-324; www.cedok.cz), was once the state travel bureau and is now a privatized agency. Its entrenched position still gives it decent access to tickets and information about domestic events, and the staff can book rail and bus tickets and hotel rooms. Čedok accepts major credit cards and is open Monday to Friday from 9am to 7pm, Saturday 9:30am to 1pm.

Avoid kiosks that look like information points but are really ticket touts for tours and concerts. Asking for directions from a Czech on the street will be more enjoyable (and useful) than the surly response you'll probably get from the usually uninformed person staffing the kiosk.

CITY LAYOUT

The **river Vltava** bisects Prague and provides the best line of orientation; you can use **Charles Bridge** as your central point. From the bridge, turn toward **Prague Castle,** the massive complex on the hill with the cathedral thrusting out. Now you're facing west.

Tips **Calling Prague**

The **country code** for the Czech Republic is **420**. In all cases, the **city codes** are connected to the local number in front so that the entire number that must be dialed locally has **nine** digits. For directory assistance in English and for information on services and rates calling abroad, dial ✆ **1181**.

To call Prague direct from the United States, dial **011** (international code), 420 (country code), and the 9-digit local number. From Britain, dial 00 (international code), 420 (country code), and the local number.

Up on the hill is the Castle District known as **Hradčany.** Running up the hill between the bridge and the castle is the district known as **Malá Strana** (literally the "Small Side," but known as Lesser Town in English). Turn around, and behind you on the right (east) bank is **Staré Město** (Old Town), and farther to the south and east **Nové Město** (New Town). The highlands even farther east used to be the royal vineyards, **Vinohrady,** now a popular neighborhood for expatriates with a growing array of accommodations and restaurants. The districts farther out are where most Praguers live, and have few attractions.

MAIN BRIDGES, SQUARES & STREETS You'll best enjoy Prague by walking its narrow streets, busy squares, and scenic bridges. After **Charles Bridge (Karlův most),** the other two bridges worth walking are **Mánes Bridge (Mánesův most),** which provides a stunning low-angle view of the castle especially at night, and the **Bridge of the Legions (most Legií),** which links the National Theater to Petřín Hill.

On the left bank coming off Charles Bridge is **Mostecká Street,** and at the end of it sits the cozy square under the castle hill, **Malostranské náměstí.** On the hill outside the main castle gate is the motorcade-worn **Hradčanské náměstí,** on the city side of which you'll find a spectacular view of spires and red roofs below.

On the east side of Charles Bridge, you can wind through most any of the old alleys leading from the bridge and get pleasantly lost amid the shops and cafes. The tourist-packed route through Old Town is **Karlova Street.** Like Karlova, almost any other route in Old Town will eventually lead you to **Staroměstské náměstí (Old Town Sq.),** the breathtaking heart of Staré Město. A black monument to Jan Hus, the martyred Czech Protestant leader, dominates the square. The tree-lined boulevard to the right behind Hus is **Pařížská (Parisian Blvd.)** with boutiques and restaurants; it forms the edge of the Jewish Quarter. Over Hus's left shoulder is **Dlouhá Street,** and in front of him to his left is the kitschy shopping zone on **Celetná.** Across the square to Hus's right, past the clock tower of Old Town Hall (Staroměstská radnice), is **Železná Street,** which leads to Mozart's Prague venue, the Estates' Theater. Farther to Hus's right is the narrow alley **Melantrichova,** which winds southeast to **Václavské náměstí (Wenceslas Sq.),** site of pro-democracy demonstrations in 1968 and 1989.

FINDING AN ADDRESS Don't worry about getting lost—everyone does temporarily, even lifelong Praguers. If you're pressed for time and can't enjoy an aimless wander, you'll find that street signs are emblazoned on red Art Nouveau frames, usually bolted to buildings. House numbers generally increase as you get farther from the Vltava or the square from which the street begins.

Note that Prague street names always precede the numbers, like Václavské nám. 25. *Ulice* (abbreviated ul. or omitted) means "street," *třída* (abbreviated tr.) means "avenue," *náměstí* (abbreviated nám.) is "square" or "plaza," *most* is "bridge," and *nábřeží* is "quay."

Prague is divided into 10 postal districts whose numbers are routinely included in addresses. The districts forming the main tourist areas are listed below with their corresponding neighborhoods.

Praha 1 Hradčany, Malá Strana, Staré Město, Josefov, northern Nové Město.

Praha 2 Southern Nové Město, Vyšehrad, western Vinohrady.

Praha 3 Eastern Vinohrady, Žižkov.

Praha 6 Western Bubeneč, Dejvice, Vokovice, Střešovice, Břevnov, Veleslavín, Liboc, Ruzyně, Řepy, Nebušice, Lysolaje, Sedlec, Suchdol.

MAPS   A detailed Prague street map is recommended if you want to venture off the main streets or retrace where you think you were during your wandering odyssey. **Kartographia Praha** produces a series of Prague city maps and also has hiking maps covering the best of the intricately marked footpaths throughout the country. Maps are called *turistická mapa* and have translated keys. You can find them at Czech-language bookstores.

NEIGHBORHOODS IN BRIEF

Prague was originally developed as four adjacent self-governing boroughs, plus a walled Jewish ghetto. Central Prague's neighborhoods have maintained their individual identities along with their medieval street plans.

Hradčany   The Castle District dominates the hilltop above Malá Strana. Here you'll find not only the fortress that remains the presidential palace and national seat of power but also the Loreto Church, Strahov Monastery, and the main national art gallery at the archbishop's palace. You can take a scenic walk down the hill via Nerudova or through the lush Petřín Hill gardens.

Malá Strana (Lesser Town)   Prague's storybook Lesser Town was founded in 1257 by Germanic merchants who set up shop at the base of the castle. Nestled between the bastion and the river Vltava, Malá Strana is laced with narrow, winding lanes boasting palaces and red-roofed town houses (see "Walking Tour 1," in chapter 8). The parliament and government and several embassies reside in palaces here. **Kampa Park,** on the riverbank just south of Charles Bridge, forms the southeastern edge of Lesser Town, and the riverside **Liechtenstein Palace** on the park's northern edge was used as the U.S. Embassy in the Tom Cruise version of *Mission: Impossible* (the real U.S. Embassy is a few blocks away). **Nerudova** is the steep, shop-lined alley leading from the town square to the castle. Alternate castle routes for the strong of heart are the New Castle Stairs (Nové zámecké schody), 1 block north of Nerudova, and the Old Castle Stairs (Staré zámecké schody), just northwest from the Malostranská

metro station. Tram no. 22 or 23 will take you up the hill if you don't want to make the heart-pounding hike.

Staré Město (Old Town)   Staré Město was chartered in 1234, as Prague became a stop on important trade routes. Its meandering streets, radiating from Staroměstské náměstí (Old Town Sq.), are still big visitor draws. Old Town is compact, bordered by the Vltava on the north and west and Revoluční and Národní streets on the east and south. You can wander safely without having to worry about straying into danger. Once here, stick to the cobblestone streets and don't cross any bridges, any streets containing tram tracks, or any rivers, and you'll know that you're still in Old Town. You'll stumble across beautiful **baroque and Renaissance architecture** and find some wonderful restaurants, shops, bars, cafes, and pubs. For a detailed walking tour, see "Walking Tour 3," in chapter 8.

Josefov   Prague's Jewish ghetto, entirely within Staré Město, was surrounded by a wall before almost being completely destroyed to make way for more modern 19th-century structures. The **Old-New Synagogue** is in the geographical center of Josefov, and the surrounding streets are wonderful for strolling. Prague is one of Europe's great historic Jewish cities, and exploring this remarkable area will make it clear why. For details, see "Walking Tour 4," in chapter 8.

What's All the U-ing About?

Czech establishments have traditionally taken on the name of a distinctive landmark nearby, the name of the house, or the name of the owner of the house. The Czech preposition for *at* is *u*. You'll find that a *u* fronts many pubs, restaurants, hotels, and other businesses, followed by the distinctive name, such as the Malá Strana restaurant U Malířů (At the Painter's), originally the home of 16th-century artist Šic. Another example is U Fleků (At Flek's), which was Mr. Flek's 1499 home brewery, now a regular stop for German tour buses.

Often the place takes the name of a statue or frieze over the entrance to the building that sets it apart from all others (much more so than just an address number). For example, the frieze above the door of the popular Old Town pub U medvídků tells patrons that they're about to drink "At the Little Bear's" house.

Nové Město (New Town) Draped like a crescent around Staré Město, Nové Město is where you'll find **Václavské náměstí (Wenceslas Sq.),** the **National Theater,** and the central business district. When it was founded by Charles IV in 1348, Nové Město was Europe's largest wholly planned municipal development. The street layout has remained largely unchanged, but many of Nové Město's structures were razed in the late 19th century and replaced with the offices and apartment buildings you see today. New Town lacks the classical allure of Old Town and Malá Strana, but if you venture beyond Wenceslas Square into Vinohrady you'll find restaurants, interesting shops, and a part of Prague that feels more like a normal city instead of a tourist attraction.

While violent crime is still relatively rare, you should take caution here at night, especially around Wenceslas Square and nearby Perlová Street, where prostitutes and drug dealers ply their trades.

2 Getting Around

BY PUBLIC TRANSPORTATION

Prague's public transportation network is one of the few sound Communist-era legacies and is still remarkably affordable. In central Prague, metro (subway) stations abound. Trams and buses offer a cheap sightseeing experience but also require a strong stomach for jostling with fellow passengers in close quarters.

TICKETS & PASSES   For single-use **tickets,** there are two choices. You can ride a maximum of five stations on the metro (not including the station of validation) or 20 minutes on a tram or bus, without transfers (on the metro you can transfer from line A to B to C within 30 min.), for 14Kč (60¢); children 6 and under ride free, 6- to 15-year-olds for 7Kč (30¢). This is usually enough for trips in the historic districts. Rides of more than five stops on the metro, or longer tram or bus rides, with unlimited

Prague Metro

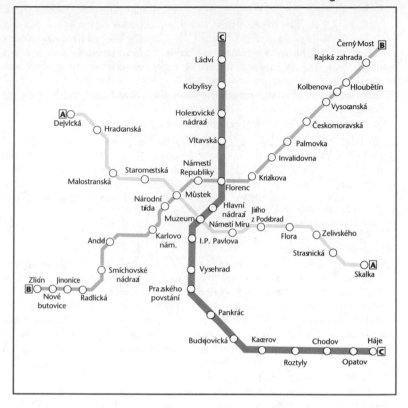

transfers for up to 75 minutes (90 min. on Sat, Sun, public holidays, and after 8pm on workdays) after your ticket is validated, cost 20Kč (85¢).

A **1-day pass** good for unlimited rides is 80Kč ($3.35), a **3-day pass** 220Kč ($9.15), a **7-day pass** 280Kč ($12), and a **15-day pass** 320Kč ($13).

You can buy tickets from yellow coin-operated machines in metro stations or at most newsstands marked TABÁK or TRAFIKA. Hold on to your validated ticket throughout your ride—you'll need to show it if a ticket collector (be sure to check for his or her badge) asks you. If you're caught without a valid ticket, you'll be asked, and not so kindly, to pay a fine on the spot while all the locals look on, shaking their heads in disgust. The fine is 500Kč ($21).

BY METRO   Metro trains operate daily from 5am to midnight and run every 2 to 6 minutes. On the three lettered lines (A, B, and C, color-coded green, yellow, and red, respectively), the most convenient central stations are Můstek, at the foot of Václavské náměstí (Wenceslas Sq.); Staroměstská, for Old Town Square and Charles Bridge; and Malostranská, serving Malá Strana and the Castle District. Refer to the metro map for details.

BY ELECTRIC TRAM & BUS   The 24 electric tram (streetcar) lines run practically everywhere, and there's always another tram with the same number traveling back. You never have to hail trams; they make every stop. The most popular trams, nos. 22 and 23 (aka the "tourist trams" and the "pickpocket express"), run past top sights like the National Theater and Prague Castle. Regular bus and tram service stops at midnight, after which selected routes run reduced schedules, usually only once per hour. Schedules are posted at stops. If you miss a night connection, expect a long wait for the next.

Buses tend to be used only outside the older districts of Prague and have 3-digit numbers.

Both the buses and tram lines begin their morning runs around 4:30am.

BY FUNICULAR   The funicular (cog railway) makes the scenic run up and down Petřín Hill every 10 minutes (15 in winter season) daily from 9am to 11:30pm with an intermediate stop at the Nebozízek restaurant halfway down the hill, which overlooks the city. It requires the 20Kč (85¢) ticket or any of the same transport passes as other modes of public transport and departs from a small house in the park at Újezd in Malá Strana.

BY TAXI

I have one word for you: *Beware.*

You can hail taxis in the streets or in front of train stations, large hotels, and popular attractions, but many drivers simply gouge visitors. In the late 1990s, the city canceled price regulations, but instead of creating price competition, it started a turf war between cabbies vying for the best taxi stands. The best fare you can hope for is 22Kč (90¢) per kilometer and 25Kč ($1.05) for the starting rate when you phone a taxi company. It will get more expensive when you stop a taxi on the street. Rates usually aren't posted outside on the taxi's door but on the dashboard—once you're inside it's a bit late to haggle. Try to get the driver to agree to a price and write it down before you get in. Better yet, go by foot or public transport.

If you must go by taxi, call reputable companies with English-speaking dispatchers: **AAA Taxi** (© **14014** or 222-333-222; www.aaataxi.cz); **ProfiTaxi** (© **844-700-800;** www.profitaxi.cz); or **SEDOP** (© **271-722-222;** www.sedop.cz). Demand a receipt for the fare before you start, as it'll keep them a little more honest.

BY RENTAL CAR

Driving in Prague isn't worth the money or effort. The roads are frustrating and slow, and parking is minimal and expensive. However, a car is a plus if you want to explore other parts of the Czech Republic.

RENTAL COMPANIES   Try **Europcar Czech Rent a Car,** Pařížská 28, Praha 1 (© **224-811-290;** www.europcar.cz), or at Ruzyně Airport, Praha 6 (© 235-364-531). There's also **Hertz,** Karlovo nám. 28, Praha 2 (© **222-231-010;** www.hertz.cz).

Tips **Getting the Most from Your Tram Fare**

If you're taking tram no. 22 or 23 to Prague Castle from Národní or anywhere farther from the castle, I recommend you get a 20Kč (85¢) ticket. It is valid for 75 minutes of tram ride on weekdays (up to 90 min. after 8pm and on weekends). Use the 14Kč (60¢) ticket only for a short travel distance (one or two tram stops) since it is only good for 20 minutes and you may get caught beyond this limit.

Budget is at Ruzyně Airport (℗ **220-113-253;** www.budget.cz) and in the Hotel Inter-Continental, náměstí Curieových, Praha 1 (℗ 222-319-595).

Local car-rental companies sometimes offer lower rates than the big international firms. Compare **CS Czechocar,** Kongresové centrum (Congress Center at Vyšehrad metro stop on the C line), Praha 4 (℗ **261-222-079** or 261-222-143; www.czechocar.cz), or at Ruzyně Airport, Praha 6 (℗ 220-113-454); or try **SeccoCar,** Přístavní 39, Praha 7 (℗ **220-800-647;** www.seccocar.cz).

Car rates can be negotiable. Try to obtain the best possible deal with the rental company by asking about discounts. Special deals are often offered for keeping the car for an extended period, for unlimited mileage (or at least getting some miles thrown in free), or for a bigger car at a lower price. You can usually get some sort of discount for a company or an association affiliation. Check before you leave home and take a member ID card with you.

Since extras can send prices into the stratosphere, find out all the charges you're likely to incur; besides the daily or weekly rental, consider the mileage charge, insurance, the cost of fuel, and tax on the total rental (19% in Prague). In addition, you may be paying for parking along the way. If you already have collision coverage on your own auto insurance, you're most likely covered when behind the wheel of a rental car; check with your insurance carrier. If you decide on European insurance, be sure it doesn't come with a $1,000 deductible. A collision-damage waiver (CDW) usually costs $7 to $13 per day. Some credit card companies, including American Express, automatically insure cardholders against collision damage at no extra charge when they rent a car using the company's card.

ROADWAYS & EMERGENCIES   Major roadways radiate from Prague like spokes on a wheel, so touring the country is easy if you make the capital your base. The Prague–Brno motorway is the most traveled, but the new Prague–Nürnberg motorway (*dálnice*) has opened a 2-hour express route into western Germany (though parts of both the German and Czech sides are not yet complete). You are advised to check the most recent map before you travel. Alternatively, see www.ceskedalnice.cz, where you will find updates on the newly built motorways. If you are going to use any of these, you have to purchase a special stamp-sticker (*dálniční známka*), which goes on your windshield. Most filling stations and post offices sell them. The sticker costs 200Kč ($8.30) for 15 days, 300Kč ($12) for 2 months, or 900Kč ($37) for the calendar year. Rented cars should come with a valid stamp already.

Czech roads are often narrow and in need of repair. Add to this drivers who live out their speedway fantasies on these pot-holed beauties, and you may want to take the train. The few superhighways that do exist are in good shape, so whenever possible, stick to them, especially at night. If you have car trouble, major highways have **SOS emergency phones** to call for assistance, located about every 1km (half-mile). There's also the **ÚAMK,** a 24-hour auto club like AAA that can provide service for a fee. You can summon its bright yellow pickup trucks on the main highways by using the emergency phones. If you're not near an SOS phone or are on a road without them, you can contact ÚAMK at ℗ **1230** (www.uamk.cz), or **ABA,** another emergency assistance company, at ℗ **1240** (www.aba.cz).

Foreign drivers are required to have an **international driver's license and proof of international insurance** (a green card issued with rental cars). Czech police are infamous for stopping cars with foreign plates, and the "fines" they exact are often negotiable. If you're stopped, expect to pay at least 1,000Kč ($41) for speeding. Those caught by the police should ask for some type of receipt (*účet* in Czech, pronounced "*oo*-chet"); this can help cut down on overpayment.

GASOLINE   Not only are rentals expensive, gasoline *(benzín)* in the Czech Republic costs much more than you're accustomed to paying—around 30Kč ($1.25) per liter, or 120Kč ($5) per gallon. Filling stations, which used to be difficult to find, are now on all major highways. Most are open 24 hours, and many have minimarkets with food and drink as well. If you're leaving the country, fill up near the border, as the price of gas in Austria and Germany is much higher still.

PARKING   Finding a parking spot in Prague can sometimes be even more challenging than driving in this maze of a city. Fines for illegal parking can be stiff, but worse are "Denver Boots," which immobilize cars until a fine is paid. If you find your car booted, call the number on the ticket, tell them where you are, wait for the clamp removers, and pay them 500Kč ($21) or more depending on your violation. The city has now installed street parking meters marked with a blue "P" in required zones; they issue slips that you place inside your car on the dashboard so they're visible through the windshield. These normally run from 20Kč to 30Kč (85¢–$1.25) per hour for up to 4 hours.

SPECIAL DRIVING RULES   Seat belts are required, you may *not*—repeat *not*—legally make a right turn when a traffic light is red, and autos must stop when a pedestrian steps into a crosswalk (however, they often don't, as you'll find when you're walking around). Children under 1.5m (about 5 ft.) tall can't ride in the front seat. On major highways, the speed limit is 130kmph (80 mph). The yellow diamond road sign denotes the right of way at an unregulated intersection. When approaching an intersection, always check to see who has the right of way, since the "main" road can change several times within blocks on the same street.

BY BIKE

Though there are no special bike lanes in the city center, and smooth streets are unheard of, Prague is a particularly fun city to bike when the crowds are thin. Vehicular traffic is limited in the city center, where small, winding streets seem especially suited to two-wheeled vehicles. Surprisingly, few people take advantage of this opportunity; cyclists are largely limited to the few foreigners who have imported their own bikes. The city's ubiquitous cobblestones make mountain bikes the natural choice. Check with your hotel about a rental, or try **Dodosport** at Na Zderaze 5 (© **272-769-387**).

FAST FACTS: Prague

American Express   For travel arrangements, traveler's checks, currency exchange, and other member services, visit the city's sole American Express office at Václavské nám. 56 (Wenceslas Sq.), Praha 1 (© **222-800-237**). It's open daily from 9am to 7pm.

Area Code   The area codes for each city are combined with the local numbers. Local phone numbers consist of 9 digits, which must be dialed from anyplace within the Czech Republic.

Babysitters   If your hotel can't recommend a sitter, phone **Agentura Domestica**, Lidická 7, Praha 5 (© **257-316-150**; www.domestica.cz), a company that provides various services, including babysitting. Make reservations in advance. The fee is 150Kč ($6.25) per hour.

Bookstores The largest English-language bookshops are **The Globe,** Pštrossova 6, Praha 1 (© **224-934-203;** www.globebookstore.cz); **Big Ben Bookshop,** Malá Štupartská 5, Praha 1 (© **224-826-565;** www.bigbenbookshop.com); and **U Knihomola,** Mánesova 79, Praha 2 (© **222-729-348**). A new addition to Prague's list of bookstores is **Neoluxor,** Václavské nám. 41, Praha 1 (© **221-111-364;** www. neoluxor.cz). See chapter 9 for complete information.

Business Hours Most **banks** are open Monday to Friday from 8:30am to 6pm. Business **offices** are generally open Monday to Friday from 8am to 6pm. **Pubs** are usually open daily from 11am to midnight. Most **restaurants** open for lunch from noon to 3pm and for dinner from 6 to 11pm; only a few stay open later. **Stores** are typically open Monday to Friday from 9am to 6pm and Saturday from 9am to 1pm, but those in the tourist center keep longer hours and are open Sunday as well. *Note:* Some small food shops that keep long hours charge up to 20% more for all their goods.

Currency Exchange Banks generally offer the best exchange rates, but **American Express** is competitive and doesn't charge commission for cashing traveler's checks, regardless of the issuer. Don't hesitate to use a credit card; card exchange rates often work to the traveler's advantage. There's an American Express office in Prague (see above).

Komerční banka has three convenient Praha 1 locations with ATMs that accept Visa, MasterCard, and American Express: Na Příkopě 33, Spálená 51 and Václavské nám. 42 (© **800-111-055,** central switchboard for all branches; www.kb.cz). The exchange offices are open Monday to Friday from 8am to 5pm, but the ATMs are accessible 24 hours.

Živnostenská banka, Na Příkopě 20, Praha 1 (© **224-121-111;** www.ziba.cz), has an exchange office open Monday to Friday from 10am to 9pm and Saturday from 3 to 7pm.

Chequepoint keeps the longest hours but offers the worst exchange rates. Central Prague locations are 28. října 13 and Staroměstské nám. 21 (both open 24 hr.); Staroměstské nám. 27 (open daily 8am–11:30pm); and Václavské nám. 32 (open daily 8am–11pm).

Doctors & Dentists If you need a doctor or dentist and your condition isn't life-threatening, you can visit the Polyclinic at Národní, Národní 9, Praha 1 (© **222-075-120**) during walk-in hours Monday to Friday from 8:30am to 5pm. For emergency medical aid call their mobile phone © 777 942-270. Dr. Stránský, the founder of this private practice, is an Ivy League–trained, straight-talking physician, born to a celebrated Czech émigré family who came back to reclaim property on National Boulevard. He turned part of the block into a Western-standard health center that acts as a clinic of record for the U.S. Embassy. You'll be asked to show proof of insurance or to pay upfront. The **Medicover Clinic,** Vyšehradská 35, Praha 2 (© **224-921-884**), provides EKGs, diagnostics, ophthalmology, house calls, and referrals to specialists. Normal walk-in hours are Monday to Saturday from 7am to 7pm.

For **emergency medical aid,** call the **Foreigners' Medical Clinic,** Na Homolce Hospital, Roentgenova 2, Praha 5 (© **257-272-146,** or 257-272-191 after hours).

Electricity Czech appliances operate on 220 volts and plug into two-pronged outlets that differ from those in America and the United Kingdom. Appliances designed for the U.S. or U.K. markets must use an adapter and a transformer (sometimes incorrectly called a converter). Don't attempt to plug an American appliance directly into a European electrical outlet without a transformer; you'll ruin your appliance and possibly start a fire.

Embassies The **U.S. Embassy,** Tržiště 15, Praha 1 (© 257-530-663), is open Monday to Friday from 8 to 4:30pm. The **Canadian Embassy,** Muchova 6, Praha 6 (© 272-101-800), is open Monday to Friday from 8:30am to 12:30pm and 1:30pm to 4:30pm. The **U.K. Embassy,** Thunovská 14, Praha 1 (© 257-402-111), is open Monday to Friday from 8:30am to 12:30 and 1:30pm to 5pm. You can visit the **Australian Honorary Consul,** Klimentská 10, Praha 1 (© 296-578-350) Monday to Friday from 9am to 1pm and 2pm to 5pm. The **Irish Embassy** is at Tržiště 13, Praha 1 (© 257-530-061) and is open Monday to Friday from 9am to 1pm and 2pm to 5pm. The **New Zealand Honorary Consul** is located at Dykova 19, Praha 10 (© 222-514-672) and visits here are by appointment.

Emergencies Dial the European Emergency Number © **112** or you can reach Prague's **police** at © **158** and **fire** services by dialing © **150** from any phone. To call an **ambulance,** dial © **155.**

Hospitals Particularly welcoming to foreigners is **Nemocnice Na Homolce,** Roentgenova 2, Praha 5 (© **257-272-146,** or 257-272-191 after hours). The English-speaking doctors can also make house calls. See "Doctors & Dentists," above, for more information. In an emergency, dial © **155** for an ambulance.

Internet Access One of Prague's trendiest places is the **Globe** ✸, Pštrossova 6, Praha 1 (© **224-916-264;** www.globebookstore.cz), a cafe-cum-bookstore that provides Internet access. You can browse for 1.50Kč (5¢) per minute. Its new location is open daily from 10am until midnight.

Check your e-mail and surf at the very centrally located new Internet cafe **Inetpoint.cz,** Jungmannova 32, Praha 1 (© **296-245-962;** www.inetpoint.cz). It is open daily 10am to 10pm and the connection charge is 25Kč ($1.05) per 15 minutes. The **Bohemia Bagel,** near the funicular train at Újezd 16 in Malá Strana, Praha 1 (© **257-310-694;** www.bohemiabagel.cz), has about a half-dozen PCs in a pleasant setting for 1Kč (5¢) per minute; it is open daily from 7am to midnight on Monday to Friday, 8am to midnight on Saturday and Sunday. Another place to access the Internet is **Cyber Cafe-Jáma** at V jámě 7, Praha 1 (© **224-222-383;** www.jamapub.cz). It is open daily 11am to 1am.

Language Berlitz has a comprehensive phrase book in Czech. A clever illustrated **Web tutorial** is found at **www.czechprimer.org.** See appendix B for basic phrases and vocabulary as well as menu terms.

Laundry & Dry Cleaning **Laundry Kings,** Dejvická 16, Praha 6 (© **233-343-743**) was Prague's first American-style, coin-operated, self-service laundromat. Each small load costs about 70Kč ($2.90). An attendant can do your wash for 180Kč

($7.50) in the same day. Laundry Kings is open Monday to Friday from 7am to 10pm and Saturday and Sunday from 8am to 10pm.

Laundryland, Londýnská 71, Praha 2 (© **222-516-692**), offers dry cleaning as well as laundry service and charges about the same as Laundry Kings. Located 2 blocks from the Náměstí Míru metro station and close to the I. P. Pavlova metro station, it's open daily from 8am to 10pm.

Liquor Laws There's no law against teenagers drinking alcohol, but it can only be sold to those who are over 18. Any adult selling liquor to younger person can be prosecuted. Pubs and clubs can stay open 24 hours.

Lost Property If you lose any of your personal property, luggage, or other belongings, try your luck at the Lost Property Office at Karolíny Světlé 5, Praha 1(©) **224-235-085.**

Luggage Storage & Lockers The **Ruzyně Airport Luggage Storage Office** never closes and charges 60Kč ($2.50) per item per day. Left-luggage offices are also available at the main train stations, **Hlavní nádraží** and **Nádraží Holešovice.** Both charge 30Kč ($1.25) per bag per day and are technically open 24 hours, but if your train is departing late at night, check to make sure someone will be around. Luggage lockers are available in all of Prague's train stations, but they're not secure and should be avoided.

Mail Post offices are plentiful and are normally open Monday to Friday from 8am to 6pm. Mailboxes are orange and are usually attached to the sides of buildings. If you're sending mail overseas, make sure it's marked "Par Avion" so it doesn't go by surface. If you mail your letters at a post office, the clerk will add this stamp for you. Postcards to the U.S. cost 14Kč (60¢), to any E.U. country 9Kč (40¢). Mail can take up to 10 days to reach its destination.

The **Main Post Office (Hlavní pošta),** Jindřišská 14, Praha 1 (© **221-131-111**), a few steps from Václavské náměstí, is open 24 hours. You can receive mail, marked "Poste Restante" and addressed to you, care of this post office. If you carry an American Express card or Amex traveler's checks, you would be wiser to receive mail care of **American Express,** Václavské nám. 56 (Wenceslas Sq.), Praha 1 (© **222-800-237**).

Newspapers & Magazines The 1995 failure of *Prognosis,* Prague's first English-language newspaper, left the weekly *Prague Post* (www.praguepost.com) with a near lock on the local market, though it's being challenged for the business audience by the *Prague Business Journal.* Published each Wednesday, the *Post* is a quick read that usually offers a couple of interesting features, along with updated listings of sightseeing and entertainment happenings. The *Prague Tribune* (www.prague-tribune.cz) is a glossy monthly with an excellent mix of news, business, and cultural features.

Přehled, a monthly listings booklet, is probably the best entertainment publication, with details on theaters, galleries, concerts, clubs, films, and events around town. It's in Czech, but the listings aren't too difficult for non-Czechs to understand.

For gays and lesbians, the best information on happenings is in *SOHO Review,* a monthly magazine listing activities and events. It's in Czech but does run some English-language information and personal ads. The *Prague Post* also occasionally updates gay and lesbian offerings.

Newsstands are located inside most every metro station, and good-size international magazine shops can be found in major hotels and on most busy shopping streets.

Pharmacies The most centrally located pharmacy *(lékárna)* is at Václavské nám. 8, Praha 1 (℡ **224-227-532**), and is open Monday to Friday from 8am to 6pm. The nearest emergency (24-hr.) pharmacy is at Palackého 5, Praha 1 (℡ **224-946-982**). If you're in Praha 2, there's an emergency pharmacy on Belgická 37 (℡ **222-519-731**).

Police Dial the European Emergency Number ℡ **112** from any phone in an emergency. For Czech police dial ℡ **158.**

Radio You can hear English-language World News on the BBC World Service (101.1 FM). More than a dozen private stations compete with publicly owned news-talk Czech Radiožurnál (94.6 FM). Radio DEEJAY (99.7 FM) is a rock station that gives Czech bands lots of play. Radio Kiss (98 FM) is an Irish-owned station with a strictly pop-oriented play list. Radio 1 (91.9 FM) plays a world-class assortment of contemporary dance and trance music, mixed with some novelty songs. Radio Free Europe (1287 kHz AM) is an American-funded news-oriented station now based in Prague's Communist-era Parliament building.

Restrooms You'll find plenty of public restrooms. Toilets are located in every metro station and are staffed by cleaning personnel who usually charge users 5Kč (20¢) and dispense a precious few sheets of toilet paper.

Be aware—even though restrooms at the city's train stations are staffed, you need to get your toilet paper by yourself from a dispenser situated on the wall before you actually enter the restroom. The charge here is 6Kč (25¢).

Restaurants and pubs around all the major sights are usually kind to nonpatrons who wish to use their facilities. Around the castle and elsewhere, public toilets are clearly marked with the letters wc. For comfort and cleanliness, try lobby-level lavatories in Prague's better-known hotels or the new restrooms in the Municipal House (Obecní dům), the Art Nouveau palace next to the Powder Tower in Old Town.

Safety In Prague's center you'll feel generally safer than in most Western cities, but always take common-sense precautions. Be aware of your immediate surroundings. Don't walk alone at night around Wenceslas Square—one of the main areas for prostitution and where a lot of unexplainable loitering takes place. All visitors should be watchful of pickpockets in heavily touristed areas, especially on Charles Bridge, in Old Town Square, and in front of the main train station. Be especially wary on crowded buses, trams, and trains. Don't keep your wallet in a back pocket and don't flash a lot of cash or jewelry. Riding the metro or trams at night feels just as safe as during the day.

Taxes A 19% **value-added tax (VAT)** is built into the price of most goods and services rather than tacked on at the register. Most restaurants also include the VAT in the prices stated on their menus. If they don't, that fact should be stated somewhere on the menu. There are no VAT refunds for the Czech Republic.

Telephone & Fax For **directory inquiries** regarding phone numbers within the Czech Republic, dial ℡ **1180.** For information about services and rates abroad, call ✆ **1181.** Dial tones are continual high-pitched beeps that sound something like busy signals in America. After dialing a number from a pay phone, you might hear a series of very quick beeps that tell you the line is being connected. Busy signals sound like the dial tones, only quicker.

There are two kinds of **pay phones** in normal use. The first accepts coins and the other operates exclusively with a phone card, available from post offices and news agents in denominations ranging from 50Kč to 500Kč ($2.10–$21). The minimum cost of a local call is 4Kč (15¢). Coin-op phones have displays telling you the minimum price for your call, but they don't make change, so don't load more than you have to. You can add more coins as the display gets near zero. Phone-card telephones automatically deduct the price of your call from the card. These cards are especially handy if you want to call abroad, as you don't have to continuously chuck in the change. If you're calling the States, you'd better get a phone card with plenty of points, as calls run about 20Kč (85¢) per minute; calls to the United Kingdom cost 15Kč (34p) per minute.

Long-distance phone charges are higher in the Czech Republic than they are in the United States, and hotels usually add their own surcharge, sometimes as hefty as 100% to 200%, of which you may be unaware until you're presented with the bill. Ask before placing a call from a hotel.

Even if you're not calling person-to-person, collect calls are charged with the hotel fees, making them pricey, too. Charging a long-distance call to your phone credit card from a public telephone is often the most economical way to phone home.

A fast, convenient way to call the United States from Europe is via services like AT&T USA Direct. This bypasses the foreign operator and automatically links you to an operator with your long-distance carrier in your home country. The access number in the Czech Republic for **AT&T USA Direct** is ✆ **00-800-222-55288.** For **MCI CALL USA,** dial ✆ **00-800-001-112.** Canadians can connect with **Canada Direct** at ✆ **00-800-001-115,** and Brits can connect with **BT Direct** at ✆ **00-800-001-144.** From a pay phone in the Czech Republic, your local phone card will be debited only for a local call.

Telephone books are printed in two editions: A separate set of White Pages contains alphabetical lists of household phone owners, while the Yellow Pages list businesses according to trade, with an alphabetical listing in more White Pages upfront. The Yellow Pages include an English-language index.

You can send **faxes** from the main post office (Hlavní pošta), Jindřišská 14, Praha 1 (✆ **221-131-111**). The fax office is open 24 hours and charges 30Kč ($1.25) per page, plus the price of the phone call. The best place to receive faxes is the American Express office, Václavské nám. 56 (Wenceslas Sq.), Praha 1 (✆ **222-800-251**).

Television There are four national broadcast TV stations. **ČT1** and **ČT2** (channels 1 and 2) are public-service stations often with reruns of Communist-era teleplays and classical music broadcasts. **TV Nova** is a private commercial station launched by New York cosmetics scion Ronald Lauder, who was involved in a lengthy lawsuit demanding over $500 million after his Czech partner allegedly cut him out of the station. Nova is loaded with American sitcoms and serials, sensational newscasts, and Western movies all dubbed into Czech. **Prima** is the upstart nationwide commercial station trying to cut into Nova's dominance with the same tactics. If you're channel surfing after 10pm, note that both Prima and Nova (which you can find on various channels depending on how your TV is programmed) have very saucy shows often including full-frontal nudity. All four stations are off the air sometime between midnight and 2am. Satellite channels at hotels and on cable include Eurosport, MTV, CNBC, CNN, and BBC World.

Time Zone Prague is on Continental Europe Time (CET), 2 hours ahead of Greenwich Mean Time (GMT) from April to the end of October and 1 hour ahead from November to the end of March (in both cases 1 hr. ahead of London). It's usually 6 hours ahead of U.S. Eastern Standard Time. Clocks here spring forward and fall back for daylight saving time, but the semiannual rituals follow a slightly different schedule than in the States (about 3 weeks earlier).

Tipping Rules for tipping aren't as strict in the Czech Republic as they are in the United States. At most restaurants and pubs, locals just round the bill up to the nearest few *koruny*. When you're presented with good service at tablecloth places, a 10% tip is proper. Washroom and cloakroom attendants usually expect a couple of koruny, and porters at airports and train stations usually receive 25Kč ($1.05) per bag. Taxi drivers should get about 10%, unless they've already ripped you off, in which case they should get a referral to the police. Check restaurant menus to see if service is included before you leave a tip.

Transport Information The **Prague Information Service,** near Wenceslas Square on Na Příkopě 20, Praha 1 (© **12444;** www.pis.cz), is open Monday to Friday from 9am to 7pm and Saturday and Sunday 9am to 6pm (Apr–Oct), and Monday to Friday 9am to 6pm and Saturday 9am to 3pm (Nov–Mar). PIS can help you get where you are going on local transport (while the travel agencies Čedok, E-Travel.cz, and AVE Travel are all good for intercity connections; see "Visitor Information," earlier in this chapter). Train and bus timetables can also be viewed at www.jizdnirady.cz or at www.idos.cz. All metro stations now have much better maps and explanations in English. You will find more on Prague's public transportation at www.dpp.cz.

4

Suggested Itineraries

Prague's most intriguing aspects are its architecture and atmosphere, best enjoyed while slowly wandering through the city's heart. So, with that in mind, your itinerary should be a loose one. If you have the time and energy, go to Charles Bridge at sunrise and then at sunset to view the grand architecture of Prague Castle and the Old Town skyline. You'll see two completely different cities.

1 The Best of Prague in 1 Day

In order to digest enough of Prague's wonders, do what visiting kings and potentates do on a 1-day visit: Walk the Royal Route (or at least part of it). From the top of the castle hill in Hradčany, tour Prague Castle in the morning. After lunch begin your slow descent through the odd hill-bound architecture of Lesser Town (Malá Strana).

Then stroll across Charles Bridge, on the way to the winding alleys of Old Town (Staré Město). You can happily get lost finding Old Town Square (Staroměstské nám.), stopping at private galleries and cafes along the way. From Old Town Square take Celetná street to Ovocný trh, and you get to Mozart's Prague venue, the Estates' Theater. Dinner and your evening entertainment are all probably within a 10-minute walk from anywhere in this area.

Start: Tram no. 22 or 23, or take a taxi ride up the castle hill.

❶ Prague Castle ✦✦✦
Since the 9th century, the castle has been the seat of the central state and church. It witnessed the first central unifying power, the Premyslids, and the reigns of the Luxembourg and the Jagiellos, as well as the Habsburg dynasty. The castle is now the official seat of the Czech president. See p. 104.

❷ St. Vitus Cathedral ✦✦✦
King John of Luxembourg and his even more famous son Charles IV laid the foundation stone in 1344 in the place of the original Romanesque rotunda. The

---

Impressions
Prague is a priceless asset, which surely deserves to be spared from the worst excesses of modern development, which have so ravaged the other cities of Europe. The challenge must be to find ways of ensuring . . . that it becomes once again the thriving prosperous heart of Europe, not merely a crumbling museum exhibit.

—Prince Charles to Prague's leaders (May 1991)

Suggested Itineraries: The Best of Prague

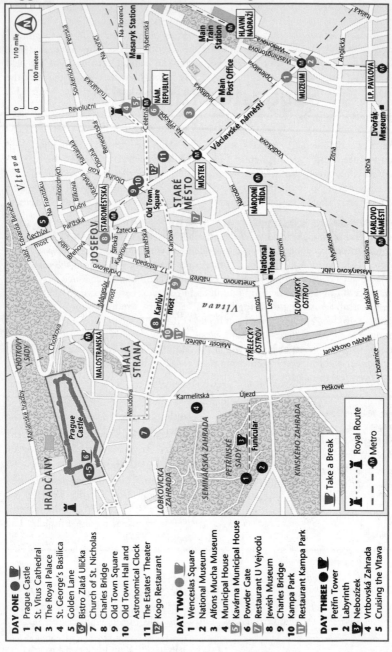

DAY ONE ● 🍷
1 Prague Castle
2 St. Vitus Cathedral
3 The Royal Palace
4 St. George's Basilica
5 Golden Lane
🍴 Bistro Zlatá Ulička
7 Church of St. Nicholas
8 Charles Bridge
9 Old Town Square
10 Old Town Hall and
   Astronomical Clock
11 The Estates' Theater
🍴 Kogo Restaurant

DAY TWO ● 🍷
1 Wenceslas Square
2 National Museum
3 Alfons Mucha Museum
4 Municipal House
🍴 Kavárna Municipal House
6 Powder Gate
🍴 Restaurant U Vejvodů
8 Jewish Museum
9 Charles Bridge
10 Kampa Park
🍴 Restaurant Kampa Park

DAY THREE ● 🍷
1 Petřín Tower
2 Labyrinth
🍴 Nebozízek
4 Vrtbovská Zahrada
5 Cruising the Vltava

first Gothic building period was led by Matyas of Arras, and then Peter Parler and his sons continued through 1399. The construction of this impressive architectural piece was not completed until 1929. See p. 105.

❸ The Royal Palace

The oldest part of the palace dates back to 1135. Famous Czech kings Premyslid Otakar II, Charles IV, Wenceslas IV, and Vladislav Jagello then initiated additional reconstructions. The central part, the late Gothic Vladislav Hall, with its ribbed-star-vaulting ceiling, was the largest secular hall in medieval Prague. Still today, every 5 years, the presidential elections take place here. See p. 109.

❹ St. George's Basilica

This is the oldest preserved church building of the castle. The originally Romanesque structure gained its baroque facade in the 17th century. Now, as a part of the National Gallery, this venue houses a permanent exhibition of Gothic Czech art. See p. 109.

❺ Golden Lane 🏛

This bizarre conglomeration of mini–town houses within the castle complex was once home to writer Franz Kafka. See p. 109.

🍴 ❻ BISTRO ZLATÁ ULIČKA

Break for lunch in one of the restaurants around the castle complex. For sandwiches I recommend the Bistro Zlatá Ulička at the top of Golden Lane.

Start making your way back through the castle's courtyards to Hradčanské náměstí, from which you'll be able to see Prague in its panoramic beauty (if it's not foggy that day). Then as you walk down Nerudova, the road leading to the Lesser Town, you'll find small shops and galleries tucked into every narrow nook.

❼ Church of St. Nicholas 🏛🏛

The dome of the Church of St. Nicholas, with its gilded baroque interior, dominates the view from Lesser Town Square (Malostranské nám). Organ concerts are held here throughout the year. Note that the interior is not heated in winter. See p. 112.

❽ Charles Bridge 🏛🏛🏛

Early on, this pedestrian path became one of the centers of town life. Now it's a promenade best known for its open-air gallery of sculptures, and, of course, the magic views of Prague Castle and Lesser Town. See p. 111.

❾ Old Town Square 🏛🏛🏛

The very center of the Old Town life, this square is constantly crowded in high season, but definitely one of the "must dos." See p. 127.

❿ Old Town Hall & Astronomical Clock 🏛Kids

In Old Town Square, you can watch a performance of the astronomical clock at the top of each hour, and if you aren't tired by now, climb to the top of the Old Town Hall tower for a panoramic view. See p. 113.

⓫ Estates' Theater

If you still have the time and you like opera, try to see *Don Giovanni,* which is frequently staged. It was here, in October 1787, that Mozart himself conducted the world premiere of his masterpiece. It is not performed every day, so check the program in advance. Tickets are available at Ticketpro outlets (p. 177) or usually at the theater, just before the performance. See p. 183.

🍴 ⓬ KOGO 🏛🏛

Whether you make it here before the theater or for a late-night, after-opera dinner, you'll not be disappointed by the well-prepared and well-presented Italian food. Havelská 27. ✆ 224-214-543. See p. 92.

2 The Best of Prague in 2 Days

On your second day, explore the varied sights of New Town, Old Town, the Jewish Quarter, and Lesser Town—what you didn't have time for the day before. Just wander and browse. Throughout Old Town you'll find numerous shops and galleries offering the finest Bohemian crystal, porcelain, and modern artwork, as well as top fashion boutiques, cafes, and restaurants. While the shops aren't that much different from those in other European cities, the setting is.

From Old Town, it's just a short walk across Charles Bridge to Lesser Town. This was once the neighborhood for diplomats, merchants, and those who served the castle, with narrow houses squeezed between palaces and embassies. Finish the day by getting a riverside view of the city and Charles Bridge from Kampa Park.

Start: Metro A, Muzeum.

❶ Wenceslas Square ✿✿

As a trade center of Prague this has been the liveliest and busiest part of the city since the 18th century, witnessing several loud political demonstrations over the years. Here you'll find excellent opportunities for shopping, dining, and day or evening entertainment. See "Historic Squares" in chapter 7.

If you're traveling with children, I recommend a visit to the National Museum at the top of the square. If you are an art lover, the Mucha Museum on the Panská street, parallel to this square, might be more compelling.

❷ National Museum

This iconic hulk of a building is another example of Czech architecture of the second half of the 19th century. Its hall of fame is devoted to the memory of outstanding Czech personalities throughout history. Expansive collections of minerals and various zoological and paleontological displays are part of the permanent exhibition here. See p. 121.

❸ Alfons Mucha Museum ✿

This is a pleasant oasis in a busy neighborhood. You can slow down here and relax by stepping into a world of this famous turn-of-the-20th-century artist and his archetypical Art Nouveau designs. See p. 120.

❹ Municipal House ✿✿

Prague's Art Nouveau jewel! At the end of Na Příkopě street, in the middle of the shopping district, this beautiful corner building, built on the site of the former Royal Court, was reconstructed almost a decade ago. It houses the Prague Symphony Orchestra and offers numerous concerts in its Smetana Hall throughout the year. See p. 124.

> ❺ **KAVÁRNA OBECNÍ DŮM (AT THE MUNICIPAL HOUSE)** ✿✿
> This is a good time to have coffee or even a little snack. Sit down and witness the unique interior and atmosphere of the Art Nouveau era. Náměstí Republiky 5. ℂ **222-002-763.** See p. 101.

❻ Powder Gate

Just next to the Municipal House, on its right side when facing it, you can't miss the Old Town Powder Tower. This is where the Royal Route ends (or starts). If you have enough energy, you can climb up the 186 stairs to have a look at Old Town's rooftops. *Note:* It is closed in winter. See p. 125.

Continue walking through the pedestrian zone of Na Příkopě and 28. října. Turn right onto Perlová street and you'll get to a little square, Uhelný trh. Skořepka street will lead you from there to

Jilská. If you get lost around these Old Town winding streets, I'm sure you'll stumble upon a pub or restaurant. I recommend:

---

7 U VEJVODŮ ★★
One of the original restaurants of the Pilsner brewery, this spot serves a tasty goulash for 99Kč ($4.10), and even though you probably won't meet many locals here anymore, you'll still have a good Czech pub experience. Jilská 4. ✆ **224-219-999**. See p. 103.

Make your way through Jilská, Malé náměstí, and U Radnice, to Maiselova street.

8 Jewish Museum
In the Jewish quarter of Josefov, you can visit the Jewish Museum with its wide array of religious artifacts, as well as Old Jewish Cemetery, and its clusters of headstones stacked grave upon grave. The adjacent Ceremonial Hall displays heart-wrenching

sketches by the children held at the Terezín concentration camp during World War II. See p. 114.

9 Charles Bridge ★★★
Try to pace your walk towards Charles Bridge so you stroll across at dusk and witness the unforgettable view of Prague panorama at twilight. See p. 111.

10 Kampa
Kampa is the Lesser Town embankment of the Vltava, with a series of quaint shops and restaurants. You can reach it by taking the stairs down from Charles Bridge (on the left side, before you exit the bridge itself).

---

11 KAMPA PARK ★★
For a super riverside view with a fine dining experience go to this Continental/seafood restaurant located at Na Kampě 8b; ✆ **296-826-102**. If you prefer an international/pizza option, try **Hergetova Cihelna** ★★, at Cihelná 2b; ✆ **296-826-103**. See p. 88 and 85.

---

3 The Best of Prague in 3 Days

On your third day, after visiting the most important Prague sights, go for a day's excursion to **Karlštejn Castle**. See p. 197 for details.

Alternatively, if you're staying in Prague, on a warm, sunny day, pack yourself a picnic and stroll over to Petřín Hill, the leafy park where kids will enjoy the tower view and mirrored labyrinth. Before you leave Lesser Town, visit its well-hidden secret, the Vrtbovská garden. Try to work in a cruise on the Vltava or pilot your own rowboat ride in the late afternoon or evening.

Start: Tram no. 12, 22, or 23 to újezd. Begin by walking up the Petřín Hill, or take the funicular from újezd halfway up to Nebozízek, or all the way up.

1 Petřín Tower
In the morning you'll probably be rested enough to climb the 299 steps up to the top platform of this reduced copy of the Eiffel Tower built in 1891. When the weather cooperates, the bird's-eye view of

Prague is worth the hike. There is an elevator, but only seniors over 70 and people with disabilities may use it. *Note:* It is closed in winter. See p. 126.

2 Labyrinth
This fun house was originally built as a pavilion for the Prague Exhibition in 1891 and later transferred to Petřín. It was fitted with mirrors and made into a maze. See p. 138.

After you find your way out, start looking for a picnic spot. You can have a walk around on the top of the hill or begin your slow descent to the town. There are plenty of benches along the way down.

If you are not ready for a picnic or a walk, use the funicular and go to the midway stop:

> **3 NEBOZÍZEK**
> This restaurant has a great hillside location, and you probably will forget what you're eating, which is not exceptional anyway, since your attention will be drawn to the view. Petřínské sady 411. $\textcircled{C}$ **257-315-329.** See p. 88.

Take tram no. 12, 22, or 23 from újezd to Karmelitská stop.

4 Vrtbovská Zahrada *

The entrance to this baroque terraced garden is not well marked, and you won't quite imagine what kind of "backyard" is hidden behind the door at no. 25 on Karmelitská. *Note:* It is closed in winter. See p. 135.

5 Cruising the Vltava

Cruising upstream and enjoying the sights of Prague as dusk descends is a memorable experience. You'll see it all from a low angle surrounded by reflections on the water, providing a new perspective on the city. Choose the 3-hour cruise, which departs from a port under Čechův Bridge at 7pm. Buffet dinner, aperitif, and live music are included in the price. See p. 139.

4 The Best of the Czech Republic in 1 Week

The Czech lands offer many historic and cultural monuments. Castles and châteaux dominating the picturesque natural landscape represent the most important part of Czech attractions. For those travelers with more time to discover Bohemia and even Moravia, see chapters 11, 12, and 13 to learn about visits to other Czech towns. Below I give you one example out of many possible itineraries.

Days 1–2: Arrive in Prague

Spend the first 2 days as recommended above in "The Best of Prague in 2 Days." Then rent a car from one of the rental agencies recommended on p. 44. Keep in mind that the speed limit is 90kmph (56 mph) on two-lane highways and 50kmph (31 mph) in villages. Before setting out, please review the other Czech rules for driving on p. 46.

Day 3: Český Krumlov ***

Leave for this romantic destination in southern Bohemia early in the morning, when the roads aren't too crowded. This will also allow you time to stroll around the city. Take Highway D1 and then E55. The trip takes about 2½ hours. Once

there, visit the castle first, then just wander, and finally relax in a local restaurant. Spend the night in one of the recommended hotels or pensions. But book early, as Krumlov is the most popular Czech destination after Prague. See details in chapter 12.

Day 4: České Budějovice, Castle Hluboká nad Vltavou **

On this day start heading for Plzeň via České Budějovice, the home of Budvar beer. Upon arrival at České Budějovice, have a quick stroll and look around one of central Europe's largest squares, where you can also have lunch. In the early afternoon, take Highway E49 and then Highway 105 north for 30 minutes (this

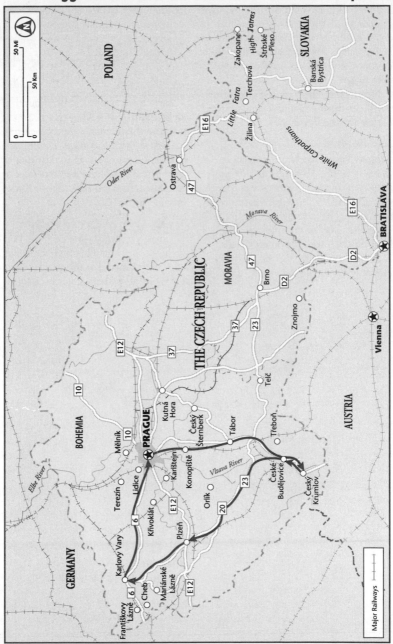

includes parking time) to the tiny town Hluboká nad Vltavou, where you'll see a castle fashioned after the Windsor Castle in England towering above the green meadows. For more information see p. 238 in chapter 12.

Next, take Highway E49 to Plzeň. You'll get there in about 2 hours. Spend the night there. See p. 231.

Day ❺: Plzeň

Explore Plzeň's center in the morning, when it is the least crowded. If you're interested in the beer-making process, visit the Pilsner Breweries in the early afternoon. Just outside the factory is a restaurant that serves traditional Czech food. See chapter 12 for more details.

After your break, hit the road again. Highway E49 will take you to the most popular Czech spa town, Karlovy Vary, in about 1 hour. Spend the night there.

Day ❻: Karlovy Vary ✿

This town was built for relaxation, which makes it the perfect place to end your Bohemian week.

Start slowly with a stroll around the city's historic center. Then, get your "cup" and taste the mineral waters which make this destination so famous. Finally, book yourself a massage or other individual spa treatment at one of the recommended spa complexes. Find out more about Karlovy Vary in chapter 12.

Day ❼: Karlovy Vary to Prague

It's time to return to Prague. Take Highway E48. You should reach the capital in 2 hours. Be warned that this two-lane highway is one of the busiest in the country.

5

Where to Stay in Prague

The range of accommodations in Prague has widened significantly since the 1989 revolution. Today you can choose the opulence of the Four Seasons Hotel, the coziness of an innovative B&B, or a more spartan stay in a hostel.

Many hotels and pensions are old properties reconstructed to a higher standard, including refined interiors and tiled bathrooms with modern fixtures. The concept of easy access for travelers with disabilities has been slower to emerge, however. Only a few places offer facilities; I've noted them below.

With a very efficient metro and tram system, it is relatively easy to stay in one part of Prague and quickly visit another quarter, but if you want to awaken with the Golden City glowing in your window, a room with a view in Old Town or Malá Strana is worth the splurge.

HOTELS Full-service hotels have begun to catch up with Western standards in the face of competition, but rooms are still more expensive than those in many European hotels of similar or better quality. The staff, while much more attentive than they were soon after the revolution, still often act as if you are invading their turf.

The selection is growing, but because there's not much room to build in the historic center, newer properties tend to be farther out. Notable exceptions are given below.

PRIVATE ROOMS & APARTMENTS Rooms in private homes are more expensive than dorms in student hostels but provide a little more privacy. Many, if not most, of these rooms will be located in the center of the city, but some are in outlying massive concrete housing blocks called *sídliště*. The exteriors are akin to those of prisons, but unlike many Western housing projects, these are relatively safe and well maintained and usually have a basic level of comfort and amenities. Some owners take special care of these rooms, and you may stumble on a homey place with old Bohemian charm. Most of the projects are close to metro stations or tram lines, so getting to the city center shouldn't take longer than 15 to 30 minutes. Expect to pay between 500Kč and 1,000Kč ($21 and $42) per person per night for accommodations in these homes.

Tips What's for Breakfast?

In most hotels and B&Bs, the room rate includes breakfast—usually heavy bread or rolls *(rohlíky)*, jam, butter, cheese spreads, and sometimes liver pâté, plus yogurt, cereal, juice, milk, and coffee or tea. Occasionally, slices of Prague ham or smoked pork *(debrecínka)*, local cheeses, and fresh fruit will join the buffet, and some offer ham and eggs cooked to order.

Tips **Websites with Online Reservations**

Most travel agencies provide online reservation service. My advice is to check the prices of accommodations on several different websites, since the competition is significant. Also, many hotels and pensions come up with special offers to visitors throughout the year. You can find out more on these well-organized websites:

- www.prague-accommodation-guide.com
- www.euroagentur.cz
- www.praguehotels.cz
- www.hotelline.cz
- www.travel.cz

Better than the private rooms where you will have to share space with your landlord are the **private apartments** offered to tourists for anywhere from 1 night to a long-term stay. These may be the best value around for privacy and location. Expect to pay between 2,000Kč and 4,000Kč ($83 and $166) per night for a studio apartment for two, depending on location. Larger apartments are also available.

Several local agencies offer assistance. The leader now is Prague-based **E-Travel.cz** (www.travel.cz or www.apartments.cz). Its office is near the National Theater at Ostrovní 7 (✆ **224-990-990;** fax 224-990-999). Another agency, especially good for those arriving late by train or air, is **AVE Travel Ltd.** (✆ **251-091-111;** www.avetravel.cz). It has outlets at the airport, open daily from 7am to 10pm; at the main train station, Hlavní nádraží, open daily from 6am to 11pm; and at the north train station, Nádraží Holešovice, open daily from 7am to 8:30pm.

PENSIONS   These guesthouses with few services are cheaper than hotels, but when compared to similar Western B&Bs, they're still relatively expensive. Some have found a niche offering a quaint stay in a quiet neighborhood.

BEST HOTEL BETS

- **Best Panoramic Views:** The pride of the former Communist tourism industry was the Hotel Forum, which has since been privatized, sold again, and renamed the **Corinthia Towers Hotel** (✆ **261-191-111**). Each north-facing room at this high-rise south of the city center provides a wide-angle view stretching to Prague Castle and beyond. See p. 77.
- **Best Malá Strana Views:** The upper floors of the **Hotel U tří pštrosů** (✆ **257-532-410**) offer some of the best old-world views over Malá Strana's red rooftops. The corner rooms are best, providing glimpses of Charles Bridge and Prague Castle. See p. 69.
- **Best Bohemian Country Setting:** The **Romantik Hotel U raka** (✆ **220-511-100**), in a secret ravine minutes from the castle in Hradčany, has cozy rustic rooms and a tastefully folksy atmosphere. See p. 66.
- **Best Hotel Closest to Prague Castle:** The **U Krále Karla** (✆ **257-532-869**), on the main castle-bound thoroughfare Nerudova, tries hard to provide a stay to

match its Renaissance motif. It's a few steps above the main turn to the castle, avoiding much of the noise, which has become a nuisance to rivals down the street. See p. 66.

- **Best for Business Travelers:** Just off náměstí Republiky near the imposing Czech National Bank, the new **Prague Marriott Hotel** (© **222-888-888**) comfortably fits the bill for those who need to get in, use their laptops, cut a deal, and then get out to see the city (especially if your firm is paying the bill). See p. 75.

- **Best Romantic Pension:** Although the **Pension Větrník** (© **220-612-404**) is well outside the city center, this family-run B&B is a very friendly and romantic place, easily accessible by tram or taxi. It's built into an antique windmill amid lush gardens, and you can't beat it for charm and price. See p. 77.

- **Best Throwback to Prague's First Republic:** The restored Art Nouveau **Hotel Paříž** (© **222-195-195**) recalls 1920s Prague, one of the wealthiest cities on earth at that time. The hotel's beauty oozes with period elegance. It's across from another newly remodeled gem, the Municipal House (Obecní dům). See p. 70.

- **Best for Families:** Consider a **private apartment** from an agency (see "Private Rooms & Apartments," above). Larger and cheaper than hotel rooms, these apartments come with kitchens so you can fix your own meals. (For more options, see "Family-Friendly Accommodations," later in this chapter.)

- **Best Health Clubs:** The **Hotel Inter-Continental Praha** (© **296-631-111**) is fully equipped with modern machines and free weights and is home to Prague's most narcissistic aerobic classes—an after-work gawking paradise for stockbrokers. See p. 69. The new **Prague Marriott** (© **222-888-888**) actually has a better-equipped fitness center but it's not yet as clubby as the Inter-Con's. See p. 75.

- **Best Tom Cruise/Leonid Brezhnev Haunt:** The **Hotel Praha** (© **224-343-305**) was once a heavily guarded bastion for visiting Communist bigwigs. The lingering chintz of the Praha has unexpectedly emerged as a refuge for luminaries who want to lie low, including the star of *Mission: Impossible.* A wacky choice. See p. 78.

1 Hradčany

VERY EXPENSIVE

Hotel Savoy ✸✸✸   One of Prague's finest hotels, the Savoy belongs to the company that manages the more venerable Palace on Wenceslas Square (p. 73), and it has attracted a demanding clientele. Just behind the Foreign Ministry and Černín Palace, and a few blocks from the castle, the Hotel Savoy welcomes you with a modern lobby. The guest rooms are richly decorated and boast every amenity as well as spacious marble bathrooms. The beds are consistently huge, which is in contrast to the customary central European style of two twin beds shoved together. As at the Palace, the pleasant staff provides an attention to detail that's a cut above that at most hotels in Prague. The Hradčany Restaurant is excellent (p. 84).

Keplerova 6, Praha 1. © **224-302-430.** Fax 224-302-128. www.hotel-savoy.cz. 59 units. From 9,600Kč ($399) double; from 12,900Kč ($537) suite. Rates include breakfast. AE, DC, MC, V. Tram: 22 or 23. **Amenities:** Restaurant; bar; "relaxation" center w/small set of exercise machines; sauna; whirlpool; concierge; business services; salon; 24-hr. room service; massage; laundry. *In room:* A/C, TV, VCR, DVD, dataport, minibar, hair dryer, safe.

EXPENSIVE

Hotel Neruda ✸✸   Another great writer/philosopher who left his mark on Prague was Jan Neruda, but the street that bears his name—Nerudova—is hardly remembered

Where to Stay in Prague

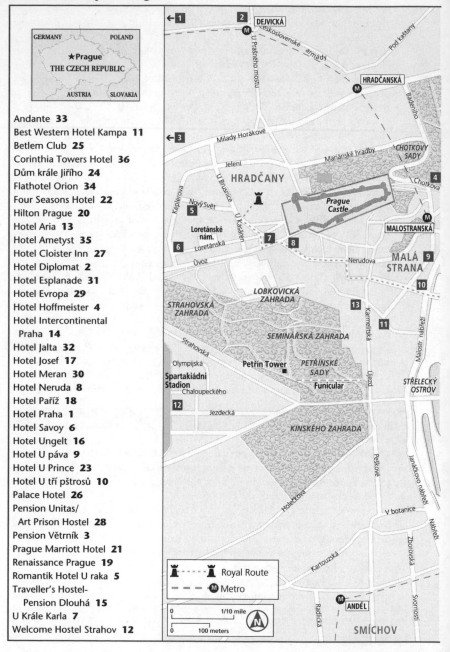

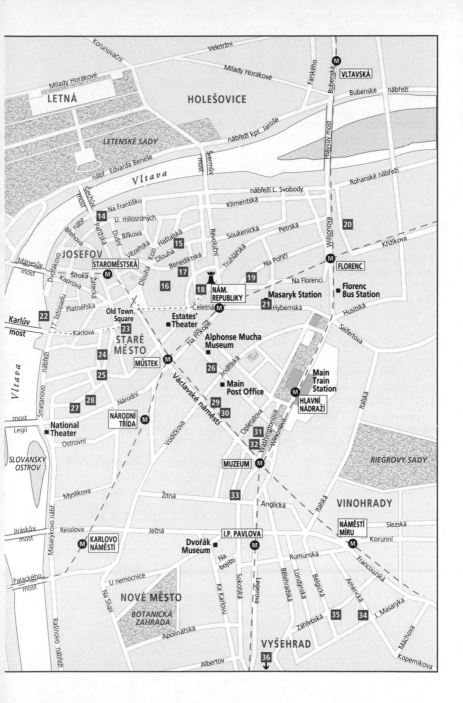

as the scene of his 19th-century literary greatness. Instead, it is a cozy alley of stores and pubs leading up to the castle. Squeezed into the long row of curiosity shops is a strong contender for the best boutique hotel in Malá Strana—the Hotel Neruda. This refurbished 20-room villa has combined a high level of modern elegance with the original accents of its 14th-century shell. Most of the fixtures—from the fresh new bathrooms to the beds and dining tables—suggest a bold sense of Prague's promising future, but enveloped within its Renaissance past. With the recent summers setting new records for heat, you will appreciate the air-conditioning, as well as the few paces up the hill for castle events.

Nerudova 44, Praha 1. (Ⓒ 257-535-557. Fax 257-531-492. www.hotelneruda-praha.cz. 20 units. From 5,550Kč ($231) double. Rates include breakfast. AE, DC, MC, V. Tram: 22 or 23 to Malostranské nám. **Amenities:** Cafe-restaurant; concierge. *In room:* A/C, TV, VCR, minibar, hair dryer, safe.

Romantik Hotel U raka 🦀 Hidden among the stucco houses and cobblestone streets of a pristine medieval neighborhood below Prague Castle is this pleasant surprise. The Romantik Hotel U raka (At the Crayfish), in a ravine beneath the Foreign Ministry gardens, has been lovingly reconstructed as an old-world farmhouse. It is the quietest getaway in this tightly packed city. The rustic rooms have heavy wooden furniture, open-beamed ceilings, and stone walls. The much-sought-after suite has a fireplace and adjoins a private manicured garden, making it a favorite with honeymooners. Water trickles through the Japanese garden that surrounds the hotel.

A few years ago, the English-speaking owners changed the name to "Romantik Hotel," which connotes to the mostly German clientele a higher standard than the previous "Pension." The owners are relaxed but attentive and will help you navigate the phalanx of nearby streets. Prague Castle is a 10-minute walk away, and you can catch a tram into the city center by walking up ancient steps at the side of the hotel. Reservations well in advance are recommended.

Černínská 10, Praha 1. (Ⓒ 220-511-100. Fax 233-358-041. www.romantikhotel-uraka.cz. 6 units (5 with shower only). From 4,500Kč ($187) double; from 5,100Kč ($212) suite. Rates include breakfast. AE, MC, V. Tram: 22 or 23. **Amenities:** Laundry service; safe in reception. *In room:* A/C, TV, minibar, hair dryer.

U Krále Karla 🦀 This castle hill property does so much to drive home its Renaissance roots, King Charles's heirs should be getting royalties. Replete with period prints, open-beamed ceilings, and stained-glass windows, the atmosphere is almost

---

(*Value* **Money-Saving Tips**
_____

Many hotels set their prices depending on the koruna's market rate against the euro, so prices change frequently.

Czech hotel reception attendants have little interest in haggling over room rates, but sometimes you can still get a deal. Try calling in advance and getting a very senior manager (preferably the owner) to book your room. Be clear that you're looking at other properties and don't be afraid to say that price does matter. If there are plenty of rooms around town, you're in a great negotiating position. You can also seek a higher discount for a longer stay.

Disneyesque in its pretense, but somehow appropriate for this location at the foot of Prague Castle. The rooms offer plenty of space, heavy period furniture, and bed frames with firm mattresses as well as clean bathrooms with a tub/shower combination or shower only. This is a fun, comfortable choice, with heavy period furniture and colorful angelic accents everywhere.

Nerudova-Úvoz 4, Praha 1. (℗ 257-532-869. Fax 257-533-591. www.romantichotels.cz. 19 units (13 with shower only). From 3,900Kč ($162) double; 7,500Kč ($312) suite. Rates include breakfast. AE, MC, V. Tram: 22 or 23 to Malostranské nám. and then up the hill. **Amenities:** Restaurant; bike or scooter rental; tour and activities desk; private limousine hire; limited room service; babysitting; laundry; dry cleaning; solarium. *In room:* TV, minibar, kitchenette, hair dryer, iron, safe.

2 Malá Strana (Lesser Town)

EXPENSIVE

Best Western–Hotel Kampa   On the edge of the park where troops once camped along the banks of the Vltava, the Kampa occupies what was a 17th-century armory. It has a choice location on a quiet, winding alley off the park, with easy access to Malá Strana and Charles Bridge. The rooms suggest a bit of Communist chintz without much attention to aesthetics, but they're comfortable enough if you don't expect first-class surroundings. The best rooms boast a park view—request one of these when booking or checking in. There's a restaurant, but you'd be better off visiting one of those nearby, like Kampa Park under Charles Bridge (p. 88). The hotel also rents its large hall for private parties and that might become a disturbing factor in your stay here. Ask beforehand about planned events at the hall.

Všehrdova 16, Praha 1. (℗ 257-404-444. Fax 257-404-333. www.euroagentur.cz. 84 units (shower only). From 5,400Kč ($225) double. Rates include breakfast. AE, DC, MC, V. Metro: Malostranská; then take tram no. 12, 22, or 23 to the Hellichova stop. **Amenities:** Restaurant w/garden; bar; room service; laundry service; dry cleaning. *In room:* TV, minibar, hair dryer, safe.

Hotel Aria 🏵🏵   This new music-themed hotel recently opened in the heart of Malá Strana just around the corner from the St. Nicholas Cathedral. Each of its four floors is tastefully decorated by Versace designers to evoke a different genre of music, famous composer, or musician. The rooms and bathrooms vary in their size and layout, and all are kept to the same exceptionally high standard evident throughout the hotel. There is an impressive library of CDs, DVDs, and books about music off the lobby, and a full-time resident musicologist available to help you choose a concert in the city. The Aria will delight newlyweds or any romantic soul with its luxurious, but cozy, atmosphere, and the extensive list of amenities, which includes a roof terrace garden with spectacular views of Malá Strana, a screening room, and music salon.

Tržiště 9, Praha 1. (℗ 225-334-111. Fax 225-334-666. www.ariahotel.net. 52 units. From 8,010Kč ($333) double; 10,230Kč ($426) suite. Rates include breakfast. AE, MC, V. Metro: Malostranská and then tram no. 12, 22, or 23 to Malostranské nám. **Amenities:** Restaurant; bar; exercise room; courtesy car from the airport; 24-hr. business center; 24-hr. room service. *In room:* A/C, Internet, PC, DVD/CD player, minibar, safe, hair dryer.

Hotel Hoffmeister   The artsy Hoffmeister opened in 1993, rising out of the ruins of dilapidated block of buildings. It's one of a kind: a full-service luxury property owned and operated by a Czech who tries hard to provide friendly customer service. As the hotel is on a busy street used by cars and trams to get to Prague Castle, your stay can be somewhat noisy at times, but the rooms are solid, distinctive, and well equipped. Each has a unique color scheme with rich fabrics, matching draperies, and

Which Quarter?

If location is important to you, there are three areas among which you should choose. If you're lucky enough to stay in one of the few rooms on the castle hill in **Hradčany,** you'll feel as if you have a privileged position where princes, potentates, and politburo wonks once roamed. You'll also pay for this privilege. You'll remember your stay in **Malá Strana** because of the quiet old-world atmosphere of this compact quarter, whose red roofs lie in the afternoon shadow of Prague Castle and fight for attention with the dome of St. Nicholas Church. A room in **Old Town (Staré Město)** will put you right in the heart of the largest saturation of shops, theaters, and restaurants. It's certainly the most lively quarter.

Elsewhere, you'll find more affordable options near fine restaurants, cafes, and services in **Vinohrady,** just above Wenceslas Square off the Náměstí Míru metro station. This part of **New Town (Nové Město)** is quickly becoming the trendy part of central Prague, with gentrified First Republic apartment buildings and greener residential neighborhoods. As for staying on **Wenceslas Square,** my advice is to avoid this increasingly rough area, unless you enjoy living on the edge.

even bed canopies. The beds have firm mattresses, while the roomy bathrooms are fitted with tub/shower combinations. For an ultimate relaxation visit the wellness center, where massages and other body treatments are on the menu. Conceived by the son of Adolph Hoffmeister, an artist and former diplomat, the hotel's bold, eclectic style is striking. Sketches by Adolph are hung around the building and depict such friends and acquaintances of the late artist as Charlie Chaplin, Salvador Dalí, George Bernard Shaw, and John Steinbeck. One corner of the building is held up by a massive abstract human figure gesturing in an Italian-style salute to the wild drivers who pass on their way up the hill.

Pod Bruskou 9, Praha 1. ✆ **251-017-111.** Fax 251-017-120. www.hoffmeister.cz. 42 units (tub/shower combination in bathrooms). From 6,000Kč ($250) double; from 8,700Kč ($362) suite. Rates include breakfast. AE, MC, V. Parking 300Kč ($12) per day. Metro: Malostranská. **Amenities:** Restaurant; cafe; bar; wellness center; concierge; car-rental service; 24-hr. room service; laundry service. *In room:* A/C, TV, dataport, minibar, hair dryer, safe.

Hotel U páva ✸ "At the Peacock" is a fine B&B in Malá Strana managed by the same group as the King Charles is. On the narrow street across from the walled Vojanov Gardens, a stone's throw from Charles Bridge, this family-run hotel has the intimacy of a farmhouse and offers room service from its decent kitchen. Original wooden ceilings, antique chairs, and comfortable beds accent the reasonably spacious rooms. The best ones on the top floor facing the front have a fantastic low-angle view of Prague Castle. The fully tiled bathrooms of adequate size have tub/shower combinations. The best rooms on the top floor facing the front have a fantastic low-angle view of Prague Castle. In 2000 the hotel underwent an expansion, and 16 rooms, a new restaurant, a sauna, and a reception area were added.

U Lužického semináře 22, Praha 1. ✆ **257-533-360.** Fax 257-530-919. www.romantichotels.cz. 27 units (tub/shower combination in bathrooms). From 4,800Kč ($200) double; from 7,500Kč ($312) suite. Rates include breakfast. AE, MC,

V. Metro: Malostranská. **Amenities:** Restaurant; cafe; bar; sauna; tour and activities desk; car rental; business services; room service; babysitting; overnight laundry. *In room:* TV, minibar, hair dryer.

Hotel U tří pštrosů   This small inn is at the foot of Charles Bridge on the left bank, where buskers try to make a living and the footsteps and conversations of visitors provide the background noise. Reopened in 1992, this hotel has preserved its painted wooden Renaissance ceilings and some antique furnishings. The rooms are rustic but comfortable. They're medium-size and simply decorated, fitted with beds with mattresses of various firmness, and tiny bathrooms. The corner suites offer spectacular views of Charles Bridge and Prague Castle. The hotel is run more like a casual B&B than a professional hotel.

Dražického nám. 12, Praha 1. © **257-532-410.** Fax 257-533-217. www.upstrosu.cz. 18 units (11 with shower only). From 4,800Kč ($200) double; from 6,000Kč ($250) suite. Rates include breakfast. AE, DC, MC, V. Metro: Malostranská. **Amenities:** Restaurant; bar; concierge; tour and activities desk; room service 7am–11pm; laundry service; dry cleaning. *In room:* TV, dataport, minibar.

Carol recs Old Town

3 Staré Město (Old Town) & Josefov

EXPENSIVE

Four Seasons Hotel ✹✹✹   This addition to Prague's short list of luxury hotels is its most impressive. Located in an imposing position on the banks of the Vltava River right next to Charles Bridge, the Four Seasons provides an elegant base for exploring Old Town and enjoying the symphonies at the nearby Rudolfinum, while taking in a wonderful panoramic view of Prague Castle across the river.

The property actually melds three historic buildings from the city's most important architectural periods—baroque, Renaissance, and Art Nouveau. The most impressive wing, the 17th-century baroque villa, houses the Presidential Suite for 43,200Kč to 84,000Kč ($1,800–$3,500) per night. At least this tariff grants a surprising amount of privacy (despite the hordes of tourists below the hotel), a cozy fireplace, a private dining room, and the privilege of peering into the castle's ornate staterooms across the way. The surrounding executive suites and guest rooms are smaller but still nicely appointed. The best have sweeping views and sunken marble tubs. In the tasteful and lower-priced Art Nouveau wing, comfortable doubles can be booked for less than $300, but the street-side views are much less impressive.

All rooms are fitted with fine solid wood furniture: some with antique pieces, others with more modern avant-garde accents. There are CD players with robust stereo systems, and high-speed Internet connections.

Veleslavínova 2a, Praha 1. © **221-427-000.** Fax 221-426-000. www.fourseasons.com. 162 units. From 7,800Kč ($324) double; from 15,600Kč ($649) suite. Rates do not include breakfast. AE, DC, MC, V. Metro: Staroměstská. **Amenities:** Restaurant; bar; health club; concierge; business services; 24-hr. room service; laundry; dry cleaning overnight. *In room:* A/C, TV, CD, DVD player, dataport, minibar, hair dryer, safe.

Hotel Inter-Continental Praha ✹   The upper suites of this hotel have hosted luminaries like Michael Jackson, Madeleine Albright and, legend has it, global terrorist Carlos the Jackal. Mr. Jackson and Ms. Albright came for the comfortably reconstructed rooms; the Jackal apparently came because during the Communist era—the hotel was a safe house with decent room and board. The 1970s design has been updated with modern rooms, a glittering fitness center, and an atrium restaurant. The standard guest rooms aren't very large but are comfortable, with decent but not exceptional upholstered furniture, computer ports, and marble bathrooms. A riverside window might give you a glimpse of the castle or at least the metronome at the top of Letná Park across the river, where a massive statue of Joseph Stalin stood in the 1950s.

Náměstí Curieových 43/5, Praha 1. ℂ 296-631-111. Fax 224-811-216. www.interconti.com. 364 units. From 4,170Kč ($173) double; from 6,420Kč ($267) suite. Rates include buffet breakfast. AE, DC, MC, V. Metro: Staroměstská. **Amenities:** 2 restaurants; cafe; indoor swimming pool; fitness center; concierge; car rental; fax and business services; salon; 24-hr. room service; massage; laundry. *In room:* TV, dataport, minibar, hair dryer.

Hotel Paříž 🦌   At the edge of náměstí Republiky and across from the Municipal House, the 100-year old Paříž provides a rare chance to put yourself back in the gilded First Republic. Each light fixture, etching, and curve at this Art Nouveau landmark recalls the days when Prague was one of the world's richest cities. The sinuous banister leading past the reception area is an intricate piece of ironwork, and the lobby is tastefully furnished in the Art Nouveau style known here as the *secese* motif. The high-ceilinged guest rooms are done in a purplish theme; they aren't plush but are comfortable and adequately equipped, with more modern furnishings than the lobby would suggest. It's the ground floor that really maintains an authentic period elegance. Now that the Municipal House is open again, offering beautiful salons, cafes, restaurants, and concert halls, you can have a 1920s experience without leaving the neighborhood.

U Obecního domu 1, Praha 1. ℂ 222-195-195. Fax 224-225-475. www.hotel-pariz.cz. 94 units (74 tub/shower combination, 20 shower only). 4,650Kč ($193) double; 8,250Kč ($343) suite. AE, DC, MC, V. Metro: Náměstí Republiky. **Amenities:** Restaurant; cafe; concierge; business services; 24-hr. room service; babysitting; laundry; dry cleaning. *In room:* A/C, TV, minibar, hair dryer, safe.

Hotel Ungelt 🦌🦌 *Value* *Kids*   In the afternoon shadow of the Týn Church, just off Old Town Square, you'll find a place not as opulent as the Paříž, but a good value. The three-story Ungelt offers full apartments that are airy, spacious, and very comfortable for families. Each unit contains a bedroom, a living room, a full kitchen, and a bathroom. The bedrooms have standard-issue beds and not-too-attractive upholstered couches, but do boast luxurious accents like huge chandeliers and antique dressers. Some also have magnificent hand-painted ceilings. Because the Ungelt is in a tightly constructed neighborhood behind the church, there are no great exterior views. However, the back rooms overlook a quaint courtyard.

Štupartská 1, Praha 1. ℂ 224-828-686. Fax 224-828-181. www.ungelt.cz. 10 units. 4,650Kč ($193) 1-bedroom suite; 5,750Kč ($239) 2-bedroom suite. Rates include breakfast. AE, MC, V. Metro: Staroměstská or line B to náměstí Republiky. **Amenities:** Bar; tour and activities desk at reception; car rental; business service; laundry. *In room:* TV, minibar, hair dryer.

Hotel U Prince 🦌 *Value*   Sometimes a location this good means a hotel that falls well short of expectations and value, but the Hotel U Prince, directly across from the Astronomical Clock in Old Town Square, has reformed itself into a worthy choice in the upper price range. A complete reconstruction of the 12th-century building has given its once ragged rooms and salons a new lease on life. They are pretty spacious and equipped with heavy period furniture, including beds with soft mattresses. The bathrooms offer tub/shower combinations. The double glazing has locked out most of the constant buzz from the square below. Colleagues of ours who stayed there said they were able to hear the tinkle of the clock's hourly bell, but it was faint enough to be soothing. Rooms in the back are even more secluded. However, the showstopper of this property is the roof terrace bar and restaurant, which offers exceptional views for dining in Prague during the high season.

Staroměstské nám. 29, Praha 1. ℂ/fax 224-213-807. www.hoteluprince.cz. 24 units. 6,190Kč ($258) double; from 7,190Kč ($299) suite. Rates include breakfast. AE, MC, V. Metro: Staroměstská. **Amenities:** 2 restaurants, including a rooftop 1 open year-round; bar; summer garden; 24-hr. room service. *In room:* A/C, minibar.

MODERATE

Betlem Club   Protestant firebrand Jan Hus launched his reformation drive at the reconstructed chapel across the street, but other than the vaulted medieval cellar where breakfast is served, little about the Betlem Club recalls those heady 15th-century days. Still, this small hotel has a great location on a cobblestone square. The rooms are unimaginatively decorated with bland modern pieces but are comfortable and fairly priced. The bathrooms are small but clean. If you come by car, you can park in spots in front of the hotel—a rarity for this parking-deficient city—but book a spot early.

Staying in a Hostel

If you need simply a dry, cheap place to lay your head, Prague has several relatively clean hostels. They aren't very private, but they do provide you with a chance to meet people from around the world. Hostels are most abundant in July and August, the school vacation period when many classrooms are converted into dorms. For the latest information, contact **AVE Travel Ltd.** (© 251-091-111; fax 251-556-005; www.avetravel.cz).

One of the best hostels is **Welcome Hostel Strahov** (building 3, Vaníčkova 5, Praha 1, on Strahov Hill; © 224-320-202; fax 224-323-489; www.hostels.com), across from the giant Strahov Stadium on the biggest hill overlooking the castle and city below. This complex of dormitories was built to house competitors for Socialist *Spartakiáda* exercise festivals that were held before the fall of Communism. Today, these concrete high-rises serve as student dormitories and are a popular choice for backpackers from all over the world. Most rooms are doubles, not one has a private bathroom, and all are open 24 hours. Expect nothing much more than a bed and a place to throw your things in a pretty clean concrete cell, but the price is right. Rates are 300Kč to 400Kč ($12–$17) per person.

Traveller's Hostel-Pension Dlouhá ✿ (Dlouhá 33, Praha 1; © 224-826-662; fax 224-826-665; www.travellers.cz) is one of the best hostels in the city center. This flagship in the local Traveller's group of hostels is open year-round, just a few blocks off Old Town Square and a few floors above the wildest dance club in town, the Roxy. There is a total of 90 beds—which can be expanded from singles to sextets—on two floors, with all sharing large, well-equipped bathrooms. This hostel attracts a mix of student backpackers and veteran tourists taking advantage of the clean, affordable, modern setting, renovated in 1997. One single and one double have en-suite bathrooms, but they are often saved as a premium for tour group leaders; ask anyway. Traveller's offers other hostels at dormitories throughout town during the high season. Check their website for each season's roster. Rates including breakfast are 650Kč ($27) per person in a double room.

Pension Unitas/Art Prison Hostel ✿, at Bartolomějská 9, Praha 1 (© 224-221-802; fax 224-217-555; www.unitas.cz), is great value for the money and located in an unbeatable location. For more details see p. 73.

Kids Family-Friendly Accommodations

Private apartments where you can fix your own meals are the most convenient option for families (p. 61), but if you would prefer more hotel-like services and settings, try:

Flathotel Orion (p. 76)   This affordable apartment-style hotel in Vinohrady has plenty of space for kids as well as kitchens for meals the way you want them.

Corinthia Towers Hotel (p. 77)   This is the only place in town with its own Western-style bowling alley complete with automatic scoring. Vyšehrad Park with playgrounds and beautiful views for picnicking is a short walk away.

Hotel Ungelt (p. 70)   A convenient location in the heart of Old Town, and large apartment suites, make this hotel a good choice for a short or long family stay.

Pension Větrník (p. 77)   This country inn has plenty of fresh air and forests for kids to run around. Mom and Dad will like the price and made-to-order meals.

Betlémské nám. 9, Praha 1. © 222-221-575. Fax 222-220-580. www.betlemclub.cz. 22 units (tub/shower combination). From 3,300Kč ($137) double; from 3,700Kč ($154) suite. Rates include breakfast. No credit cards. Metro: Národní třída. **Amenities:** Babysitting; laundry; safe. *In room:* TV, minibar.

Hotel Cloister Inn ★ *Value*   Between Old Town Square and the National Theater, this property has been renovated into a good-value, midrange hotel. The original rooms of this unique spot were developed from holding cells used by the Communist secret police, the StB; the cells themselves were converted from a convent. It sounds ominous, but the Cloister Inn rooms are actually very inviting. A new proprietor has taken over management from the secret police and the Sisters of Mercy (the nuns, not the rock group). He has refurbished and expanded the hotel with smart colors and comfortable Nordic furniture. The rooms offer enough space, beds with comfortable firm mattresses, and reasonably sized bathrooms with shower only. All is maintained to a high standard. It is just 3 minutes by foot from both Charles Bridge and Wenceslas Square.

Konviktská 14, Praha 1. © 224-211-020. Fax 224-210-800. www.cloister-inn.cz. 73 units (showers only). From 3,300Kč ($137) double. Rates include breakfast. AE, DC, MC, V. Metro: Národní třída. **Amenities:** Concierge; tour and activities desk; safe. *In room:* TV, hair dryer, safety box.

Dům krále Jiřího   The "House at King George's" perches above two pubs on a narrow side street. The rooms are pretty bare but have a bit more charm than they used to. The ceilings are high, and the dark wooden furniture is another improvement. Charles Bridge is a few dozen steps and a swing to the left from the pension, but this narrow alley has become more like Bourbon Street than the Royal Route. Ask for a room in back if you want to deaden the clamor of the pubs below. Breakfast is served in the wine cellar, which lacks character despite a recent remodeling.

Liliová 10, Praha 1. © 353-232-100. Fax 353-222-999. www.hotel.cz/kraljiri. 11 units. From 2,700Kč ($112) double or suite. Rates include breakfast. AE, MC, V. Metro: Staroměstská. *In room:* TV, fridge.

Pension Unitas/Art Prison Hostel *Value*   With a quirky history (same building complex as Hotel Cloister Inn) and an unbeatable location at this price, the Unitas is great value for the money. On a side street between Old Town Square and the National Theater stands this former convent, which was conveniently seized for use as secret police holding cells under the Communists. One of their most frequent guests, before the place was turned into a postrevolution pension, was none other than the pesky dissident and soon-to-be-president Václav Havel. But once the bizarre allure of staying in Havel's former hoosegow wears off, you realize that this is a pretty artful attempt at providing decent accommodations at a good price. The cells and rooms range from doubles to quads, with comfy mattresses and clean linen provided. A recent rebranding of the complex added some funky wall murals to give it the added subtitle of being an Art Prison Hostel. There is no curfew, and the complimentary breakfast of cold cuts, rolls, and cheese is fresh and plentiful. The joint bathrooms are clean enough to pass. If you feel you are becoming a bit too bohemian from too many backpacking days on the road, there is a well-equipped laundry room. There's also a safe and luggage room to store your valuables.

Bartolomějská 9, Praha 1. ℭ **224-221-802.** Fax 224-217-555. www.unitas.cz. 36 units (shared bathroom facilities). From 1,200Kč ($50) double in pension; from 490Kč ($20) per person in double room in hostel. Rates include breakfast. AE, MC, V. Metro: Národní třída. **Amenities:** Coin-op laundry.

4 Nové Město (New Town)

NEAR WENCESLAS SQUARE
VERY EXPENSIVE

Hotel Jalta *✦*   Recently reconstructed, the Jalta has put on a fresh face and a new attitude. The lobby is pretty cold and unwelcoming, but the rooms have high ceilings and decent upholstered chairs. An infusion of Japanese money has improved the hotel furnishings, which were formerly depressing Communist-issue pieces.

The Jalta is just below the statue of King Wenceslas, where the masses gathered to ring out the Communist government in 1989. The rooms facing the square have balconies, allowing a broad view of the busy square and a chance to imagine the scene on those historic, revolutionary November nights.

Václavské nám. 45, Praha 1. ℭ **222-822-111.** Fax 222-822-833. www.jalta.cz. 94 units. 9,000Kč ($374) double; 10,800Kč ($449) suite. Rates include breakfast. AE, DC, MC, V. Metro: Můstek or Muzeum. **Amenities:** 2 restaurants; concierge; room service; laundry service; casino. *In room:* A/C, TV, minibar, hair dryer, safe.

Palace Hotel *✦✦*   The Palace has long been the quintessential Prague address for visiting dignitaries and celebrities like Josephine Baker, Enrico Caruso, Steven Spielberg, the Rolling Stones, and Britain's Prince Charles. Surpassed in comfort only by the Savoy in Hradčany, the Palace is a block from Wenceslas Square. The 1903 Art Nouveau building offers a more stoic "Viennese" approach to the era's architectural fashion than the more ornate Paříž (p. 70) and Esplanade (see below) nearby. The lobby boasts accents like buttery-wood paneling and furniture with subtle flowered upholstery, but the overall effect is that of contemporary wealth sampling the past rather than building a museum to it. The staff makes a point of remembering guests' names and provides excellent service.

The soothing, delicately colored guest rooms are some of the largest luxury accommodations in Prague, each with an Italian marble bathroom. The special Lady Queen suites have luxurious dressing tables at which to prepare for an elegant night on the Golden City's social circuit. Two rooms are available for travelers with disabilities.

Panská 12, Praha 1. ✆ **224-093-111.** Fax 224-221-240. www.palacehotel.cz. 124 units (tub/shower combination). From 10,770Kč ($448) double; 11,880Kč ($495) suite. Rates include breakfast. AE, DC, MC, V. Metro: Můstek. **Amenities:** 2 restaurants; cafe; concierge; business services; 24-hr. room service; laundry service. *In room:* A/C, TV, VCR, minibar, safe.

EXPENSIVE

Hotel Esplanade ✦   Though the Esplanade doesn't get as much attention as the other Art Deco hotels around Old Town, a recent overhaul has put it into the top class. Constructed during the First Republic, the Esplanade began life as a bank and the offices of an Italian insurance company on a side street at the top of the square. The first owners must have had extravagant tastes, as indicated by the ornate accents that remain: An original multicolored flowered chandelier hangs from an atrium dome in the French restaurant that used to be the bank lobby. Huge oil paintings hang throughout, with intricate ceiling details framing every guest room. Individual private dining salons are available for special luncheons and meetings.

The halls have a musty feel, but the guest rooms are bright and airy, some with standard beds, others with French Provincial headboards and tables, and others with elaborate canopies. Suite no. 101 is packed with antique wooden chairs, intricate inlaid tables, and a fascinating (but busy) embossed wall covering. Top-floor room nos. 711 and 712 offer a panorama of Prague. The quality of each room varies, so ask to see what you're offered before you commit. The main train station across the street may put you off, but the doorman claims the hotel is completely safe.

Washingtonova 19, Praha 1. ✆ **224-501-111.** Fax 224-229-306. www.esplanade.cz. 74 units (47 shower only). From 3,870Kč ($161) double; from 6,870Kč ($286) suite. Rates include breakfast. AE, DC, MC, V. Metro: Muzeum. **Amenities:** Restaurant; bar; cafe/lounge; sauna; concierge; car-rental desk; room service; massage; babysitting; laundry; dry cleaning; executive-level rooms. *In room:* TV, dataport, minibar, hair dryer, safe.

MODERATE

Andante ✦ *Value*   This best-value choice near Wenceslas Square is tucked away on a dark side street, about 2 blocks off the top of the square. Despite the less-than-appealing neighborhood, this is the most comfortable property at this price. It lacks the character of the old Hotel Evropa (p. 75) but is better cared for. With modern beds and good firm mattresses, as well as high-grade Scandinavian furniture and colorful decorations, the rooms gain in comfort what they lose in adventure. They offer plenty of space and white, well-kept bathrooms with tub/shower combinations, some with shower only.

Ve Smečkách 4, Prague 1. ✆ **222-210-021.** Fax 222-210-591. www.andante.cz. 32 units (some with shower only, some with tub only). 3,300Kč ($137) double; 4,560Kč ($190) suite. Rates include breakfast. AE, MC, V. Metro: Muzeum. **Amenities:** Restaurant; tours arranged w/the reception desk; business services; limited room service. *In room:* TV, minibar, hair dryer, iron, safety box available at the reception desk.

Hotel Meran   This used to be part of the Hotel Evropa (see below), now known better for its cafe than its spartan accommodations. The Meran is the brighter, narrower building next door, and it is on its own again. Family run, and cozier than the bigger Art Deco landmark which draws so much attention to its gilded facade, the Meran has had a face-lift to make it a fair but not spectacular midrange choice on Wenceslas Square, a walkable distance to the main train station. The lobby interior has retained some original Art Nouveau accents, although the rooms have few. They are unimaginatively decorated and seem cramped. The tiny bathrooms have tub/shower combinations or shower only. The front windows overlook the place where hundreds of thousands demonstrated night after night until the Communist government fell in a peaceful coup in 1989.

Václavské nám. 27, Praha 1. ℭ **222-244-373.** Fax 224-230-411. www.hotelmeran.cz. 20 units with bathroom (tub or shower). From 3,450Kč ($144) double. Rates include breakfast. AE, DC, MC, V. Metro: Muzeum or Můstek. **Amenities:** Concierge; exchange. *In room:* TV.

INEXPENSIVE

Hotel Evropa   Born in 1889 as the Hotel Archduke Stephan, the Evropa was recast in the early 1900s as an Art Deco hotel. However, this is yet another classic that has seen much better days. Though the statue-studded exterior, still one of the most striking landmarks on Wenceslas Square, has recently been polished, the rooms are aging; most don't have bathrooms and some are just plain shabby. The best choice is a room facing the square with a balcony.

The hotel's famous cafe, a wood-encased former masterpiece that no longer glows, furthers the theme. Still, this is an affordable way to stay in one of Wenceslas Square's once-grand addresses.

Václavské nám. 25, Praha 1. ℭ **224-215-387.** Fax 224-224-544. www.evropahotel.cz. 90 units, 20 with bathroom (tub only). 2,600Kč ($108) double without bathroom; 4,000Kč ($166) double with bathroom. Rates include continental breakfast. AE, MC, V. Metro: Můstek or Muzeum. **Amenities:** Restaurant; concierge; safe; luggage storage.

NEAR NÁMĚSTÍ REPUBLIKY/BANKING DISTRICT
EXPENSIVE

Hotel Josef 🐾🐾   The Josef stands as the new home for tasteful minimalism in the new Bohemia. It is the hippest of Prague's new hip hotels. British-based architect Eva Jiřičná brings a new study on the interior use of glass to her native land with its own long history of the glazier's craft. Every piece of space breathes with life and light, breaking the stuffy mold of most high-end hotels.

She uses modern glass walls, tables, and chairs bathed with the light of modern lighting fixtures to offset funky yellows and greens, and even rust-colored bedspreads thrown in. There is a daring and dramatic effect in every room. Superior rooms are so bold as to offer transparent bath nooks, shower stalls, and washrooms with a full view of grooming activities for your partner to absorb in the main sleeping chamber. Room no. 801, a penthouse suite with a magnificent vista of the Prague skyline, is highly sought-after for those who want to absorb the golden city in its full glory.

Rybná 20, Praha 1. ℭ **221-700-111.** Fax 221-700-999. www.hoteljosef.com. 110 units. From 5,190Kč ($216) double. Rates include breakfast. AE, DC, MC, V. Metro: Náměstí Republiky. **Amenities:** Restaurant; health club; concierge; car rental; courtesy limo; business center; room service; babysitting; laundry. *In room:* A/C, TV, DVD, CD player, dataport, minibar, hair dryer, safe.

Prague Marriott Hotel 🐾🐾🐾 *Kids*   A major addition to the thin ranks of full-service business hotels, the Marriott provides just what you would expect—a high-standard. The large rooms have bright colors, tasteful, homogenized furniture and comfortable beds as well as phones, faxes, laptop connections, and other services. The bathrooms are spacious and immaculately maintained. As well as being newer and slightly better appointed, the Marriott is about 10 paces closer to the Czech central bank than its sister, the Hotel Renaissance, right off náměstí Republiky. In an effort to attract families, the Marriott offers Sunday family brunches in the Brasserie Praha, where kids are welcome and PC games are available.

V Celnici 8, Praha 1. ℭ **222-888-888.** Fax 222-888-889. www.marriott.com. 328 units. 6,870Kč ($286) double; 8,070Kč ($336) executive-level double; from 8,970Kč ($373) suite. Rates for suites and executive rooms include breakfast. AE, DC, MC, V. Valet parking $31 per day. Metro: Náměstí Republiky. **Amenities:** Restaurant; cafe; bar; indoor swimming pool; well-equipped fitness center; saunas; whirlpools; gym; spa rooms; concierge; fully equipped business center; salon; 24-hr. room service; laundry and dry-cleaning service. *In room:* A/C, TV, dataport, minibar, hair dryer, safe.

Renaissance Prague 𝒢𝒢𝒢   The Renaissance, opened in 1993 and now run by Marriott, also has the standard comforts of a top-level business hotel. Like the Marriott, it is around the corner from the central bank and caters to conferences and entrepreneurs. Each room is strategically lit, with warm woods and earth tones but without any of the accents found at the Old Town's Art Nouveau hotels. The rooms are reasonably sized and well kept, with comfortable modern beds and clean, fully tiled bathrooms. The top two floors of the eight-level building have rooms with pitched ceilings, adding some variety. Suites on the top floor are spacious and have walk-in closets and sizable bathrooms. A few standard rooms are wheelchair-accessible.

V Celnici 7, Praha 1. ℂ **221-821-111.** Fax 221-822-200. www.renaissancehotels.com. 314 units. From 6,270Kč ($261) double; from 8,370Kč ($348) suite. Rates for suites and executive rooms include breakfast. AE, DC, MC, V. Metro: Náměstí Republiky. **Amenities:** 3 restaurants; bar; indoor swimming pool; small exercise room; sauna; whirlpool; concierge; business center; 24-hr. room service; massage; laundry; dry cleaning. *In room:* A/C, TV, dataport, minibar, hair dryer, safe.

5 Vinohrady

EXPENSIVE

Hotel Ametyst   The most expensive full-service hotel in an affordable part of town, the Ametyst is less expensive than hotels of similar quality in the older districts, but you can get a better deal at one of the nearby pensions. On a quiet back street about 5 blocks from náměstí Míru, it's spotless and decorated in a warm contemporary style. The top-floor rooms are especially bright and cheery, with pitched ceilings and balconies overlooking the peaceful residential neighborhood. The hotel is clearly geared toward its German visitors, so you won't find many signs in Czech, much less English.

Jana Masaryka 11, Praha 2. ℂ **222-921-921.** Fax 222-921-999. www.hotelametyst.cz. 84 units (some with tub only, some with shower only). 6,450Kč ($268) double. Rates include breakfast. AE, DC, MC, V. Metro: Náměstí Míru. **Amenities:** 2 restaurants; bar; small fitness center; sauna. *In room:* TV, minibar, hair dryer, safe.

INEXPENSIVE

Flathotel Orion 𝒢 *Kids*   The best family value close to the city center, the Orion is an apartment hotel with each unit sporting a well-equipped kitchen. All accommodations have either one bedroom (sleeps two) or two bedrooms (sleeps up to six). The spacious guest rooms are comfortable but not very imaginative, bordered in pale blue with leather armchairs and dark wooden bed frames without much on the walls. The beds vary in the firmness of their mattresses. The bathrooms are small, basic white and modern, as are the kitchens. In this friendly neighborhood, fruit and vegetable shops and corner grocery stores can be found around náměstí Míru, just up the street.

Americká 9, Praha 2. ℂ **353-232-100.** Fax 353-222-999. www.hotel.cz/orion. 26 apts with bathroom (tub/shower combination). 2,580Kč ($107) 1 bedroom; 3,320Kč ($138) 2 bedrooms. Breakfast 160Kč ($6.65). AE, MC, V. Metro: Náměstí Míru. **Amenities:** Finnish sauna for 200Kč ($8.30) per hour; tours and activities arrangements at reception; room service; laundry and dry-cleaning service. *In room:* TV, kitchen, fridge, coffeemaker.

Tips A Note on Floors

Remember that Europe's floor-numbering system differs from America's. European buildings have a ground floor (the first floor in the U.S.), then a first floor (the second floor in the U.S.), a second floor, and so on.

6 Elsewhere in Prague

EXPENSIVE

Corinthia Towers Hotel *(Kids)*   Opened in the mid-1980s, this hotel was one of the last "achievements" of Communist central planners. Reserved occasionally for delegates attending Party Congress meetings at the Palace of Culture next door (now the Congress Center), the hotel juts up from a hill with a gorgeous panorama of the city. The medium-size rooms used to be like those in a 1980s upper-middle-range Sheraton, but have undergone renovation. They are fitted with solid furniture and the beds have firm mattresses, but the decoration is pretty bland. The bathrooms are reasonably sized and have tub/shower combinations.

The hotel is American in its approach, with an AMF bowling alley in the basement. Though the city center isn't within walking distance, the Vyšehrad metro station is just below the hotel entrance.

Note: The Maltese company which now owns the Corinthia Towers is itself partly owned by a Libyan state firm on the U.S. State Department's list for trade sanctions. A U.S. citizen staying at this place is technically breaking a federal law, although no known cases have been prosecuted. Check with the U.S. Embassy's consular section if you are concerned about staying here.

Kongresová 1, Praha 4. © **261-191-111.** Fax 261-225-011. www.corinthia.cz. 583 units. 7,200Kč ($300) double; from 11,850Kč ($493) suite. Rates include breakfast. AE, DC, MC, V. Metro: Vyšehrad. **Amenities:** 2 restaurants; cafe; well-equipped fitness center w/pool, sauna, exercise machines; game room; concierge; activities desk; salon; 24-hr. room service; babysitting; laundry; bowling alley. *In room:* A/C, TV, minibar.

Hilton Prague *(Overrated)*   With its jarring 1980s galleria style, the Hilton looks like a huge ice cube outside and a greenhouse inside. The guest rooms are relatively cushy and functional, somewhat like those in an upscale U.S. motel. The building is packed with amenities that include a tennis club, pool, fitness center, and casino. The 700-plus rooms make this place (originally launched by former state travel wonks Čedok, but now run by Hilton) a natural choice for the largest conferences and conventions. Then-U.S. President Clinton and his entourage took over this place during his well-staged 1994 visit. The location just outside the city center isn't ideal, but the hotel's overpriced Mercedes can take you where you want to go.

Pobřežní 1, Praha 8. © **224-841-111.** Fax 224-842-378. www.hilton.com. 788 units (tub/shower combination). 7,680Kč ($319) double; from 10,380Kč ($432) suite. AE, DC, DISC, MC, V. Metro: Florenc. **Amenities:** Cafe/restaurant; indoor swimming pool; putting greens; tennis club; health club; sauna; concierge; car rental; business center; 24-hr. room service; massage; laundry; dry cleaning; casino. *In room:* A/C, TV, minibar, hair dryer.

INEXPENSIVE

Pension Větrník *(Value)(Kids)*   A mostly scenic half-hour tram ride (or metro-tram combo) from the city center takes you to this romantic, secret, country hideaway. After getting off the tram, walk back behind a bunch of large concrete dorms to find a painstakingly restored 18th-century white windmill house. Once you buzz at the metal gate (be careful to avoid the buzzer for the door to the family residence), Miloš Opatrný will greet you. Lush gardens and a tennis court lead to a quaint guesthouse with a stone staircase and spacious rooms with big beds, open-beamed ceilings, and modern amenities. The plain bedcovers and odd-shaped table lamps could stand some improvement, however. The bathrooms are roomy, with stand-up showers, and the windows are shuttered and boast flower boxes.

Opatrný, a former foreign-service chef, takes pride in whipping up a traditional Czech country dinner (100Kč–200Kč/$4.15–$8.30) and serving it personally in a small medieval stone cellar with a crackling fire. There's a patio for drinks outside during pleasant weather. You can't get more romantic than this, especially for the price.

U Větrníku 40, Praha 6. ⓒ 220-612-404. Fax 220-513-390. www.pensionvetrnik.wz.cz. 6 units (4 shower only, 2 tub/shower combination). 2,100Kč ($87) double; 3,150Kč ($131) suite. Rates include breakfast. MC. Metro: Line A to Hradčanská station, then tram no. 1 or 18 to Větrník. **Amenities:** Private tennis court in the courtyard, lit for night play (hope for the right weather!). *In room:* TV, hair dryer.

7 Near the Airport

EXPENSIVE

Hotel Diplomat ⓕ   Prague's primary airport business hotel, the clean and functional Diplomat, isn't next to Ruzyně Airport but about 15 minutes on the way into town. Another in the Vienna International Hotels group that manages the more fashionable Savoy and Palace in Prague, the Diplomat achieves what it sets out to do: provide an array of business services and spacious rooms with comfortable beds. The colorful decorations and furnishings give the rooms a warm atmosphere. The bathrooms are of adequate size, fitted with tub/shower combinations, and well maintained. *Note:* The rates are adjusted according to the daily Czech koruna/euro exchange rate.

Evropská 15, Praha 6. ⓒ 296-559-111. Fax 296-559-215. www.diplomatpraha.cz. 398 units (tub/shower combination). 7,050Kč ($293) double; 10,800Kč ($449) suite. Rates include breakfast. AE, DC, MC, V. Metro: Dejvická. **Amenities:** 3 restaurants; cafe/bar; conference center; health club w/sauna; whirlpool; concierge; tour and activities desk; car rental; business services; shopping arcade; 18-hr. room service; laundry/dry cleaning; executive-level rooms. *In room:* A/C, TV, dataport, minibar, coffeemaker, hair dryer.

Hotel Praha ⓕ   The Hotel Praha is the most grotesque of the central-planners' whims. During the post-invasion 1970s, this terraced behemoth was built into a prime hill in the richest part of western Prague as a guesthouse for visiting party bosses, destroying any romantic notion that Communism was all-for-one and one-for-all. It had all the brass, chrome, and marble veneer that Brezhnev and Castro could ever have wanted, resulting in a building that looks unintentionally kitschy. Before you dismiss the Praha as a relic, you might be interested to know that Tom Cruise, Johnny Depp, and other celebrities have stayed here while filming in Prague. The draws are the fortresslike setting, massive guest rooms and bathrooms, private balconies, magnificent views of the city, and proximity to the airport.

Sušická 20, Praha 6. ⓒ 224-343-305. Fax 224-311-218. www.htlpraha.cz. 124 units (tub/shower combination). From 7,140Kč ($297) double; from 8,850Kč ($368) suite. Rates include breakfast. AE, DC, MC, V. Metro: Dejvická. **Amenities:** 2 restaurants; indoor pool; 2 tennis courts; exercise room; sauna; concierge; tour and activities desk; car rental; business center; shopping arcade; 24-hr. room service; massage; babysitting; dry-cleaning and laundry service. *In room:* A/C, TV, dataport, minibar, hair dryer, iron, safe.

6

Where to Dine in Prague

So you don't know much about Czech food? The country's culinary reputation doesn't resound much beyond the borders of Bohemia, but there are still plenty of tasty treats.

The schnitzels, strudels, and goulashes of neighboring Germany and Hungary are familiar to almost everyone. Czech cuisine borrows from these countries and adds twists like tasty *svíčková na smetaně*, sirloin slices in a baked, vegetable-based cream sauce served over tender, spongy, sliced dumplings.

If prepared with care, Czech dishes are as delicious as they are hearty. A few innovative restaurateurs have added character to the generally dull diet of soups, meat, game, potatoes, and dumplings, proving that even Czech cuisine can be delicate. I've included a selection of the best of these.

But if there's a gastric draw to Bohemia, it's the **beer.** Pubs are so much a part of the local life here that the food is just an accompaniment. I've included a "The Pick of the Pubs" section listing those places that offer decent meals at fantastic prices—and serve the best brew on earth.

With the influx of postrevolutionary tourism came the inevitable explosion of restaurants. The majority of better Prague restaurants now serve either a selection of continental European standbys or more exotic niche cuisine. As a result, you can find anything from Indonesian to Lebanese to Greek to Tex-Mex, a surprising variety when you consider the vacuum of just a few years ago. Below, I steer you to the finest local cuisine, international standouts, and best budget bets.

CZECH MEALS Whenever someone mentions this country's heavy food, Czechs delight in the fact that obesity is much more of a problem in the United States. Statistically they're right. It seems that the walking-hiking-biking lifestyle of Czechs goes a long way toward keeping their waistlines trim. Still, statistics also show that the incidence of heart disease and colon cancer is much greater in the Czech Republic than in the United States. Fortunately, you'll probably be visiting for only a few days or weeks, so check your calorie counters at the border, loosen your belts, and get ready to sample the best of Bohemia (you'll walk enough to burn some of the extra calories, anyway).

Starters, outside the ubiquitous ham rolls and unappetizing gelatin appetizers shoved in your face by waiters, are usually soups, often garlic, onion, or beef broth with noodles. The herb soups are often the most piquant part of the meal, but the meat-based broths, whether chicken or beef, are frequently served without filtering the heavy renderings.

As for **main courses,** no self-respecting Czech restaurant could open its doors without serving at least some version of the three national foods: *vepřo, knedlo,* and *zelo* (pork, dumplings, and cabbage). The **pork** (*vepřové maso*) is usually a shoulder or brisket that is baked and lightly seasoned, smoked, or breaded and fried like a schnitzel (řízek). Unlike German sauerkraut, the **cabbage** (zelí) is boiled with a light sugar sauce. The **dumplings** are light and spongy if made from flour and bread (houskové knedlíky), or dense and pasty if made from flour and potatoes (bramborové knedlíky). This "VKZ" combo cries out for an original **Budweiser (Budvar), Kozel,** or **Pilsner Urquell** to wash it down.

Other standard main courses are the above-mentioned svíčková, roast beef (rošátěná), baked chicken (grilované kuře), and smoked ham and other spicy cured meats (uzeniny). A local favorite is **cmunda,** found at the pub U medvídků (p. 103): a steaming potato pancake topped with sweet boiled red cabbage and spicy Moravian smoked pork. Also popular is **wild game,** such as venison, goose, rabbit, and duck, and the more exotic, like the wild boar goulash served at U modré kachničky (probably the best Czecho-centric restaurant; p. 89). Czech sauces can be heavy and characterless but more frequently they are prepared with daring doses of spice.

There's also usually a good selection of indigenous freshwater fish, such as trout, perch, and carp, the Christmas favorite. People worry about the safety of waterways, but most fish served in Prague come from controlled fish farms. Since the country has no coastline, you'll find most **seafood** at the more expensive restaurants, but a growing selection of salmon, sea bass, shark, and shellfish is shipped in on ice.

Side dishes, usually ordered separately, are rice, fries, potato croquettes or potato pancakes, and the stalwart sliced dumplings (sponges for all that sauce on your plate). The svíčková dish (sirloin in a cream sauce) is accompanied by a sour chutney from cranberry, to cut through the dense flavors.

As for **dessert,** try a palačinka, a crepe-thin pancake filled with chocolate, fruit, or marmalade and whipped cream. Another favorite is ovocné knedlíky, whole dumplings filled with strawberries, apricots, or cherries, rolled in sweet butter, topped with powdered sugar and cream.

RESERVATIONS Not long ago, getting reservations at a decent Prague restaurant was as easy as finding a health-conscious meal or a friendly waiter: Fat chance! However, the number of solid restaurants has grown substantially, and the chances of getting a table as a walk-in are much better. If you don't want to gamble, you can generally get a reservation at the better restaurants on the same day, by early afternoon. Some popular, smaller places need a few days' notice, and I've noted these below.

Unfortunately, there still are very few Prague restaurants worth organizing your day around. So, as with the rest of your touring strategy, let the winding roads take you where they may and don't be afraid to stumble into a cozy-looking pub or restaurant. Just don't set your expectations too high. Below are some of the best choices in each neighborhood.

SERVICE Czech service is improving proportionally to the growth of competition. Still, many restaurants have yet to master the art of nonintrusive service. Waiters barge in at inappropriate moments or are nowhere to be found when you need them. The concept of better tips for better service is catching on, and waiters are generally much more attentive and pleasant in restaurants where they tell you upfront that service is not included in the bill.

TIPPING & TAX Tips of about 10% of the bill's total are catching on, though just rounding up the bill to a logical point is still more traditional. Tipping was frowned on by the Communists, and waiters, as you might guess, became lazy, looking for reasons to avoid your table and make your stay as long as possible in order to thin the workload. Today, good service, if you should be lucky enough to get it, demands a decent tip.

At most restaurants, menu prices include the 19% value-added tax (VAT). When they don't, the menu must say so. It's also common for some restaurants to levy a small cover charge in the evening, usually about 10Kč (40¢) per person, although some places raise it three or five times that, even with no entertainment.

DINING CUSTOMS Traditional Czech custom is simply to find whatever seats are available without the assistance of a hostess or maitre d', but newer restaurants have started to employ staff to seat you. Barring this, just point at the table you want and nod at a nearby waiter to make sure it's available. Don't be afraid to sit in open seats at the large tables where others are already seated, as is the case in many pubs and casual restaurants. However, it's customary to ask *"Je tu volno?"* ("Is this spot free?") before joining a large table. Likewise, don't be surprised if others ask to sit at your table. Just nod or say *"Ano, je"* ("Yes, it's free"), and make some new friends.

BEST DINING BETS

- **Best Czech Cuisine:** In an intricate flower-embellished setting, **U modré kachničky** (© 257-320-308) brings delicacy to Czech fare, including savvy spins on heavy sauces and wild game. See p. 89.
- **Best Pub Guláš (Goulash):** Old Town's boisterous **U Vejvodů** (© 224-219-999) dishes out a fine spicy goulash along with Pilsner Uruqell. See p. 103.
- **Best Homemade Italian Pasta:** Feel the Italian *ambiente* and enjoy the great taste of southern Europe and its cuisine at family-run **Il Ritrovo** (© 224-261-475). See p. 99.
- **Best American Bistro:** With the death of Planet Hollywood and the California-esque Avalon, **Red Hot & Blues** (© 222-314-639) remains the last best hope for Yankee food in Prague. The menu is mostly Tex-Mex and Cajun, with a good burger thrown in. See p. 93.
- **Best Seafood:** Old Town's **Rybí trh** (© 224-895-447) ships in fresh monkfish, salmon, shellfish, and just about anything else that swims in saltwater, and serves them in an airy space in the courtyard behind Týn Church. See p. 90.
- **Best Bagels:** Bohemia Bagel (© 257-310-694) at Újezd in Malá Strana and at Masná Street in Staré Město (© 224-812-560) has filled what was a curious vacuum. See p. 89.
- **Best Hot Dog:** I bet you have never had a hot dog like they make in a stand on **náměstí Míru** square. When strolling around Vinohrady, take a break here. There are plenty of benches. See p. 94.
- **Best Kosher:** Astonishingly, it was several years after the revolution before a real kosher restaurant returned to Prague's Jewish Quarter. The **King Solomon Strictly Kosher Restaurant** (© 224-818-752), across from the Pinkas Synagogue, finally gets it right. See p. 92.
- **Best for Kids/Best Pizza:** You can please the kids and satisfy your own cravings at **Pizzeria Rugantino** (© 222-318-172), a friendly and energetic Old Town room run by an Italian family that loves kids. See p. 95.
- **Best Pancakes (Crepes):** The **Creperie Café Gallery Restaurant** at the foot of Charles Bridge (© 221-108-240) is for those who have a sweet tooth. See p. 99.
- **Best for Vegetarians:** The **Radost FX Café** (© 224-254-776) dishes out veggie burgers, burritos, and salads to the trendy post-club crowd until 5am. See p. 99.

1 Restaurants by Cuisine

AMERICAN

Buffalo Bill's (Nové Město, $$,
   p. 96)
Red Hot & Blues ☞ (Staré Město, $$,
   p. 93)

BAGELS

Bohemia Bagel ☞☞ (Malá Strana, $,
   p. 89)

CAFES/TEAROOMS

Cafe Evropa (Nové Město, $, p. 102)
Café Resto Le Patio ☞ (Staré Město
   & Josefov, $, p. 101)
Dahab ☞☞ (Staré Město, $, p. 101)
Dobrá čajovna ☞ (Nové Město, $,
   p. 102)
Globe ☞☞ (Nové Město, $, p. 102)
Grand Café (Staré Město & Josefov,
   $, p. 101)
Kavárna Medúza (Vinohrady, $,
   p. 102)
Kavárna Obecní dům ☞☞ (Staré
   Město & Josefov, $, p. 101)
Kavárna Slavia ☞ (Staré Město &
   Josefov, $, p. 101)
La Dolce Vita ☞ (Staré Město &
   Josefov, $, p. 102)
Ovocný bar (fruit bar) Hájek
   (Nové Město, $, p. 94)
Velryba (Staré Město & Josefov, $,
   p. 102)

CAJUN

Red Hot & Blues ☞ (Staré Město, $$,
   p. 93)

COLUMBIAN

Don Pedro ☞ (Nové Město, $$,
   p. 96)

CONTINENTAL

Jarmark ☞ (Nové Město, $, p. 97)
Kampa Park ☞☞ (Malá Strana, $$,
   p. 88)
Nebozízek (Malá Strana, $$, p. 88)

U medvídků ☞☞ (Staré Město, $,
   p. 103)
U modré kachničky ☞☞ (Malá
   Strana, $$, p. 89)
U Vejvodů ☞☞ (Staré Město, $,
   p. 103)

CZECH

Café-Restaurant Louvre (Nové Město,
   $, p. 97)
Dutýhlava-Klub architektů (Staré
   Město, $, p. 95)
Hergetova Cihelna ☞☞ (Malá Strana,
   $$, p. 85)
Nebozízek (Malá Strana, $$, p. 88)
Osmička ☞ (Vinohrady, $, p. 99)
Potrefená husa (The Wounded Goose)
   ☞ (Nové Město, $, p. 97)
Restaurant U Čížků ☞ (Nové Město,
   $$, p. 96)
Střelecký Ostrov ☞ (Staré Město, $$,
   p. 93)
U medvídků ☞☞ (Staré Město, $,
   p. 103)
U modré kachničky ☞☞ (Malá
   Strana, $$, p. 89)
U Vejvodů ☞☞ (Staré Město, $,
   p. 103)
Vinárna U Maltézských rytířů
   (At Knights of Malta) ☞
   (Malá Strana, $$, p. 89)

DELI

Lahůdky Zlatý Kříž (Nové Město,
   p. 94)

FRENCH

Brasserie Le Molière (Vinohrady, $$,
   p. 98)
Café Resto Le Patio ☞ (Staré Město
   & Josefov, $, p. 101)
Chez Marcel (Staré Město, $, p. 95)
Creperie Café Gallery Restaurant
   (Staré Město, $, p. 95)
La Provence (Staré Mě, $$, p. 92)

Key to Abbreviations: $$$$ = Very Expensive $$$ = Expensive $$ = Moderate $ = Inexpensive

Le Bistrot de Marlene ❦ (Praha 6,
$$$, p. 100)
Le Café Colonial ❦❦ (Staré Město,
$$, p. 93)
U Malířů ❦ (Malá Strana, $$$$,
p. 85)

HEALTH CONSCIOUS
Country Life (Staré Město, $, p. ###)

INDIAN
Taj Mahal ❦ (Vinohrady, $$, p. 98)

INDONESIAN
Saté (Hradčany, $, p. 84)

INTERNATIONAL
Bellevue ❦❦❦ (Staré Město, $$$,
p. 90)
Bonante (Vinohrady, $$$, p. 97)
Café-Restaurant Louvre (Nové Město,
$, p. 97)
Dutýhlava-Klub architektů
(Staré Město, $, p. 95)
Hergetova Cihelna ❦❦ (Malá Strana,
$$, p. 85)
Hradčany Restaurant ❦ (Hradčany,
$$$, p. 84)
Mlýnec (Staré Město, $$$, p. 90)
Osmička ❦ (Vinohrady, $, p. 99)
Potrefená husa (The Wounded Goose)
❦ (Nové Město, $, p. 97)
Reykjavik (Staré Město, $$, p. 93)
Střelecký Ostrov ❦ (Staré Město, $$,
p. 93)
Vinárna V zátiší ❦❦ (Staré Město,
$$$, p. 90)
Zahrada v Opeře (Garden at the
Opera) ❦ (Nové Město, $$,
p. 96)

INTERNET CAFES
Bohemia Bagel ❦❦ (Malá Strana, $,
p. 89)
Cyber Cafe-Jáma (Nové Město, $,
p. 103)
Globe ❦❦ (Nové Město, $, p. 102)
Inetpoint.cz (Nové Město, $, p. 102)

ITALIAN
Ambiente Pasta Fresca (Staré Město,
$$, p. 92)
Il Ritrovo ❦ (Vinohrady, $, p. 99)
Kogo ❦❦ (Staré Město, $$, p. 92)

KOSHER
King Solomon Strictly Kosher Restau-
rant ❦ (Staré Město, $$, p. 92)

LEBANESE
Fakhreldine (Nové Město, $$, p. 96)

MEXICAN/TEX-MEX
Buffalo Bill's (Nové Město, $$,
p. 96)
Don Pedro ❦ (Nové Město, $$,
p. 96)
Red Hot & Blues ❦ (Staré Město, $$,
p. 93)

MIDDLE EASTERN
Dahab ❦❦ (Staré Město, $, p. 101)

PASTA
Hergetova Cihelna ❦❦
(Malá Strana, $$, p. 85)
Pizzeria Rugantino ❦❦
(Staré Město, $, p. 95)

PIZZA
Pizzeria Rugantino ❦❦ (Staré Město,
$, p. 95)

SANDWICHES
Bohemia Bagel ❦❦ (Malá Strana, $,
p. 89)

SEAFOOD
Kampa Park ❦❦ (Malá Strana, $$,
p. 88)
Reykjavik (Staré Město, $$, p. 93)
Rybí trh ❦ (Staré Město, $$$, p. 90)

SPORTS BAR
Jágr's Sports Bar (Staré Město, $,
p. 98)
Sport Bar Praha-Zlatá Hvězda (Staré
Město, $, p. 98)

STEAKS
U bílé krávy (Vinohrady, $$, p. 99)

VEGETARIAN

Country Life (Staré Město, $, p. 94)
Dahab 𝒢𝒢 (Staré Město, $, p. 101)
Radost FX Café 𝒢𝒢 (Vinohrady, $, p. 99)

WILD GAME

U modré kachničky 𝒢𝒢 (Malá Strana, $$, p. 89)

YUGOSLAV

Dolly Bell (Vyšehrad, $$, p. 100)

2 Hradčany

EXPENSIVE

Hradčany Restaurant 𝒢 INTERNATIONAL   Matching the crisp English setting of the hotel in which it resides, the Austrian-managed Hradčany is the most elegant choice this side of the castle. The menu lists vary depending on the season. At this writing, they offer delicious roasted veal with corn or tasty rump steak with pistachio crust. For dessert try their apple mousse. The service sets the standard for Prague, and the new lunch sitting is sure to attract a solid clientele to this jewel beyond the castle gates.

In the Hotel Savoy, Keplerova 6, Praha 1. ℂ **224-302-150.** Reservations recommended. Main courses lunch 450Kč–650Kč ($19–$27), dinner 590Kč–790Kč ($24–$33). AE, DC, MC, V. Daily noon–3pm and 6–11pm. Tram: 22 or 23, 2 stops past Prague Castle.

INEXPENSIVE

Saté INDONESIAN   The Saté has made quite a business out of simple Indonesian dishes at low prices. It's just down the street from the Castle Square (Hradčanské nám.) and past the massive Černín Palace. The unassuming storefront near the Swedish

---

A Few Dining Warnings

Some Czech restaurants are notorious for placing seemingly free bowls of nuts or olives on the table or offering platters of appetizers or aperitifs that appear to be compliments of the house. They're not. What's worse is that when the bill comes, you might find that you're paying the equivalent of $5 for a bowl of stale cashews. Always ask before nibbling.

Many places, especially in the evening, tack on an extra 30Kč or 50Kč ($1.25 or $2) per person as a cover charge, even if they don't offer live entertainment. If this charge is mentioned at all, it'll be written discreetly on the menu as *couvert.*

Finally, as more Czech restaurants begin to accept credit cards, stories of waiters adding a digit or two to your total have increased. One protection is to write out the total in words on the credit card bill, the way you would on a personal check. Also ask for the carbons and keep a good record of where you've used your card to check against your bank statement to ensure that someone hasn't been using your number. The restaurants in this chapter don't seem to engage in these practices, but be on guard, especially if you veer from these suggested establishments.

(*Value*) **Money-Saving Tips**

Stick to the pubs or restaurants with an exclusively Czech menu, and remember that generally the farther from the castle or Old Town you go, the cheaper your meal will be. Imported foods or those prepared in a "foreign" fashion will always be more expensive.

You can also save money by looking for fixed-price menus, two-for-one specials, and deals in the local English-language newspapers. Don't eat anything without first determining its price (see "A Few Dining Warnings," above). For very cheap meals, try the places covered in "Inexpensive Meals on the Run" (p. 94).

Embassy doesn't stand out, so look closely. The pork saté comes in a peanut sauce along with a hearty *mie goreng* (traditional Indonesian fried noodles). This casual place is a good choice if you've just visited the castle and need to refuel and rest your feet.

Pohořelec 152/3, Praha 1. (✆) **220-514-552.** Main courses 42Kč–220Kč ($1.75–$9.15). No credit cards. Daily 11am–10pm. Tram: 22 or 23.

3 Malá Strana (Lesser Town)

VERY EXPENSIVE

U Malířů (✸ *Overrated*) FRENCH   The 1991 rebirth of the *vinárna* (wine bar) in the Malá Strana house "At the Painter's" brought French-trained Czech chef Jaromír Froulík's gourmet fare to Prague. Surrounded by Romance-age murals and gorgeously appointed tables in three intimate dining rooms, you're faced with some tough choices. Half-baked salmon filets swim in caper sauce, tiger shrimps come with oranges, lamb steak is glazed with red-pepper sauce, and baked quail bathe in Sherry. The crispy breast of duck is a safe choice. Some in the diplomatic corps still hiss that they've had better French at the less stuffy Le Bistro de Marlene across the river, but if you want a truly old-world evening of elegant romance and French specialties, U Malířů is worth it.

Maltézské nám. 11, Praha 1. (✆) **257-530-000.** www.umaliru.cz. Reservations necessary. Main courses 480Kč–2,390Kč ($20–$99); fixed-price menus 1,190Kč ($50) and 1,790Kč ($74). AE, DC, MC, V. Daily 7pm–2am. Metro: Malostranská.

MODERATE

Hergetova Cihelna (✸✸) INTERNATIONAL/PASTA/CZECH   This late addition to a list of Prague's top dining experiences quickly became a popular spot on the riverbank. The building, dating from the 18th century, which used to serve as a brick factory *(cihelna)*, was in very bad shape before its extensive reconstruction started in 2000. Now the interior is divided into a restaurant, cocktail bar, cafe, and music lounge, and the modern furniture from top Czech designer Barbora Škorpilová is simple and comfortable. From the large summer terrace you can experience one of the most exciting and unforgettable views of the river and Charles Bridge. The food is a good standard; I enjoyed their homemade Czech potato soup with forest mushrooms and garlic called *bramboračka* and Czech *svíčková* (sirloin) served in a cream sauce with dumplings and cranberries.

Where to Dine in Prague

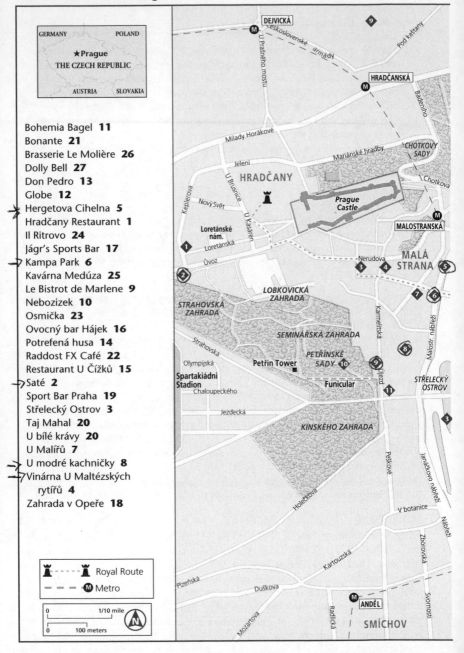

Bohemia Bagel **11**
Bonante **21**
Brasserie Le Molière **26**
Dolly Bell **27**
Don Pedro **13**
Globe **12**
Hergetova Cihelna **5**
Hradčany Restaurant **1**
Il Ritrovo **24**
Jágr's Sports Bar **17**
Kampa Park **6**
Kavárna Medúza **25**
Le Bistrot de Marlene **9**
Nebozizek **10**
Osmička **23**
Ovocný bar Hájek **16**
Potrefená husa **14**
Raddost FX Café **22**
Restaurant U Čížků **15**
Saté **2**
Sport Bar Praha **19**
Střelecký Ostrov **3**
Taj Mahal **20**
U bílé krávy **20**
U Malířů **7**
U modré kachničky **8**
Vinárna U Maltézských
rytířů **4**
Zahrada v Opeře **18**

$\Tbar$ ---- $\Tbar$ Royal Route
— — —Ⓜ Metro

0   1/10 mile
0   100 meters

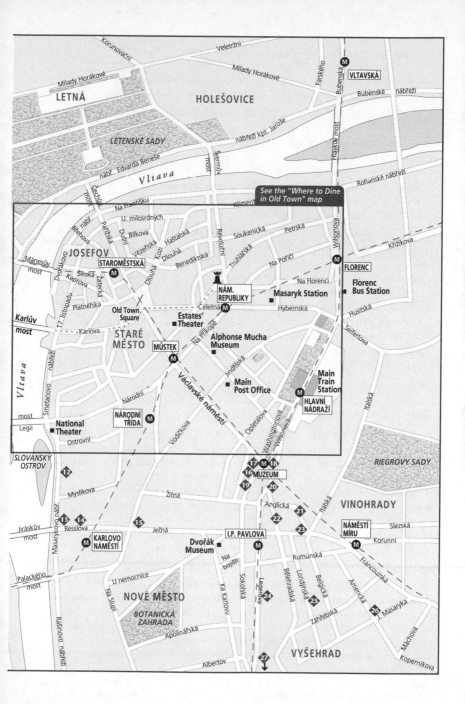

See the "Where to Dine in Old Town" map

(Kids) Family-Friendly Restaurants

Bohemia Bagel (p. 89)   The one on Masná street provides a small garden with outside seating, and a playroom for children, which makes family dining much more pleasant and relaxed. Bagels and sandwiches are on the menu together with selections for small children.

Jarmark (p. 97)   A wide selection of food served buffet-style, fresh salads and fruit juices, as well as comfortable casual seating make this place suitable for family dining.

Pizzeria Rugantino (p. 95)   A long list of crispy individual pizzas and salads, a seldom-seen nonsmoking section, and childproof tables make this noisy Old Town stop a staple for families.

Red Hot & Blues (p. 93)   This is a casual spot for burritos and burgers as well as spicier Louisiana treats for parents and a tasty Sunday brunch in the courtyard.

Osmička (p. 99)   Just above the National Museum in Vinohrady, this artful cellar has a huge menu ranging from heavy Czech to chicken dishes and fresh salads. There's little smoke and the waitstaff is pleasant.

Ovocný bar (fruit bar) **Hájek** (p. 94)   This is ice-cream and fruit salad heaven for the whole family. Take a break here while fighting the crowds on Václavské náměstí.

Cihelná 2b, Praha 1. (C) **296-826-103**. www.cihelna.com. Main courses 215Kč–695Kč ($8.90–$28). AE, MC, V. Daily 11:30am–1am. Metro: Malostranská.

Kampa Park 🕷🕷 CONTINENTAL/SEAFOOD   The best thing about Kampa Park is the summertime riverside view from its patio below Charles Bridge. In high season, the terrace is lively, with grills churning out solid portions of beef, pork, ribs, halibut, sea bass, and other barbecued favorites. Desserts like the fresh strawberry cappuccino have won raves from kids. During colder weather, this left-bank chalet is even more sublime, as candlelit tables provide glimpses of the stone bridge through the windows. Kampa Park boasts solid portions of fresh salmon, beefsteaks, and venison.

Na Kampě 8b, Praha 1. (C) **296-826-102**. www.kampagroup.com. Reservations recommended. Main courses 345Kč–795Kč ($14–$33). AE, DC, MC, V. Daily 11:30am–1am. Metro: Malostranská.

Nebozízek CZECH/CONTINENTAL   Nebozízek relies too much on its unique location to draw crowds and not enough on its food. In its case, the allure is the hillside setting looking east over Prague—not the absolutely best vantage point for a city panorama but pretty nonetheless. You get to this white Victorian house midway up Petřín Hill by taking the funicular to the interim stop (see chapter 3). The standard Continental menu has no real standouts, but the pepper steak and roast pork are solid. The view draws curious tourists, so tables are difficult to get—make reservations early.

Petřínské sady 411, Praha 1. (C) **257-315-329**. www.nebozizek.cz. Reservations recommended. Main courses 150Kč–560Kč ($6.25–$23). AE, MC, V. Daily 11am–11pm. Tram: 22 or 23 to Újezd, then take funicular up the hill.

✳ **U modré kachničky** 𝄞𝄞 CZECH/CONTINENTAL/WILD GAME At the "Blue Duckling," on a narrow Malá Strana street, is our choice for the most innovative attempt at refining standard Czech dishes into true Bohemian haute cuisine. This series of small dining rooms with vaulted ceilings and playfully frescoed walls is packed with antique furniture and pastel-flowered linen upholstery. The menu is loaded with an array of wild game and quirky spins on Czech village favorites. President and former prime-minister Václav Klaus took visiting leaders here when he wanted to prove that Czechs, too, have a unique style. Starters include lightly spiced venison pâté and gooseliver on toast. The roast rabbit, one of my mom's favorite dishes, is cooked to tender perfection and served with spinach and potato dumplings. You can choose from five different duck specialties. Finally, the ubiquitous *palačinky* crepes are thin and tender and filled with fruit, nuts, and chocolate.

Nebovidská 6, Praha 1. © **257-320-308.** www.umodrekachnicky.cz. Reservations recommended for lunch, required for dinner. Main courses 290Kč–690Kč ($12–$28). AE, MC, V. Daily noon–4pm and 6:30–11:30pm. Metro: Malostranská. There is an even more popular sister to the first "kachnička," at Michalská 16, Praha 1 (© **224-213-418**). Reservations recommended. Main courses 240Kč–685Kč ($10–$28). AE, MC, V. Daily 11:30am–11:30pm. Metro: Můstek.

Vinárna U Maltézských rytířů (At Knights of Malta) 𝄞 CZECH This restaurant on the ground floor and in the cellar of a charming house provides one of the friendliest and most reasonable home-cooked Czech meals in central Prague. Nadia Černíková's apple strudel keeps the regulars coming back. Her husband, Vítězslav Černík, once noticing a hungry and lost American (my husband), came out to guide him into the restaurant through the scaffolding erected for the reconstruction of this 16th-century burgher's house on a narrow Malá Strana side street. The atmosphere makes you feel as if you've been invited into the family's home for a cozy candlelit dinner. The menu offers a fine and affordable chateaubriand for two, a thick filet of pikeperch in wine leaf, and a breast of duck with saffron apples. Save room for the flaky strudel served with egg cognac.

Prokopská 10, Praha 1. © **257-533-666.** www.umaltezskychrytiru.cz. Reservations recommended. Main courses 230Kč–770Kč ($9.55–$32). AE, MC, V. Daily 1–11pm. Metro: Malostranská.

INEXPENSIVE

Bohemia Bagel 𝄞𝄞 *Kids* BAGELS/SANDWICHES Bohemia Bagel emerged in 1997 at the base of Petřín Hill as the answer to the bagel-less morning blues. The roster of golden-brown, hand-rolled, stone-baked bagels is stellar. There's plain, cinnamon raisin, garlic, onion, poppy, tomato basil, cheese, or apple and nut providing a sturdy but tender frame for Scandinavian lox and cream cheese or maybe jalapeño-cheddar cheese (on which you can dollop Tex-Mex chili for the Sloppy Bagel). There are also turkey club, marinated chicken breast, and egg sandwiches. A Fatouš cucumber or tomato salad, daily quiche, gourmet coffee, and even a bloody mary round out the board. The earthy contemporary setting is comfortable.

There's another **Bohemia Bagel** on Staré Město, just off Old Town Square at Masná 2, Praha 1; © **224-812-560.** This one is bigger, includes an Internet cafe with 15 terminals (Internet connection $1.75 per hour), a small garden with outside seating, and a playroom for children. The same menu is offered with the same opening hours. On www.bohemiabagel.cz you can order bagels and other food for at least 500Kč ($20) to be delivered in Praha 1 within an hour. Take the metro to Staroměstská.

Újezd 16, Praha 1. © **257-310-694.** Bagels and sandwiches 30Kč–145Kč ($1.25–$6). No credit cards. Mon–Fri 7am–midnight; Sat–Sun 8am–midnight. Tram: 6, 9, 12, 22, or 23 to Újezd stop.

4 Staré Město (Old Town)

Try to time your walks so that you can enjoy lunch and dinner in the Old Town Square; this is your best chance to find a table in a good restaurant. The picturesque area boasts the largest concentration of dining choices and flat streets good for growling bellies and aching feet.

EXPENSIVE

Bellevue ✿✿✿ INTERNATIONAL   With its excellent view of Prague Castle, the Bellevue is my perennial top choice. The ambitious owners (who also run Vinárna V zátiší and Mlýnec, both reviewed below) have put all their energy into the Bellevue's intelligent menu: beef, nouvelle sauces, well-dressed fish and duck, delicate pastas, and artistic desserts. For a tamer but extraordinary treat, try the filet of fallow deer. Al dente pastas share a plate with lobster-and-spinach purée, garlic and herbs, or tomatoes and olives. The greens on the side are always fresh and never overcooked. Desserts feature hot bitter chocolate tart, or wild berries in port and cognac served with vanilla and walnut ice cream. The consistent food and presentation and the pleasant and perfectly timed service make your meal at Bellevue one to remember.

Smetanovo nábřeží 18, Praha 1. ⓒ **222-221-443**. www.pfd.cz. Reservations recommended. Main courses 590Kč–890Kč ($24–$37); fixed-price menu 1,990Kč ($82) or 2,290Kč ($95). AE, DC, MC, V. Mon–Sat noon–3pm and 5:30–11pm; Sun 7–11pm (live jazz dinner). Metro: Staroměstská.

Mlýnec ✿ INTERNATIONAL   The Mill is owned by the V zátiší group, which is also responsible for Bellevue and V zátiší (see reviews above and below). Mlýnec is a more casual venture with a very comfortable, clubby, cabaret setting. I particularly recommend the lime leaves salmon with ginger-carrot purée.

Novotného lávka 9, Praha 1. ⓒ **221-082-208**. www.pfd.cz. Main dishes 395Kč–745Kč ($16–$31). AE, MC, V. Daily noon–3pm and 5:30–11pm. Tram: 17 or 18. Metro: Staroměstská.

Rybí trh ✿ SEAFOOD   That strange smell wafting from deep inside the courtyard behind Týn Church is the most extensive selection of fresh seafood in Prague, served at the "Fish Market." From starters like oysters on the half shell and jumbo shrimp to main choices like monkfish, salmon, eel, shark, and many others, you select your favorite fish and method of preparation at the bright counter near the entrance. You can eat it with the standard pilaf and other accompaniments, with numerous spices and sauces, either in the comfortably modern indoor area or the medieval courtyard during nicer weather. Despite the name, the dining room has the trappings of a modern bistro rather than an old fish market. This isn't a bad choice for seafood lovers.

Týnský Dvůr 5, Praha 1. ⓒ **224-895-447**. www.rybitrh.cz. Reservations recommended. Main courses 299Kč–1,500Kč ($12–$62). AE, MC, V. Daily 11am–midnight. Metro: Můstek.

Vinárna V zátiší ✿✿ INTERNATIONAL   Best described as "Bellevue Light," this laid-back version of our riverfront favorite provides the same quality and similar ingredients, with a few lighter choices such as the vegetarian dish gratinéed tagliatelle with broad beans. There are some fish choices as well. V zátiší ("still life") has a casual elegance, like the living room of a beachfront Mediterranean villa, with cushy upholstered wrought-iron chairs and plenty of artfully arranged flora.

Liliová 1, Praha 1. ⓒ **222-220-629**. www.pfd.cz. Reservations recommended. Main courses 495Kč–795Kč ($20–$33); fixed-price menu 1,275Kč or 1,575Kč ($53 or $65). AE, DC, MC, V. Daily noon–3pm and 5:30–11pm. Metro: Národní třída.

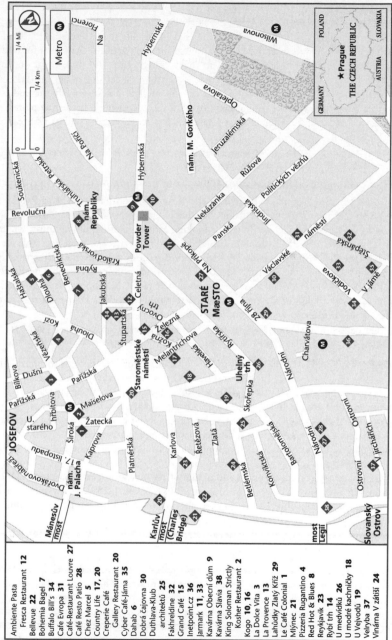

Ambiente Pasta
Fresca Restaurant **12**
Bellevue **22**
Bohemia Bagel **7**
Buffalo Bill's **34**
Cafe Evropa **31**
Café-Restaurant Louvre **27**
Café Resto Patio **28**
Chez Marcel **5**
Country Life **17, 20**
Creperie Café
Gallery Restaurant **20**
Cyber Café-Jáma **35**
Dahab **6**
Dobrá čajovna **30**
Duthlava-Klub
architektů **25**
Fakhreldine **32**
Grand Café **15**
Inetpoint.cz **36**
Jarmark **11, 33**
Kavárna Obecní dům **9**
Kavárna Slavia **38**
King Soloman Strictly
Kosher Restaurant **2**
Kogo **10, 16**
La Dolce Vita **3**
La Provence **13**
Lahůdky Zlatý Kříž **29**
Le Café Colonial **1**
Mlýnec **21**
Pizzeria Rugantino **4**
Red Hot & Blues **8**
Reykjavik **23**
Rybí trh **14**
U medvídků **26**
U modré kachničky **18**
U Vejvodů **19**
Velryba **37**
Vinárna V zátiší **24**

MODERATE

Ambiente Pasta Fresca ITALIAN   This pasta joint on the Royal Route, just off Old Town Square, is the best of the Ambiente family of "living restaurants." While Ambiente's Vinohrady locations once warranted the trip out of the city center for what used to be the only ribs and Tex-Mex in town, other joints have since caught on to ethnic menus, which go beyond the basic Czech fare. What this outlet on Celetná offers is location, location, location, and usually enough tables to satisfy the endless tourist rush hour. In a candlelit basement trattoria, the menu is limited to pastas—albeit served about 50 different ways—salads, a few meaty entrees, and garlic bread if you're still hungry.

Celetná 11, Praha 1. ℂ **224-230-244**. www.ambi.cz. Reservations recommended. Main courses 158Kč–580Kč ($6.50–$24). AE, MC, V. Daily 11am–midnight. Metro: Můstek.

King Solomon Strictly Kosher Restaurant ⍟ KOSHER   Under the supervision of the Orthodox Council of Kaschrus, the King Solomon has brought to Prague a truly kosher restaurant, across from the Pinkas Synagogue. The restaurant's dozen booths are camped under an industrial-looking atrium. During dining hours, which strictly adhere to the Sabbath, you can choose from a variety of fresh vegetable and meat dishes following kosher dietary rules. Saturday meals must be arranged separately and paid for before the Sabbath. The broad menu ranges from a vegetable béchamel for 250Kč ($10) to a stuffed roast quail for 1,600Kč ($66). Selections of Israeli, American, and Moravian kosher wine include the restaurant's pride: a Frankovka red from the Aaron Günsberger Moravian cellars in Rakvice.

Široká 8, Praha 1. ℂ **224-818-752**. www.kosher.cz. Reservations recommended. Main courses 250Kč–1,600Kč ($10–$67). AE, MC, V. Sun–Thurs noon–11pm; Fri dinners and Sat lunch by arrangement only. Metro: Staroměstská.

Kogo ⍟⍟ (Value) ITALIAN   This modern, upscale trattoria has become the local Italian favorite for the many brokers and bankers who work nearby. Tucked away on a side street adjacent to the Estates' Theater, Kogo manages to combine the warmth and boisterousness of a family restaurant with a high culinary standard in its pastas, meaty entrees, and desserts. Try the fresh, zesty mussels in white wine and garlic (*cozze al vino bianco e aglio*) or the tangy grilled salmon for $16. The wine list is extensive, and the tiramisu, if you get it before the nightly supply runs out, is light and sweet without being soggy.

Kogo has a second location in the atrium of the newly reopened Slovanský Dům shopping and culture center at Na Příkopě 22 (ℂ **221-451-259**). This venue, which maintains the menu of its parent, has become a favorite hangout of the 30-something set. However, it lacks the cozy ambience of the original.

Havelská 27, Praha 1. ℂ **224-214-543**. www.kogo.cz. Reservations recommended. Main courses 190Kč–480Kč ($7.90–$20). AE, MC, V. Daily 9am–midnight. Metro: Můstek.

La Provence FRENCH   A French country wine cellar meets urban kitsch in this loud subterranean haunt. Tables have been squeezed in, making a once-comfortable setting a little too intimate. Still, the din of the crowd allows you to discuss private matters without too much eavesdropping. A lunch choice of the local banking crowd, La Provence offers a wide array of French Provencal dishes, and the spiciest scampi in Prague. Escargots, easily accessible on a tray in drawn butter, are garlicky and surprisingly good. Salads, from Caesar to Niçoise, are large and fresh, with tangy niva (a kind of Czech blue cheese) and croutons; they come with fresh French bread and garlic butter. Weekends often attract drag queens from the Banana Café upstairs for a funky lip-synch floor show, which I doubt the bankers would appreciate at lunch.

Štupartská 9, Praha 1. ℂ 296-826-155. www.laprovence.cz. Reservations recommended. Main courses 345Kč–595Kč ($14–$24). AE, MC, V. Daily noon–11pm. Metro: Náměstí Republiky.

Le Café Colonial &&& FRENCH
This is a safe place for a break at any time of the day, but it is especially convenient after a stroll around the Jewish quarter (Josefov) and Staré Město. The menu features risotto and pasta dishes, which are good without being overwhelming. This is a favorite spot of Prague's rapidly growing professional women's community.

Široká 6, Praha 1. ℂ 224-818-322. www.lecafecolonial.cz. Main courses 195Kč–265Kč ($8–$11). AE, MC, V. Daily 10am–midnight. Metro: Starom[e]stská.

Red Hot & Blues & Kids AMERICAN/CAJUN/MEXICAN
As a pudgy former resident of the region that inspired Red Hot & Blues, my husband was skeptical about this early postrevolutionary Prague attempt at Creole/Cajun cooking. And while you won't find a crawfish or chef Paul Prudhomme lurking about, the étoufée is excellent and the spicy Cajun shrimp delivers a punch. Tex-Mex regulars, plus burgers and nachos, round out the menu. Sunday brunch, best enjoyed in the small courtyard, includes tangy huevos rancheros on crispy tortillas. The casual French Quarter feel makes this a family-friendly choice. From 7 to 10:30pm you can hear live jazz.

Jakubská 12, Praha 1. ℂ 222-314-639. www.redhotandblues.com. Main courses 139Kč–499Kč ($5.80–$20). AE, MC, V. Daily 9am–midnight; Sat–Sun brunch 9am–4pm. Metro: Náměstí Republiky.

Reykjavik SEAFOOD/INTERNATIONAL
On one of the busiest pedestrian intersections, Reykjavik is a safe choice just off Charles Bridge. It's decorated inside like a clubby brasserie with plenty of cozy wood and curiosities, and the narrow menu consistently features Icelandic salmon and steaks from the north country. During summer you can dine on a platform out in front as the throngs of tourists pass by on Karlova Street on their way to Charles Bridge or Old Town Square.

Karlova 20, Praha 1. ℂ 222-221-218. www.reykjavik.cz. Main courses 265Kč–525Kč ($11–$21). AE, DC, MC, V. Daily 11am–midnight. Metro: Staroměstská.

Střelecký Ostrov & CZECH/INTERNATIONAL
The island sitting in the middle of the Vltava near the National Theater has been a destination for artisans, romantics, and political activists throughout the centuries. From here the Czech labor movement held its rallies and found its footing in the 19th century, and the unique riverside perspectives of the castle and National Theater have been featured in many paintings and photographs, and even in rock band INXS's melancholy "Never Tear Us Apart" video. The floods of 2002 brought misery here, destroying a fine Italian restaurant. In its place is now one of the more elegant attempts at delivering Czech cuisine to an upscale local and international clientele. The riverside terrace is the restaurant's calling card in the summer, a fine place for lunch with gorgeous snapshots of the gold-topped National Theater, as the boaters row below. The brick-cellar dining room is cozy on a winter's night before the curtain goes up in theaters across the water.

Main courses boast a standard version of the Czech national dish *svíčková* (sirloin in cream sauce), plus plenty of wild game dishes, including venison in cranberry, lamb in rosemary, duck with cabbage and a pleasant pheasant in plum sauce. Nothing is too inventive here, but all is well prepared, warm, and satisfying.

If you are having the evening meal in the cellar, leave time for an aperitif or night-cap in the tasteful and modern upstairs bar.

Střelecký ostrov 336, Praha 1. (©) **224-934-026**. www.streleckyostrov.cz. Reservations recommended. Main courses 235Kč–790Kč ($9.75–$32). AE, MC, V. Mon–Fri noon–midnight; Sat–Sun 11am–midnight. Metro: Národní třída and tram 6, 9, 22, or 23 to Národní divadlo stop; about halfway on the *Most Legíí* bridge go downstairs to access Střá elecký ostrov, a little island on the Vltava.

Value **Inexpensive Meals on the Run**

The Czech-style delicatessen **Lahůdky Zlatý Kříž**, Jungmannovo nám. 19 (entrance from Jungmannova 34), Praha 1 (© **221-191-801**), offers the typical Czech snack food *chlebíčky*—a slice of white bread with ham or salami and cheese or potato salad. You have to eat standing up, but prices are pure Czech. Or take it with you and go eat in the cozy garden behind the corner of this building (enter from the square). It's open Monday to Friday from 6:30am to 7pm and Saturday from 9am to 3pm. No credit cards are accepted.

Vegetarians will like **Country Life**, Melantrichova 15, Praha 1 (© **224-213-373**), a health-food store run by the Seventh-Day Adventists; it offers a strictly meatless menu to go. You'll find tofu, tomato, cucumber, and shredded cabbage salads; zesty wheat-bread pizzas topped with red pepper, garlic, and onions; and vegetable burgers on multigrain buns with garlic-yogurt dressing. Selections are 25Kč to 75Kč ($1.05–$3.10). It's open Monday to Thursday from 9am to 8:30pm, Friday 9am to 6pm, Sunday 11am to 8:30pm. No credit cards are accepted.

Ovocný bar (fruit bar) **Hájek** at Václavské nám. 52, Praha 1 (© **222-211-466**), upstairs from an ice-cream stall, welcomes all for coffee and delicious deserts, ice cream, and fruit salads priced from 13Kč to 90Kč (54¢–$3.75). This sweet oasis has been popular with the locals for decades. It's open Monday to Saturday 9am to 8pm, Sunday 10am to 8pm.

If you are visiting Prague's Vinohrady quarter, you can't avoid its main square, náměstí Míru, with St. Ludmila's Church. On the right side of the church, when facing it, near the metro entrance, there is usually a stand with the **best hot dog** in Prague. The dog is topped with ketchup or two kinds of tasty Czech mustard and served on a fresh white roll. It costs 14Kč (60¢) and it is available Monday to Friday from 9:30am until the supply for that day lasts.

And in a pinch in Praha 1, there's always **McDonald's,** including two at the top and bottom of Wenceslas Square (nos. 56 and 9), one at Vodičkova 15 just off the square, and another at Mostecká 21, about 100m (328 ft.) after you get off Charles Bridge in Malá Strana. **KFC** is at Vodičkova 32, Wenceslas Square 56, and at Kaprova 14 near Old Town Square. There's a **KFC/Pizza Hut** combo at Na Poříčí 42, next to the Hotel Axa, with a play area for kids upstairs. **Pizza Hut** is at Celetná 10, about 50 paces from Old Town Square on the right.

INEXPENSIVE

Chez Marcel FRENCH   Off a small, secluded Old Town square, this casual French country restaurant attracts a young French Embassy crowd and is a good option for post-theater or late dining. On the menu are large portions of salmon and beef tips, tangy soups, cold appetizers like thinly sliced marinated salmon, and unique salads. There's also steak and fries for those who don't want to venture into the chalkboard's daily specials. There's a little more room to breathe here than at La Provence, but the menu isn't as eclectic. Chez Marcel is affiliated with the Brasserie Le Molière (p. 98) in Vinohrady, which offers an even wider selection of daily specials.

Haštalské nám. 12, Praha 1. Ⓒ **222-315-676.** Main courses 90Kč–300Kč ($3.75–$12). No credit cards. Mon–Fri 8am–1am; Sat–Sun 9am–1am. Metro: Staroměstská.

Creperie Café Gallery Restaurant FRENCH   This more convenient and affordable faux French eatery rests at the foot of Charles Bridge on the Old Town side. Occupying a wing of the St. Francis church complex, the Creperie maintains its links to the Knights of Malta, and does well to approximate the feel of a cozy farmhouse, with old wooden chairs and with hand-stitched pillows thrown on sturdy benches. The savory *galettes* are filled with spinach, tangy niva cheese, or chicken, and provide a sufficient light lunch for most in the middle of a heavy day of trudging. The sweet crepes with chocolate, fruit compote, or whipped cream are good for an afternoon break or dessert following an evening stroll across the bridge. The dining room is split into two halves, so try to get a table on the right side of the foyer where the bar is, or you may be forgotten by the waitstaff who congregate around the tavern.

Křížovnické nám. 3, Praha 1. Ⓒ **221-108-240.** www.npivovar.cz/creperie. Crepes and *galettes* 75Kč–129Kč ($3.10–$5.30). AE, MC, V. Daily 10am–midnight. Metro: Staroměstská.

Dutýhlava–Klub architektů CZECH/INTERNATIONAL   Tucked into the alcoves of a 12th-century cellar across the courtyard from Jan Hus's Bethlehem Chapel, this eclectic clubhouse for the city's progressive architects' society is the best nonpub deal in Old Town. Among the exposed air ducts and industrial swag lights hovering above the tables in the stone dungeon, you can choose from baked chicken, pork steaks, pasta, stir-fried chicken, and even vegetarian burritos. It's not really spectacular, but the large portions and variety will satisfy a range of tastes. The wicker seating in the courtyard makes a summer night among the torches enjoyable, though the alfresco menu is limited.

Betlémské nám. 5a, Praha 1. Ⓒ **224-401-214.** Reservations recommended. Main courses 80Kč–130Kč ($3.35–$5.40). AE, MC, V. Daily 11:30am–midnight. Metro: Národní třída.

Pizzeria Rugantino 🕶🕶 Kids PIZZA/PASTA   Pizzeria Rugantino serves generous iceberg salads and the best selection of individual pizzas in Prague. Wood-fired stoves and handmade dough result in a crisp and delicate crust. The Diabolo with fresh garlic bits and very hot chiles goes nicely with a salad and a pull of Krušovice beer. The constant buzz, nonsmoking area, heavy childproof wooden tables, and lots of baby chairs make this a family favorite.

Dušní 4, Praha 1. Ⓒ **222-318-172.** Individual pizzas 100Kč–250Kč ($4.15–$10). No credit cards. Mon–Sat 11am–11pm; Sun 5–11pm. Metro: Staroměstská.

5 Nové Město (New Town)

MODERATE

Buffalo Bill's MEXICAN/AMERICAN   This cellar cantina near Wenceslas Square is cramped, always full, and about the best you can do in Prague if you crave fajitas, chimichangas, or burritos. Buffalo Bill's has found its niche among those who have to have a crispy taco fix from time to time and Czechs who want to try their first. Unlike in Warsaw, which has had the fortune (or misfortune) of PepsiCo-installed Taco Bells, you still have to pay a premium for a Bohemian taco. Buffalo Bill's caters the annual July 4th party at the U.S. Embassy, at which Alan Alda said while filling his shell in the grub line, "My God, Prague and a taco."

Vodičkova 9, Praha 1. ⓒ **224-948-624.** Reservations recommended on weekends. Main courses 150Kč–350Kč ($6.25–$15). AE, MC, V. Daily noon–midnight. Metro: Můstek.

Don Pedro ⓡ COLOMBIAN/MEXICAN   A unique fusion of Austin, Prague, and the back streets of Bogota, Don Pedro has brought more fire to the often mundane Czech palate. This small and simply decorated storefront dining room on the riverfront in New Town (near the Jiráskův bridge) is one part Czech pub, two parts tropical bodega. The menu ranges from Tex-Mex staples like quesadillas and chimichangas to more exotic Colombian fare with lots of steaks, fried yucca, and plantains. There are taster menus available for people to swap and share the dishes, including plenty of delicious guacamole—relatively hard to find in these parts.

Masarykovo nábřeží 2, Praha 2. ⓒ **224-923-505.** www.donpedro.cz. Main courses 165Kč–250Kč ($6.85–$10). AE, MC, V. Daily 11:30am–11:30pm. Metro: Karlovo nám.

Fakhreldine LEBANESE   This outlet of London's popular Lebanese restaurant delivers a quality exotic menu in an elegant dining room. Entrees include charcoal-grilled lamb, marinated veal, and steak. Better yet, put together a mix of appetizers in a fantastic variety of tastes to constitute a meal. These include raw lamb, grilled Armenian sausages, the spicy eggplant dish baba ghanouj, and Lebanese cream cheese. The hummus isn't too pastelike, as it is in many Middle Eastern eateries, and meals come with fresh unleavened naan bread. Three kinds of baklava and cardamom-scented coffee are a great final course. Service is sharp and attentive.

Štěpánská 32, Praha 1. ⓒ **222-232-616.** Main courses 250Kč–350Kč ($10–$15). AE, DC, MC, V. Mon–Sat noon–midnight. Metro: Muzeum.

Restaurant U Čížků ⓡ ⟨Value⟩ CZECH   One of the city's first private restaurants, this cozy cellar–cum–hunting lodge on Charles Square can now be identified by the long line of German tour buses parked outside. The fare is purely Czech, and the massive portions of game, smoked pork, and other meats will stay with you for a while. The traditional *Staročeský talíř*, with a variety of local meat preparations, dumplings, and cabbage, is about as authentic as it gets. The excellent value earns this pioneer a star.

Karlovo nám. 34, Praha 2. ⓒ **222-232-257.** www.restaurantucizku.cz. Reservations recommended. Main courses 120Kč–290Kč ($5–$12). AE, MC, V. Daily 11:30am–10:30pm. Metro: Karlovo nám.

Zahrada v Opeře (Garden at the Opera) ⓡ INTERNATIONAL   Czech designer Bořek Šípek, the man who remodeled former president Havel's offices in Prague Castle, has created a pleasant earthy interior mixing dark and light wood, rattan chairs, and intricate floral arrangements. In this calm oasis, you can relax and enjoy an excellent meal. Highly recommended among the light (but lively) salads and fish and vegetarian dishes is the filet of salmon boiled in champagne with an egg yolk tarragon sauce and served with ginger rice and sautéed vegetables.

Legerova 75, Praha 1 (behind the Radio Free Europe building). ⟨ **224-239-685.** www.zahradavopere.cz. Main courses 150Kč–530Kč ($6.25–$22). AE, MC, V. Daily 11:30am–1am. Metro: Muzeum.

INEXPENSIVE

Café-Restaurant Louvre CZECH/INTERNATIONAL   A big, breezy upstairs hall, Café-Restaurant Louvre, previously known as Gany's, is great for breakfast, coffee, an inexpensive pretheater meal, or an upscale game of pool. A fabulous Art Nouveau interior, with huge original chandeliers, buzzes with the noise of local coffee talk, the shopping crowd, business lunches, and students. Starters include smoked salmon, or Greek *tzatziki* (yogurt and cucumber). Main dishes range from grilled steak of salmon to lamb filets with rosemary. Avoid the always-overcooked pasta dishes and stick to the basic meats and fish. In the snazzy billiards parlor in back, you can enjoy drinks and light meals.

Národní třída 20, Praha 1. ⟨ **224-930-949.** www.cafelouvre.cz. Reservations accepted. Main courses 79Kč–259Kč ($3.30–$11). AE, DC, MC, V. Daily 8am–11:30pm. Metro: Národní třída.

Jarmark 𝕽 *Kids* CONTINENTAL   This is one cafeteria that serves a really tasty variety of meats, sides, and salads and, of course, beer. Oh, but this one is not, *repeat not,* all-you-can-eat for one price despite its convenient come-and-shove-it-in system. Upon entering Jarmark, everyone gets a ticket, which is validated at each pit stop you make among the various rows of steaming hot tables, veggie carts, and drink dispensers. For less than $5 you can strap on the feedbag for the heartiest entrees on the board, including roast beef and the traditional Czech roast pork. The seating is spread throughout the bowels of an early-20th-century, multipurpose shopping arcade and pleasure palace, which has found a new life, keeping visitors dry and well fed.

Vodičkova 30, Dům U Nováků. ⟨ **224-233-733.** Reservations not accepted. Main courses 70Kč–150Kč ($2.90–$6.25). AE, MC, V. Daily 11am–10pm; Mon–Fri breakfast 8–10am. Metro: Můstek.

Potrefená husa (The Wounded Goose) 𝕽 *Value* CZECH/INTERNATIONAL Local brewers launched this chain of taverns which combine the convivial atmosphere of a traditional Bohemian *hospoda,* or pub, with the amenities of a trendy sports bar. This outlet on the river in New Town has its own open fireplace (roaring in the colder months), and discreetly placed TVs for monitoring the latest NHL action featuring, no doubt, the latest Czech star. The most interesting offerings on the menu are the thick homemade soups—mainly vegetable-based—served in *chléb* (whole, hollowed-out round bread loaves), and yes, it's cool to eat the bread after the soup is done. There are also standard grilled meats, pastas, salads, and plenty of varieties of beer on draft or in bottles.

Resslova 2, Praha 2. ⟨ **224-918-691.** www.pivovary-staropramen.cz. Main courses 100Kč–300Kč ($4.15–$12). AE, MC, V. Daily 11:30am–1am. Metro: Karlovo nám.

6 Vinohrady

EXPENSIVE

Bonante *Value* INTERNATIONAL   My favorite choice above Wenceslas Square in Vinohrady, Bonante is especially great for shunning the cold of an autumn or winter evening near the roaring fire in the brick-cellar dining room. As its name suggests, this place is a bridge between French cuisine and other Continental foods. You can start with a fish soup with salmon and mussels, or deep-fried jalapeños. There are several

Sports, Spuds & Suds

The **Sport Bar Praha-Zlatá Hvězda** (ⓒ **222-210-124**), on Ve smečkách 12, Praha 2, is about 3 blocks from the top of Wenceslas Square. Here you'll find a big screen, big burgers, and big games—with local prices. A burger and fries run 99Kč ($4.10), while a half liter of local brew costs as little as 35Kč ($1.45). There's a rock music club in the basement and billiard tables for those times when the games drag on.

Challenging the Sport Bar Praha on his own home ice is former Pittsburgh Penguins (now New York Rangers) Czech-born hockey star Jaromír Jágr, who has opened **Jágr's Sports Bar** along with Czech partners in the Blaník Passage on Wenceslas Square at Václavské nám. 56 (ⓒ **224-032-481**). During the season, images of Jágr and his mates from the NHL fill the 35 screens in this glass-and-neon disco-esque space, live and on tape, along with soccer, tennis, and other favorite Czech sports.

vegetarian and low-calorie chicken-based selections. Jazz combos play on most nights from a small stage in the corner. When reserving, ask for a table within view of, but not too close to, the fireplace. If you do break into a sweat, it's not because of the check, as Bonante provides one of the best values in a full-service restaurant in Prague.

Anglická 15, Praha 2. ⓒ **224-221-665.** www.bonante-restaurant.cz. Reservations recommended. Main courses 195Kč–695Kč ($8.10–$28). AE, MC, V. Daily 11:30am–11pm. Metro: I. P. Pavlova or Náměstí Míru.

MODERATE

Brasserie Le Molière FRENCH   While it's not a standout, this restaurant is a decent choice for those staying in the neighborhood. This bistro, with only a few Parisian banquettes in a classical corner room, was nearly empty the last time I was there. You're greeted by a perky, polyglot waitress lugging the chalkboard with the day's specials in French, which constitute the entire menu, and a heavy slate with the wine list. The first courses were foie gras and a transparent smoked salmon that was much too bland. Entrees included boiled veal in an onion-carrot mixture with au gratin potatoes and braised chicken leg in herb-cream sauce. The cheese plate consisted of a few unspectacular chunks of brie and Camembert.

Americká 20, Praha 2. ⓒ **222-513-340.** Main courses 250Kč–450Kč ($10–$19). AE, V. Mon 7–10:30pm; Tues–Sat 7pm–midnight. Metro: Náměstí Míru.

Taj Mahal ✦ INDIAN   As European curry shops go, this falls well short of what you might expect in a city with a larger Indian population, such as London. But if nothing but a scorching hot vindaloo will do, then the Taj at least comes close—and at a decent price. Other than a few images of India on the walls, its sparse decor seems more like Calcutta back streets than Agra's Taj Mahal. Still, on many nights (especially Fri and Sat in summer), sitar music gives the place a life it doesn't otherwise have. The standard Indian fare can be served with varying degrees of spice, and the Czech beer washes away the heat.

Škrétova 10, Praha 2 (behind the National Museum). ⓒ **224-225-566.** www.tajmahal.cz. Reservations recommended. Main courses 175Kč–395Kč ($7.30–$16). AE, MC, V. Mon–Fri noon–11pm; Sat–Sun 1–11pm. Metro: Muzeum.

U bílé krávy *Value* STEAKS   "At the White Cow" is a Czech version of a French steakhouse with the Charolais beef from Burgundy as the main draw. Decked out as a faux farmhouse, the setting is woodsy and warm, except for the cow murals peering over your shoulder. The meat portions, while tender and tasty, are smallish, as are the salads, and the vegetables aren't as fresh as they might be. Not a bad price for a good steak, though.

Rubešova 10, Praha 2. © 224-239-570. www.bilakrava.cz. Reservations recommended in high season. Main courses 173Kč–385Kč ($7.20–$16). AE, MC, V. Daily 11am–11pm. Metro: I. P. Pavlova.

INEXPENSIVE

Il Ritrovo *ITALIAN   This restaurant, in an old, gray-stucco apartment house off the beaten path in a quiet Vinohrady neighborhood, reminds me of my late Italian aunt's house. It's a small, cozy place with modest wooden chairs and familiar Italian maps and reproductions decorating the walls, the trappings of a place run by a family of proud immigrants. The food never disappoints. The antipasto bar usually is packed with marinated vegetables, spiced olives, mushrooms, and salad. Il Ritrovo's long list of homemade pasta choices would have put even my aunt to shame. The second plates of veal and beef are just passable, however. The tiramisu was dense, and almost as thick as the espresso served with it.

Lublaňská 11, Praha 2. © 224-261-475. Reservations recommended. Main courses 120Kč–250Kč ($5–$10). MC, V. Daily noon–3pm and 6–11pm. Metro: I. P. Pavlova.

Osmička *Value Kids* CZECH/INTERNATIONAL   Osmička is an interesting hybrid in Vinohrady on a side street a few blocks above the National Museum. At first sight, the "Number 8" reveals a tourist-geared cellar restaurant with tawny eclectic colors, local art for sale on the walls, and a menu dominated by Italian standbys, fresh salads, and a variety of sandwiches. But once a Czech sits down, he or she quickly recognizes the neighborhood secret: This is still a good ol' Bohemian *hospoda* with *vepřo-knedlo-zelo* and other indigenous fare at local prices—served on new solid wood furniture by nicer-than-normal staff. The staff tries hard to make guests, including families, feel welcome; they took the time to negotiate the right combo for our sometimes finicky boys. If you're staying in Vinohrady, Osmička should be on your itinerary. Look closely for the dark metal triangle marking the location, next to one of the only golf pro shops in town.

Balbínova 8, Praha 2. © 222-826-888. www.osmicka.com. Main courses 54Kč–328Kč ($2.15–$14). MC, V. Mon–Fri 11am–midnight; Sat noon–midnight. Metro: I. P. Pavlova or Náměstí Míru.

Radost FX Café *Value* VEGETARIAN   *En vogue* and full of vegetarian offerings, Radost is a clubhouse for hip new Bohemians, but it attracts plenty of international visitors, too. The veggie burger served on a grain bun is well seasoned and substantial, and the soups, like lentil and onion, are light and full of flavor. Sautéed vegetable dishes, tofu, and huge Greek salads round out the health-conscious menu. The dining area is a dark rec room seemingly furnished by a rummage sale of upholstered armchairs, chaise longues, and couches from the 1960s. Guests eat off coffee tables. Too cool.

Bělehradská 120, Praha 2. © 224-254-776. www.radostfx.cz. Main courses 60Kč–285Kč ($2.50–$11). AE, MC, V. Daily 11:30am–5am. Metro: I. P. Pavlova.

7 Elsewhere in Prague

EXPENSIVE

Le Bistrot de Marlene ✿ FRENCH   Le Bistrot de Marlene, at the Villa Schwaiger residence in one of the best Prague residential districts, Bubeneč, is packed with locals and visitors in search of the finest casual French cuisine in town. Chef Marlene Salomon has kept the menu short and simple, focusing on high-quality meats and produce. Many starters are worth recommending, including eggplant terrine and basil, or tuna carpaccio. Of the main courses, the roasted *dorade royale* (sea bream) and the filet of veal are best. Most everything comes with a side of vegetables, which are simply steamed or baked with layers of cheese.

Schwaigerova 59/3, Praha 6. ℭ 224-921-853. www.bistrotdemarlene.cz. Reservations recommended. Main courses 398Kč–630Kč ($17–$26). AE, MC, V. Mon–Fri noon–2:30pm and 7–10:30pm. Metro: Hradčanská.

MODERATE

Dolly Bell YUGOSLAV   This is the best Yugoslav restaurant in town, memorably set like a surreal library, with cluttered upside-down tables fixed to the ceiling above diners' heads. The Serbian food looks and sounds Czech but comes out much more lively and well spiced than northern Slav fare. Excellent appetizers are the flaky cheese and meat pies and thick stews and soups. There's a Balkan moussaka with layers of potatoes and ground beef, topped with béchamel sauce. Main meats are seared or skewered on a spit.

Neklanova 20, Praha 2. ℭ 249-354-868. Main courses 100Kč–250Kč ($4.10–$10). AE, DC, MC, V. Daily 2–11pm. Metro: Vyšehrad.

8 Cafe Society

In their heyday in the late 19th and early 20th centuries, Prague's elegant *kavárny* (cafes) rivaled Vienna's as places to be seen and perhaps have a carefree afternoon chat. But the Bohemian intellectuals, much like the Parisian Left Bank philosophers of the 1920s, laid claim to many of the local cafes, turning them into smoky parlors for pondering and debating the anxieties of the day.

Today, most of Prague's cafes have lost the indigenous charm of the Jazz Age or, strangely enough, the Communist era. During the Cold War, the venerable Café Slavia, across from the National Theater, became a de facto clubhouse in which dissidents passed the time, often within listening range of the not-so-secret police. It's here that Václav Havel and the arts community often gathered to keep a flicker of the Civic Society alive.

The eighth anniversary of the Velvet Revolution marked the rebirth of an old friend. For on that day, the remodeled **Kavárna (Cafe) Slavia** (p. 101) opened again, raised from the dead after a half-decade's absence prolonged by a Boston real estate speculator who apparently was sitting on the property until she could extract a better price. Then-President Havel intervened to plead the cafe's case. After a long legal battle, his wish was granted. "A small victory for reason over stupidity," he said in a proclamation read at the gala opening.

New Bohemian haunts have also popped up, now serving better exotic blends of espresso and cappuccino. The gorgeous **Kavárna Obecní dům** has been returned to its pristine splendor. Cafe life may return to Prague yet again.

Meanwhile, as post-Communist Prague seeks to keep up with the new times, a swath of Internet cafes has also opened (p. 102).

STARÉ MĚSTO (OLD TOWN) & JOSEFOV

Café Resto Le Patio ☞ CAFE/FRENCH   This is a unique place offering an exciting atmosphere made of furniture and accessories dating back to old colonial times. After you have your cup of coffee or something from the lovely French cuisine offered on the menu, don't forget to look around, since you can buy any tagged piece hanging or standing near you.

Národní 22, Praha 1. ℂ 224-934-375. www.patium.com. Main courses 180Kč–420Kč ($7.50–$18). AE, MC, V. Mon–Sat 8am–11pm; Sun 11am–11pm. Metro: Národní třída.

Dahab ☞☞ CAFE/MIDDLE EASTERN   This tearoom was founded last year by Prague's king of tea, Luboš Rychvalský, who introduced Prague to Eastern and Arabic tea cultures soon after the 1989 revolution. Dahab ("gold" or "oasis" in Arabic) provides a New Age alternative to the clatter of the *kavárnas*. The soothing atmosphere is perfect for relaxing quietly over a cup of tea or coffee. You can choose from about 20 sorts of tea and more than 10 kinds of coffee. Arabic soups, hummus, tahini, couscous, pita bread, and tempting sweets are on the menu.

Dlouhá 33 at Rybná, Praha 1. ℂ 224-827-375. www.dahab.cz. Main courses 125Kč–329Kč ($5.20–$14). AE, MC, V. Daily noon–1am. Metro: Náměstí Republiky.

Grand Café CAFE FARE   The biggest draw of this quaint cafe, the former Café Milena, is a great view of the Orloj, an astronomical clock with an hourly parade of saints on the side of Old Town Square's city hall. With a new management came wider selection of main courses as well as higher prices. Make sure you get a table at the window.

Staroměstské nám. 22, Praha 1 (1st floor). ℂ 221-632-520. www.grandcafe.cz. Cappuccino 89Kč ($3.70); main menu 190Kč–490Kč ($7.90–$20). AE, MC, V. Daily 10am–midnight. Metro: Staroměstská.

Kavárna Obecní dům ☞☞ CAFE FARE   An afternoon here feels like a trip back to the time when Art Nouveau was the newest fashion, not history. The reopening of the entire Municipal House in the spring of 1997 was a treat for those who love this style of architecture, and the *kavárna* might be its most spectacular public room. Witness the lofty ceilings, marble wall accents and tables, altarlike mantle at the far end, and huge windows and period chandeliers. Coffee, tea, and other drinks come with pastries and light sandwiches.

In the Municipal House, náměstí Republiky 5, Praha 1. ℂ 222-002-763. www.vysehrad2000.cz. Cakes and coffees from 50Kč–135Kč ($2.10–$5.65). AE, MC, V. Daily 7:30am–11pm. Metro: Náměstí Republiky.

Kavárna Slavia ☞ CAFE FARE   You'll most certainly walk by this Prague landmark, which reopened after a 6-year hiatus across from the National Theater, so why not stop in? The restored crisp Art Deco room recalls the Slavia's 100 years as a meeting place for the city's cultural and intellectual corps. The cafe still has a relatively affordable menu accompanying the gorgeous riverfront panoramic views of Prague Castle.

Impressions

Today's opening of Café Slavia, one of the places that played such a fundamental role in my life, I understand as a step toward renovation of the natural structure of Czech spiritual life.

—Former president Václav Havel's proclamation
at the Slavia's reopening (Nov 17, 1997)

Národní at Smetanovo nábřeží, Praha 1. ⓒ 224-218-493. Coffees and pastries 20Kč–40Kč (85¢–$1.65); salad bar and light menu items 40Kč–120Kč ($1.65–$5). AE, MC, V. Daily 8am–midnight. Metro: Národní třída.

La Dolce Vita ⓡ CAFE FARE   Half a block off Pařížská in Prague's Jewish Quarter, Josefov, is the city's finest Italian cafe. Lively banter, attractive regulars, strong pulls on the espresso machine, and pretty good Italian pastries keep the place humming.

Široká 15, Praha 1. ⓒ 224-226-546. Cappuccino 60Kč ($2.50); pastries 80Kč–140Kč ($3.35–$5.85). No credit cards. Daily 8am–11pm. Metro: Staroměstská.

Velryba CAFE FARE   This is the city center's cafe for young intellectuals. Journalists and actors set the mood in this bareish basement on a back street off Národní třída, where the emphasis is on good friends and hard talk. Pretty decent pasta dishes are served.

Opatovická 24, Praha 1. ⓒ 224-912-391. Light meals 62Kč–135Kč ($2.50–$5.60). No credit cards. Daily 11am–midnight. Metro: Národní třída.

NOVÉ MĚSTO (NEW TOWN)
Cafe Evropa CAFE FARE   Once a grande dame of Wenceslas Square, the Evropa has fallen into disrepair, but its wooden and etched-glass grandeur is still worth a coffee and a look.

Václavské nám. 25, Praha 1. ⓒ 224-228-117. Coffee 45Kč ($1.85); pastries 50Kč–100Kč ($2.10–$4.15). AE, MC, V. Daily 9:30am–11pm. Metro: Můstek.

Dobrá čajovna ⓡ CAFE FARE   On the walk toward the National Museum on the right side of Wenceslas Square, there is an island of serenity in the courtyard at no. 14. Inside the Dobrá čajovna (Good Tearoom), a pungent bouquet of herb teas, throw pillows, and sitar music welcomes visitors to this very understated Bohemian corner. The extensive tea menu includes green Japanese tea for 55Kč ($2.30) a cup.

Václavské nám. 14, Praha 1. ⓒ 224-231-480. 40Kč–120Kč ($1.65–$5) for a pot of tea. No credit cards. Mon–Fri 10am–9:30pm; Sat–Sun 2–9:30pm. Metro: Můstek.

Globe ⓡⓡ LIGHT FARE   A mainstay for younger English-speaking expats, the Globe is split into a fairly well-stocked bookstore and a usually crowded literary cafe serving pastas, sandwiches, salads, and chewy brownies along with stiff espresso. This new location is bigger than the first one was in Praha 7, and it has several terminals for Internet connections costing 1.50Kč (6¢) per minute.

Pštrossova 6, Praha 1. ⓒ 224-934-203. www.globebookstore.cz. Salads, sandwiches, pastas, and desserts 50Kč–145Kč ($2.10–$6.05). No credit cards. Daily 10am–midnight. Metro: Národní třída.

VINOHRADY
Kavárna Medúza CAFE FARE   With the feeling of an old attic, the Medúza, near several Vinohrady hotels and pensions, has a comfortable mix of visitors and students. The cappuccino comes in bowls, not cups, and the garlic bread hits the spot.

Belgická 17, Praha 2. ⓒ 222-515-107. Cappuccino 25Kč ($1.05); pastries/light meals 39Kč–95Kč ($1.60–$3.95). No credit cards. Mon–Fri 10am–1am; Sat–Sun noon–1am. Metro: Náměstí Míru.

INTERNET CAFES
A great place to surf the Internet for 1.50Kč (6¢) per minute and have a good cup of coffee in a pleasant atmosphere is **Globe,** the bookstore and cafe (above). Also offering Internet connections for 1.80Kč (7¢) per minute is **Bohemia Bagel** (p. 89). Check your e-mail and surf at the very centrally located new Internet cafe **Inetpoint.cz,**

Jungmannova 32, Praha 1 (© **296-245-962**). It's open daily 10am to 10pm and the connection charge is 25Kč ($1.05) per 15 minutes. Another place to get on the Internet is **Cyber Cafe-Jáma** at V jámě 7, Praha 1 (© **224-222-383**).

9 The Pick of the Pubs

Besides being the center of extracurricular activity, *hospody* are the best places for a fulfilling, inexpensive meal and a true Czech experience—not to mention the best brews, or "liquid bread" as they are sometimes called. Food selections are typically the same: *svíčková, guláš, roštěná na roštu* (see "Czech Meals," p. 79), or breaded fried hermelín cheese *(smažený sýr)*. All can be ordered with fries, rice, potato pancakes *(bramborák)*, or boiled potatoes. Reservations aren't usually accepted, though you may call ahead and make one, since these places are getting popular.

Below I've listed two top Old Town pub choices based on atmosphere, authenticity, and price. For more pub selections, see chapter 10.

U medvídků *☞☞* CZECH/CONTINENTAL   Bright and noisy, the "House at the Little Bears" serves a better-than-average *vepřo, knedlo,* and *zelo* with two colors of cabbage. The pub on the right after you enter is half as cheap and livelier than the restaurant to the left. It's a hangout mixing locals, German tour groups, and foreign journalists who come for the original Czech **Budweiser** beer, the genuine article. In high season, an "oompah" band plays in the beer wagon in the center of the pub.

Na Perštýně 7, Praha 1. © **224-211-916**. www.umedvidku.cz. Main courses 90Kč–250Kč ($3.70–$10). AE, MC, V. Daily 11:30am–11pm. Metro: Národní třída.

U Vejvodů *☞☞* CZECH/CONTINENTAL   Long gone from this place are the once-familiar hordes of neighborhood locals lording over the tables for hours as their beer tickets mount. The brewers of **Pilsner** have moved in with tables and booths among the alcoves and balconies, along with big-screen TVs showing the latest Czech sports triumph, and a wider range of cuisine beyond the pigs' knuckle and pickled eggs of yesteryear. Now a mug of Pilsner Urquell costs about 26Kč ($1), and it can be enjoyed with goulash or goose, and even trout or salmon. You can find multiple choices of fresh salads, though the lettuce will often disappoint.

Jilská 4, Praha 1. © **224-219-999**. www.restauraceuvejvodu.cz. Main courses 99Kč–595Kč ($4.15–$24). AE, MC, V. Mon–Sat 10am–4am; Sun 11am–3am. Metro: Národní třída.

7

Exploring Prague

While Prague's classical music and the Czech Republic's unmatched beer are among some of the better reasons to visit, the primary pleasure for many is simply strolling Prague's winding cobblestone streets and enjoying the unique atmosphere. Only by foot can you explore the countless nooks and crannies. It would be hard to think of another world capital where there is so much in such a compact area.

Exquisite examples from the history of European architecture—from Romanesque to Renaissance, from baroque to Art Nouveau to cubist—are crammed next to one another on twisting narrow streets. Seen from Charles Bridge, this jumble of architecture thrusts from the hills and hugs the riverbanks, with little of the 20th century's own excesses obscuring the grandeur from the past millennium. The most revered areas remain relatively free of the blindingly electric technicolored world—however, splotches of graffiti and seemingly constant reconstruction often taint the mood.

While Prague's leaders have been slow to tap into the city's true potential as a primary European tourist destination, there have been some marked improvements in recent years. Buildings within the city center, the walking zone Na Příkopě, and Václavské náměstí, have undergone several changes and renovations.

In 2000 Slovanský Dům re-opened after a massive reconstruction. One of the Prague's most popular cultural and social meeting places for more than a century, today this site houses one of the city's most modern cinema complexes, several new restaurants, and shops.

1 Prague Castle (Pražský Hrad) & Charles Bridge (Karlův most)

The huge hilltop complex known collectively as **Prague Castle (Pražský Hrad)** ⭐⭐⭐, on Hradčanské náměstí, encompasses dozens of houses, towers, churches, courtyards, and monuments. (It's described in detail in "Walking Tour 2: Prague Castle

⟨Value⟩ Saving Money on Entrance Fees

If you like museums, galleries, castles, or churches, you may consider getting a **Prague Card.** This pass is valid for 3 days and allows you to visit up to 40 top attractions in the city, including the Prague Castle.

The price is 590Kč ($24) adults and 410Kč ($17) students under 26, and you can buy it at the Čedok office or the PIS information center at Na Příkopě 20, Praha 1. For more information and the whole list of sights go to www.praguecard.biz.

> ## (Tips) What's Going on Around Town?
>
> The **Prague Information Service** maintains a listing of current exhibits on its website at www.pis.cz. Also, the English newspaper the **Prague Post** offers a good and updated list of cultural and social events in Prague. See www.prague post.com.

Half Day

(Pražský Hrad)" in chapter 8; see also the map on p. 106.) A visit to the castle can easily take an entire day or more, depending on how thoroughly you explore it. Still, you can see the top sights—St. Vitus Cathedral, the Royal Palace, St. George's Basilica, the Powder Tower, and Golden Lane—in the space of a morning or an afternoon.

Although the individual attractions are closed, you can also explore the castle complex at night, as it's generally lit until midnight, or make a return trip to see the Gothic art in St. George's Convent. The complex is always guarded and is said to be safe to wander at night, but keep to the lighted areas of the courtyards just to be sure.

If you're feeling particularly fit, you can walk up to the castle, or you can take metro line A to Malostranská or Hradčanská or tram no. 22 or 23.

TICKETS & CASTLE INFORMATION   Tickets are sold at the **Prague Castle Information Center** in the second courtyard after you pass through the main gate from Hradčanské náměstí. The center also arranges tours in various languages and sells tickets for individual concerts and exhibits. The castle is located at Hradčanské náměstí, Hradčany, Praha 1 (© **224-373-368;** Fax 224-310-896; www.hrad.cz). Admission to the grounds is free. A combination ticket for tour A to six main attractions (St. Vitus Cathedral, Royal Palace including "The Story of Prague Castle" permanent exhibition, St. George's Basilica, Powder Tower, Golden Lane, and Daliborka Tower), without a guide costs 350Kč ($15) adults, 175Kč ($7) students; with an English-speaking guide, 440Kč ($18) adults, 265Kč ($11) students. Tour B (St. Vitus Cathedral, Royal Palace, Golden Lane, and Daliborka Tower) costs 220Kč ($9.20)adults, 110Kč ($5) students; Tour C (only Golden Lane and Daliborka Tower) costs 50Kč ($2) adults and students. For guided tours (groups of five and more), supplement 90Kč ($4) per person (only Tues–Sun 9am–4pm). All tours are free for children under 6. Tickets are valid for 2 days. The castle is open daily 9am to 5pm (to 4pm Nov–Mar). Metro: Malostranská, then tram no. 22 or 23, up the hill two stops.

TOURING ST. VITUS CATHEDRAL (CHRÁM SV. VÍTA) 🎬🎬🎬

St. Vitus Cathedral (Chrám sv. Víta), named for a wealthy 4th-century Sicilian martyr, isn't just the dominant part of the castle, it's the most important section historically. In April 1997, Pope John Paul II paid his third visit to Prague in 7 years, this time to honor the thousandth anniversary of the death of 10th-century Slavic evangelist St. Vojtěch. He conferred the saint's name on the cathedral along with St. Vitus's, but officially the Czech state calls it just St. Vitus.

Built over various phases beginning in A.D. 926 as the court church of the Premyslid princes, the cathedral has long been the center of Prague's religious and political life. The key part of its Gothic construction took place in the 14th century under the direction of Mathias of Arras and Peter Parléř of Gmuend. In the 18th and 19th centuries, subsequent baroque and neo-Gothic additions were made. The **Golden Portal** entrance from the third courtyard is no longer used; however, take a look above the

Prague Attractions

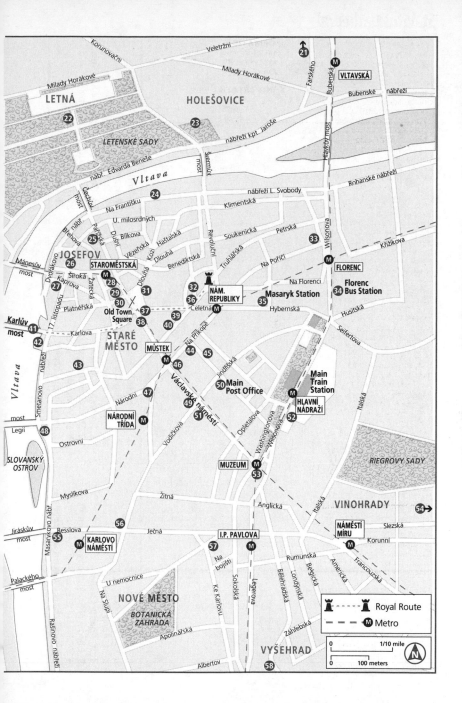

St. Vitus Cathedral

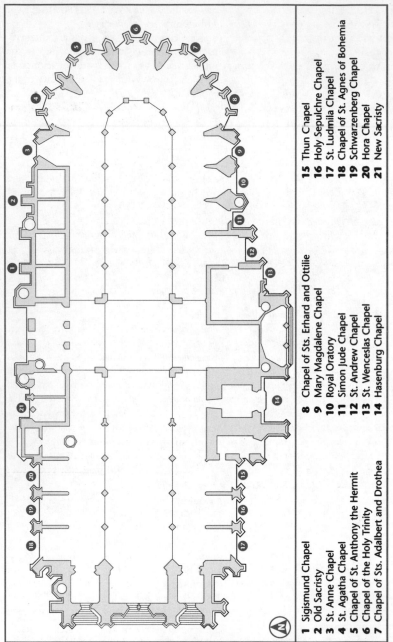

1 Sigismund Chapel
2 Old Sacristy
3 St. Anne Chapel
4 St. Agatha Chapel
5 Chapel of St. Anthony the Hermit
6 Chapel of the Holy Trinity
7 Chapel of Sts. Adalbert and Drothea

8 Chapel of Sts. Erhard and Ottilie
9 Mary Magdalene Chapel
10 Royal Oratory
11 Simon Jude Chapel
12 St. Andrew Chapel
13 St. Wenceslas Chapel
14 Hasenburg Chapel

15 Thun Chapel
16 Holy Sepulchre Chapel
17 St. Ludmila Chapel
18 Chapel of St. Agnes of Bohemia
19 Schwarzenberg Chapel
20 Hora Chapel
21 New Sacristy

arch. The 1370 mosaic *The Last Judgment* has been painstakingly restored with the help of computer-aided imagery provided by American art researchers.

As you enter the cathedral through the back entrance into the main aisle, the colored light streaming through the intricate **stained-glass windows** that rise to the Gothic ceiling above the high altar may dazzle you. The center windows, restored in the 2 years after World War II, depict the Holy Trinity, with the Virgin Mary to the left and St. Wenceslas kneeling to the right.

Of the massive Gothic cathedral's 21 chapels, the **St. Wenceslas Chapel (Svatová-clavská kaple)** ✪ stands out as one of Prague's few must-see, indoor sights. Midway toward the high altar on the right, it's encrusted with hundreds of pieces of jasper and amethyst and decorated with paintings from the 14th to the 16th centuries. The chapel sits atop the gravesite of Bohemia's patron saint, St. Wenceslas.

Just beyond this, the **Chapel of the Holy Rood (Kaple sv. Kříže)** leads to the entrance of the underground **royal crypt.** In the early 1900s, the crypt was reconstructed, and the remains of the kings and their relatives were replaced in new sarcophagi. The center sarcophagus is the final resting place of Charles IV, the favorite Bohemian king who died in 1378 and is the namesake of much of Prague. In the back row are Charles's four wives (all in one sarcophagus), and in front of them is George of Poděbrady, the last Bohemian king, who died in 1471.

CONTINUING THROUGH THE CASTLE COMPLEX

For more than 700 years, beginning in the 9th century, Bohemian kings and princes resided in the **Royal Palace (Královský palác),** located in the third courtyard of the castle grounds. Vaulted **Vladislav Hall (Vladislavský sál),** the interior's centerpiece, hosted coronations and is still used for special occasions of state such as inaugurations of presidents. The adjacent Diet was where kings and queens met with their advisers and where the Supreme Court was held. From a window in the Ludwig Wing, where the Bohemia Chancellery met, the Second Defenestration took place (see "Beware of Open Windows: The Czech Tradition of Defenestration," below). In 2004, a new part of the permanent exhibition called **"The Story of Prague Castle"** has been presented within the Royal Palace. This project shows the transformation of the castle from the prehistoric period up to the present. For information and booking, contact ☏ **224-373-102** (www.pribeh-hradu.cz). It is open daily from 9am to 5pm and the 90-minute presentation costs 140Kč ($5.85) adults, 80Kč ($3.35) students. The castle's "A tour" ticket includes admission to this exposition as well.

St. George's Basilica (Kostel sv. Jiří), adjacent to the Royal Palace, is Prague's oldest Romanesque structure, dating from the 10th century. It also houses Bohemia's first convent. No longer serving a religious function, the convent contains a gallery of Gothic Czech art (see "Museums & Galleries," later in this chapter) that you should see on a separate visit, if you have the time.

Inside the sparse and eerie basilica you will find relics of the castle's history along with a genealogy of those who have passed through it. If you look carefully at the outer towers, you'll notice that they're slightly different from each other: They have an Adam and Eve motif. The wider south tower represents Adam, while the narrower north tower is Eve.

Golden Lane (Zlatá ulička) and Daliborka Tower ✪ is a picturesque street of tiny 16th-century houses built into the castle fortifications. Once home to castle sharpshooters, the houses now contain small shops, galleries, and refreshment bars. In

1917, Franz Kafka is said to have lived briefly at no. 22; however, the debate continues as to whether Kafka actually took up residence or just worked in a small office there.

The Prague Castle Picture Gallery (**Obrazárna Pražského hradu**) displays European and Bohemian masterpieces, but few are from the original imperial collection, which was virtually destroyed during the Thirty Years' War. Of the works that have

Beware of Open Windows: The Czech Tradition of Defenestration

About 600 years before Prague's popular uprising brought down Communism, the Czech people began a long tradition of what might be considered a unique form of political protest.

In 1402, Jan Hus, a lecturer from Prague University, became the leading voice in a growing condemnation of the Catholic Church. From a pulpit in Old Town's Bethlehem Chapel (later destroyed but reconstructed in the 1950s), Hus gained popular support for his claims that the omnipotent power of the mostly German-dominated clergy had to be contained. In 1414, he was invited to the Catholic ecclesiastical Council of Konstanz to explain his beliefs. Though the emperor had promised Hus safe conduct, on arriving he was promptly arrested, and a year later he was burned at the stake. The Protestant Hussite supporters declared him a martyr and rallied their calls for change around his death.

On July 30, 1419, a group of radical Hussites stormed the New Town Hall on Charles Square and demanded the release of other arrested pro-reform Hussites. After town councilors rejected the demand, the Hussites tossed them out of third-story windows, killing several. This became known as the First Defenestration, from the Latin for "out of the window." The incident sparked a 15-year battle known as the Hussite Wars, which ended in the defeat of the radical Protestants in 1434.

By the 17th century, the Austrian Catholics who came to power in Prague tolerated little dissent, but as Protestant Czechs became ever more wealthy, they began criticizing the Habsburg monarchy. This bubbled over again on May 23, 1618, when a group of Protestant nobles entered Prague Castle, seized two pro-Habsburg Czechs and their secretary, and tossed them out of the eastern window of the rear room of the Chancellery—the Second Defenestration. In the Garden on the Ramparts below the Ludwig Wing, two obelisks mark where they landed. This act led, in part, to the conflict known as the Thirty Years' War, which ended again in victory in 1648 for the Catholics. The Habsburgs remained in power for another 270 years, ruling over Prague as a provincial capital until the democratic Czechoslovak state was born.

Though Prague's 1989 overthrow of the totalitarian Communist regime gained the name the Velvet Revolution for its nonviolent nature, scattered calls for another defenestration (some serious, some joking) were heard. Contemporary Czech politicians surely know to keep away from open windows.

> **Fun Fact A Bridge Tale**
>
> Why has Charles Bridge stood for so long? One great yarn that has lived through the ages states that when the lovingly cut stones were being laid, the master builders mixed eggs into the mortar to strengthen the bond. At the time of the construction, one village tried to impress the king by sending carts full of hard-boiled eggs. The gift might have been a welcome snack for the builders, but it did little to strengthen the mortar.

survived from the days of Emperors Rudolf II and Ferdinand III, the most celebrated is Hans von Aachen's *Portrait of a Girl* (1605–10), depicting the artist's daughter.

The **Powder Tower (Prašná věž, aka Mihulka)** forms part of the northern bastion of the castle complex just off the Golden Lane. Originally a gunpowder storehouse and a cannon tower, it was turned into a laboratory for the 17th-century alchemists serving the court of Emperor Rudolf II.

CROSSING THE VLTAVA: CHARLES BRIDGE

Dating from the 14th century, **Charles Bridge (Karlův most)** 𝄞𝄞𝄞, Prague's most celebrated structure, links Prague Castle to Staré Město. For most of its 600 years, the 510m-long (1,673-ft.) span has been a pedestrian promenade, though for centuries walkers had to share the concourse with horse-drawn vehicles and trolleys. Today, the bridge is filled with folks walking among artists and busking musicians.

The best times to stroll across the bridge are early morning and around sunset, when the crowds have thinned and the shadows are more mysterious. The 30 statues lining the bridge are explained in detail in "Walking Tour 1: Charles Bridge & Malá Strana (Lesser Town)," in chapter 8.

2 Other Top Sights

HRADČANY

Loreto Palace (Loreta)   Loreto Palace was named after the town of Loreto, Italy, where the dwelling of the Virgin Mary was said to have been brought by angels from Palestine in the 13th century. After the Roman Catholics defeated the Protestant Bohemians in 1620, the Loreto faction was chosen as the device for a re-Catholicization of Bohemia. The Loreto legend holds that a cottage in which the Virgin Mary lived had been miraculously transferred from Nazareth to Loreto, an Italian city near Ancona. The Loreto Palace is thought to be an imitation of this cottage, and more than 50 copies have been constructed throughout the Czech lands.

The Loreto's facade is decorated with 18th-century statues of the writers of the Gospel—Matthew, Mark, Luke, and John—along with a lone female, St. Anne, mother of the Virgin Mary. Inside the **Church of the Nativity** are fully clothed remains of two Spanish saints, St. Felicissimus and St. Marcia. The wax masks on the skeletons' faces are particularly macabre.

Inside the **Chapel of Our Lady of Sorrows** is a painting of a bearded woman hanging on a cross. This is St. Starosta, or Vilgefortis, who, after taking a vow of virginity, was forced to marry the king of Sicily. It's said that God, taking pity on the woman, gave her facial hair to make her undesirable, after which her pagan father had her crucified. Thus, Starosta went into history as the saint of unhappily married women. The painting was created in the 1700s. Also on display is a portrait of St. Apolena (or Appollonia), a 3rd-century deacon who had her teeth knocked out as part of a torture for refusing to renounce Christianity. She's often represented in art by a gold tooth or pincer. As the patron saint of dentists, Apolena is sometimes referred to as the "saint of toothaches."

Loretánské nám. 7, Praha 1. ℂ 220-516-740. www.loreta.cz. Admission 90Kč ($3.75) adults, 70Kč ($2.90) students, free for children under 6. Tues–Sun 9am–12:15pm and 1–4:30pm. Tram: 22 or 23 from Malostranská.

Strahov Monastery and Library (Strahovský klášter) 🐾 The second-oldest

monastery in Prague, Strahov was founded high above Malá Strana in 1143 by Vladislav II. It's still home to Premonstratensian monks, a scholarly order closely related to the Jesuits, and their dormitories and refectory are off-limits. What draws visitors are the monastery's ornate libraries, holding more than 125,000 volumes. Over the centuries, the monks have assembled one of the world's best collections of philosophical and theological texts, including illuminated (decorated with colored designs) manuscripts and first editions.

The ceiling of the 1679 **Theological Hall** is a stunning example of baroque opulence, with intricate leaf blanketing the walls and framing the 18th-century ceiling frescoes. The rich wood-accented **Philosophical Library**'s 14m-high (46-ft.) ceiling is decorated with a 1794 fresco entitled *The Struggle of Mankind to Know Real Wisdom,* by A. F. Maulpertsch, a Viennese master of rococo. Intricate woodwork frames the immense collection of books. Ancient printing presses downstairs are also worth visiting, as are several altars and the remains of St. Norbert, a 10th-century, German-born saint who founded the Premonstratensian order. His bones were brought here in 1627, when he became one of Bohemia's 10 patron saints. Paths leading through the monastery grounds take you to a breathtaking overlook of the city.

Strahovské nádvoří 1, Praha 1. ℂ 220-517-278. www.strahovskyklaster.cz. Admission 80Kč ($3.35) adults, 50Kč ($2) students. Daily 9am–noon and 1–5pm. Tram: 22 or 23 from Malostranská metro station.

MALÁ STRANA (LESSER TOWN)
Church of St. Nicholas (Chrám sv. Mikuláše) 🐾🐾 *(Moments* This church is one

of the best examples of high baroque north of the Alps. However, K. I. Dienzenhofer's 1711 design didn't have the massive dome that now dominates the Lesser Town skyline below Prague Castle. Dienzenhofer's son, Kryštof, added the 78m-high (256-ft.) dome during additional work completed in 1752. Smog has played havoc with the exterior, yet the gilded interior is stunning. Gold-capped marble-veneered columns frame altars packed with statuary and frescoes. A giant statue of the church's namesake looks down from the high altar.

Malostranské nám. 1, Praha 1. ℂ 257-534-215. www.psalterium.cz. Daily 9am–5pm (4pm in winter); concerts are usually held at 5pm. Admission 50Kč ($2) adults, 25Kč ($1) students. Concerts 390Kč ($16). Metro: Line A to Malostranská.

STARÉ MĚSTO (OLD TOWN)
Estates' Theater (Stavovské divadlo) Completed in 1783 by wealthy Count F.

A. Nostitz, the neoclassical theater became an early symbol of the emerging high Czech culture—with the Greek theme *Patriae et Musis* (the Fatherland and Music) etched above its front columns. In 1799, the wealthy land barons who formed fiefdoms known as The Estates gave the theater its current name.

Wolfgang Amadeus Mozart staged the premier of *Don Giovanni* here in 1787 because he said that Vienna's conservative patrons didn't appreciate him or his passionate and sometimes shocking work. They also wanted mostly German opera, but Praguers were happy to stage the performance in Italian. "Praguers understand me," Mozart was quoted as saying.

In 1834, Czech playwright J. K. Tyl staged a comedy called *Fidlovačka,* in which the patriotic song "Kde domov můj?" ("Where Is My Home?") was a standout. It later became the Czech national anthem. In the heady days at the end of World War II in 1945, the Estates' Theater was renamed Tyl Theater but, when a total reconstruction of the building was completed in 1991, its previous name was reinstated.

Czech director Miloš Forman returned to his native country to film his Oscar-winning *Amadeus,* shooting the scenes of Mozart in Prague with perfect authenticity at the Estates' Theater.

The theater doesn't offer daily tours, but tickets for performances—and the chance to sit in one of the many elegant private boxes—are usually available. Tour events are occasionally scheduled, and individual tours for this and other major monuments can be arranged through **Pražská informační služba** (www.pis.cz; fax **221-714-151**).

Ovocný trh 1, Praha 1. © **224-901-448.** www.nd.cz. Metro: Line A or B to Můstek.

Old Town Hall (Staroměstská radnice) & Astronomical Clock (Orloj) *Kids*

Crowds congregate in front of Old Town Hall's Astronomical Clock *(orloj)* to watch the glockenspiel spectacle that occurs hourly from 8am to 8pm. Built in 1410, the clock has long been an important symbol of Prague. According to legend, after the timepiece was remodeled at the end of the 15th century, clock artist Master Hanuš was blinded by the Municipal Council so that he couldn't repeat his fine work elsewhere. In retribution, Hanuš threw himself into the clock mechanism and promptly died. The clock remained out of kilter for almost a century.

It's not possible to determine the time of day from this timepiece; you have to look at the clock on the very top of Old Town Hall's tower for that. This astronomical clock, with all its hands and markings, is meant to mark the phases of the moon, the equinoxes, the seasons, the days, and numerous Christian holidays.

When the clock strikes the hour, a kind of politically incorrect medieval morality play begins. Two doors slide open and the statues of the Twelve Apostles glide by, while the 15th-century conception of the "evils" of life—a Death skeleton, a preening Vanity, a corrupt Turk, and an acquisitive Jew—shake and dance below. At the end of World War II, the horns and beard were removed from the moneybag-holding Jew, who's now politely referred to as Greed.

Staroměstské nám., Praha 1. © **724-508-584.** www.pis.cz. Admission to tower 50Kč ($2) adults; 40Kč ($1.65) students, children under 10, and seniors. Mar–Oct Mon 11am–6pm, Tues–Sun 9am–6pm; Nov–Feb Mon 11am–5pm, Tues–Sun 9am–5pm. Metro: Line A to Staroměstská.

JOSEFOV

Within Josefov, you'll find a community that for centuries was forced to fend for itself and then experienced horrific purges under Nazi occupation in World War II.

A View with a Warning

It's worth climbing the Town Hall's tower for an excellent view over the red rooftops of Staroměstské náměstí and the surrounding area. But be warned: The steps are narrow, steep, and quite physically demanding, so those less courageous should take the newly installed elevator.

Impressions

Upon my word, if fate drove me to the furthest corner of the Earth, I could not otherwise but wander back after a while to ancient Vyšehrad and refresh my mind with the view.

—Karel Hynek Mácha (Czech poet, buried at Vyšehrad Cemetery)

Although more than 118,000 Jews were recorded as living in the Czech lands of Bohemia and Moravia in 1939, only 30,000 survived to see the end of the Nazi occupation. Today, the Jewish community in the entire country numbers about 3,000 people, most of whom live in Prague.

Josefov's synagogues are lovingly regarded as monuments to the survival of Judaism in central Europe, and the Old Jewish Cemetery, with generations buried upon one another, is an odd relic of the cohesion of Prague's ghetto. Prague's Jewish Quarter is described in detail in "Walking Tour 4: Josefov (Jewish Quarter)" in chapter 8.

The **Jewish Museum in Prague** (www.jewishmuseum.cz) is the name of the organization managing all the Jewish landmarks in Josefov. It provides guided package tours with an English-speaking guide as part of a comprehensive admission price. The package includes the Ceremonial Hall, Old Jewish Cemetery, Old-New Synagogue, Pinkas Synagogue, Klaus Synagogue, Maisel Synagogue, and Spanish Synagogue. From April to October, tours leave on the hour starting at 9am with the last tour at 5pm, but there must be at least 10 people in a group. Off season, the tours are between 9am and 4:30pm. The package costs 500Kč ($20) for adults and 340Kč ($14) for students, free for children under 6.

The Maisel Synagogue now serves as the exhibition space for the **Jewish Museum.** In October 1994, the State Jewish Museum closed; the Torah covers, 100,000 books, and other exhibits once housed there were given to the Jewish community, who then proceeded to return many items to synagogues throughout the country. The Nazis destroyed much of Prague's ancient Judaica during World War II. Ironically, those same Germans constructed an "exotic museum of an extinct race," thus salvaging thousands of objects, such as the valued Torah covers, books, and silver now displayed at the Maisel Synagogue.

Old Jewish Cemetery (Starý židovský hřbitov) ⊛

Just 1 block from the Old-New Synagogue, this is one of Europe's oldest Jewish burial grounds, dating from the mid–15th century. Because the local government of the time didn't allow Jews to bury their dead elsewhere, graves were dug deep enough to hold 12 bodies vertically, with each tombstone placed in front of the last. The result is one of the world's most crowded cemeteries: a 1-block area filled with more than 20,000 graves. Among the most famous persons buried here are the celebrated Rabbi Loew (Löw; d. 1609), who created the legend of Golem (a giant clay "monster" to protect Prague's Jews); and banker Markus Mordechai Maisel (d. 1601), then the richest man in Prague and protector of the city's Jewish community during the reign of Rudolf II.

U Starého hřbitova; the entrance is from Široká 3. © 222-317-191. Admission 300Kč ($12) adults, 200Kč ($8.30) students, free for children under 6. Apr–Oct Sun–Fri 9am–6pm; Nov–Mar Sun–Fri 9am–4:30pm. Metro: Line A to Staroměstská.

Old-New Synagogue (Staronová synagóga) ⊛

First called the New Synagogue to distinguish it from an even older one that no longer exists, the Old-New Synagogue, built around 1270, is Europe's oldest remaining Jewish house of worship. The faithful have prayed here continuously for more than 700 years, carrying on even after a massive 1389 pogrom in Josefov that killed over 3,000 Jews. Its use as a house of worship was interrupted only between 1941 and 1945 because of the Nazi occupation. The synagogue

Moments The Art of Getting Lost

Prague is popular—too popular, really—and you can find yourself in the middle of a special moment only to have it punctured by an umbrella or the loud voice of a tour guide from Ohio. So my advice to visitors trying to get a peek into the real life of Czechs is simple: Get lost. Get really, really lost.

You won't stray too far, since "tourist Prague" encompasses a relatively small area. And you know the landmarks: the castle, the bridge, the river, Old Town Square. So leave the map behind.

My favorite times to get lost in Prague are early morning and late at night. One foggy morning, I woke up early, grabbed a coffee in the breakfast room of my Communist-era hotel, and headed out. I'm not sure which direction I went—left, I think. I strolled several blocks into unfamiliar territory. I found a wonderful bookshop where I picked up a Czech version of Maurice Sendak's *Where the Wild Things Are*. Then I ducked into an old camera shop in search of film. The shop carried not only the latest German and Japanese cameras but also fascinating, old Eastern European cameras that looked to my American eyes like some discarded cosmonaut space garbage. Next, I discovered a little hut of a church that was dark and wonderful; two old Czech women dusted while I looked around. I'd love to tell you where these memorable places were, but you see, I was lost.

Another great way to get lost is to hop on a tram and let the driver take you where he's going. Get off when you see an intriguing neighborhood, if you're hungry, or if you have to go to the bathroom. Or, if you're adventurous, follow someone. For 40 minutes I trailed an old woman doing her shopping. Wow, did she get me lost! I followed her into a local food shop, not one of the big chains filled with processed foods and produce from Germany, but a little "czecha" shop. I bought some candy, which I still have—for me candy is the best kind of souvenir.

Late in the evening, as you wander aimlessly through Old Town, you'll half expect to see ghosts darting about. The lanterns along the uneven cobblestone streets don't really help you navigate; instead, I'm convinced that their function is to set a mysterious, quiet mood. That peacefulness is occasionally interrupted by the sounds of late-night revelers. You may be tempted to join them for a *pivo* (beer).

Roaming the streets of Prague is like unraveling a big ball of twine. When you get lost, you're likely to find something special, some experience that will make you feel "of" the place, rather than just passing through.

So remember where you are. Then get lost.

—*by Bill Boedeker*

Prague's Most Powerful Daughter: The Rise & Surprise of Madeleine Albright

Marie Jana Koerbelová took an unlikely path to becoming one of the most powerful women in the world. Born in Prague in 1937, she first learned about the horrors of politics gone wrong at an early age when in 1938 her diplomat father, Josef Koerbel, fled with the family to London as Hitler invaded Czechoslovakia.

After the war, the family moved to Belgrade, where Josef was appointed Czechoslovak ambassador to Yugoslavia (he also served as a delegate at the founding of the United Nations). Maria was sent to boarding school in Switzerland, where she learned to speak French. Prague's 1948 Communist coup turned the family into refugees again, for Josef feared that his pro-democracy credentials meant that he'd be singled out in the impending totalitarian purges. Eventually the family received asylum in the United States. At age 11, Marie Jana Koerbelová, renamed Madeleine Korbel for American ears, began a new life in Colorado, where her father took a teaching position at the University of Denver.

Her father's fierce devotion to democracy and his interest in world politics influenced Madeleine tremendously, by her own account. After her marriage to New York newspaper scion Joseph Albright (whom she later divorced), Madeleine Albright began to study and forge a career in foreign policy while raising three daughters. Her writings and teachings often focused on the land of her birth and the horrors it had suffered.

After becoming an immensely popular professor at Georgetown University and advising former Czech president Havel following the Velvet Revolution, she was picked by then-U.S. President Clinton as ambassador to the United Nations.

is also one of Prague's great Gothic buildings, built with vaulted ceilings and retro-fitted with Renaissance-era columns. It is not part of the Jewish Museum, so you can visit this synagogue separately.

Červená 2. ⓒ 222-317-191. Admission 200Kč ($8.30) adults, 140Kč ($5.805) students. (If part of the package for Jewish Museum, 500Kč/$20 adults, 340Kč/$14 students.) Free for children under 6. Sun–Thurs 9:30am–5pm; Fri 9am–4pm. Metro: Line A to Staroměstská.

ELSEWHERE IN PRAGUE

Vyšehrad   This sprawling rocky hilltop complex is the cradle of the Bohemian state. From this spot, legend has it, Princess Libuše looked out over the Vltava valley toward present-day Prague Castle and predicted the founding of a great kingdom and capital city. Vyšehrad was the first seat of the first Czech kings in the Premyslid dynasty before the dawn of the 20th century.

On her first official visit to Prague as ambassador in 1994, she walked into the palatial foreign ministry where her father had once worked. "This is a really emotional moment for me," she said to journalists as she entered Černín Palace, fighting back tears. She has since played tour guide for the Clintons in Prague and has dazzled Czechs in her native language, albeit frozen in a girlish tone and vocabulary.

In early 1997, Ambassador Albright became Secretary of State Albright, the first woman ever to serve in such a high government post. "Nothing compares to the feeling of coming to my original home, Prague, as Secretary of State of the United States, for the purpose of saying to you, 'Welcome home,'" she said in both languages in an emotional 1997 speech celebrating the country's invitation to join NATO.

Raised a Catholic, she said she discovered only in early 1997 that her parents hid their Jewish heritage during the war and never told their children of their true background. During that 1997 trip, Albright visited the Pinkas Synagogue, where the names of her paternal grandparents are inscribed on the wall, alongside the names of thousands of Czech Jews who died in the Holocaust.

Albright's remaining link to Prague is the house U labutí ("At the Swans"), tucked in the corner at Hradčanské nám. 11 adjacent to the castle, where she lived as a small girl.

Just before his 1977 death, Albright's father had foreshadowed 1989's revolutionary events when he wrote this as the last paragraph of his final book, *Twentieth Century Czechoslovakia*: "The spark is still there. One cannot doubt that it will flicker one day again into flame, and freedom will return to this land that is so essentially humane."

You can find out more about Albright's feelings regarding her original homeland in her book titled *Madam Secretary*.

This was also the first Royal Route. Before the kings could take their seat at the more modern Prague Castle, they first had to pay homage to their predecessors on Vyšehrad and then follow the route to Hradčany for the coronation.

Today, the fortifications remain on the rocky cliffs, blocking out the increasing noise and confusion below. Within the confines of the citadel, lush lawns and gardens are crisscrossed by dozens of paths leading to historic buildings and cemeteries. Vyšehrad is still somewhat of a hidden treasure for picnics and romantic walks, and from here you'll see one of the most panoramic views of the city.

Vyšehrad Cemetery (Vyšehradský hřbitov) is the national cemetery within the ancient citadel on the east side of the Vltava. It's the final resting place of some 600 honored Czechs, including composers Antonín Dvořák and Bedřich Smetana and Art Nouveau painter Alfons Mucha. The complex of churches and gardens is a pleasant getaway from the city crush. The cemetery is on Soběslavova 1, Praha 2 (✆ **241-410-348;** www.praha-vysehrad.cz). To get here, take tram no. 3 or 16 from Karlovo náměstí to Výtoň south of New Town.

3 Museums & Galleries

Many fine private art galleries showing contemporary work by Czech and other artists are in central Prague, within walking distance of Staroměstské náměstí. Although their primary interest is sales, most welcome browsing. See "Art Galleries" in chapter 9 for information on the city's top art galleries.

As for public museums and galleries, note that many museums are closed on Monday.

NATIONAL GALLERY SITES

The national collection of fine art is grouped for display in the series of venues known collectively as the **National Gallery (Národní Galerie).** Remember that this term refers to several locations, not just one gallery.

The most extensive collection of classic European works spanning the 14th to the 18th centuries is found at the Archbishop's Palace complex in the **Šternberský palác** across from the main gate to Prague Castle.

Veletržní Palace houses most of the country's 20th-century art collection and now also shows the important national revival works from Czech artists of the 19th century. Much of the rest of the national collection is divided between Kinský Palace on Old Town Square and the Gothic collection at St. Agnes Convent near the river in Old Town.

The key Prague sites within the national gallery system are listed below.

HRADČANY

St. Agnes Convent (Klášter sv. Anežky České)   A complex of early Gothic buildings and churches dating from the 13th century, the convent, tucked in a corner of Staré Město, began exhibiting much of the National Gallery's collection of Gothic art in 2000. Once home to the Order of the Poor Clares, it was established in 1234 by St. Agnes of Bohemia, sister of Wenceslas I. The Blessed Agnes became St. Agnes when Pope John Paul II paid his first visit to Prague in 1990 for her canonization.

The museum contains many bronze studies that preceded the casting of some of the city's greatest public monuments, including the equestrian statue of St. Wenceslas atop the National Theater. Downstairs, a Children's Workshop offers hands-on art activities, most of which incorporate religious themes. The grounds surrounding the convent are pretty nice, too. The convent is at the end of Anežka, off Haštalské náměstí.

U Milosrdných 17, Praha 1. ⓒ 224-810-628. www.ngprague.cz. Admission 100Kč ($4.15) adults, 50Kč ($2) children. Tues–Sun 10am–6pm. Metro: Line A to Staroměstská.

St. George's Convent at Prague Castle (Klášter sv. Jiří na Pražském hradě) Dedicated to displaying traditional Czech art, the castle convent is especially packed with Gothic and baroque Bohemian iconography as well as portraits of patron saints. The most famous among the unique collection of Czech Gothic panel paintings are those by the Master of the Hohenfurth Altarpiece and the Master Theodoricus. The collections are arranged into special exhibits usually revolving around a specific place, person, or historical time.

Jiřské nám. 33. ⓒ 257-531-644. www.ngprague.cz. Admission 100Kč ($4.15) adults, 50Kč ($2) students, free for children under 6. Tues–Sun 9am–5pm. Metro: Line A to Malostranská or Hradčanská.

Šternberk Palace (Šternberský palác) ⚐   The jewel in the National Gallery crown (also known casually as the European Art Museum), the gallery at Šternberk Palace, adjacent to the main gate of Prague Castle, displays a wide menu of European

Fun Fact **Did You Know?**

- Charles University, central Europe's first post-secondary school, opened in Prague in 1348.
- Albert Einstein was a professor of physics in Prague from 1911 to 1912.
- The word *robot* was coined by Czech writer Karel Čapek and comes from a Slavic root meaning "to work."
- Contact lenses were invented by a Czech scientist.
- The word *dollar* came from the Tolar coins used during the Austrian empire; the coins were minted in the western Bohemian town of Jáchymov from silver mined nearby.

art throughout the ages. It features 5 centuries of everything from Orthodox icons to Renaissance oils by Dutch masters. Pieces by Rembrandt, El Greco, Goya, and Van Dyck are mixed among numerous pieces from Austrian imperial court painters. Exhibits such as Italian Renaissance bronzes rotate throughout the seasons.

Hradčanské nám. 15, Praha 1. ℃ **233-090-570.** www.ngprague.cz. Admission 150Kč ($6.25) adults, 70Kč ($2.90) students and children. Tues–Sun 10am–6pm. Metro: Line A to Malostranská or Hradčanská.

STARÉ MĚSTO (OLD TOWN)

Kinský Palace (Palác Kinských) ☞ The reconstructed rococo palace houses graphic works from the National Gallery collection, including pieces by Georges Braque, André Derain, and other modern masters. Pablo Picasso's 1907 *Self-Portrait* is here and has virtually been adopted as the National Gallery's logo. Good-quality international exhibits have included Max Ernst and Rembrandt retrospectives, as well as shows on functional arts and crafts.

Staroměstské nám. 12, Praha 1. ℃ **224-810-758.** www.ngprague.cz. Admission is different for each exhibition. Tues–Sun 10am–6pm. Metro: Line A to Staroměstská.

Veletržní Palace (National Gallery) This 1925 constructivist palace, built for trade fairs, was remodeled and reopened in December 1995 to hold the bulk of the National Gallery's collection of 20th-century works by Czech and other European artists. Three atrium-lit concourses provide a comfortable setting for some catchy and kitschy Czech sculpture and multimedia works. Alas, the best cubist works from Braque and Picasso, Rodin bronzes, and many other primarily French pieces have been relegated to the second floor. Other displays are devoted to peculiar works by Czech artists that demonstrate how creativity flowed even under the weight of the iron curtain. The first floor features temporary exhibits from traveling shows.

Veletržní at Dukelských hrdinů 47, Praha 7. ℃ **224-301-111.** www.ngprague.cz. Admission 250Kč ($10) adults, 120Kč ($5) students for 4 floors of the palace; 200Kč ($8.30) adults, 100Kč ($4.15) students for 3 floors; 150Kč ($6.25) adults, 70Kč ($2.90) students for 2 floors; 100Kč ($4.15) adults, 50Kč ($2) students for 1 floor. Free for children under 6. Tues–Sun 10am–6pm. Metro: Line C to Vltavská. Tram: 17.

OTHER MUSEUMS & GALLERIES

MALÁ STRANA

Franz Kafka Museum ☞ A new long-term exhibition here presents first editions of Kafka's work, his letters, diaries, and manuscripts. This unique project, which was originally introduced in Barcelona in 1999, has been brought to the writer's birthplace and the city where he had strong ties. The exhibit is divided into two sections: the first, Existential Space, explains the huge influence of the city on Kafka's life and therefore his writing. The second uses 3-D installations as well as good audiovisual technology to depict the author's "Imaginary Topography of Prague."

Hergetova Cihelna, Cihelná 2b, Praha 1. © **257-535-507.** www.kafkamuseum.cz. Admission 120Kč ($5) adults, 60Kč ($2.50) students. Daily 10am–6pm. Metro: Malostranská.

Museum Kampa–Sovovy mlýny ⊛

This building on Kampa island served for most of its history, due to the location, as a mill. Throughout the centuries it was struck by floods, fires, and destructive wars. The premises underwent several transformations and reconstructions. In September 2003, the Sovovy mlýny was opened as a museum of modern art by Czech-born American Meda Mládková and her foundation. She has been collecting works of Czech and central European artists since the 1950s. Her dream reached its pinnacle when she presented the permanent exhibition of František Kupka's drawings and Otto Gutfreund's sculptures.

U Sovových mlýnů 503/2, Praha 1. © **257-286-147.** www.museumkampa.cz. Admission 120Kč ($5) adults, 60Kč ($2.50) students, free for children under 6. Daily 10am–6pm. Metro: Malostranská.

STARÉ MĚSTO (OLD TOWN)

Bedřich Smetana Museum (Muzeum B. Smetany)

Opened in 1936 (in what was the former Old Town waterworks) and jutting into the Vltava next to Charles Bridge, this museum pays tribute to the deepest traditions of Czech classical music and its most patriotic composer, Bedřich Smetana. The exhibits show scores, diaries, manuscripts, and gifts presented to the composer while he was the preeminent man of Prague music in the mid–19th century. You can buy tickets for the concerts held here on-site or at **Prague Information Service,** Na Příkopě 20, Praha 1 (© **12-444**).

Novotného lávka 1, Praha 1. © **222-220-082.** www.nm.cz. Admission 50Kč ($2) adults, 20Kč (85¢) students and children. Wed–Mon 10am–noon and 12:30–5pm. Metro: Staroměstská. Tram: 17 or 18.

NOVÉ MĚSTO (NEW TOWN)

Alfons Mucha Museum (Muzeum A. Muchy) ⊛

This museum opened in early 1998 near Wenceslas Square to honor the high priest of Art Nouveau, Alphonse (Alfons in Czech) Mucha. Though the Moravian-born, turn-of-the-20th-century master spent most of his creative years in Paris drawing luminaries like actress Sarah Bernhardt, Mucha's influence can still be seen throughout his home country. The new museum, around the corner from the Palace Hotel, combines examples of his graphic works, posters, and paintings, and highlights his influence in jewelry, fashion, and advertising. Those who remember the 1960s and 1970s will flash back to one of Mucha's most famous works, the sinuous goddess of Job rolling papers.

Panská 7, Praha 1. © **224-216-415.** www.mucha.cz. Admission 120Kč ($5) adults, 60Kč ($2.50) students and children. Daily 10am–6pm. Metro: Můstek.

Dvořák Museum (Muzeum A. Dvořáka)

The favorite 19th-century Czech composer, Antonín Dvořák, lived here during his golden years. Built in 1712, the two-story rococo building, tucked away on a Nové Město side street, was Dvořák's home for 24 years until his death in 1901. In the 18th century when the building was erected, this part of Prague was frontier land. Czechs willing to open businesses so far from the center were called "Americans" for their pioneer spirit. This building came

My, what an inefficient way to fish.

Ring toss, good. Horseshoes, bad.

Faster! Faster! Faster!

We take care of the fiddly bits, from providing over 43,000 customer reviews of hotels, to helping you find our best fares, to giving you 24/7 customer service. So you can focus on the only thing that matters. Goofing off.

travelocity
You'll never roam alone.

travelocity.com   1-888-TRAVELOCITY   AOL Keyword: Travel

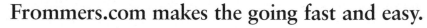

to be known as "America." Opened in 1932, the museum displays an extensive collection, including the composer's piano, spectacles, Cambridge cap and gown, photographs, and sculptures. Several rooms are furnished as they were around 1900. Upstairs, a small recital hall hosts chamber-music performances in high season, with concerts usually at 8pm.

Ke Karlovu 20, Praha 2. ℂ 224-918-013. Admission 40Kč ($1.65) adults, 20Kč (85¢) students, free for children under 6. Concert tickets 220Kč–395Kč ($9.10–$16). Apr–Sept Tues–Sun 10am–1:30pm and 2–5:30pm; Oct–Mar 9:30am–1:30pm and 2–5pm. Metro: Line C to I. P. Pavlova.

National Museum (Národní muzeum) *Kids*   The National Museum, dominating upper Václavské náměstí, looks so much like an important government building that it even fooled the Soviet soldiers, who fired on it during their 1968 invasion, thinking it was the seat of government. If you look closely at the columns you can still see shell marks. This grandiose statement of nationalist purpose opened in 1893, as the national revival gained momentum. The exterior is rimmed with names of the great and good of the homeland (albeit with several foreign guests such as astronomer Johannes Kepler). Inside the grand hall on the first floor is the lapidarium with statues depicting the most important figures in Czech history, including the father of the republic, Tomáš Masaryk. Also on the first floor is an exhaustive collection of minerals, rocks, and meteorites from the Czech and Slovak republics.

The other floor's exhibits depict the ancient history of the Czech lands through zoological and paleontological displays. Throughout the prehistory exhibit are cases of human bones, preserved in soil just as they were found. Nearby, a huge model of a woolly mammoth is mounted next to the bones of the real thing, and half a dozen rooms are packed with more stuffed-and-mounted animals than you can shake a spear at.

Václavské nám. 68, Praha 1. ℂ 224-497-111. www.nm.cz. Admission 100Kč ($4.15) adults, 50Kč ($2) students, free for children under 6; free for everyone 1st Mon of each month. May–Sept daily 10am–6pm; Oct–Apr daily 9am–5pm. Closed 1st Tues each month. Metro: Line A or C to Muzeum station.

ELSEWHERE IN PRAGUE
Bertramka (W. A. Mozart Museum) *K*   Mozart loved Prague, and when he visited, he often stayed at this villa owned by the Dušek family. Now a museum, it contains displays of his written work and his harpsichord. There's also a lock of Mozart's hair, encased in a cube of glass. Much of the Bertramka villa was destroyed by fire in the 1870s, but Mozart's rooms, where he finished composing the opera *Don Giovanni*, were miraculously left untouched. Chamber concerts are often held here, usually starting at 5pm.

Mozartova 169, Praha 5. ℂ 257-318-461. www.bertramka.cz. Admission 110Kč ($4.60) adults, 80Kč ($3.35) students, free for children under 6. Concert tickets 350Kč ($16) adults, 250Kč ($10) students. Daily 9am–6pm (Nov–Mar 9:30am–4pm). Tram: 4, 6, 7, 9, 10, 14, or 16 from Anděl metro station.

Museum of the City of Prague (Muzeum hlavního města Prahy) *K*   Not just another warehouse of history where unearthed artifacts unwanted by others are chronologically stashed, this delightfully upbeat museum encompasses Prague's illustrious past with pleasant brevity. Sure, the museum holds the expected displays of medieval weaponry and shop signs, but the best exhibit in the Renaissance building is an intricate miniature model of 18th-century Prague. It's fascinating to see Staré Město as it used to be and the Jewish Quarter before its 19th-century face-lift. A reproduction of the original calendar face of the Old Town Hall astrological clock is

also on display, as are a number of documents relating to Prague's Nazi occupation and the assassination of Nazi commander Reinhard Heydrich. The museum is 1 block north of the Florenc metro station.

Na Poříčí 52, Praha 8. © 224-816-773. www.muzeumprahy.cz. Admission 80Kč ($3.35) adults, 30Kč ($1.25) students, free for children under 6; 1Kč (5¢) for children, parents with children, and seniors 1st Thurs each month. Tues–Sun 9am–6pm (to 8pm 1st Thurs each month). Metro: Line B or C to Florenc.

National Technical Museum (Národní technické museum) *Kids*   The Czechs are justifiably proud of their long traditions in industry and technology. Before Communism, this was one of the world's most advanced industrialized countries. At the National Technical Museum it's clear why. The depository holds nearly one million articles, although it can show only about 40,000 at a time. The array of machines, vehicles, instruments, and design documents is displayed in awesome detail. You can see the harbingers of radio and TV technology, the development of mechanization, and the golden age of rail service. (During the Austrian monarchy, velvet-lined cars were standard—only to be replaced by the frayed vinyl upholstery used by today's Czech Rail.)

Kostelní 42, Letná, Praha 7. © 220-399-111. www.ntm.cz. Admission 70Kč ($2.90) adults, 30Kč ($1.25) students, free for children under 6. Tues–Fri 9am–5pm; Sat–Sun 10am–6pm. Tram: 1, 8, 25, or 26 from Hradčanská metro to Letná Park.

4 Churches & Cemeteries
CHURCHES
STARÉ MĚSTO (OLD TOWN)
Bethlehem Chapel (Betlémská kaple)   This is the site where, in the early 15th century, the firebrand Czech Protestant theologian Jan Hus raised the ire of the Catholic hierarchy with sermons critical of the establishment. He was burned at the stake as a heretic in 1415 at Konstanz in present-day Germany and became a martyr for the Czech Protestant and later nationalist cause. A memorial to Hus dominates the center of Old Town Square. The chapel was completed in 1394 and reconstructed in the early 1950s. In the main hall you can still see the original stone floors and the pulpit from where Hus preached; it's now used as a ceremonial hall for Czech national events.

Betlémské nám. 4, Praha 1. © 224-248-595. Admission 40Kč ($1.65) adults, 20Kč (85¢) students, free for children under 6. Apr–Oct daily 10am–6:30pm; Nov–Mar daily 10am–5:30pm. Metro: Line B to Národní třída.

Church of St. Nicholas (Kostel sv. Mikuláše)   At the site of a former Gothic church built by German merchants, this St. Nicholas church was designed in 1735 by the principal architect of Czech baroque, K. I. Dienzenhofer. He's the same Dienzenhofer who designed Prague's other St. Nicholas Church, in Lesser Town (see above). This church isn't nearly as ornate as the other but has a more tumultuous history. The Catholic monastery was closed in 1787, and the church was handed over for use as a concert hall in 1865. The city's Russian Orthodox community began using it in 1871, but in 1920 management was handed to the Protestant Hussites. One notable piece inside is the 19th-century crystal chandelier with glass brought from the town of Harrachov. Concerts are still held here; for details, see "Classical Concerts Around Town," in chapter 10.

Old Town Sq. at Pařížská, Praha 1. © 224-190-994. Free admission, except for occasional concerts. Daily 10am–4pm; Sun Mass at 10:30am, noon, and 3pm. Metro: Line A to Staroměstská.

Týn Church or the Church of Our Lady Before Týn (Kostel paní Marie před Týnem)   Huge, double, square towers with multiple black steeples make this church

Old Town Square's most distinctive landmark. The "Týn" was the fence marking the border of the central marketplace in the 13th century. The church's present configuration was completed mostly in the 1380s, and it became the main church of the Protestant Hussite movement in the 15th century (though the small Bethlehem Chapel in Old Town where Hus preached is the cradle of the Czech Protestant reformation). The original main entrance to the church is blocked from view when you look from Old Town Square because the Habsburg-backed patricians built in front of it with impunity. A massive reconstruction to fortify the aging church is nearing completion; unfortunately, at press time, it was still impossible to see the interior.

Aside from the church's omnipresent lurch over the square and the peculiar way buildings were erected in front of it, it's well known as the final resting place of Danish astronomer Tycho de Brahe, who died in 1601 while serving in the court of Austrian Emperor Rudolf II. Brahe's tombstone bearing his effigy as an explorer of many worlds is behind the church's main pulpit. The brilliant floodlights washing over the front of the church at night cast a mystical glow over the whole of Old Town Square.

Staroměstské nám., Praha 1, entrance from Štupartská. Mass Wed, Thurs, and Fri 6pm; Sat 8am; Sun 9:30am and 9pm. Metro: Line A to Staroměstská.

MALÁ STRANA (LESSER TOWN)
Church of Our Lady Victorious—Holy Child of Prague (Klášter Pražského jezulátka)
This 1613 early baroque church of the Carmelite order is famous throughout Italy and other predominantly Catholic countries for the wax statue of infant Jesus displayed on an altar in the right wing of the church. The Holy Child of Prague was presented to the Carmelites by the Habsburg patron Polyxena of Lobkowicz in 1628 and is revered as a valuable Catholic relic from Spain. Copies of the "Bambino" are sold at the little museum in the church as well as on the Lesser Town streets, angering some of the faithful.

Karmelitská 9, Praha 1. Museum of the Holy Child of Prague. ℭ 257-533-646. Fee admission. Mon–Sat 8:30am–6:30pm; Sun 9:30am–8pm. Metro: Line A to Malostranská.

CEMETERIES
New Jewish Cemetery (Nový židovský hřbitov)
Though it's neither as visually captivating nor as historically important as Prague's Old Jewish Cemetery (p. 114), the ivy-enveloped New Jewish Cemetery is popular because writer Franz Kafka is buried here. To find his grave, enter the cemetery and turn immediately to your right. Go along the wall about 90m (295 ft.) and look down in the first row of graves. There you'll find Kafka's final resting place. If you don't have a yarmulke (skullcap), you must borrow one from the man in the small building at the entrance. He's quite happy to lend one, but don't forget to return it. If you only come to see Kafka, you may find yourself staying longer; the cemetery is a soothing and fascinating place.

Izraelská 1, Praha 3. ℭ 272-241-893. Apr–Sept Sun–Thurs 9am–5pm, Fri 9am–1pm; Oct–Mar Sun–Thurs 9am–4pm, Fri 9am–1pm. Metro: Line A to Želivského.

Olšanské Cemeteries (Olšanské hřbitovy)
Olšanské hřbitovy is the burial ground of some of the city's most prominent former residents, including the first Communist president, Klement Gottwald, and Jan Palach, who burned himself to death in protest of the 1968 Soviet invasion. Olšanské hřbitovy is just on the other side of Jana Želivského Street from the New Jewish Cemetery.

Vinohradská St., Praha 3. Daily dawn–dusk. Metro: Line A to Flora or Želivského.

The Art of Prague's Architecture

Prague's long history, combined with its good fortune in having avoided heavy war damage, makes it wonderful for architecture lovers. Along with the standard must-see castles and palaces comes a bountiful mixture of styles and periods. Buildings and monuments from the Middle Ages to the present are interspersed with one another throughout the city.

The best examples of Romanesque architecture are parts of **Prague Castle**, including St. George's Basilica. In Staré Město you'll see the best examples of the 3-century-long Gothic period: the **Convent of St. Agnes**, Na Františku; the **Old-New Synagogue**, Pařížská třída; **Old Town Hall** and the **Astronomical Clock**, Staroměstské náměstí; **Powder Tower**, Celetná ulice; and **Charles Bridge**. A few Renaissance buildings still stand, including **Golden Lane**, **Malá Strana Town Hall**, and **Pinkas Synagogue** (Široká ulice) in Staré Město.

Many of Prague's best-known structures are pure baroque and rococo, enduring styles that reigned in the 17th and 18th centuries. Buildings on Staroměstské náměstí and Nerudova Street date from this period, as does **St. Nicholas Church**, Malostranské náměstí, in Malá Strana, and the **Loreto Palace**, Loretánské náměstí, in Hradčany.

Renaissance styles made a comeback in the late 19th century. Two neo-Renaissance buildings in particular—the **National Theater**, Národní třída, and the **National Museum**, Václavské náměstí, both in Praha 1, have endured and are among Prague's most identifiable landmarks.

An exciting addition to the architectural lineup is the painstakingly refurbished 1911 Art Nouveau **Municipal House (Obecní dům)** ☆☆ at náměstí Republiky, Praha 1. Every opulent ceiling, sinuous light fixture, curling banister, etched-glass window, and inlaid ceramic wall creates the astonishing atmosphere of hope and accomplishment from the turn of the 20th century. This is Prague's outstanding monument to itself. The music salon, Smetana Hall (home to the Prague Symphony), has a gorgeous atrium roof with stained-glass windows. After World War I, with independence won, the democratic Czechoslovak Republic was declared here by the first National Council (parliament) in 1918. You can arrange private guided tours by calling the building's directors at ✆ **222-002-100** well in advance. The information center is located down a ramp from the ground-floor main entrance.

5 Historic Buildings & Monuments

Education has always occupied an important place in Czech life. Professors at **Charles University**—the city's most prestigious and oldest university, founded in 1348—have been in the political and cultural vanguard, strongly influencing the everyday life of all citizens. During the last 50 years, the university has expanded into some of the city center's largest riverfront buildings, many of which are between Charles Bridge (Karlův most) and Čech's Bridge (Čechův most).

Other excellent examples of whimsical Art Nouveau architecture are the **Hotel Evropa,** on Václavské náměstí, and the main train station, **Hlavní nádraží,** on Wilsonova třída, both in Praha 1.

Prague's finest cubist design, the **House at the Black Mother of God (Dům U Černé Matky boží),** at Celetná and Ovocný trh in Old Town, is worth a look. The building is named for the statuette of the Virgin Mary on its well-restored exterior. It now houses a Museum of Cubism and modern art gallery. You'll also find a full cubist neighborhood of buildings directly under Vyšehrad Park near the right bank of the Vltava.

The city's most unappealing structures are the functional socialist designs built from 1960 until the end of Communism. Examples are the entrance and departure halls of **Hlavní nádraží,** Wilsonova třída, Praha 1; the **Máj department store** (now a British Tesco), Národní třída 26, Praha 1; and the **Kotva department store,** náměstí Republiky, Praha 1.

However, the absolute worst are the prefabricated apartment buildings (*paneláky*) reached by taking metro line C to Chodov or Háje. Built in the 1970s, when buildings grew really huge and dense, each is eight or more stories tall. Today, half of Prague's residents live in *paneláks,* which rim the city.

One postrevolution development—the **Rašín Embankment Building** ⊛, Rašínovo nábřeží at Resslova, Praha 2—continues to fuel the debate about blending traditional architecture with progressive design. Known as the **Dancing Building,** the Prague headquarters of the Dutch insurance group ING opened in 1996.

Co-designed by Canadian-born Frank Gehry, who planned Paris's controversial American Center, the building's method of twisting concrete and steel together had never before been tried in Europe or elsewhere. An abstract Fred Astaire, dusting off his white tie and tails, embraces an eight-story ball-gowned Ginger Rogers for a twirl above the Vltava. The staggered design of the windows gives the structure motion when seen from afar. The only way to get the full effect is from across the river. The kicker is that the building is made out of prefabricated concrete, proving that the Communist *panelák* apartment houses could have been made more imaginatively. Ex-president Havel used to live next door in a modest apartment in the neoclassical building built and owned by his family.

STARÉ MĚSTO (OLD TOWN)

Powder Tower (Prašná brána ["Powder Gate"])   Once part of Staré Město's system of fortifications, the Old Town Powder Tower (as opposed to the Powder Tower in Prague Castle) was built in 1475 as one of the walled city's major gateways. The 42m-tall (138-ft.) tower marks the beginning of the Royal Route, the traditional 1km (half-mile) route along which medieval Bohemian monarchs paraded on their way to being crowned in Prague Castle's St. Vitus Cathedral. It also was the east gate to the Old Town on the road to Kutná Hora. The tower was severely damaged during the Prussian invasion of Prague in 1737.

The present-day name comes from the 18th century, when the development of Nové Město rendered this protective tower obsolete, and it began to serve as a gunpowder storehouse. Early in the 20th century, the tower was the daily meeting place of Franz Kafka and his writer friend Max Brod. On the tower's west side, facing Old Town, you'll see a statue of King Přemysl Otakar II, under which is a bawdy relief depicting a young woman slapping a man who's reaching under her skirt. The remains of the original construction are visible on the first floor above the ground.

Náměstí Republiky, gate to Celetná St., Praha 1. ⓒ 724-063-723. www.pis.cz. Admission 50Kč ($2) adults, 40Kč ($1.65) students, free for children under 6. Apr–Oct daily 10am–6pm. Metro: Line B to Náměstí Republiky.

NOVÉ MĚSTO (NEW TOWN)

Můstek Metro Station   It's not the metro station itself, which is 20-something years old, that warrants an entry here. But descend to Můstek's lower escalators and you'll see the illuminated stone remains of what was once a bridge that connected the fortifications of Prague's Old and New Towns. In Czech, *můstek* means "little bridge," but the ancient span isn't the only medieval remains that modern excavators discovered. Metro workers had to be inoculated when they uncovered viable tuberculosis bacterium, which had lain here dormant, encased in horse excrement, since the Middle Ages.

Na Příkopě, the pedestrian street above Můstek metro station, literally translates as "on the moat," a reminder that the street was built on top of a river that separated the walls of Staré Město and Nové Město. In 1760, it was filled in. The street follows the line of the old fortifications all the way down to the Gothic Powder Tower at náměstí Republiky.

Václavské nám., Praha 1. Metro: Line A.

National Theater (Národní divadlo) 🞳🞳   Lavishly constructed in the late Renaissance style of northern Italy, the gold-crowned National Theater, overlooking the Vltava, is one of Prague's most recognizable landmarks. Completed in 1881, the theater was built to nurture the Czech National Revival Movement—a drive to replace the dominant German culture with homegrown Czech works. To finance construction, small collection boxes with signs promoting the prosperity of a dignified national theater were installed in public places.

Almost immediately upon completion, the building was wrecked by fire and rebuilt, opening in 1883 with the premiere of Bedřich Smetana's opera *Libuše*. The magnificent interior contains an allegorical sculpture about music and busts of Czech theatrical personalities created by some of the country's best-known artists. The motto *"Národ sobě"* ("A Nation to Itself") is written above the stage. Smetana conducted the theater's orchestra here until 1874, when deafness forced him to relinquish his post.

The theater doesn't have daily tours, but tickets for performances are usually available (see chapter 10) and tour events are occasionally scheduled.

Národní třída 2, Praha 1. ⓒ 224-901-668. www.pis.cz. Metro: Line B to Národní třída.

ELSEWHERE IN PRAGUE

Petřín Tower (Rozhledna)   A one-fifth-scale copy of Paris's Eiffel Tower, Prague's Petřín Tower was constructed out of recycled railway track for the 1891 Prague Exhibition. It functioned as the city's primary telecommunications tower until the space-age Žižkovská věž (tower) opened across town. Those who climb the 59m (194 ft.) to the top are treated to striking views, particularly at night.

Petřínské sady, atop Petřín Hill, Praha 1. ✆ **257-320-112.** www.pis.cz. Admission 50Kč ($2) adults, 40Kč ($1.65) students, free for children under 6. Jan–Mar Sat–Sun 10am–5pm; Apr and Sept daily 10am–7pm; May–Aug daily 10am–10pm; Oct daily 10am–6pm; Nov–Dec Sat–Sun 10am–5pm. Tram: 12, 22, or 23 to Újezd, then ride the funicular to the top.

MODERN MEMORIALS

One of the city's most photographed attractions is the colorful graffiti-filled **Lennon Wall,** on Velkopřevorské náměstí. This quiet side street in Malá Strana's Kampa neighborhood near Charles Bridge is across from the French Embassy on the path leading from Kampa Park.

The wall is named after singer John Lennon, whose huge image is spray-painted on the wall's center. Following his 1980 death, Lennon became a hero of freedom, pacifism, and counterculture throughout Eastern Europe, and this monument was born. During Communist rule, the wall's pro-democracy and other slogans were regularly whitewashed, only to be repainted by the faithful. When the new democratically elected government was installed in 1989, it's said that the French ambassador, whose stately offices are directly across from the wall, phoned Prague's mayor and asked that the city refrain from interfering with the monument. Today young locals and visitors continue to flock here, paying homage with flowers and candles. Lennon's picture has been repainted, larger and more angelic. It is now surrounded by graffiti more ridiculous than political.

The 1989 revolution against Communism is modestly remembered at the **Národní Memorial,** Národní 16, under the arches, midway between Václavské náměstí and the National Theater. This marks the spot where hundreds of protesting college students were seriously beaten by riot police on the brutal, icy night of November 17, 1989.

Just 5 years later, only about 100 Czechs showed up to commemorate the fifth anniversary of the Velvet Revolution at the place that became the cradle of the rebellion. Then-President Václav Havel laid flowers at the tiny monument, but all around him were examples of how things have changed. A shiny new red Ferrari with Czech plates streaked past the group and screeched to a halt about a block farther on. Throwing a blistering U-turn, it sped back. The driver, wearing designer sunglasses, stuck his head out to see just a guy and some flowers. Disappointed, he slid back into the car and peeled back down Národní as the police shook their heads and said in awe, "What a car."

On the 10th anniversary of the revolution, Havel invited the last "Cold Warriors"—leaders Bush, Sr.; Thatcher; Kohl; and Gorbachev—to Prague for a walk down "Revolution Lane."

The street has itself become a monument to the country's new capitalism. Where armed police and dogs once lined up outside the rotting Máj department store, people now flock to find bargains at the British-owned Tesco. Fashion boutiques, a plastic surgeon's private office, and sparkling new branches of private banks take spots once occupied by such "businesses" as the Castro Grill at the Cuban Culture Center.

It all obscures a small bronze monument whose peace-sign hands recall the night when Czechoslovakia's bloodless revolution began.

6 Historic Squares

The most celebrated square in the city, **Old Town Square (Staroměstské nám.)** ★★★ is surrounded by baroque buildings and packed with colorful craftspeople, cafes, and entertainers. In ancient days, the site was a major crossroads on central European merchant routes. In its center stands a memorial to Jan Hus, the 15th-century martyr who crusaded against Prague's German-dominated religious and political establishment. It was unveiled in 1915, on the 500th anniversary of Hus's execution. The monument's most compelling features are the dark asymmetry and fluidity of the figures. Take metro line A to Staroměstská. The square and Staré Město are described in more detail in Walking Tour 3 in chapter 8.

Officially dedicated in 1990, **Jan Palach Square (náměstí Jana Palacha),** formerly known as Red Army Square, is named for a 21-year-old philosophy student who set himself on fire on the National Museum steps to protest the 1968 Communist invasion. An estimated 800,000 Praguers attended his funeral march from Staroměstské náměstí to Olšanské Cemeteries (see above). To get to the square, take metro line A to Staroměstská at the Old Town foot of Mánesův Bridge. There is now a pleasant riverside park with benches. Charles University's philosophy department building is on this square; on the lower-left corner of the facade is a memorial to the martyred student: a replica of Palach's death mask.

One of the city's most historic squares, **Wenceslas Square (Václavské nám.)** 🌟🌟 was formerly the horse market (Koňský trh). The once muddy swath between the buildings played host to the country's equine auctioneers. The top of the square, where the National Museum now stands, was the outer wall of the New Town fortifications, bordering the Royal Vineyards. Unfortunately, the city's busiest highway now cuts the museum off from the rest of the square it dominates. Trolleys streamed up and down the square until the early 1980s. Today the half-mile-long boulevard is lined with cinemas, shops, hotels, restaurants, casinos, and porn shops.

The square was given its present name in 1848. The giant equestrian statue of St. Wenceslas on horseback surrounded by four other saints, including his grandmother, St. Ludmila, and St. Adalbert, the 10th-century bishop of Prague, was completed in 1912 by prominent city planner J. V. Myslbek, for whom the new Myslbek shopping center on Na Příkopě was named. The statues' pedestal has become a popular platform for speakers. Actually, the square has thrice been the site of riots and revolutions—in 1848, 1968, and 1989. At the height of the Velvet Revolution, 250,000 to 300,000 Czechs filled the square during one demonstration. Take metro line A or B to Můstek.

Built by Charles IV in 1348, **Charles Square (Karlovo nám.)** once functioned as Prague's primary cattle market. New Town's Town Hall (Novoměstská radnice), which stands on the eastern side, was the site of Prague's First Defenestration—a violent protest sparking the Hussite Wars in the 15th century (see "Beware of Open Windows: The Czech Tradition of Defenestration," earlier in this chapter). Today, Charles Square is a peaceful park in the center of the city, crisscrossed by tramlines and surrounded by buildings and shops. It is the largest square in town. To reach it, take metro line B to Karlovo náměstí.

7 Václav Havel's Prague

Havel's extraordinary life acts as a magnet, drawing to Prague those who are interested in understanding one of the most dominant factors of recent history—the Cold War.

While it is easy to ascribe Havel's valiant struggle to pure altruism and a desperate desire to end totalitarian rule in his homeland, many believe a more intimate force was at work—his inextricable relationship to a beautiful, complex character—not his first wife Olga (to whom he addressed his famous letters from prison), but the city of Prague itself.

To begin to understand Havel (and even close friends say they can't grasp the full depth of his character), you must first try to see Prague in all its complex ironies. Even during the darkest days of Communist rule, Havel remained faithful to the city of his birth, although it would have been much easier to run away—as did many other dissidents and artists—to fame and fortune in the West.

Havel's family roots run deeply in Prague. He was reared in the city's grand palaces and dingy theaters, and received his political education in Prague's smoky cafes and closely observed living rooms. (For more on Havel's background, see below.)

Described below (and on the accompanying map on p. 130) are some of Havel's most notable haunts both before and after 1989. Luckily for those who want to track his footsteps, Havel's Prague is now somewhat more accessible (albeit heavily reconstructed from the prerevolutionary days)—and you won't have to worry about any StB (Communist-era secret agents) watching over your shoulder.

THE HAVEL FAMILY

Havel's father and namesake, a wealthy real estate developer and patron of Prague's newly liberated, post-Austrian Jazz Age, built the **Lucerna Palace** (Štěpánská 61 or Vodičkova 36, Praha 1; metro: Můstek), an early-20th-century pleasure palace, in 1921. This fully enclosed complex of arcades, theaters, cinemas, nightclubs, restaurants, and ballrooms became a popular spot for the city's nouveau riche to congregate. The young Havel spent his earliest years on the Lucerna's polished marble floors until the Communists expropriated his family's holdings after the 1948 putsch. Soon thereafter, the glitter wore off this monument to early Czech capitalism and the Lucerna lost its soul to Party-sanctioned singalongs and propaganda films.

After the fall of Communism and the mass return of nationalized property, the new government gave the Lucerna back to the Havel estate. Unfortunately, this led to an ugly family feud over the division of shares in the palace. Eventually the then-president and his second wife worked out a settlement with younger brother Ivan and his wife, but only after the battle became a daily feature in the tabloid press.

The Lucerna is trying to regain its original grandeur. While today you'll see plenty of wear and tear, it still houses some restaurants and stores (see **Jarmark** and **Botanicus** on p. 97 and 174 respectively). A statue of Havel senior can be seen on the staircase leading to the main **Lucerna movie theater,** where many blockbuster films premier today.

To get to **Barrandov Terrace** you'll need to take one of the tourist boats from the center of Prague and head south on the Vltava (see details of boat tours below). After about half an hour you will pass under the bridge of the superhighway at the southern edge of the city. About a mile farther, look to your right. You will see a creaking remnant of a once-spectacular Art Deco resort tucked into the cliff. This is Barrandov Terrace, another heart-wrenching example of the elder Havel's grandiose plans destroyed by Communist-era squalor.

The flowing white balconies of the Barrandov Terrace were Prague's answer to 1920s Hollywood. Havel's uncle, Miloš Havel, commissioned Jazz Age architect Max Urban to build his dream—a top-notch riverside restaurant and cafe. It was meant to capture the glamour of the films produced at nearby Barrandov Studios, whose productions at the time rivaled Hollywood films in style and panache.

Sadly, Barrandov Terrace, like the Lucerna Palace, became a prime target of Communist expropriation, leading to its neglect and eventual closure. Unlike Lucerna, however, when the property was returned to the Havels after the 1989 revolution, its

Václav Havel's Prague

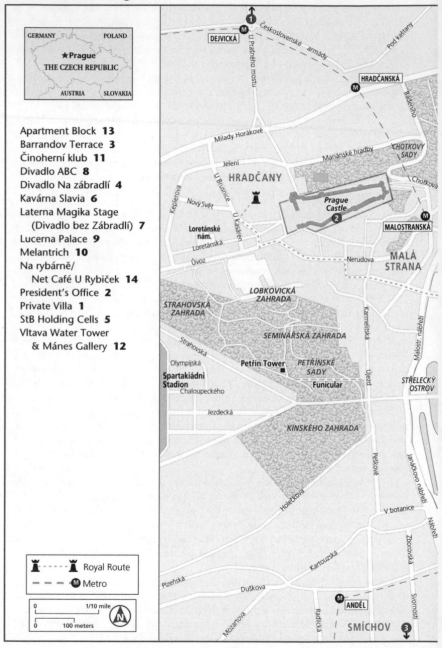

Apartment Block **13**
Barrandov Terrace **3**
Činoherní klub **11**
Divadlo ABC **8**
Divadlo Na zábradlí **4**
Kavárna Slavia **6**
Laterna Magika Stage
  (Divadlo bez Zábradlí) **7**
Lucerna Palace **9**
Melantrich **10**
Na rybárně/
  Net Café U Rybiček **14**
President's Office **2**
Private Villa **1**
StB Holding Cells **5**
Vltava Water Tower
  & Mánes Gallery **12**

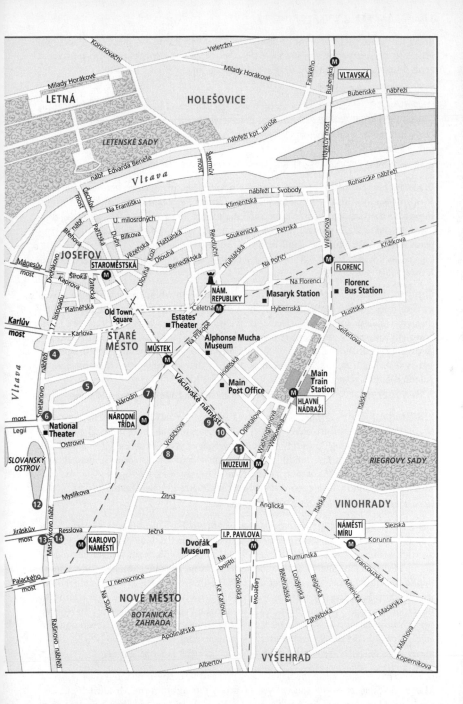

decay had gone past the point of no return and it was left to rot. Security fences prevent any close investigation on foot, but the view of the complex from the river is enough to make you ache for Prague's golden age of the First Republic.

THEATER & POLITICS

Divadlo ABC   Havel's first theater job was as a stagehand here in the late 1950s. This is one of the many intimate theaters in Prague where excitement was found in the spoken word rather than expensive visuals. Czech musicals and dry comedies are still performed here.

Vodičkova 28, Praha 1. © 224-215-943. Tickets cost 90Kč–270Kč ($3.75–$11). Metro: Můstek.

Divadlo Na zábradlí   Havel became the resident playwright here in the early 1960s. It was on this stage that his play *The Garden Party* launched 25 years of subtly subversive dramas, which were to become the subtext of many dissident struggles during the Cold War. At present, dramas (for example, Chekhov's *Ivanov*) are on the program here every evening at 7pm. Performances are in Czech.

Anenské nám. 5, Praha 1. © 222-868-868. Tickets run from 90Kč–250Kč ($3.75–$10). Metro: Staroměstská. Tram: 17 or 18.

Činoherní klub   After the early days of the revolution when Laterna Magika played a major role, the first attempts at forming a true political movement were made in this tiny club theater on a back street near Wenceslas Square. It is here that the Civic Forum (Občanské Fórum) movement took shape under Havel's understated leadership. This small theater, founded in the 1960s by a group of young and progressive actors and directors, has always been popular for its nonconventional performances. Talented Czech actors perform here nightly at 7:30pm.

Ve Smečkách 26, Praha 1. © 296-222-123. Tickets cost 30Kč ($1.25) or 220Kč ($9.15). Metro: Muzeum.

StB Holding Cells   Housed in a former convent, the StB Holding Cells were used by the StB (Communist secret police) to interrogate and hold political prisoners. Havel stayed in room P6 during one of his frequent visits between 1977 and 1989. After the revolution, the holding cells became a spartan but popular hostel with months-long waiting lists of tourists who wanted to stay in Havel's hovel. After its renovation, you can now be a guest of **Pension Unitas/Art Prison Hostel** (p. 73).

Bartolomějská 9, Praha 1. © 224-221-802. Metro: Národní třída.

Laterna Magika Stage (Divadlo bez Zábradlí)   This became Havel's "War Room," where he and a hearty band of artists and intellectuals plotted the peaceful overthrow of the government in late 1989. From this platform, Havel chaired 10 nights of debates among striking actors and artists on how best to rally the masses to their democratic cause. The resignation of the Politburo at the end of November 1989 set off rapturous celebrations in the theater. The remodeled place no longer retains the stench of cigarettes and stale beer nor, unfortunately, the aura of those heady November revolutionary days. Performances in Czech (mostly comedies by Czech and foreign playwrights) take place here every evening at 7pm.

Národní třída 4, Praha 1. © 224-946-436. Tickets cost up to 290Kč ($12). Metro: Národní třída.

Melantrich   Midway up the right side of Wenceslas Square at no. 36 (now the British Marks and Spencer store), you will see a balcony jutting from the Melantrich publishing house. This is where, in late November 1989, Havel made his first appearances in front of the hundreds of thousands who were clamoring for his leadership in a peaceful coup d'état. His mumbling yet stoically defiant speeches solidified his position as the popular choice to guide Czechoslovakia out of the dark days. Soon, Alexander Dubček—leader of 1968's failed attempt to deliver "Socialism with a Human Face" which led to his banishment after the Warsaw Pact invasion—joined Havel along with blacklisted singers and artists to mark the beginning of the end of 4 decades of totalitarian rule.

Václavské nám. 36, Praha 1. Metro: Můstek.

Kavárna Slavia   Of all the Prague pubs, restaurants, and cafes that Havel patronized, this was his most recognized haunt. Its reputation as the hangout of choice for Prague's dissidents and secret police became a staple in Western media accounts of life on this side of the iron curtain.

Smetanovo nábřeží 2, Praha 1. ℂ 224-218-493. Metro: Národní třída.

Vltava Water Tower & Mánes Gallery   Jutting from the quay on the right (east) bank of the Vltava next to Jiráskův Bridge stands this brooding, dark, defunct water tower with a bulbous dome. Inside the dome, secret police agents spent days peering into Havel's meager top-floor flat on the opposite street corner. Havel has spoken often of the ways he used to taunt his hunters during his effective house arrests, and of the suffocation of knowing they were almost always there, watching his comings and goings and those of his guests.

Just below the tower stands an unspectacular building of white boxes, the art gallery and meeting hall **Mánes.** Havel calls this his favorite building in Prague. In a BBC documentary filmed several years after he became president, Havel described his love for this place of art right under his wardens' noses. The Mánes now shows many avant-garde artists who were taboo before the revolution.

Masarykovo nábřeží 250, Praha 1. ℂ 224-930-754. Tram: 17 or 21.

Apartment Block   While standing on the river side of the street from Jiráskův Bridge, look past the Frank Gehry–inspired Dancing Building. Next door you will find a discreet apartment block with a small tilted globe on its roof. The top-floor windows were the focus of secret agents' binoculars from the water tower across the way. This was Havel's base, his small, Bohemian bunker, from where he wrote his subversive essays and plotted his peaceful putsches. Until 1995 he and his wife Olga lived as president and first lady in this relatively tiny place, refusing to accept the accommodations of state at Prague Castle. Later the couple bought a stylish villa in the high-rent district on the west side of town (financed by Havel's royalties and property). They chose to live in one of the castle's residences until the villa was reconstructed.

Rašínovo nábřeží 78, Praha 2. Metro: Karlovo Nám. Tram: 17 or 21.

Na rybárně–Net Café U Rybiček   At this fishmonger around the corner from his dissident-era apartment, Havel spent hours debating politics over a plate of trout and a bottle of tart Czech Frankovka wine. After the revolution, the back room became a shrine to visiting dignitaries and rock stars, who were treated to a down-market "state dinner" and then signed the wall in a bizarre piece of presidential protocol. Among the autographs still found here are Mick Jagger's and Frank Zappa's, two of Havel's favorite rockers.

Gorazdova 17, Praha 2. ℂ 224-918-885. Metro: Karlovo Nám. Tram: 17 or 21.

THE PRESIDENTIAL YEARS

From the baroque balcony at the **President's Office** in Prague Castle (tram no. 22 or 23) that hovers over the courtyard opposite St. Vitus Cathedral in Prague Castle, Havel delivered a stirring inauguration speech following his first investiture on December 29, 1989. To a world transfixed by his unlikely journey from prison to presidential palace, he proclaimed the rebirth of "a humane republic that serves the individual and that therefore holds the hope that the individual will serve it in turn."

Havel's Everyman image was largely destroyed when he moved out of his modest riverside flat and into a **Private Villa** (Dělostřelecká 1, Praha 6; metro: Hradčanská, then tram no. 1, 8, or 18 to U Brusnice stop) in 1995. With this move, Havel returned to the tightly knit circle of wealthy Prague homeowners. Unfortunately, the high walls surrounding the villa make it nearly impossible to have the brief encounters with Havel frequently experienced by visitors to his old home.

8 Parks & Gardens

Havel's Market (Havelský trh), on Havelská ulice, a short street running perpendicular to the main route connecting Staroměstské náměstí with Václavské náměstí, is a great open-air place to shop for picnic supplies. Here you'll find seasonal homegrown fruits and vegetables at inexpensive prices. Vyšehrad (see earlier in this chapter) is my family's favorite place for a picnic. The market is open Monday to Friday from 8am to 6pm.

HRADČANY

The **Royal Garden (Královská zahrada)** ✹ at Prague Castle, Praha 1, once the site of the sovereigns' vineyards, was founded in 1534. Dotted with lemon trees and surrounded by 16th-, 17th-, and 18th-century buildings, the park is consciously and conservatively laid out with abundant shrubbery and fountains. Entered from U Praša ného mostu Street, north of the castle complex, it's open daily from 10am to 6pm in the summer season.

The castle's **Garden on the Ramparts (Zahrada na Valech)** ✹ is on the city-side hill below the castle. Beyond beautifully groomed lawns and sparse shrubbery is a tranquil low-angle view of the castle above and the city below. Enter the garden from the south side of the castle complex, below Hradčanské náměstí. The garden is open daily from 10am to 6pm in the summer season.

In 2000, Prince Charles himself was present when the gardens under Prague Castle towards Malá Strana were reopened after years of cleaning and reconstruction. **Ledeburská, Pálffyovská, Kolowratská,** and **Malá Furstenberská** ✹ are open during summer season daily from 10am to 6pm.

MALÁ STRANA

Looming over Malá Strana, adjacent to Prague Castle, lush green **Petřín Hill (Petřínské sady)** is easily recognizable by the miniature replica of the Eiffel Tower that tops it (p. 138). Gardens and orchards bloom in spring and summer. Throughout the myriad monuments and churches are a mirror maze and an observatory (p. 138). The Hunger Wall, a decaying 6m-high (20-ft.) stone wall that runs up through Petřín to the grounds of Prague Castle, was commissioned by Charles IV in the 1360s as a medieval welfare project designed to provide jobs for Prague's starving poor. Take tram no. 12, 22, or 23 to Újezd.

On Petřín's steep slope, near Malostranské náměstí, is located **Vrtbovská zahrada** 𝒜. Its entrance is through Karmelitská 25, Praha 1 (© **257-531-480;** www.vrtbovska.cz). This is supposed to be the most beautiful terraced garden north of the Alps. It was built in the 18th century's baroque style by architect Kaňka, and Matyas Braun provided some of his sculptures. This very special site was totally neglected during the old regime (it partially served as a playground for a local nursery). Its now relaxing atmosphere has been enjoyed for only a couple of years since then. The garden is open daily April to October from 10am to 6pm. Admission is 40Kč ($1.65) adults, 25Kč ($1) students. Take tram no. 12, 22, or 23 to Malostranské náměsti.

Near the foot of Charles Bridge in Malá Strana, **Kampa Park (Na Kampě)** was named by Spanish soldiers who set up camp here after the Roman Catholics won the Battle of White Mountain in 1620. The park as it is today wasn't formed until the Nazi occupation, when the private gardens of three noble families were joined. It's a fine place for an inner-city picnic, though the lawns are packed in high season.

Part of the excitement of **Waldstein (Wallenstein) Gardens (Valdštejnská zahrada)** at Letenská, Praha 1 (© **257-072-759**) is its location, behind a 9m (30-ft.) wall on the back streets of Malá Strana. Inside, elegant gravel paths dotted with classical bronze statues and gurgling fountains fan out in every direction. Laid out in the 17th century, the baroque park was the garden of Gen. Albrecht Waldstein (or Wallenstein; 1581–1634), commander of the Roman Catholic armies during the Thirty Years' War. These gardens are the backyards of Waldstein's Palace—Prague's largest—which replaced 23 houses, three gardens, and the municipal brick kiln. The gardens are open March to October, daily from 10am to 6pm.

ELSEWHERE IN PRAGUE

The plain above the western side of the Vltava north of Prague Castle is a densely tree-covered swath, maintained as a park since 1858. **Letná Park (Letenské sady)** provides many quiet spaces for a picnic, and a summer beer garden at the north end serves up brew with a view. The garden is connected to two restaurants in a recently renewed, 19th-century, neo-Renaissance château (Letenský zámeček), where you can get a pub-style meal or formal dinner. Take tram no. 1, 8, 25, or 26 from Hradčanská metro station. Farther north is the massive nature reserve **Stromovka** (metro: Nádraží Holešovice, then tram no. 5 or 17). Acres of densely tree-lined paths, mostly flat and paved, comprise a shaded set of corridors for long strolls, jogging, and even in-line skating.

My favorite inner-city getaway is **Vyšehrad Park** 𝒜 above the Vltava south of the city center. This 1,000-year-old citadel encloses a peaceful set of gardens, playgrounds, footpaths, and the national cemetery next to the twin-towered Church of Sts. Peter and Paul, reconstructed from 1885 to 1887. The park provides a fantastic wide-angle view of the whole city. Take metro line C to Vyšehrad or tram no. 3 or 16 to Výtoň. The park is open at all times.

9 Prague with Kids

Traveling with children can be an exhausting experience, if you don't plan ahead. Prague offers many options, including museums, theaters, cinemas, and many parks with playgrounds. If your brood gets tired of walking, take in a tram ride. The kids will quickly forget about sore legs. Also, the Vltava River offers the possibility of exploring the city from yet another angle. Below are some places to take your family to make visiting Prague enjoyable.

Prague with Kids

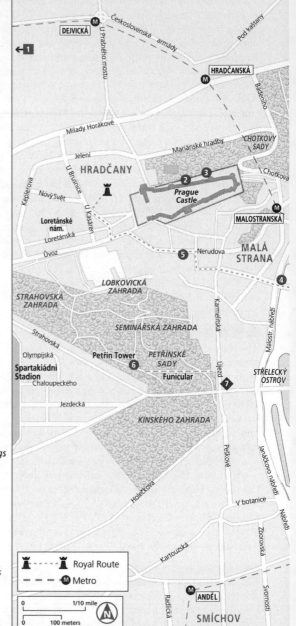

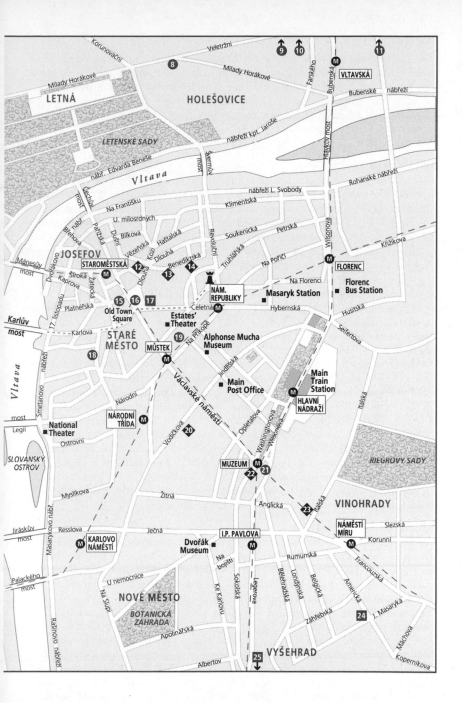

ON HRADČANY

The Toy Museum (Museum hraček) (© 224-372-294; www.barbiemuseum.cz), situated within the complex of Prague Castle, at Jiřská 4, is a place to come with your family to see and feel the nostalgia of the past. This is the world's second-largest exposition of toys, where you can find everything from pieces dating back to ancient Greece up to a collection of the most popular toys of our time. It is open daily from 9:30am to 5:30pm. Admission is 60Kč ($2.50) adults, 30Kč ($1.25) students, free for children under 6.

ON PETŘÍN HILL

Kids will enjoy the funicular ride to the top of Petřín Hill, capped by the **Petřín Tower,** a miniature replica of the Eiffel Tower. Once there, look for the **Labyrinth (Bludiště)** (© 257-315-212; www.pis.cz), a mirror maze that you walk through. Like the tower replica, the Labyrinth was built for the 1891 Prague Exhibition, an expo that highlighted the beauty and accomplishments of Bohemia and Moravia.

Inside the Labyrinth is a gigantic painting/installation depicting the battle between Praguers and Swedes on the Charles Bridge in 1648, a commemoration of the fighting that ended the Thirty Years' War. In 1892, the building's other historic exhibits were replaced with mirrors, turning the Labyrinth into the fun house it is today. It's open April and September daily from 10am to 7pm; May to August daily from 10am to 10pm; October daily from 10am to 6pm; and November to March Saturday and Sunday from 10am to 5pm. Admission is 50Kč ($2) for adults and 40Kč ($1.65) for children above 10 years, 10Kč (40¢) children under 10.

Also in the park is the **Štefánik Observatory** (© 257-320-540; www.observatory.cz), built in 1930 expressly for public stargazing through a 90-year-old telescope. It is open April to August Tuesday to Friday from 2 to 7pm and 9 to 11pm, and Saturday and Sunday from 10am to noon, 2 to 7pm, and 9 to 11pm; September Tuesday to Friday 2 to 6pm and 8 to 10pm, Saturday and Sunday 10am to noon, 2 to 6pm, and 8 to 10pm; March and October Tuesday to Friday 7 to 9pm, Saturday and Sunday 10am to noon, 2 to 6pm, and 7 to 9pm; January, February, November, and December Tuesday to Friday 6 to 8pm, Saturday and Sunday 10am to noon and 2 to 8pm. Admission is 30Kč ($1.25) for adults and 20Kč (85¢) for children.

The funicular departs from a small house in the park just above the middle of Újezd in Malá Strana; tram no. 12, 22, or 23 will take you to Újezd.

ELSEWHERE IN PRAGUE

Budding astronomers can try to catch the stars at the **Planetárium** in Stromovka Park, Královská obora, Praha 7 (© 233-376-452; www.planetarium.cz). There are shows daily under the dark dome, including one in which highlighted constellations are set to music and another that displays that night sky. The shows are in Czech, but the sky is still fun to watch. To reach the planetarium, take tram no. 1, 12, 14, 15, or 17 to Výstaviště and walk through the park to your left about 315m (1,033 ft.). Admission is from 40Kč ($1.65) to 120Kč ($5). It's open Monday to Thursday from 8:30am to noon and from 1pm until the end of the last program at 8pm. Saturday and Sunday hours are from 9:30am to noon and from 1pm until the end of the evening program (8pm).

In the **Výstaviště** fairgrounds adjacent to Stromovka Park is **Křižík's Fountain (Křižíkova fontána).** A massive system of water spigots spout tall and delicate streams of color-lit water in a spectacular light show set to recorded classical and popular music. Small children are especially fascinated. There's also a small amusement park on the fairgrounds. The water/music program (© **220-103-280;** www.krizikova fontana.cz) runs April to October from 7 to 11pm, and in the summer it's 8 to 11pm. Admission is 180Kč ($7.50), free for children under 6. Take tram no. 1, 12, 14, 15, or 17 to Výstaviště.

In the same complex—the Výstaviště fairgrounds—is located a new attraction called **Sea World (Mořský svět)** (© **220-103-275;** www.morsky-svet.cz). This permanent exhibition of sea fish and animals as well as simulations of the underwater world appeals to children and adults. Sea World is open daily 10am to 7pm and tickets cost 120Kč ($5) adults, 70Kč ($2.90) children. Take tram no. 1, 12, 14, 15, or 17 to Výstaviště.

If you are visiting Prague with kids, leaving the city center for a short trip makes for a good break. Try a trip to the **Prague Zoo,** which is situated in Prague 7-Trója, U Trojského zámku 120 (© **296-112-111;** www.zoopraha.cz). Take bus no. 112 from the last stop on the C line, Nádraží Holešovice, all the way to the zoo park. It is open April to October daily 9am to 6pm; June to August 9am to 7pm; March 9am to 5pm; January, February, November, and December 9am to 4pm. On weekends the place is packed with Praguers; it's better to plan the trip on a weekday. A family ticket for 1 day costs 270Kč ($11) from April to September, 200Kč ($8.30) from October to March.

The **Museum of Children's Drawings** is situated in Dům U Zelené Žáby at U Radnice 13/8, Praha 1 (© **224-234-482;** www.muzeumuzaby.cz). Close to Old Town Square, this reconstructed house shows various children's artwork. On Sunday, this family-friendly place becomes a hands-on experience, allowing young visitors to create their own masterpieces. Admission fee is 40Kč ($1.65) adults, 20Kč (85¢) children. It's open Tuesday through Sunday from 1 to 6pm.

10 Sightseeing Options

BUS TOURS

Prague streets can often become gridlocked, making any tour by car or bus frustrating. But if you want to take a guided English-language bus tour, among the best are those given by **Prague Sightseeing Tours,** Klimentská 52, Praha 1 (© **222-314-655;** www.pstours.cz). Its 3½-hour Grand City Tour leaves April to October, daily at 9:30am and 2pm (only 9:30am during winter), from the company's bus stop at náměstí Republiky. The tour costs 660Kč ($28) adults, 590Kč ($25) students, 330Kč ($14) children.

Better for the kids is the green, open-air, electric **Ekoexpres** (an electric bus in the shape of a train) (© **222-517-741;** www.ekoexpres.cz) that usually leaves hourly from behind the Jan Hus monument on Old Town Square. An hour's drive around the tourist areas of Old Town and up the hill to Prague Castle with a recorded narration in several languages costs 250Kč ($10) for adults and teenagers. Children up to age 12 travel free with their parents.

CRUISE-SHIP TOURS

Tourist cruise ships are the only commercial vessels allowed to pass through the city. This is an enjoyable, relaxing way to see Prague.

Evropská vodní doprava (© **224-810-030;** www.evd.cz), with a four-ship fleet, offers the most interesting sightseeing excursions. From April to October, several tours, including some serving decent inexpensive meals, disembark from Čechův, most at the northern turn of the Vltava, and sail past all the key riverside sights. A daily lunch tour with a smorgasbord and traditional Czech music leaves at noon, travels to the south end of the city, and returns by 2pm. The price, including meal, is 640Kč ($26). A 1-hour tour, without meal, sails to Charles Bridge and back, leaving every hour from 10am to 6pm. It costs 220Kč ($9.10). A 2-hour tour, without meal, leaves at 3pm and costs 350Kč ($15). A dinner cruise to the south end of town leaves at 7pm and returns by 10pm. The price, including meal, is 740Kč ($30) for adults, 500Kč ($20) for children.

Pražská paroplavba (© 224-931 013; www.paroplavba.cz) offers similar tours on the Vltava, but you can also take their boat to Prague Zoo in Troja, which the kids appreciate. It leaves daily at 9:30am, 12:30pm, and 3:30pm from their port at Rašínovo nábřeží, between the Palackého and Jiráskův bridge. The 75-minute trip costs 90Kč ($3.75) adults, 60Kč ($2.50) children above 6.

RENTING A ROWBOAT

Many people rent rowboats and paddleboats on the Vltava, which is free from commercial boat traffic. The remarkably romantic (if not sparkling clean) river slowly snakes through the middle of town and gleams beneath the city's spires.

Rent-A-Boat "Slovanka," on Slovanský ostrov (Slavic Island), is the only company at press time that offers lanterns for evening jaunts. This is an extremely romantic time to row, when the amber lights of the city flicker above you. The docks are at the bottom of the steps on the small island 2 blocks south of the National Theater. Enter from just behind the theater. Rowboat rates are 60Kč ($2.50) per hour during daylight for up to four people, or 80Kč ($3.35) per hour with lanterns after dark. Paddleboats are 80Kč ($3.35) per hour. Boats are available March to October (sometimes in Nov if it's pleasant) from 10am to 11pm or even midnight, weather permitting.

Moments An Old-Fashioned Tram Ride

Prague has had a system of tramlines since horses pulled the cars in the mid–18th century. The Communist-era tram cars aren't very attractive, and the new futuristic designs are built for efficiency rather than charm. You have to go back in time to have fun in a Prague tram . . . and you can, thanks to the **Historic Tram Tour (Elektrické dráhy DP)**, Patočkova 4, Praha 6 (© **296-124-902;** fax 296-124-901; www.dpp.cz).

If you send a fax with details 1 day ahead, the city transport department will arrange a private tour using one of the 19th-century wooden tram cars that actually traveled on regular lines through Prague. Up to 24 people can fit in one car, which sports wood-planked floors, cast-iron conductors' levers, and the "ching-ching" of a proper tram bell. The ride costs 3,840Kč ($160) per hour. Up to 60 people can fit into a double car for 5,440Kč ($226) per hour. You can also order a cold smorgasbord with coffee, beer, or champagne; a waiter to serve it; and an accordion player if you wish. You can choose the route the tram takes—the no. 22 route is best.

WALKING TOURS

Sylvia Wittmann's tour company, **Wittmann Tours,** Mánesova 8, Praha 2 (*©* **222-252-472;** www.wittmann-tours.com), offers daily walks around Prague's compact Jewish Quarter. A thousand years of history are discussed during the 3-hour stroll. From May to October, tours led by an English-speaking guide depart Sunday to Friday from Pařížská 28 at 10:30am and 2pm. From March 15 to April, and from November to December, tours depart at 10:30am. The tour's cost, including entrance fees to sights, is 630Kč ($26) for adults and 500Kč ($20) for students, free for children under 6 years. Wittmann Tours also offers a bus tour to the Terezín concentration camp costing 1,150Kč ($48) for adults, 1,000Kč ($41) for students, free for children under 10. The bus leaves from the same spot on Pařížská daily at 10am from May to October. March 15 through April, and November through December, the tour is available on Tuesday, Thursday, Saturday, and Sunday only. Make an advance reservation online or by calling the office. See chapter 11 for more on Terezín.

The group called **City Walks** (*©* **222-244-531;** www.praguewalkingtours.com) organizes guided walks around the city and visits of its main as well as lesser-known attractions. With them you will discover some of Prague's many secrets and mysteries. Groups leave daily from a meeting point on the Old Town Square; tickets are available on the spot from the guide. Each walk costs 300Kč ($12) adults, 250Kč ($10) students. A special "All in One/Insider Tour" costs 450Kč ($19) adults, 350Kč ($15) students, free for children under 6. The meeting point for this one is at the horse statue on Václavské náměstí.

BY PLANE

Točná Airport (*©* **241-773-454**) organizes short charter sightseeing flights from a little airstrip on the edge of Prague. The days and times are negotiable, but you have to call 2 days ahead to set up a flight. For example, an 18-minute flight above Karlštejn Castle and back costs 1,890Kč ($68) per person. Each flight can carry up to three passengers.

To get to the airport, take the metro to Kačerov, then bus no. 205 to the last stop, Komořany, and walk 10 minutes through the forest.

BY BALLOON

Točná Airport (*©* **241-773-454**) offers 1-hour flights over Prague and its surroundings in a balloon—weather permitting! The trip costs 6,300Kč ($262) per person. Call *©* **604-320-044** for a reservation and details.

Also, with **Ballooning CZ,** Na Vrcholu 7, Praha 3 (*©* **222-783-995** or 603-337-005; www.ballooning.cz), you can fly like a bird. An hour in a balloon will cost you 4,700Kč ($195) Monday to Friday or 5,200Kč ($216) on weekends. The take-off is usually from Konopiště, so your trip there can be easily combined with a visit to Konopiště Castle.

11 Staying Active

ACTIVITIES

BIKING   Central European Adventure Tours, Jáchymova 4, Praha 1 (*©*/fax **222-328-879;** http://cea51.tripod.com), rents touring bikes and arranges whatever transport you need for them. The best biking is outside Prague, on the tertiary roads and paved paths in the provinces. They will suggest routes and provide maps. A 1-day guided biking trip around Karlštejn Castle and Koněpruské Caves costs 680Kč ($28). Call ahead to make arrangements. Tickets and information are also available at the PIS office, Na Příkopě 20, Praha 1.

GOLF Czechs are rediscovering golf on the new tournament-caliber course with a world-class view at the **Praha Karlštejn Golf Club,** 30 minutes south of Prague. For details and directions, see chapter 11. You can improve your game during cold weather at the **Erpet Golf Center,** Strakonická 510, Praha 5 (© **257-321-177;** www.erpet.cz). Opened in 1994, the renovated innards of a Communist-era sports hall now has a tropical setting of driving platforms, with pitching and putting greens on Astroturf and interactive video simulators. It's open daily from 8am to 11pm. Take metro line B to Smíchovské nádraží. The price is 300Kč ($12) per hour, including the use of a well-equipped fitness center.

HEALTH & FITNESS CLUBS On the 25th floor of the Corinthia Towers Hotel, Kongresová 1, Praha 4, the **Level 25 Health and Fitness Centrum** (© **261-191-326**) provides weight machines, free weights, exercise bikes, step machines, a small pool, a sauna, and a solarium. The modern facility also offers tanning beds, squash courts, a whirlpool, and massages. It's open to nonguests, but you need to reserve in advance by phone. A 1-day pass is 560Kč ($23)

Daily 10am to 4pm. Squash courts can be rented for 500Kč ($20) per hour. The club is open Monday to Friday from 7am to 10:30pm and Saturday and Sunday from 8am to 10:30pm. Take metro line C to Vyšehrad.

The **Erpet Golf Center** (Fitness Center), Strakonická 510, Praha 5 (© **257-321-177;** www.erpet.cz), has modern fitness machines, free weights, electronic rowers, and treadmills. There's also a relaxation center, with a dry sauna and a co-ed whirlpool that's usually open to the public. Use of the fitness and relaxation centers costs 300Kč ($12) for 3 hours. It's open Thursday through Tuesday from 9am to 11pm, Wednesday from 9am to 9pm. Take metro line B to Smíchovské nádraží.

JOGGING Prague's sometimes thick smog makes jogging more like smoking, but on clear days—and there are many in summer—the air is bearable. For the most scenic run, jog on the paths atop the **Vyšehrad citadel,** accessible by tram no. 3 or 16 from Karlovo náměstí. The parks at Kampa and Letná are also good places to run. The paths crisscrossing Petřín Hill offer a challenging uphill route. The best no-traffic, long-distance runs—flat, long, and mostly tree-lined—are found at **Stromovka Park.**

If you want to run through central Prague, use the traffic-restricted walking zones as often as you can. For an approximately 2.5km (1.5-mile) circuit, start at Můstek at the end of Wenceslas Square, run down Na Příkopě through the Powder Tower (Prašná brána) to Celetná Street all the way to Old Town Square, run around the Hus monument, run back to Železná Street past the Estates' Theater on to Rytířská Street, and run back to Můstek. This route is virtually free of cars, but your feet will be pounding the bricks. Try running in early morning or late evening before the crowds block your way.

SWIMMING Summer doesn't last long in Prague, and when it arrives, many city dwellers are only too happy to cool off in one of the city's many pools. In addition to the hotel pools listed in chapter 5, there's the **Džbán Reservoir,** in the Šárka nature reserve, Praha 6. Džbán is fronted by a grassy "beach" that can—and often does—accommodate hundreds of bathers. There's a special section for nude swimming and

Moments **The Prague International Marathon**

"The narrow streets in the first two miles enforce a leisurely early pace, and the violinists on the Charles Bridge are the first live musicians along the way. After that, jazz, funk, samba, reggae and classical music groups help the runners as the miles begin to take their toll."

—George A. Hirsch, Publisher, *Runner's World*

The **Prague International Marathon (PIM),** Prague's premier annual civic-pride event, has grown by leaps and bounds since it was first run in 1995. The 42.2km (26.2-mile) race attracted just under 1,000 runners in its first year, but in 2004 they had more than 8,000 runners from 60 countries. That number combined with the **Fun Run,** a 6km (4-mile) race for families, totals about 40,000 people or even more.

Many come to take advantage of the unique chance to run through Prague's cobblestone streets without having to dodge *Škodas* and trams. Others, especially nonrunners, love the festive atmosphere in Old Town Square, the music groups that line the race routes, and, of course, the great Czech beer that flows across the finish line.

My husband, John, a consummate couch potato, was so inspired by the event that he was motivated to train just enough to run the 1999 marathon (although he missed his goal of breaking 4 hr. and has yet to attempt it again).

The marathon route takes runners through the very heart of old Prague. The final stage of the race winds through the quirky streets of Old Town and eventually ends back at Old Town Square. Public transport on race day is free for participants who show their start number. A free massage and plenty of affordable *pivo* (beer) is available in the finish area, along with plenty of other energy-restoring liquids.

For those who would like to give it a shot, the race takes place usually on the third Sunday in May, starting at 9am in Old Town Square (Staroměstské nám.). Marathoners can register for the race in person at the **PIM EXPO,** at Záhořanského 3, Praha 2. You can also register in advance by phone or online (© **224-919-209;** www.pim.cz). The registration fee for the full marathon is 1,900Kč ($79); for family fun runs, the cost is about 300Kč ($12). All marathon runners must get their timing chip (shorter distances are not officially timed).

sunbathing. To reach Šárka, take tram no. 26 from the Dejvická metro station. If you prefer a swimming pool or the weather doesn't cooperate, visit one of Prague's best aqua centers. The **Letňany Lagoon,** Tupolevova 665, Praha 9-Letňany (© **283-921-799;** www.letnanylagoon.cz) has got a full-length pool as well as Jacuzzi and toboggan, which is a good fun for the whole family. You can also get a little refreshment and a drink while around the pool. The Lagoon is open Monday, Wednesday, and Friday 6 to 9am and noon to 10pm; Tuesday 7 to 9am and 4 to 10pm; Thursday 7 to 9am and noon to 10pm; Saturday and Sunday 9am to 10pm. Admission is 140Kč ($5.85) adult, 70Kč ($2.90) children for 2 hours. To get there take bus no. 210 from metro line C Holešovice to the Tupolevova stop at Letňany.

TENNIS At the **First Czech Lawn Tennis Club Praha** at Štvanice Island (© **222-316-317;** www.cltk.cz), you can play on the courts where Martina Navrátilová and Ivan Lendl trained. The rental rate is from 340Kč ($14) to 620Kč ($26) per hour per court. It's best to make a reservation if the weather's nice and for the morning (off-peak) hours.

SPECTATOR SPORTS

For information on games, tickets, and times for hockey and soccer games, check the *Prague Post* sports section. Sports tickets for major events can be bought from **Ticketpro** (www.ticketpro.cz).

ICE HOCKEY Although Czech stars like Jaromír Jágr and Dominik Hašek have left home to play in the NHL, Czech hockey still has a lot of up-and-comers. Prague's team **Sparta Praha** plays their national rivals from mid-September to April at **T-Mobile Arena,** Za elektrárnou 419, Praha 7 (© **266-724-454;** www.hcsparta.cz). Admission is 100Kč to 160Kč ($4.15–$6.65). Take metro line C to Holešovice and then tram no. 1, 12, 15, or 25 to Výstaviště.

Sazka Arena, Ocelářská 460, Praha 9 (© **266-121-122**), the newest and most modern sports arena in Europe, has been christened by hosting the Ice-Hockey World Championship in 2004. This multipurpose venue for up to 18,000 spectators offers mainly ice-hockey games of local hockey team **HC Slavia,** but serves for cultural, social, and other sports events throughout the year as well. Check www.sazkaticket.cz for program and tickets. Take tram no. 3 to the Sazka Arena stop.

SOCCER **AC Sparta Praha,** the top local soccer team, has a fanatical following, and games draw rowdy crowds to **Toyota Arena,** Milady Horákové 98, Praha 7 (© **296-111-400;** www.sparta.cz). Tickets for big matches often sell out long before game time, but seats are usually available up to the last moment for lesser matches. Game tickets are usually 50Kč to 230Kč ($2–$9.60) for a domestic league game, 450Kč to 1,600Kč ($19–$66) for an international match. Take metro line A to Hradčanská and then take tram no. 1, 8, 25, or 26 to the stadium.

8

Strolling Around Prague

Forget bus tours and taxis—walking is really the only way to explore Prague. Most of the oldest areas are walking zones with limited motor traffic. It's best to wear very comfortable, preferably flat, shoes. The crevasses between the bricks in the street have been known to eat stiletto heels. You might want to get in shape for all this walking before you leave home.

Below are some recommended routes, but don't worry about following the maps too closely—getting lost among the twisting narrow streets is also a wonderful way to discover Prague. Let the turns take you where they may; they usually lead to something memorable.

WALKING TOUR 1	CHARLES BRIDGE & MALÁ STRANA (LESSER TOWN)

Start:	Old Town Bridge Tower (Staroměstská mostecká věž).
Finish:	Church of St. Nicholas (Kostel sv. Mikuláše).
Time:	About 3 to 4 hours.
Best Times:	Early morning or around sunset, when crowds are thinner and the shadows most mysterious.
Worst Time:	Mid-afternoon, when the bridge is packed.

Dating from the 14th century, Charles Bridge is Prague's most celebrated structure. As the primary link between Staré Město and the castle, it has always figured prominently in the city's commercial and military history. For most of its 600 years, the 510m-long (1,673-ft.) span has been a pedestrian promenade, as it is today.

The first sculpture, St. John of Nepomuk, was placed upon the bridge in 1683. It was such a hit that the church commissioned another 21 statues, which were created between 1698 and 1713. Since then the number has increased to 30. The locations of each statue are shown on the accompanying map.

As you stand in the shadow of the tower on the Old Town side of the bridge, first turn to your right, where you'll find an 1848 statue in tribute to Charles IV, who commissioned the bridge's construction between Prague's oldest quarters. Now walk toward the bridge entrance straight ahead, but first look up at the:

❶ Old Town Bridge Tower (Staroměstská mostecká věž)
This richly ornate 1357 design was made for Charles IV by Peter Parléř, the architect who drafted the Gothic plans for St. Vitus Cathedral. The original east side of the tower remains pristine, with coats of arms of the Bohemian king and Holy

Tips Organized "City Walks"

Nine thematic walking tours are on the menu of a company called **City Walks**. It's run by experienced English-speaking guides, who will help you discover Prague, its past and present, from different perspectives. To find out more about the tours, see p. 141, call © **222-244-531**, or go to www.praguewalking tours.com.

Roman Empire. Shields also depict each territory under the auspices of the Bohemian crown at that time.

Above the east-side arch, seated to the right of the standing statue of St. Vitus, is Charles himself, and on the left is a statue of his ill-fated son, Wenceslas IV (Václav IV), who lost the crown of the empire.

The tower's western side was severely damaged in a battle against invading Swedish troops in 1357. During the Thirty Years' War, the heads of 12 anti-Habsburg Protestants were hung for public viewing from iron baskets on the tower.

The observation platform inside the tower has been reopened.

As you pass through the archway, the first statue on the right is of the:

❷ Madonna

She is attending to a kneeling **St. Bernard,** flanked by cherubs. Like most of the statues on the bridge, this is a copy; the originals were removed to protect them from weather-related deterioration.

With your back to the Madonna statue, directly across the bridge is a statue of:

❸ St. Ives

He is the patron saint of lawyers and is depicted as promising to help a person who petitioned him. **Justice,** with a sword on his right, is also portrayed. If you see his outstretched hand holding a glass of beer, you'll know that Prague's law students have just completed their finals.

Cross back again and continue to do so after you view each statue.

❹ St. Dominic & St. Thomas Aquinas

These two figures are shown receiving a rosary from the hands of the Madonna. Below the Madonna are a cloud-enshrouded globe and a dog with a torch in its jaws, the symbol of the Dominican order.

❺ St. Barbara, St. Margaret & St. Elizabeth

These statues were sculpted by two brothers who worked under the watchful eye of their father, Jan Brokoff, who signed the work as a whole. Franz Kafka has written about the finely sculpted hands of St. Barbara, the patron saint of miners, situated in the center of the monument. To art experts, however, the sculpture of St. Elizabeth (on the left) is the most artistically valuable figure in this group.

❻ The Bronze Crucifix

It was produced in Dresden, Germany, and was bought by the Prague magistrate and placed on Charles Bridge in 1657. The statue's gilded Hebrew inscription, which translates as "holy, holy, holy God," is believed to have been paid for with money extorted from an unknown Jew who had mocked a wooden crucifix that formerly stood on this site.

❼ The Lamenting of Christ

This sculpture depicts Jesus lying in the Virgin Mary's lap, with St. John in the center and Mary Magdalene on the right. Executions were regularly held on this site during the Middle Ages.

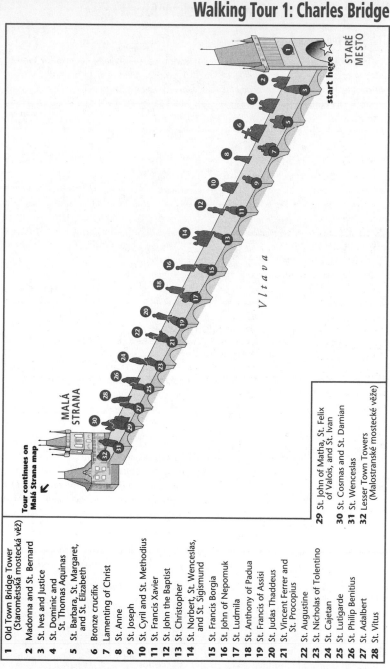

STARÉ
MĚSTO

start here

MALÁ
STRANA

Tour continues on
Malá Strana map

V l t a v a

1 Old Town Bridge Tower
   (Staroměstská mostecká věž)
2 Madonna and St. Bernard
3 St. Ives and Justice
4 St. Dominic and
   St. Thomas Aquinas
5 St. Barbara, St. Margaret,
   and St. Elizabeth
6 Bronze crucifix
7 Lamenting of Christ
8 St. Anne
9 St. Joseph
10 St. Cyril and St. Methodius
11 St. Francis Xavier
12 St. John the Baptist
13 St. Christopher
14 St. Norbert, St. Wenceslas,
   and St. Sigismund
15 St. Francis Borgia
16 St. John of Nepomuk
17 St. Ludmila
18 St. Anthony of Padua
19 St. Francis of Assisi
20 St. Judas Thaddeus
21 St. Vincent Ferrer and
   St. Procopius
22 St. Augustine
23 St. Nicholas of Tolentino
24 St. Cajetan
25 St. Lutigarde
26 St. Philip Benitius
27 St. Adalbert
28 St. Vitus
29 St. John of Matha, St. Felix
   of Valois, and St. Ivan
30 St. Cosmas and St. Damian
31 St. Wenceslas
32 Lesser Town Towers
   (Malostranské mostecké věže)

Walking Tour 1: Malá Strana (Lesser Town)

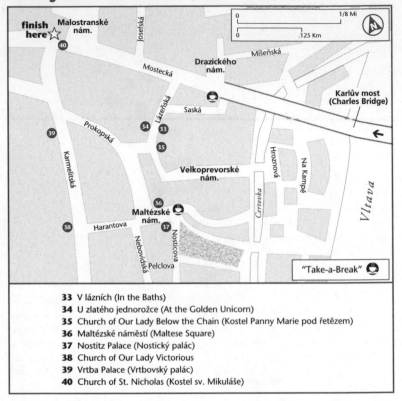

33 V lázních (In the Baths)
34 U zlatého jednorožce (At the Golden Unicorn)
35 Church of Our Lady Below the Chain (Kostel Panny Marie pod řetězem)
36 Maltézské náměstí (Maltese Square)
37 Nostitz Palace (Nostický palác)
38 Church of Our Lady Victorious
39 Vrtba Palace (Vrtbovský palác)
40 Church of St. Nicholas (Kostel sv. Mikuláše)

❽ St. Anne

The Virgin Mary's mother holds the baby Jesus as the child embraces the globe in this statue from 1707.

❾ St. Joseph

This statue of Joseph with Jesus dates from 1854 and was put here to replace another that was destroyed by gunfire 6 years earlier by anti-Habsburg rioters.

❿ St. Cyril & St. Methodius

These Catholic missionaries are credited with introducing Christianity to the Slavs.

⓫ St. Francis Xavier

This 18th-century cofounder of the Jesuit order is depicted carrying four pagan princes on his shoulders—an Indian, a Tartar, a Chinese, and a Moor—symbolizing the cultures targeted for proselytizing. This is widely regarded as one of the most outstanding Czech baroque sculptural works.

⓬ St. John the Baptist

The saint is depicted here with a cross and a shell, symbols of baptism.

⓭ St. Christopher

The patron saint of raftsmen is shown carrying baby Jesus on his shoulder. The statue stands on the site of the original bridge watch-house, which collapsed into the river along with several soldiers during the Great Flood of 1784.

⑭ St. Norbert, St. Wenceslas & St. Sigismund

All three are patron saints of Bohemian provinces.

⑮ St. Francis Borgia

He was a Jesuit general and is depicted with two angels holding a painting of the Madonna. Look on the lower part of the sculpture's pedestal, where you'll see the three symbols of the saint's life: a helmet, a ducal crown, and a cardinal's hat.

⑯ St. John of Nepomuk

He was thrown to his death in chains from this bridge, and this, the oldest sculpture on the span, was placed here to commemorate him. The bronze figure, sporting a gold-leaf halo, was completed in 1683. The bridge's sole bronze statue, St. John is now green with age and worn from years of being touched for good luck.

⑰ St. Ludmila

She points to a Bible from which St. Wenceslas is learning to read. In her left hand, St. Ludmila holds the veil with which she was suffocated. The statue's relief depicts the murder of St. Wenceslas.

⑱ St. Anthony of Padua

Dedicated in 1707, this statue depicts the preacher with baby Jesus and a lily. The relief is designed around a motif inspired by the saint's life.

⑲ St. Francis of Assisi

The first Roman Catholic martyr to be incorporated into the Bohemian liturgy, the contemplative saint is shown here between two angels.

⑳ St. Judas Thaddeus

He is depicted holding both the Gospel and the club with which he was fatally beaten.

㉑ St. Vincent Ferrer

He is shown boasting to **St. Procopius** of his many conversions: 8,000 Muslims and 25,000 Jews.

㉒ St. Augustine

Holding a burning heart and walking on "heretical" books, this statue of St. Augustine is a 1974 copy of a 1708 work. On the pedestal is the emblem of the Augustinians.

㉓ St. Nicholas of Tolentino

He is depicted as handing out bread to the poor. Behind him is a house with a Madonna, a mangle, and a lantern on its top-floor balcony. Walk quickly. Legend holds that if the lantern goes out while you pass by the statue, you'll die within the year.

㉔ St. Cajetan

The saint stands here in front of a column of cherubs while holding a sacred heart. Behind the statue, a triangle symbolizes the Holy Trinity.

㉕ St. Lutigarde

This figure was created in 1710 by 26-year-old M. B. Braun, and it is widely considered to be the most valuable sculpture on Charles Bridge. St. Lutigarde, a blind nun, is depicted here as able to see Christ on the cross, in order that she might kiss his wounds.

㉖ St. Philip Benitius

He was the general of the Servite order and is the only marble statue on the bridge. He's portrayed with a cross, a twig, and a book. The papal tiara lying at his feet is a symbol of the saint's refusal of the papal see in 1268.

㉗ St. Adalbert (1709)

The first bishop of Bohemia is blessing the Czech lands after returning from Rome.

㉘ St. Vitus

Attired as a Roman legionary, he stands on a rock between the lions to which he fell victim.

㉙ St. John of Matha, St. Felix of Valois & St. Ivan

This statue was commissioned for the Trinitarian order, which rescued Christians from Turkish captivity. In the huge rock is a prison, in front of which there's a dog and a Turk with a cat-o'-nine-tails guarding the imprisoned Christians. With money for their freedom, St. John is standing on the summit of the rock. St. Ivan is seated on the left, and St. Felix is loosening the bonds of the prisoners.

⑳ St. Cosmas & St. Damian

They are the patron saints of physicians and were known for dispensing free medical services to the poor. The statues, which were commissioned by Prague's medical faculty, are attired in gowns and hold containers of medicines.

㉛ St. Wenceslas

This statue was commissioned in 1858 by Prague's Klar Institute for the Blind.

Follow the brick path toward the archway at the end of the bridge, but on your way, look up at the:

㉜ Lesser Town Towers (Malostranské mostecké věže)

The small tower on the left was built in the 12th century before Charles ever began construction on the bridge. It was a plain Romanesque structure, but Renaissance accents were added in the 16th century. The taller tower was built in the 15th century and completed the connection of the archway with the smaller tower built in the early 1400s.

After passing through the tower, you'll enter Mostecká Street.

TAKE A BREAK
At the first entrance on the left side of the street, at no. 3, is **Kavárna U Mostecké věže**, a comfortable place to stop right after you get off the bridge. Hot and cold drinks with sweets and ice cream are served in the downstairs restaurant or in the backyard garden with its rattan furniture. Coffee and tea are 30Kč ($1.25), pancakes 69Kč ($2.85). You can have salads, fondue, and steaks as well. It's open daily from 10am to 9pm.

Head back up Mostecká and take the first left to Lázeňská Street. At no. 6, on the left, you'll find a graying former hotel and bathhouse:

㉝ V lázních (In the Baths)

This was a well-known stop for visitors to Prague in the 1800s. The pub and baths, which once hosted writer François-Rene de Chateaubriand, were in operation on this spot from the earliest periods of Lesser Town's existence.

Just up Lázeňská at no. 11, on the right side, is the hotel:

㉞ U zlatého jednorožce (At the Golden Unicorn)

This was another favored stop for honored guests, including Beethoven. A plaque on the front bears the composer's face. The hotel was originally built into the heavy walls that once ringed Malá Strana.

On the other side of the street, at the curve of Lázeňská, you come to the:

㉟ Church of Our Lady Below the Chain (Kostel Panny Marie pod řetězem)

One of the best Romanesque designs in Prague, this church was built for the Order of the Maltese Knights, replacing the oldest church in Malá Strana after it burned in 1420. You can see remnants of the original inside the church courtyard.

After exiting the church back onto the street, go about 20 steps straight on Lázeňská to:

㊱ Maltese Square (Maltézské náměstí)

On the first corner of the square to the left is one of the city's most posh French restaurants packed into a former pub, U Malířů or "At the Painter's" (see the review in chapter 6).

TAKE A BREAK
At no. 10 on the square is the **Restaurace Vinárna U vladaře (At the Governor's)**, open daily from 11:30am to midnight. You can sit out front on the terrace and order coffee and dessert or a meal from a full Czech-style menu. Inside, on the left, is a more formal restaurant serving traditional Czech food. On the right is what used to be a horse stable, **The Konírna**, with vaulted ceilings, cozy and heavy wooden furniture, and a full menu of hearty Czech food. Main dishes cost between 150Kč and 680Kč ($6.25 and $28), coffee around 50Kč ($2).

Across Maltézské náměstí is the large:

③⑦ Nostitz Palace (Nostický palác)

This palace represents a grand, 17th-century, early baroque design attributed to Francesco Caratti. A Prague family who strongly supported the arts used to own it. Its ornate halls once housed a famed private art collection. You can still hear chamber concerts through its windows.

Crossing back through the little Maltese Square, you'll enter Harantova Street on the way to Karmelitská. After crossing Karmelitská Street and walking another 135m (443 ft.), you'll come to the:

③⑧ Church of Our Lady Victorious (Kostel Panny Marie Vítězné)

This is the home of the famed wax statue of the baby Jesus, the *Bambino di Praga*, seen as an important religious relic in Italy and other predominantly Catholic countries.

From the church entrance, continue up Karmelitská Street to see a complex of houses on the left side at no. 25, collectively known as:

③⑨ Vrtba Palace (Vrtbovský palác)

In 1631, Sezima of Vrtba seized a pair of Renaissance houses and connected them to create his palace among the vineyards at the bottom of Petřín Hill. The lush, terraced gardens (Vrtbovská zahrada) surrounding this complex add to its beauty.

Proceed up Karmelitská, where you'll come finally to Malostranské náměstí. To the left, around the uphill side of the square, is the imposing dome of the:

④⓪ Church of St. Nicholas (Kostel sv. Mikuláše)

This high-baroque gem was designed by K. I. Dienzenhofer and completed by his son in 1752. Relax among the statues and take in the marble-and-gilt interior. In the square surrounding the church are numerous restaurants and cafes, good places to stop for an afternoon break or your evening meal.

WALKING TOUR 2   PRAGUE CASTLE (PRAŽSKÝ HRAD)

Start:	The castle's front entrance, at Hradčanské náměstí.
Finish:	Daliborka Tower.
Time:	Allow approximately 2½ hours, not including rest stops.
Best Times:	Weekdays from 9am to 5pm (to 4pm Nov–Mar).
Worst Times:	Weekends, when the crowds are thickest.

The history and development of Prague Castle and the city of Prague are inextricably entwined; it's impossible to envision one without the other. Popularly known as the "Hrad," Prague Castle dates to the second half of the 9th century, when the first Czech royal family, the Premyslids, moved their seat of government here. Settlements on both sides of the Vltava developed under the protection of the fortified castle.

Walking Tour 2: Prague Castle

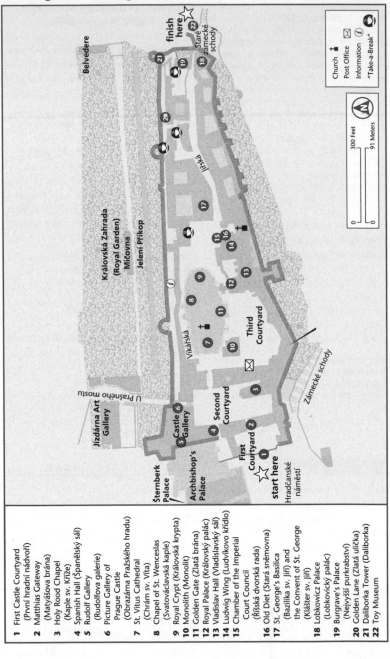

1. First Castle Courtyard
(První hradní nádvoří)
2. Matthias Gateway
(Matyášova brána)
3. Holy Rood Chapel
(Kaple sv. Kříže)
4. Spanish Hall (Španělský sál)
5. Rudolf Gallery
(Rudolfova galerie)
6. Picture Gallery of
Prague Castle
(Obrazárna Pražského hradu)
7. St. Vitus Cathedral
(Chrám sv. Víta)
8. Chapel of St. Wenceslas
(Svatováclavská kaple)
9. Royal Crypt (Královská krypta)
10. Monolith (Monolit)
11. Golden Gate (Zlatá brána)
12. Royal Palace (Královský palác)
13. Vladislav Hall (Vladislavský sál)
14. Ludwig Wing (Ludvíkovo křídlo)
15. Chamber of the Imperial
Court Council
(Říšská dvorská rada)
16. Old Diet (Stará sněmovna)
17. St. George's Basilica
(Bazilika sv. Jiří) and
the Convent of St. George
(Klášter sv. Jiří)
18. Lobkowicz Palace
(Lobkovický palác)
19. Burgrave's Palace
(Nejvyšší purkrabství)
20. Golden Lane (Zlatá ulička)
21. Daliborka Tower (Daliborka)
22. Toy Museum

Begin your tour from the castle's front entrance at Hradčanské náměsti. Walk through the imposing rococo gateway, topped by the colossal Battling Giants statues (1911 copies of 18th-c. granite works), to the:

❶ First Castle Courtyard (První hradní nádvoří)

An informal changing of the guard occurs here daily on the hour. It involves only five guards doing little more than some impressive heel clicking and rifle twirling. The guards wore rather drab khaki outfits until 1989, when Václav Havel asked costume designer Theodor Pištěk, who costumed the actors in the film *Amadeus,* to redress them. Their smart new blue outfits were reminiscent of those worn during the First Republic.

Directly ahead is the:

❷ Matthias Gateway (Matyášova brána)

Built in 1614 as a free-standing gate, it was later incorporated into the castle itself. The gateway bears the coats of arms of the various lands ruled by Emperor Matthias. Once you pass through it, you'll see a stairway on the right leading to the staterooms of the president of the republic. They're closed to the public.

The gateway leads into the Second Castle Courtyard (Druhé hradní nádvoří). Ahead, on the eastern side of the square, is the:

❸ Holy Rood Chapel (Kaple sv. Kříže)

Originally constructed in 1763, this chapel was redesigned in 1856. The chapel is noted for its high-altar sculpture and ceiling frescoes.

On the western side of the courtyard is the opulent:

❹ Spanish Hall (Španělský sál)

This hall was built in the late 16th century. During 1993 restorations, officials at the castle discovered a series of 18th-century *trompe-l'oeil* murals that lay hidden behind the mirrors lining the hall's walls.

Adjoining the Spanish Hall is the:

❺ Rudolf Gallery (Rudolfova galerie)

This official reception hall once housed the art collections of Rudolf II. The last remodeling of this space—rococo-style stucco decorations—occurred in 1868.

On the northern side of the square is the:

❻ Picture Gallery of Prague Castle (Obrazárna Pražského hradu)

Containing both European and Bohemian masterpieces, the gallery holds few works from the original imperial collection, which was virtually destroyed during the Thirty Years' War. Of the works that have survived from the days of Emperors Rudolf II and Ferdinand III, the most celebrated is Hans von Aachen's *Portrait of a Girl* (1605–10), depicting the artist's daughter.

A covered passageway leads to the Third Castle Courtyard (Třetí hradní nádvoří), dominated by hulking:

❼ St. Vitus Cathedral (Chrám sv. Víta)

Begun in 1334, under the watchful eye of Charles IV, Prague's most celebrated Gothic cathedral has undergone three serious reconstructions. The tower galleries date from 1562, the baroque onion roof was constructed in 1770, and the entire western part of the cathedral was begun in 1873.

Before you enter, notice the facade, decorated with statues of saints. The bronze doors are embellished with reliefs; those on the central door depict the construction history of the cathedral. The door on the left features representations from the lives of St. Adalbert (on the right) and St. Wenceslas (on the left).

Inside the cathedral's busy main body are several chapels, coats of arms of the city of Prague, a memorial to Bohemian casualties of World War I, and a Renaissance-era organ loft with an organ dating from 1757.

Light It Up: The Rolling Stones Give Satisfaction

Are the lights flickering in Spanish Hall? If they are, someone might be playing with the remote control that operates the lighting.

In the summer of 1995, the Rolling Stones played to a crowd of more than 100,000 people in their second Prague concert since the Velvet Revolution. After finishing, the Stones gave Václav Havel, then president and a big fan, a bright gift: They paid for a $32,000 overhaul of the lighting in four of the castle's grand halls, including the Spanish Hall and Vladislav Hall. The director and lighting designer of their record-breaking Voodoo Lounge Tour managed the project.

The result? Well, it's a somewhat more dignified spectacle than the raucous light show that was part of the mythical Voodoo Lounge Tour on stage. Mick Jagger, Keith Richards, Charlie Watts, and Ron Wood presented Havel with a remote control to operate the chandeliers and spotlights that now strategically cast their beams on baroque statues and tapestries.

According to legend, St. Vitus died in Rome but was then transported by angels to a small town in southern Italy. Since his remains were brought here in 1355, Vitus, the patron saint of Prague, has remained the most popular saint among the faithful in the country. Numerous Czech Catholic churches have altars dedicated to him.

The most celebrated chapel, on your right, is the:

8 Chapel of St. Wenceslas (Svatováclavská kaple)

The chapel is built atop the saint's tomb. A multitude of polished semiprecious stones decorates the chapel's altar and walls. Other spaces are filled in with 14th-century murals depicting Christ's sufferings and the life of St. Wenceslas.

Below the church's main body is the:

9 Royal Crypt (Královská krypta)

The crypt contains the sarcophagi of kings Václav IV, George of Poděbrady, Rudolf II, and Charles IV and his four wives. The tomb was reconstructed in the early 1900s, and the remains of the royalty were placed in new encasements.

Charles's four wives share the same sarcophagus.

Exit the cathedral from the same door you entered and turn left into the courtyard, where you'll approach the:

10 Monolith (Monolit)

The marble obelisk measuring over 11m (36 ft.) tall is a memorial to the victims of World War I. Just behind it is an equestrian statue of St. George, a Gothic work produced in 1373.

Continue walking around the courtyard. In the southern wall of St. Vitus Cathedral, you'll see a ceremonial entrance known as the:

11 Golden Gate (Zlatá brána)

The tympanum over the doorway is decorated with a 14th-century mosaic, *The Last Judgment,* which is being carefully restored, bit by bit. The doorway's 1950s-era decorative grille is designed with zodiac figures.

An archway in the Third Castle Courtyard connects St. Vitus Cathedral with the:

12 Royal Palace (Královský palác)

Until the second half of the 16th century, this was the official residence of royalty. Inside, to the left, is the **Green Chamber**

(Zelená světnice), where Charles IV presided over minor court sessions. A fresco of the court of Solomon is painted on the ceiling.

The adjacent room is:

⑬ Vladislav Hall (Vladislavský sál)

This ceremonial room has held coronation banquets, political assemblies, and knightly tournaments. Since 1934, elections of the president of the republic have taken place here below the exquisite 12m (40-ft.), rib-vaulted ceiling.

At the end of Vladislav Hall is a door giving access to the:

⑭ Ludwig Wing (Ludvíkovo křídlo)

In this wing, built in 1509, you'll find two rooms of the Chancellery of Bohemia (Česká kancelář), once the administrative body of the Land of the Crown of Bohemia. When the king was absent, Bohemia's nobles summoned assemblies here. On May 23, 1618, two hated governors and their secretary were thrown out of the eastern window of the rear room. This act, known as the Second Defenestration, marked the beginning of the Thirty Years' War (see the box "Beware of Open Windows: The Czech Tradition of Defenestration," in chapter 7).

A spiral staircase leads to the:

⑮ Chamber of the Imperial Court Council (Říšská dvorská rada)

The chamber met here during the reign of Rudolf II. In this room the 27 rebellious squires and burghers who fomented the defenestration were sentenced to death. Their executions took place on June 21, 1621, in Staroměstské náměstí. All the portraits on the chamber walls are of Habsburgs. The eastern part of Vladislav Hall opens onto a terrace from which there's a lovely view of the castle gardens and the city.

Also located in the palace is the:

⑯ Old Diet (Stará sněmovna)

The Provincial Court once assembled here. It's interesting to notice the arrangement of the Diet's 19th-century furniture, which is all centered on the royal throne. To the sovereign's right is the chair of the archbishop and benches for the prelates. Along the walls are seats for the federal officials; opposite the throne is a bench for the representatives of the Estates. By the window on the right is a gallery for the representatives of the royal towns. Portraits of the Habsburgs adorn the walls.

Stairs lead down to St. George's Square (náměstí Svatého Jiří), a courtyard at the eastern end of St. Vitus Cathedral. If the weather is nice, you might want to:

> **TAKE A BREAK**
> **Cafeteria U kanovníku,** in the courtyard between St. Vitus and St. George's (náměstí Sv. Jiří 3), has a terrace garden with tables under trees, where you can enjoy light fare and hot Czech food. They offer coffee from 37Kč to 80Kč ($1.55–$3.35) and great French bread sandwiches for 110Kč ($4.60) daily from 10am to 6pm.

This square is dominated by:

⑰ St. George's Basilica (Bazilika sv. Jiří) & the Convent of St. George (Klášter sv. Jiří)

Benedictine nuns founded the convent in A.D. 973. In 1967, the convent's premises were acquired by the **National Gallery,** which now uses the buildings to warehouse and display its collection of Bohemian art from Gothic to baroque periods. See chapter 7 for complete information.

Leave the basilica and continue walking through the castle compound on Jiřská Street, the exit at the southeastern corner of St. George's Square.

About 60m (197 ft.) ahead on your right is the entrance to:

⑱ Lobkowicz Palace (Lobkovický palác)

This 16th-century manor now houses the Permanent History Exhibition of the National Museum, a gallery devoted exclusively to the history of the Czech lands.

Opposite Lobkowicz Palace is:

⑲ Burgrave's Palace (Nejvyšší purkrabství)

This 16th-century building, now considered the House of Czech Children, is used for cultural programs and exhibitions aimed toward children.

Walk up the steps to the left of Burgrave's Palace to:

⑳ Golden Lane (Zlatá ulička)

This picturesque street of 16th-century houses built into the castle fortifications was once home to castle sharpshooters. The charm-filled lane now contains small shops, galleries, and refreshment bars. Franz Kafka supposedly lived or worked at no. 22 for a brief time in 1917.

TAKE A BREAK
At the top of Golden Lane is the **Bistro Zlatá ulička**, serving sandwiches for 55Kč ($2.30), goulash for 65Kč ($2.70), and cakes, plus coffee, wine, and spirits. There are several cozy tables in the back, but the place is often packed in high season. It's open daily from 9:30am to 6pm.

Turn right on Golden Lane and walk to the end, where you'll see:

㉑ Daliborka Tower (Daliborka)

This tower formed part of the castle's late Gothic fortifications dating from 1496. The tower's name comes from Squire Dalibor of Kozojedy, who in 1498 became the first unlucky soul to be imprisoned here.

Turn right at Daliborka Tower, then left, and go through the passageway and down Jiřská Street. Here, at no. 6, you can visit the:

㉒ Toy Museum

Especially appreciated by children, this museum unsurprisingly holds a permanent exhibition of toys. Wooden and tin toys are on display here along with a collection of Barbie dolls.

After going down the old castle steps (Staré zámecké schody), you will reach the Malostranská station on line A of Prague's metro.

WALKING TOUR 3   STARÉ MĚSTO (OLD TOWN)

Start:	Municipal House (Obecní dům), at náměstí Republiky.
Finish:	Havel's Market (Havelský trh).
Time:	Allow approximately 1 hour, not including any breaks or museum visits.
Best Times:	Sunday to Thursday from 9am to 5pm and Friday from 9am to 2pm, when the museums and market are open.
Worst Times:	Weekend afternoons when the crowds are thickest, Monday when the museums are closed, and after 6pm when the market is closed.

Staré Město, founded in 1234, was the first of Prague's original five towns. Its establishment was the result of Prague's growing importance along central European trade routes. Staré Město's ancient streets, most meandering haphazardly around Staroměstské náměstí, are lined with many stately buildings, churches, shops, and theaters.

Walking Tour 3: Staré Město (Old Town)

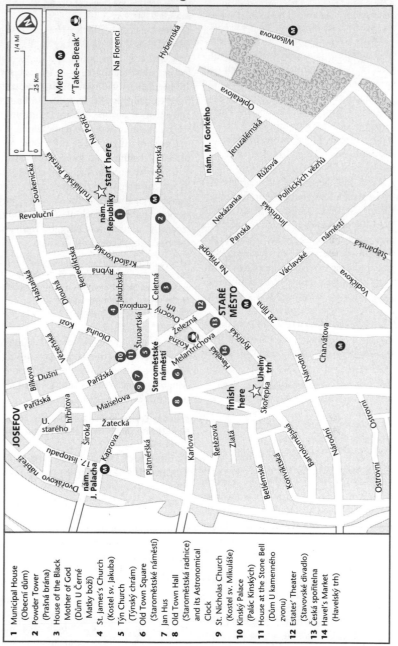

Metro **M**

"Take-a-Break" **●**

1/4 Mi
.25 Km

JOSEFOV

STARÉ MĚSTO

start here

finish here

1 Municipal House
   (Obecní dům)

2 Powder Tower
   (Prašná brána)

3 House of the Black
   Mother of God
   (Dům U Černé
   Matky boží)

4 St. James's Church
   (Kostel sv. Jakuba)

5 Týn Church
   (Týnský chrám)

6 Old Town Square
   (Staroměstské náměstí)

7 Jan Hus

8 Old Town Hall
   (Staroměstská radnice)
   and its Astronomical
   Clock

9 St. Nicholas Church
   (Kostel sv. Mikuláše)

10 Kinsky Palace
   (Palác Kinských)

11 House at the Stone Bell
   (Dům U kamenného
   zvonu)

12 Estates' Theater
   (Stavovské divadlo)

13 Česká spořitelna

14 Havel's Market
   (Havelský trh)

Although this tour is far from exhaustive, it takes you past some of Old Town's most important buildings and monuments. Go to náměstí Republiky 5, at the metro station. Begin at the:

❶ Municipal House (Obecní dům)

One of Prague's most photographed cultural and historical monuments, the Municipal House was built between 1906 and 1911 with money raised by Prague citizens. In the spring of 1997, it reopened after a long reconstruction, and historians say that it has been returned faithfully to its original grandeur.

From the beginning, this ornate Art Nouveau building has been an important Czech cultural symbol—the document granting independence to Czechoslovakia was signed here in 1918. The **Prague Symphony** performs in Smetana Hall, the building's most impressive room, with a gorgeous stained-glass ceiling. The detail of every decoration tells a story (see p. 124 for more information).

Inside you'll find a spacious period cafe, a French restaurant, and a Czech pub in the cellar with a fascinating ceramic still-life mural.

With your back to the Municipal House main entrance, walk around to your right under the arch of the:

❷ Powder Tower (Prašná brána, literally Powder Gate)

Once part of Staré Město's system of fortifications, the Powder Tower was built in 1475 as one of the walled city's major gateways. After New Town was incorporated into the City of Prague, the walls separating Old Town from the new section became obsolete. So did the Powder Tower, which was re-commissioned as a gunpowder storehouse.

The tower marks the beginning of the **Royal Route,** the traditional path along which medieval Bohemian monarchs paraded on their way to being crowned in Prague Castle's St. Vitus Cathedral.

Continue through the arch down Celetná Street (named after calt, a bread baked here in the Middle Ages) to the corner of Ovocný trh, where you'll find the:

❸ House at the Black Mother of God (Dům U Černé Matky boží)

At Celetná 34, this building is important for its cubist architectural style. Cubism, an angular artistic movement, was confined to painting and sculpture in France and most of Europe. As an architectural style, cubism is exclusive to Bohemia.

Constructed in 1912, this house features tall columns sculpted with rectangular and triangular shapes on either side of an ornate wrought-iron gate. The house is named for the Virgin Mary emblem on the corner of the building's second floor that was salvaged from the last building to stand on this site.

With your back to the House of the Black Mother of God, cross Celetná into Templová, walk 2 short blocks, and turn left onto Jakubská. At the corner, on your right, you'll see:

❹ St. James's Church (Kostel sv. Jakuba)

Prague's second-longest church contains 21 altars. When you enter, look up just inside the church's front door. The object dangling from above is the shriveled arm of a 16th-century thief.

Return to Celetná and continue walking about 90m (295 ft.). On the right, below the towering spires, is:

❺ Church of Our Lady Before Týn (Kostel paní Marie před Týnem - Týnský chrám)

This is one of the largest and prettiest of Prague's many churches. Famous for its twin spires that loom over nearby Staroměstské náměstí, the church was closely connected to the 14th-century Hussite movement for religious reform. After Roman Catholics crushed the reformers, many of the church's Hussite symbols were removed, including statues, insignia, and the tower bells that were once known by Hussite nicknames. Note the tomb of Danish astronomer Tycho de Brahe (d. 1601), near the high altar.

Exit the church and continue a few more steps along Celetná, which opens up into:

⑥ Old Town Square (Staroměstské náměstí)

Surrounded by baroque buildings and packed with colorful cafes, craftspeople, and entertainers, Staroměstské náměstí looks the way an old European square is supposed to look.

This square has long been a focal point of Czech history and politics. Since the city's inception it has served as a meeting place for commerce, from the simple bartering of the Middle Ages to the privatization deals of the 1990s.

Old Town Square has also seen its share of political protest and punishment. Protestant Hussites rioted here in the 1400s. In the 1620s, the Catholic Habsburg rulers beheaded 27 Protestants here and hung some of the heads in baskets above Charles Bridge. A small white cross has been embedded in the square near the Old Town Hall for each of the beheaded.

In the 20th century, the square witnessed a whirlwind of political change. In 1918, the Czechs celebrated the founding of the new sovereign Republic of Czechoslovakia here. But then in 1939, the Nazis celebrated their occupation of the country on the same site. The Soviets then celebrated kicking the Nazis out of Prague in 1945. But in 1968 the Reds rolled their tanks through Prague again, this time as unwelcome invaders.

In 1948, Klement Gottwald led a celebration in honor of the Communist seizure of power. No wonder the Czechs chose nearby Wenceslas Square to celebrate the return of their government in 1989.

To begin your walk around the square, go straight toward the massive black stone monument in the center. Here you'll find the statue of:

⑦ Jan Hus

Jan Hus was a fiery 15th-century preacher who challenged the Roman Catholic hierarchy and was burned at the stake for it. The statue's pedestal has been used as a soapbox by many a populist politician trying to gain points by associating himself with the ill-fated Protestant, although today you're more likely to find the international youth holding sway.

The struggle between the supporters of Hus, known as Hussites, set the stage for the religious wars that tore Bohemia apart in the 15th and 17th centuries. The Hussite Church still lives today as the Protestant Czech Brethren, but since Communism its numbers have dwindled. Membership in the Catholic Church has also declined.

From here, turn around and walk left toward the clock tower.

⑧ Old Town Hall (Staroměstská radnice)

Try to time your walk so you can pass the hall and its **Astronomical Clock** at the top of the hour. It may be an understated show, but each hour a mechanical parade of saints and sinners performs for the crowd watching below (p. 113). If you have time and your knees are up to it, try making the steep, narrow walk up to the top of the tower for a picturesque view of Old Town's red roofs.

Walking past the right side of the clock tower toward the northwest corner of the square, you'll come to:

⑨ St. Nicholas Church (Kostel sv. Mikuláše)

This is the 1735 design of Prague's baroque master architect K. I. Dienzenhofer. The three-towered edifice isn't as beautiful or as ornate inside as his St. Nicholas Church in Lesser Town, but the crystal fixtures are worth a look.

From the front of the church, walk behind the back of the Hus monument, through the square, to the broad palace with the reddish roof and balcony in front. This is:

⑩ Kinský Palace (Palác Kinských)

From the rococo balcony jutting from the palace's stucco facade, Communist leader Klement Gottwald declared the proletariat takeover of the Czechoslovak government in February 1945. Italian architect Lurago designed the building for Count Goltz. It was later taken over by the Habsburg Prince Rudolf Kinský in 1768. It now houses a fine modern art collection in the **National Museum** complex of palaces (see chapter 7).

Next to this is the:

⓫ House at the Stone Bell (Dům U kamenného zvonu)

The medieval Gothic tower was built in the 14th century for the father of Charles IV, John of Luxembourg.

From here, head back toward Old Town Hall, but then about midway to the tower, turn left toward the square's south end and begin walking down Železná. Continue down this car-restricted walking zone about 300m (984 ft.); then, on the left you'll see the pale green:

⓬ Estates' Theater (Stavovské divadlo)

Mozart premiered his opera *Don Giovanni* in this late-18th-century grand hall. More recently, director Miloš Forman filmed many scenes in the story of the composer's life here.

Make sure to walk down Rytířská in front of the theater to get a full view of this beautifully restored building, which just reopened after the revolution.

From the front of the theater, walk about 10 steps back up Železná and take the first left on Havelská.

TAKE A BREAK
At Havelská 27, you can stop for a tasty pasta, lasagna, tiramisu, or thick Italian espresso at the **Kogo** (p. 92). There are tightly packed tables inside, but if the weather is nice, sit in the more comfortable archway. Hours are daily from 9am to midnight. Salads and appetizers from 160Kč ($6.65). You won't be disappointed by their homemade pasta (from 192Kč/$8).

Continue down Havelská. On the left you'll see:

⓭ Czech Savings Bank (Česká spořitelna)

After serving as the museum to late Communist president Klement Gottwald, the large neo-Renaissance building with statue inlays is once again a bank. The 1894 building was originally intended to be a bank, but after the 1948 coup it was seized by the government and turned into a repository for Communist propaganda. After the 1989 revolution, the building was returned to the bank, which restored the intricate friezes and frescoes depicting bankers' propaganda of early Czech capitalism. This is the largest Czech savings bank and worth a peek.

Your next destination is the popular street market that overtakes the remainder of Havelská Street. Simply continue on to:

⓮ Havel's Market (Havelský trh)

At this popular local meeting place, you'll find vegetables, fruit, drinks, soaps, toiletries, artwork, and leather goods. Prices here are generally lower than in most shops. Have fun browsing.

The nearest metro is Můstek, line A or B.

WALKING TOUR 4	JOSEFOV (JEWISH QUARTER)

Start:	Lesser Square (Malé náměstí).
Finish:	Café Bar La Dolce Vita.
Time:	Allow approximately 2 hours, not including rest stops or museum visits.
Best Times:	Sunday to Friday from 9am to 5pm, when the cemetery and sights are open.
Worst Time:	Saturday, the Sabbath, when everything is closed.

Josefov, Prague's former Jewish ghetto, lies within Staré Město. The wall that once surrounded the ghetto was almost entirely destroyed to make way for 19th-century structures. Prague is considered one of Europe's great Jewish cities: Jews have been here since the end of the 10th century, and by 1708 more Jews were living here than anywhere else in Europe.

Today, Prague's Jewish community numbers less than 3,000. In 1992, the Jewish community elected Rabbi Karol Sidon as their leader, and he has led a very public fight against anti-Semitism as reported incidents of attacks against Jews and Jewish property have increased. In addition, the government has recently tried to return to Jewish citizens property confiscated by the Nazis and then the Communists. However, many claims are still unresolved.

This tour may seem short, but the sights are gripping and provide much to ponder, so budget your time loosely. Start at:

❶ Lesser Square (Malé náměstí)

This square is adjacent to Staroměstské náměstí. Though it can't boast as much history as its larger companion, excavations have proven that Malé náměstí was a prime piece of real estate as far back as the 12th century. Archaeologists turned up bits of pottery, evidence of medieval pathways, and human bones from the late 1100s, when developers committed the medieval equivalent of paving over a cemetery to build a shopping mall.

From Malé náměstí, turn left onto U radnice. One block ahead, in the courtyard across from the Magistrate Building and tucked against St. Nicholas Church, you'll see:

❷ Franz Kafka's House

In this building, which now houses Restaurace Franze Kafky, the famous author was born. There used to be a small gallery and shop here to re-create the history of his life, but it's now a restaurant. The best way to get a look at Kafka's life is by visiting the Kafka Museum in Hergetova Cihelna (p. 119).

An unflattering cast-iron bust of Kafka, unveiled in 1965, sits just to the right of the entrance, at the corner of Maiselova and U radnice. Walk straight ahead onto:

❸ Maiselova Street

This is one of the two main streets of the walled Jewish quarter, founded in 1254.

As elsewhere in Europe, Prague's Jews were forced into ghettos following a formal Roman Catholic decision that the Jews had killed Jesus. By the 16th century, Prague's 10,000 isolated Jews comprised 10% of the city's population.

The ban on Jews living outside the ghetto was lifted in 1848. Eighty percent of the ghetto's Jews moved to other parts of the city, and living conditions on this street and those surrounding it seriously deteriorated. The authorities responded by razing the entire neighborhood, including numerous medieval houses and synagogues. The majority of the buildings here now date from the end of the 19th century; several on this street sport stunning Art Nouveau facades.

About halfway down the street, on your right, is the:

❹ Maisel Synagogue (Maiselova synagóga)

This neo-Gothic temple is built on a plot of land donated by Mordechai Maisel, a wealthy inhabitant of Prague's old Jewish town. The original synagogue was destroyed by fire in 1689 but was rebuilt. During the Nazi occupation of Prague, it was used to store furniture seized from the homes of deported Jews. Today, the building holds no religious services; it's home to the Jewish Museum's collection of silver ceremonial objects, books, and Torah covers confiscated from Bohemian synagogues by the Nazis during World War II.

Walking Tour 4: Josefov (Jewish Quarter)

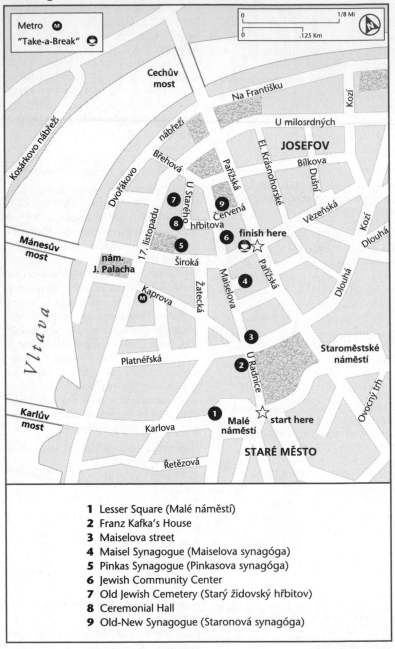

1 Lesser Square (Malé náměstí)
2 Franz Kafka's House
3 Maiselova street
4 Maisel Synagogue (Maiselova synagóga)
5 Pinkas Synagogue (Pinkasova synagóga)
6 Jewish Community Center
7 Old Jewish Cemetery (Starý židovský hřbitov)
8 Ceremonial Hall
9 Old-New Synagogue (Staronová synagóga)

Continue walking down Maiselova and turn left onto Široká. Walk past the former entrance to the Old Jewish Cemetery, through which you can catch a first glimpse of its shadowy headstones, to:

➎ Pinkas Synagogue (Pinkasova synagóga)

This is Prague's second-oldest Jewish house of worship. After World War II, the walls of the Pinkas Synagogue were painted with the names of more than 77,000 Czech Jews who perished in Nazi concentration camps. The Communist government subsequently erased the names, saying that the memorial was suffering from "moisture due to flooding." After the revolution, funds were raised to restore and maintain the commemoration. It's here that then-U.S. Secretary of State Madeleine Albright came in 1997 to see the proof that her paternal grandparents, Arnošt Koerbel and Olga Koerbelová, were killed in the Holocaust. Albright said that she hadn't been aware of her Jewish ancestry until earlier in 1997. Her father, a Czechoslovak diplomat who fled Prague with his young family twice when Madeleine was a small girl (first from the Nazis, then from the Communists), raised his children as Catholics. See the box "Prague's Most Powerful Daughter: The Rise & Surprise of Madeleine Albright," in chapter 7, for more information.

Backtrack up Široká and turn left onto Maiselova. The pink rococo building on the right side at Maiselova 18 is the:

➏ Jewish Community Center

This is an information and cultural center for locals and visitors. It once was the Jewish Town Hall. Activities of interest to Prague's Jewish community are posted here, and the staff provides visitors with details about Jewish tours. Also inside is Prague's only truly kosher restaurant, which, alas, is open only to members.

On the Community Center wall facing the Old-New Synagogue is a clock with a Hebrew-inscribed face. It turns left, counter to what's considered "clockwise."

Continue walking 1 block along Maiselova and turn left onto U Starého hřbitova, heading to the:

➐ Old Jewish Cemetery (Starý židovský hřbitov)

This is Europe's oldest Jewish burial ground, where the oldest grave dates to 1439. Because the local government of the time didn't allow Jews to bury their dead elsewhere, as many as 12 bodies were placed vertically, with each new tombstone placed in front of the last. Hence, the crowded little cemetery contains more than 20,000 graves.

Like other Jewish cemeteries around the world, many of the tombstones have small rocks and stones placed on them—a tradition said to date from the days when Jews were wandering in the desert. Passersby, it's believed, would add rocks to gravesites so as not to lose the deceased to the shifting sands. Along with stones, visitors often leave small notes of prayer in the cracks between tombstones.

Buried here is Rabbi Löw, who made from the mud of the Vltava River the legendary Golem, a clay "monster" to protect Prague's Jews. Golem was a one-eyed or three-eyed monster, depending on how you look at him. Legend has it that the rabbi would keep Golem around to protect the residents from the danger of mean-spirited Catholics outside the walls of the Jewish ghetto.

Löw's grave, in the most remote corner opposite the Ceremonial Hall, is one of the most popular in the cemetery; you'll see that well-wishers and the devout cram his tombstone with notes. Across the path from the rabbi is the grave of Mordechai Maisel, the 16th-century mayor of Josefov whose name was given to the nearby synagogue built during his term in office.

As you exit the cemetery you'll pass the:

➑ Ceremonial Hall

Inside the hall, where rites for the dead were once held, is a gripping reminder of the horrors of World War II. Displayed here are the sketches by children who were held at the Terezín concentration camp west of Prague (see chapter 11). These drawings, which are simple, honest, and painful in their playful innocence, are of the horrific world where parents and other relatives were packed up and sent to die.

Backtrack along U Starého hřbitova, cross Maiselova, and walk into the small alley called Červená. You're now standing between two synagogues. On the right is the High Synagogue (Vysoká synagóga), now an exhibition hall for the Jewish State Museum. On your left is the:

⑨ Old-New Synagogue (Staronová synagóga)

Originally called the New Synagogue to distinguish it from an even older one that no longer exists, the Old-New Synagogue, built around 1270, is the oldest Jewish temple in Europe. The building has been prayed in continuously for more than 700 years, except from 1941 to 1945, during the Nazi occupation in World War II. The synagogue is also one of the largest Gothic buildings in Prague, built with vaulted ceilings and fitted with Renaissance-era columns.

Until a 19th-century planning effort raised the entire area about 3m (10 ft.), much of Josefov and Staré Město used to be flooded regularly by the Vltava. The Old-New Synagogue, however, has preserved its original floor, which you reach by going *down* a short set of stairs.

You can attend services here. Men and women customarily sit separately during services, though that's not always rigorously enforced.

Continue to the end of the Červená alley and turn right onto Pařížská (Paris St.), Prague's most elegant thoroughfare, built around the turn of the 20th century. Follow Pařížská back toward Staroměstské náměstí, but take the first left and go 1 block. On the left you'll find:

WINDING DOWN
La Dolce Vita, at Široká 15, half a block off Pařížská, is one of the city's finest Italian cafes. Its marble interior contains five tables on the ground floor, and 10 tables on a veranda overlooking the action below. The cafe offers traditional Italian sandwiches, gelato, and espresso drinks, served by an Italian-speaking Czech waitstaff. The cafe is open daily from 8:30am to midnight. Cappuccino costs 60Kč ($2.50); homemade Italian desserts or cheesecake are 80Kč ($3.35). See p. 102.

Returning to Pařížská and turning left will lead you back to Staroměstské náměstí.

9

Prague Shopping

The rapid influx of visitors, the post-Communist wage growth, and a new consumer economy fueled by the shopping habits of the Czech nouveau riche have resulted in expensive boutiques and specialty shops popping up like mushrooms in Prague. Shopping malls now offer everything from designer baby clothes to Bruno Magli shoes. The selection of world-renowned labels is beginning to rival that of many western European cities, though shops tend to have a tiny inventory compared with the same outlets in Paris or London. Still, since labor and rent make operations cheaper here, you might find a bargain for the same items offered at points farther west.

For those looking for a piece of Czech handiwork, you can find some of the world's best crystal and glass, often at shockingly low prices. Antiques shops and booksellers abound, and the selection of classical, trendy, and offbeat art is immense at the numerous private galleries. Throughout the city center you'll find quaint, obscure shops, some without phones or advertising.

1 The Shopping Scene

SHOPPING AREAS

The L-shaped half-mile running from the middle of **Wenceslas Square** around the corner to the right on **Na Příkopě** and to the Myslbek Center has become Prague's principal shopping street. In this short distance you'll find three multilevel shopping gallerias, with stores like Britain's **H&M, Next, Kenvelo, Pierre Cardin, Adidas,** and **Revlon.** Between the centers is a wide array of boutiques and antiques shops; in high season there's also a crafts market at the low end of the square.

A handful of fine private **art galleries** is concentrated on the stretch of **Národní třída** running from just east of the National Theater to Wenceslas Square. The wide tree-lined Pařížská, from Old Town Square to the Hotel Inter-Continental, is flanked with top-level boutiques, travel agencies, and airline offices, as well as eclectic local shops.

In the streets surrounding **Old Town Square,** you'll find a wide variety of expensive shops like Mapin & Webb jewelers, with bizarre nooks offering woodcarvings, garnets, handmade toys, and typical Czech glass and porcelain.

In **Malá Strana,** you'll find artists and craftspeople selling their jewelry, prints, handicrafts, and faux Red Army surplus on Charles Bridge and the Old Castle Steps (Staré zámecké schody).

HOURS & TAXES

Prague's centrally located shops rely on tourist business and keep fairly long hours. Most are open Monday to Friday from about 9am to 6pm and Saturday from 9am to

Prague Shopping

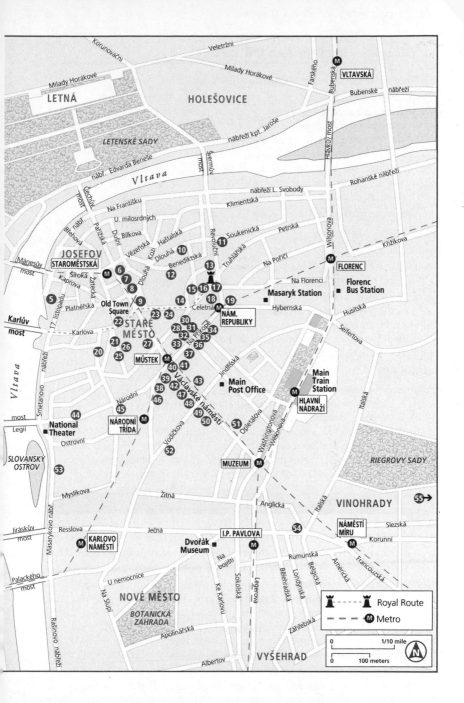

Tips How to Claim Your VAT Refund

Recouping some of your tax money is easy; just follow these steps:

- When paying for your goods, ask the store for a Global Refund Cheque.
- Within 30 days of the date of purchase, present the voucher to a Czech Customs official to get a stamp. At the airport, the Customs Stamps official is located *before* Passport Control.
- Hand the stamp in *after* Passport Control to one of the Cash Refund Offices. Their staff will then refund your VAT, free of charge. Alternatively, you can use a direct crediting of a chosen credit card, or have a bank check sent to a chosen address.

For more information go to **www.globalrefund.cz**.

1pm, and sometimes much later. Many open on Sunday as well, though usually for a shorter time. Note that some small food shops that keep long hours charge up to 20% more for all their goods.

Prices for goods in shops include the government's 19% **value-added tax (VAT).** All tourists from **outside the E.U.** can save up to 16% of this tax. To make use of this concession, buy from stores with the TAX FREE sign. To qualify, the purchase price must exceed 2,000Kč ($83), including the VAT in 1 day in one store.

SHIPPING
Don't trust the post office when it comes to shipping valuable goods. If your package is larger than a breadbox, contact the international company **DHL,** Aviatická 12 (Ruzyně Airport), Praha 6 (✆ **220-300-111** or 800-103-000; www.dhl.cz). They charge 1,960Kč ($81) for a 1-kilogram (2.2-lb.) parcel to the U.K. and 2,000Kč ($83) to the United States. You can use the DHL terminal at the Ruzyně Airport, open nonstop, or visit the Express Center at Václavské nám. 47 (the entrance is from Opletalova St.), open Monday to Friday 8am to 6:30pm and Saturday 9am to 3pm.

2 Shopping A to Z
ANTIQUES
Antikvariát Pařížská   This is a musty market with valuable pieces of Czechoslovak and Czech history. Pictures, graphics, coins, medals, paper currency, and maps are offered. Open daily from 10am to 6pm. Pařížská 8, Praha 1. ✆ 222-321-442. Metro: Staroměstská.

Antique-Andrle Vladimír   A wide selection of Eastern Orthodox icons distinguishes this shop halfway up on Wenceslas Square. The proprietor produces papers showing that each icon was legitimately obtained (despite heavy restrictions in many countries) and legal for export. There's also a large selection of antique watches and other accessories. Open Monday to Saturday from 10am to 7pm and Sunday from 10am to 6pm. Václavské nám. 17, Praha 1. ✆ 224-009-166. Metro: Můstek. Also at Křížovnická 1, Praha 1. ✆ 222-311-625. Metro: Staroměstská. www.antiqueandrle.cz.

Art Deco Galerie   This dandy store sells the trappings of Prague's golden age and is filled with colored perfume bottles and clothing from the 1920s and 1930s. Furniture and household items include Art Deco clocks and lamps. Open Monday to Friday from 2 to 7pm. Michalská 21, Praha 1. ☎ 224-223-076. Metro: Můstek.

Art Décoratif   Another Art Nouveau throwback, this outlet is housed in the purely authentic hull of the refurbished Municipal House, but most things offered aren't originals. Still, there's a fine selection of Alfons Mucha reproductions, jewelry, and lamps from the era. Open daily from 10am to 8pm. U Obecního domu (on the right side of the Municipal House while facing it), Praha 1. ☎ 222-002-350. Metro: Náměstí Republiky.

Galerie Peron   This one-room antiques shop has a bit of everything: small and mostly decorative statuettes, vases, oil paintings, and curios from fine Bohemia salons of yesteryear. If you want something easy to pack, there's plenty to fit the bill. Open Monday to Friday from 11am to 7pm, Saturday and Sunday from noon to 6pm. U Lužického semináře 12, Praha 1. ☎ 257-533-507. www.peron.cz. Metro: Malostranská.

ART GALLERIES
The Czech Museum of Fine Arts   This museum presents works of contemporary Czech and other Eastern European artists. Coffee-table books and catalogs with detailed descriptions in English and color reproductions usually accompany well-planned exhibitions. Open Tuesday to Sunday from 10am to 6pm. Husova 19 and 21, Praha 1. ☎ 222-220-218. www.cmvu.cz. Metro: Národní třída or Můstek.

Galerie Art Praha/Centrum sběratelů   A showroom for a collectors' group, this gallery on Old Town Square offers innovative works from some of the more progressive Czech and Slovak artists of the 20th century. Open daily from 10:30am to 7pm. Staroměstské nám. 20, Praha 1. ☎ 224-211-087. www.galerieartpraha.cz. Metro: Staroměstská.

Galerie Platýz-Ranný Architects   This eclectic space displays and sells modern Czech paintings, sculpture, and graphics by artists who show their works on a rotating basis. Open Monday to Friday from 10:30am to 7pm and Saturday from 10am to 5pm. Národní 37, Praha 1. ☎ 224-210-755. Metro: Národní třída or Můstek.

BOOKS
Big Ben Book Shop   At the far side of the courtyard behind Týn Church near Old Town Square, Big Ben is a good place to find that commemorative or educational book on Prague in English. There are also city tours to take home on videocassette and a wealth of maps to guide you into the hinterlands, plus a good selection of children's literature. Open Monday to Friday from 9am to 6:30pm, Saturday 10am to 5pm, and

---

Tips Special Shopping Notes

In an effort to keep precious pieces of Czech heritage in the country, the government now requires export permits for a large range of objects, including glass and graphics over 50 years old, miniature art objects valued at more than 3,000Kč ($125), and paintings valued at more than 30,000Kč ($1,250). Most antiques shops provide export permits; ask for one if necessary.

In many markets, customers are expected to bring their own bags. If you don't have one, ask for a *taška;* it'll cost a couple of koruny.

(*Value*) **Prague's Best Buys**

Blood-red **garnets** are the official Czech national gem, and the ones that you can buy here are among the world's finest, as well as one of the country's top exports. Most garnets are mined near Teplice, about 63km (39 miles) northwest of Prague. There are at least five specific kinds. Bohemian garnets are the Pyrope type, an amalgam of calcium and magnesium that's almost always deep red. You can get a small necklace for as little as 700Kč ($29) or densely packed brooches or bracelets for more than 30,000Kč ($1,250), depending on whether they're set in silver or gold. Be warned that fake garnets are common, so purchase your stones from a reputable shop like the ones recommended below.

Fine **crystal** has been produced in the Bohemian countryside since the 14th century. In the 17th and 18th centuries, it became the preferred glass of the world's elite, drawing royals and the rich to Karlovy Vary to buy straight from the source. The king of Siam made a fabled trip to this western Czech spa town in the 1930s just to choose place settings for his palace. Bohemian factories are responsible for artistic advances in gilding, cutting, and coloring. Today, the quality remains high, and you can still purchase contemporary glass for prices that are much lower than those in the West. See below for a list of Prague's most prominent glass retailers.

Antiques and **antiquarian books and prints** are widely available and are distinctive souvenirs, sold by specialist Antikvariáts. These antiques shops are located throughout the city, but you'll find many in Old Town and Malá Strana.

Since beer is a little heavy to carry home and the local wine isn't worth it, take home a bottle of **Becherovka,** the nation's popular herbal liqueur from Karlovy Vary. You'll find the distinctive green decanter in shops around the city; it costs about 400Kč ($17) per liter.

Sunday from noon to 5pm. Malá Štupartská 5, Praha 1. © **224-826-565**. www.bigbenbookshop. com. Metro: Můstek.

Globe Bookstore and Coffeehouse Opened in 1993, Prague's first English-language literary hangout boasts the city's largest collection of used paperback literature and nonfiction. The atmosphere in the California-style cafe allows for a trendy afternoon read accompanied by stiff espresso, sandwiches, pastas, salads, desserts, and a full bar. Along with the great selection of books, you'll find a section with current international magazines, as well as newspapers. They offer Internet services for just 1.50Kč (6¢) per minute and laptop hookups. Open daily from 10am to midnight. Pštrossova 6, Praha 1. © **224-934-203**. www.globebookstore.cz. Metro: Národní třída.

Neoluxor-Palác knih Luxor This building on Wenceslas Square, which used to house a popular cafe and nightclub, is now the biggest book megastore in central Europe. On four floors full of books, magazines, and maps—mostly in Czech though—you will find sections with paperbacks, books on art, history, design, or books on Prague in English. Take your book and relax in their cafe on the first floor, where cappuccino costs only 35Kč ($1.50). Open Monday to Friday 8am to 8pm, Saturday 9am to 7pm, and Sunday 10am to 7pm. Václavské nám. 41, Praha 1. ℂ **221-111-364.** www.neoluxor.cz. Metro: Muzeum or Můstek.

COSMETICS & FRAGRANCES

Soon after the revolution, some of the world's most noted perfumeries and cosmetics boutiques became pioneers in Prague. **Elizabeth Arden,** Rybná 2, Praha 1 (ℂ **222-325-471;** metro: náměstí Republiky), is open Monday to Friday from 9:30am to 6:30pm and Saturday from 9:30am to 2pm. **Estée Lauder,** Železná 18, Praha 1 (ℂ **224-232-023;** metro: Můstek), is open Monday to Friday from 10am to 7pm and Saturday from 10am to 4pm. **Perfumery Lancôme,** Jungmannovo nám. 20, Praha 1 (ℂ **224-217-189;** metro: Můstek), is open Monday to Friday from 9am to 7pm and Saturday from 10am to 4pm. **Christian Dior,** at V Celnici 4, Praha 1 (ℂ **224-224-447;** metro: náměstí Republiky), is open Monday to Friday 10am to 8pm, Saturday and Sunday 10am to 6pm.

CRYSTAL & GLASS

Cristallino ℱ   This store offers one of the largest assortments of Bohemia crystal and glass, as well as some porcelain and jewelry. Designs come from top Czech glass makers and vary from classic patterns to modern glassware. Remember, if you're buying goods for more than 3,000Kč ($125), ask for the Global Refund Cheque and get a stamp. Open daily 9am to 8pm April to December, 9am to 7pm January to March. Celetná 12, Praha 1. ℂ **224-225-173.** www.cristallino.cz. Metro: Můstek.

Moser ℱℱℱ *Value*   The Moser family began selling Bohemia's finest crystal in central Prague in 1857, drawing customers from around the world. Even the king of Siam made a special trip to the Karlovy Vary factory in the 1930s to pick his place settings. Soon after, the Nazis took over, and the Jewish Mosers fled. Following the war, the Communists seized the company but kept the Moser name. Surprisingly, the quality and reputation suffered little. The dark-wood showroom upstairs is worth a look if only to get the feeling of Prague at its most elegant. Open Monday to Friday from 9am to 8pm, Saturday and Sunday from 10am to 7pm. Na Příkopě 12, Praha 1. ℂ **224-211-293.** www.moser-glass.com. Metro: Můstek. 2nd Prague shop is at Malé nám. 11, Praha 1. ℂ **224-222-012.** Metro: Můstek.

DEPARTMENT STORES & SHOPPING MALLS

Černá Růže ℱ   Situated in one of many newly reconstructed palaces in Prague's walking zone, this shopping center offers stores selling well-known brands (**Adidas, Pierre Cardin, Daniel Hechter**), as well as some new Czech boutiques and small shops. After your shopping you can rest at the Pizzeria Bondy on the third floor. The center is open Monday to Friday 10am to 8pm, Saturday 10am to 7pm, and Sunday 11am to 7pm. Na Příkopě 12, Praha 1. ℂ **221-014-111.** www.cernaruze.cz. Metro: Můstek.

Koruna Palace   At the bottom of Wenceslas Square, the venerable Koruna Building, which used to house Prague's cheapest stand-up buffet, has had its towering passages reconstructed into a series of shops and cafes. After a few chocolate éclairs at the Coffee/Donuts bar upstairs, you can check out some fashion items at **Kenvelo** or new **Swatch** watch. The basement **Bontonland Megastore** is Prague's largest record/tape shop, based on the Richard Branson's Virgin concept but without offering any real savings. Open Monday to Saturday from 9am to 8pm and Sunday from 10am to 8pm. Václavské nám. at Na Příkopě 1, Praha 1. ℂ **224-219-526.** www.koruna-palace.cz. Metro: Můstek.

Kotva   Once the symbol of Communist consumer pride (admittedly an oxymoron), Kotva is the country's largest department store, with five floors ("For a Thousand Wishes") and a large supermarket in the basement. The sporting-goods department is well stocked, and you can find just about everything you'd expect in a major department store. Open Monday to Friday from 9am to 8pm, Saturday from 10am to 7pm, and Sunday from 10am to 6pm. Náměstí Republiky 8, Praha 1. ℂ 224-801-111. www.od-kotva.cz. Metro: Náměstí Republiky.

Obchodní Centrum Nový Smíchov ℛℛ   This modern shopping mall built on the defunct site of one of the city's most famous factories is Prague's new temple to post-Communist consumption. In just a few minutes' metro ride from Old Town or Malá Strana, you can find many items cheaper than in western Europe or the States. Here, the French retail hypermarket **Carrefour** now draws Czechs by the thousands. On the three levels of surrounding concourses, international jeans shops stand shoulder to shoulder with fashion and cosmetic boutiques like **Zara, Marella,** and **Body Basics.** Shoe shops include the homegrown post-Communist return of **Bat[av]a** (originally launched last century in Moravia), and the German favorite **Salamander.** Entertainment offerings include a multiplex cinema screening international films dubbed or subtitled in Czech, plus arcade games, billiards, cafes, and fast-food and full-menu restaurants. Open daily 9am to 9pm (shops); 7am to midnight (Carrefour); 11am to 11pm (restaurants and entertainment). Plzeňská 8, Praha 5. ℂ 251-511-151. www.novysmichovoc.cz. Metro: Anděl.

Palác Flora ℛ   This new addition to the city's shopping malls is located in the residential area of Vinohrady. The modern building has been erected right above Flora metro station, so it is easily accessible from the center. Inside you will find a wide selection of shops, restaurants, and cafes and an entertainment center that includes 3-D and 2-D cinemas. Boutiques and fashion shops (**Mango, Mexx, Guess, Bata**) occupy the second floor. Open Monday to Friday 9am to 9pm, Saturday and Sunday 10am to 10pm. Vinohradská 149, Praha 3. ℂ 255-741-700. www.edb.cz. Metro: Flora.

Palác Myslbek   Two British clothing stores, **Hennes&Mauritz** and **Next,** are part of this atrium, as well as **Calvin Klein Jeans** and **Guess.** They're open Monday to Saturday from 9:30am to 7pm and Sunday from noon to 6pm. Na Příkopě 19–21, Praha 1. ℂ 224-835-000. www.myslbek.com. Metro: Můstek.

Pavilon   This brightly reconstructed town market was central Prague's first highbrow galleria, with boutiques ranging from **Tommy Hilfiger** and **Sergio Tacchini** to **La Perla.** There's a **Sony** shop and a **Belgian Butcher,** a decent Italian gelato/espresso shop, in the center courtyard, and a fair-priced grocer downstairs. Open Monday to Saturday from 9:30am to 9pm and Sunday from noon to 6pm. Vinohradská 50, Praha 2. ℂ 222-097-111. www.pavilon.cz. Metro: Náměstí Míru.

Vintage Treasure & Trash

Those looking for acres of antiques and secondhand goods can trek to **Holešovice tržnice** every Saturday from 9am to 5pm. Take the metro to Vltavská, in Praha 7, and follow the signs coming out of the station. People from all over the country come to the capital to unload their attics. Anything from pictures of Soviet leader Josef Stalin to family silver collections can be found here.

Tesco   In 1996, British retailer Tesco bought the Communist-era Máj department store from the U.S. discount chain Kmart. It has turned the Máj into a well-organized modern shopping center. The best reasons to shop at Tesco are the gifts (including fine Leander rose porcelain), snacks on the ground floor (like a Little Caesar's pizza), and a fine grocery store in the basement. Tesco kept Kmart's vaunted American junk-food wall full of nachos, microwave popcorn, and peanut butter, but most of the goods are from local suppliers. Open Monday to Friday from 8am to 9pm (food department from 7am), Saturday from 9am to 8pm (food department from 8am), and Sunday from 10am to 8pm (food department from 9am). Národní třída 26, Praha 1. ℂ 222-003-111. Metro: Národní třída.

FASHION

Adam Steiner   The tailor-made suits have gone up by about 50% to begin at 15,000Kč ($625) after the *Wall Street Journal* featured Adam as the best value for tailoring in Eastern Europe. You can buy fine clothes with the Pierre Cardin or Burberry labels, as well as other conservative business clothes, shirts, tops, and underwear off the rack. Open Monday to Friday from 9am to 7pm and Saturday from 10am to 6pm. Václavské nám. 24, Praha 1. ℂ 224-220-594. Metro: Můstek.

Boutique Pařížská 18   A collection of fashion accessories of well-known names, including Sergio Rossi, Dolce&Gabbana, Versace, Ermenegildo Zegna, and Giorgio Armani, is displayed at this address, where the prices are Parisian, too. Open Monday to Friday 10am to 7:30pm, Saturday 10am to 7pm, and Sunday 11am to 6pm. Pařížská 18, Praha 1. ℂ 224-216-407. www.prospektamoda.cz. Metro: Staroměstská.

Hugo Boss–Men   Germany's king of men's suits, Boss has become a status symbol for the 20-something stockbrokers who've made a killing on Czech privatization. Expect to pay at least 20,000Kč ($832) for one of his wedge-cut dandies. Open Monday to Friday from 10am to 8pm, Saturday from 11am to 7pm, and Sunday from 1 to 6pm. Jungmannovo nám. 18, Praha 1. ℂ 224-222-144. Metro: Můstek. Boss's shop for women: Pařížská 28, Praha 1. ℂ 222-314-584. Metro: Staroměstská.

Taiza   Since Osmany Laffita, a Cuban wizard of fashion, opened his first boutique in Prague in 1999, he has established his name also in Paris and New York. He sticks to his motto, "Be unique, be desired, and stay elegant!" and is celebrating a huge success. He has become the personal designer for former first lady Mrs. Havel, and is very popular among Czech actresses. The boutique is open Monday to Saturday from 10am to 8pm, and Sunday from 1pm to 8pm. Na Příkopě 31, Praha 1. ℂ 225-113-308. www.taiza.com. Metro: Můstek.

Versace   Italy's most famous and flamboyant designer may be gone, but his ferociously unique tastes live on through his worldwide chain of boutiques. The Prague shop offers selections from new lines and off-the-rack repros on the heels of the season's premieres, as well as some of Versace's most daring Italian-villa home furnishings, including gilded vases and gold lamé pillows. Open Monday to Friday from 10am to 7pm and Saturday from 10am to 6pm. U Prašné brány 3, Praha 1. ℂ 224-810-016. www.prospektamoda.cz. Metro: Náměstí Republiky.

Zara   This Spanish clothing brand for women, men, and children features very trendy styles. It's open Monday to Saturday 10am to 8pm and Sunday 10am to 6pm. Na Příkopě 15, Praha 1. ℂ 224-239-860. www.zara.com. Metro: Můstek.

GARNETS

Český Granát *(Value)*   This shop has an excellent reputation for good-quality jewelry at reasonable prices. Traditional, conservative earrings and pendants are spiked with some interesting and unusual designs. Most pieces are set in 24-karat gold or gold-plated silver. Open Monday to Saturday from 10am to 7pm and Sunday from 10am to 7pm. Celetná 4, Praha 1. ℂ 224-228-281. Metro: Můstek.

Granát *(Value)*   Granát Turnov, the monopoly that controls the Czech Republic's favorite gem industry, is *the* place to visit if you're serious about shopping for garnets. Expect to pay between 1,000Kč and 2,500Kč ($41 and $104) for a midpriced ring or bracelet. Open Monday to Friday from 10am to 6pm and Saturday from 10am to 1pm. Dlouhá 30, Praha 1. ℂ 222-315-612. Metro: Náměstí Republiky.

Halada   Garnets fill the cases of Prague's premier jeweler. Czechs swear by Halada for quality, price, and selection. There is also an outlet of this store among the displays on the ground floor of Tesco. Open daily from 9am to 7pm. Na Příkopě 16, Praha 1. ℂ 224-221-304. Metro: Můstek.

Royal Jewelry-Zlatnictví   The designs of the pendants and brooches sold here are some of the most unusual in the city. All items are set in 14- or 18-karat gold and range from 500Kč to about 50,000Kč ($20–$2,080) and up. Open Monday to Saturday from 9am to 9pm and Sunday from 11am to 9pm. Václavské nám. 8, Praha 1. ℂ 224-222-404. Metro: Můstek.

GIFTS & SOUVENIRS

Celetná Crystal *(Value)*   A wide selection of world-renowned Czech crystal, china, arts and crafts, garnets, and jewelry is displayed in a spacious three-floor showroom right in the heart of Prague. Open daily 10am to 10pm. Celetná 15, Praha 1. ℂ 222-324-022. www.czechcrystal.com. Metro: Náměstí Republiky.

Galerie Marionetta *(Kids)*   At this shop you can cast any play in wooden puppets and toys—planes, trains, automobiles, animals, and almost anything fun made from wood. Open daily from 10am to 10pm. U Lužického semináře 7, Praha 1. ℂ 257-535-091. Metro: Malostranská.

Dr. Stuart's Botanicus *(Finds)*   This chain of natural scent, soap, and herb shops is an amazing Anglo-Czech success story. Started by a British botanist and Czech partners on a farm northeast of Prague, Dr. Stuart's has found 101 ways to ply a plant into a sensuous gift and a lucrative trade. There are several outlets throughout Prague, with this one at the Havelský market probably most convenient for tourists. Open Monday to Friday from 10am to 6pm and Saturday from 10am to 4pm. Michalská 4, Praha 1. ℂ 224-212-977. www.botanicus.cz. Metro: Můstek.

Dům Porcelánu Praha *(Value)*   Traditional Czech "onion" *(cibulák)* china is the calling card for this representative shop of the porcelain factory in Dubí near the German border. The folksy blue-on-bone cobalt onion patterns have become a familiar sight in country kitchens around the world. Open Monday to Friday from 9am to 7pm, Saturday from 9am to 2pm, and Sunday from 2 to 5pm. Jugoslávská 16, Praha 2. ℂ 221-505-320. www.cibulak.cz. Metro: Náměstí Míru or I. P. Pavlova.

Karlovarský porcelán "Thun" *(Value)*   On display here are some of the best pieces from the 21,000 tons of decorative and domestic porcelain produced annually in Karlovy Vary. Open daily from 10am to 8pm. Pařížská 2, Praha 1. ℂ 224-811-023. www.thun.cz. Metro: Staroměstská.

Sparky's *Kids*   This toy store in the center of the city is a welcoming spot for the whole family. The younger ones will find terrific souvenirs of Prague here. Open Monday to Saturday from 10am to 7pm, Sunday to 6pm. Havířská 2 (short street between Na Příkopě and the Estates' Theater), Praha 1. ℂ 224-239-309. www.sparkys.cz. Metro: Můstek.

HATS

Model   Prague's best haberdasher sells every type of topper, from mink to straw, at prices that are distinctly un-Western. In addition to the hundreds of handcrafted hats on display, the haberdashery can specially produce a hat according to your specifications in just 3 days. Both men's and women's hats are sold. Open Monday to Friday from 9am to 7pm, Saturday from 10am to 6pm, and Sunday 10am to 5pm. Václavské nám. 28, Praha 1. ℂ 224-216-805. Metro: Můstek.

JEWELRY

Dušák (Watchmaker and Goldsmith)   Dušák features Cartier, Gucci, Omega, Rado, and Certina chronographs and does repairs, too. Open Monday to Friday from 10am to 7pm, Saturday from 9am to 6pm, and Sunday from 1 to 6pm. Na Příkopě 17, Praha 1. ℂ 224-213-025. www.dusak.cz. Metro: Můstek.

Halada   Beyond garnets, Halada has one of the best arrays of market-priced gold, silver, platinum, and fine gems in this city, which 16 years ago used to ration wedding rings as a subsidized entitlement (no joke). Open daily from 9am to 7pm. Na Příkopě 16, Praha 1. ℂ 224-221-304. Metro: Můstek.

MUSIC

Bontonland Megastore   Selling everything from serious Bohemian classics to Seattle grunge, the store is in the Koruna Palace, which is open Monday to Saturday from 9am to 8pm and Sunday from 10am to 7pm. Václavské nám. at Na Příkopě 1, Praha 1. ℂ 224-473-080. www.bontonland.cz. Metro: Můstek.

MUSICAL INSTRUMENTS

Dům hudebních nástrojů *Value*   You can buy all kinds of instruments here, from tiny harmonicas to a magnificent Petrof piano. Open Monday to Friday from 9am to 7pm, Saturday from 10am to 3pm. Jungmannovo nám. 17, Praha 1. ℂ 224-222-501. www.guitarpark.cz. Metro: Můstek.

Praha Music Center   Bring home an instrument from the land where it is said that "every Czech is a musician." Affordable Eastern European–made stringed instruments are sold here. Open Monday to Friday from 9am to 6pm. Revoluční 14, Praha 1. ℂ 222-311-693. www.pmc.cz. Metro: Náměstí Republiky.

PHOTOGRAPHY

Jan Pazdera   Camera repairs and cheap darkroom equipment make this a Prague photo-snapper's favorite. The bulk of the selection is secondhand cameras, including Pentaxes and Russian Smenas. You can also find old telescopes, Carl Zeiss microscopes, light meters, and enlargers. Open Monday to Friday from 10am to 6pm. Vodičkova 28, pasáž ABC, Praha 1. ℂ 224-216-197. Metro: Můstek.

PUPPETS

Obchod loutkami *Kids*   Although there are no ventriloquist dummies, many kinds of puppets are available here, including hand, glove, rod, and marionettes. Obchod

> ### *Value* An Open-Air Market
>
> On the short, wide street perpendicular to Melantrichova, between Staroměst-
> ské náměstí and Václavské náměstí, **Havel's Market (Havelský trh),** Havelská
> ulice, Praha 1 (named well before Havel became president), features dozens of
> private vendors selling seasonal homegrown fruits and vegetables at the best
> prices in the city center. Other goods, including detergent, flowers, and cheese,
> are also for sale. Open Monday to Friday from 8am to 6pm. Take metro line A
> or B to Můstek.

loutkami isn't cheap, but its creations are expertly made and beautifully sculpted. Hundreds of characters from trolls to barmen are available in the store as well as online. Open daily from 10am to 8pm. Nerudova 47, Praha 1. ℂ **257-532-735.** www.marionettes.cz. Metro: Malostranská.

Obchod U Šaška *(Kids)*   This store sells high-quality, imaginatively designed clowns, ghouls, witches, and other marionettes, including a good likeness of the Good Soldier Švejk. Open daily from 10:30am to 7pm. Jilská 7, Praha 1. ℂ **224-235-579.** Metro: Můstek.

SHOES

✳ Bat'a   Czechoslovakia's favorite footwear émigré, Canadian Tomáš Bat'a, has made his post-Communist return with a vengeance, taking a sizable chunk of the market long after the Nazis and then the Communists cut the original Moravian family factory to pieces. His huge outlet on the site where his father started selling shoes earlier this century on Wenceslas Square has been remodeled for modern comfort. Bat'a goods include travel bags, leather accessories, sports outfits, and top-line brands of athletic shoes. Open Monday to Friday from 9am to 9pm, Saturday from 9am to 8pm, and Sunday from 10am to 8pm. Václavské nám. 6, Praha 1. ℂ **224-218-133.** www.bata.cz. Metro: Můstek.

SPORTING GOODS

Gigasport   With row upon row of clothes and equipment, Gigasport is Prague's mega–sporting goods retailer. However, the prices aren't much better than what you'd find abroad, and the company's overzealous security staff forces you to park all your belongings in cubbyholes (you have to have correct change to use them). Open daily from 9:30am to 7pm. Palác Myslbek, Na Příkopě 19, Praha 1. ℂ **224-233-552.** www.gigasport-cr.cz. Metro: Můstek.

WINE & BEER

Wine, Budvar, and Becherovka are sold in shops all over Prague, but one of the cheapest places to buy these popular drinks is **Tesco** (see "Department Stores & Shopping Malls," earlier in this chapter). Expect to pay about 300Kč ($12) for a medium bottle of Becherovka and 150Kč ($6.25) for six bottles of Budvar. They also have a decent selection of domestic and foreign wines.

10

Prague After Dark

For many Czechs, the best nighttime entertainment is boisterous discussion and world-class brew at a noisy pub. Visitors with a penchant to blend in with the locals can learn a lot about this part of the world with an evening at the corner *hospoda.* Many are fascinated just by a quiet stroll over the ancient city's cobblestones lit by the mellow lamps of Charles Bridge and Malá Strana. Others seek the dark caverns of a fine jazz club or the black light and Day-Glo of a hot dance club.

But Prague's longest entertainment tradition, of course, is classical music. Sadly, many visitors leave disappointed at the level of the performances, especially the operas. Some of your choices can be entertaining and others thoroughly disappointing. Government cutbacks amid post-Communist budget realities have forced directors to skimp, while many great young voices have migrated to more lucrative stints abroad or to the rock operas and musicals that have sprung up around town.

A safe bet is Mozart's ***Don Giovanni,*** usually presented about twice a month in its original 2-centuries-old home, the **Estates' Theater.** This production, which has modern accents, can be choppy, but the beautifully restored setting makes even a mediocre performance worth attending.

Serious music lovers are better off at one of the numerous performances of the **Czech Philharmonic** at the Rudolfinum, the **Prague Symphony Orchestra** at Obecní dům, or top **chamber ensembles**

at salons and palaces around the city. A pipe organ concert heard while sitting in the pews of one of the city's baroque churches can be inspirational.

For a more daring night, the cutting-edge **Laterna Magika** has been wowing audiences with its multimedia performance art since the Communists made the surprising decision to allow limited freedom of expression in the 1980s. See "Theaters," later in this chapter.

TICKETS Events rarely sell out far in advance, except for major nights during the Prague Spring Music Festival or a staging of *Don Giovanni* in the high season. To secure tickets before arriving, contact the travel bureau **Čedok** in Prague, at Na Příkopě 18, Praha 1 (© **224-197-777;** www.cedok.cz; or in Britain, at 314–322 Regent St., London W1B 3BG © **020-7580-3778;** www.cedok.co.uk). You can also contact the Prague ticket agency **Ticketpro,** Klimentská 22, Praha 1 (© **296-329-999;** www.ticketpro.cz). This largest computerized ticket service sells seats online to most events around town. You can purchase tickets using Visa, MasterCard, Diners Club, or American Express, or reserve them on the Web and pay when you arrive.

Once in Prague, you can get tickets for most classical performances at the box office in the modern Nová scéna annex to the **National Theater** at Národní třída 2, Praha 1 (© **224-901-448;** www.nd.cz). You can purchase tickets either at theater box offices or from any one of the dozens of ticket agencies. The largest handle most of the entertainment offerings and include a service charge. Ask how much this is before buying, as sometimes rates are hiked substantially. Large, centrally located agencies are **Prague Tourist Center,** Rytířská 12, Praha 1 (✆ **296-333-333**), open daily from 9am to 8pm; **Bohemia Ticket,** Na Příkopě 16, Praha 1 (✆ **224-215-031;** www.bohemiaticket.cz),

open Monday to Friday from 10am to 7pm, Saturday from 10am to 5pm, and Sunday from 10am to 3pm; and **Čedok,** Na Příkopě 18, Praha 1 (✆ **800-112-112** toll free or 224-197-777; www.cedok.cz), open Monday to Friday from 9am to 7pm and Saturday from 10am to 2pm. You can buy event tickets in person at these computerized outlets.

1 The Performing Arts

Mozart reportedly shocked the Viennese when he once scoffed at his Austrian patrons, claiming that "Praguers understand me." His trips to the outpost in the Austrian Empire became the subject of music folklore. His defiant 1787 premiere of *Don Giovanni* is the high-water mark in Prague's cultural history—not that there haven't been fine performances since. Czech composers Dvořák and Smetana each moved the resurgent nation to tears in the 19th century, while Martinů and Janáček ushered in a new industrial-age sound to classical compositions in the first half of the 20th century. You can still hear many works in grand halls throughout Prague; they're worth a visit just to immerse yourself in the grandeur of the setting, let alone the musical accompaniment.

OPERA

Even if you're not fond of opera, buying a seat at any of the theaters below is a relatively affordable gamble. Prices range from about 400Kč to 1,200Kč ($16–$50) and are often available up to curtain time.

While performances of Mozart's operas at the Estates' Theater are probably the visitor's best overall choices because of the setting, the **National Opera,** performing in the gold-crowned 19th-century National Theater, remains the country's best-loved company. Once the fiefdom of heavy-handed Bedřich Smetana, and then home to soprano Emma Destinová, who sang with the great Enrico Caruso, the National Opera has now fallen on harder times. Yet it still occasionally dazzles with Czech works like Smetana's peppy *Prodaná nevěsta (The Bartered Bride).* The choreography is fun for the whole family, and explanations of the plot are provided in English. Once in a while, internationally acclaimed soloists stop by. Seasons tend to concentrate on Czech works, though foreign-composed operas are also scheduled.

The **Prague State Opera (Státní opera Praha),** in the aging State Opera House near the top of Wenceslas Square, has reorganized after its 1992 split with the National Opera and now concentrates primarily on Italian classics, though a few Czech favorites are included each season. Its staging of Puccini's *Tosca* is solid but staid and without sufficient emotion at the tragic ending. Verdi's works like *La Traviata* and *Aïda* have received mixed reviews—the performances have had high standards but the sets seem cheap.

The National Opera's large-scale productions are condensed and transported to the cozier confines of Prague's most beautiful concert hall, the **Estates' Theater.** In addition to the quintessential house performance in original Italian of *Don Giovanni,* other works by the master staged here are a Czech version of *The Magic Flute* and *The Wedding of Figaro* in Italian. At other times, the theater often stages Czech versions of international classic stage plays or chamber ballets.

Tips **Dressing the Part**

Czechs are, generally, a casual live-and-let-live people. Ex-president Havel, who had collected an extensive official wardrobe, is etched in everyone's memory as the dissident playwright wearing old frayed sweaters. Journalists still often show up for news conferences with the president or prime minister in T-shirts. But if you plan on attending the opera or theater, **proper evening wear is highly recommended.** There may be no worse faux pas in Bohemia than dressing bohemian for a classical performance. For men: a dark suit, or at least a coat and tie. For women: a mid-length dress or pantsuit.

See "Landmark Theaters & Concert Halls," below, for details on the theaters discussed here.

CLASSICAL MUSIC

This small capital boasts three full orchestras, yet all are financially strapped, so the repertoire tends to be conservative, with most concerts providing popular time-tested works. You can get information about all of them at the ticket agencies listed above. Tickets range from 100Kč to 600Kč ($4.15–$25) during the regular season and up to 2,000Kč ($83) for the opening night of the **Prague Spring Festival.** You can find dozens of concerts by the full orchestras or chamber groups each month, but the pickings are thin in July and August, when the musicians are on their holiday. See "Landmark Theaters & Concert Halls," below, for details.

Of the city's three orchestras, the **Czech Philharmonic** is the one that commands a fairly solid international reputation, though it's not considered first-rate. The Philharmonic, which calls the restored **Rudolfinum** home, went through turmoil in 1996 with the resignation of its first non-Czech musical director/chief conductor, German-born Gerd Albrecht. Despite acute money problems, the Philharmonic improved under Albrecht's demanding baton. Though many critics delighted in saying that Albrecht had tightened the ensemble and imposed disciplined precision, he had his detractors, including high government officials and orchestra members. In a hail of accusations and counteraccusations of Czech and German nationalism (mostly fanned by the press in both countries), Albrecht resigned, claiming that he'd lost his artistic freedom. Vladimír Ashkenazy, a Russian-born pianist who has promised to make the Czech orchestra world-class again, has since replaced him. In 2002 the Philharmonic opened the Prague Spring Music Festival for the first time in several years. In August 2003 the post of chief conductor was taken by Czech-born American Zdeněk Mácal, who came back to Prague after leading the New Jersey Symphony Orchestra for several years.

The **Prague Symphony Orchestra** has positioned itself as the fresher alternative to the Philharmonic, with French Serge Baudo as chief conductor. It focuses more on 20th-century music but has too often fallen back on Bach. Its freshly remodeled home in the **Smetana Hall** of the Municipal House (Obecní dům) ☞☞ cries out for a new concert approach, as its bold Art Nouveau elegance is more reminiscent of Shostakovich's power than Brahms's delicacy.

The **Prague Radio Symphony Orchestra** is primarily a studio band but does make regular concert appearances. The group plays sufficiently good versions of classical and contemporary works in the Rudolfinum or Obecní dům.

Prague After Dark

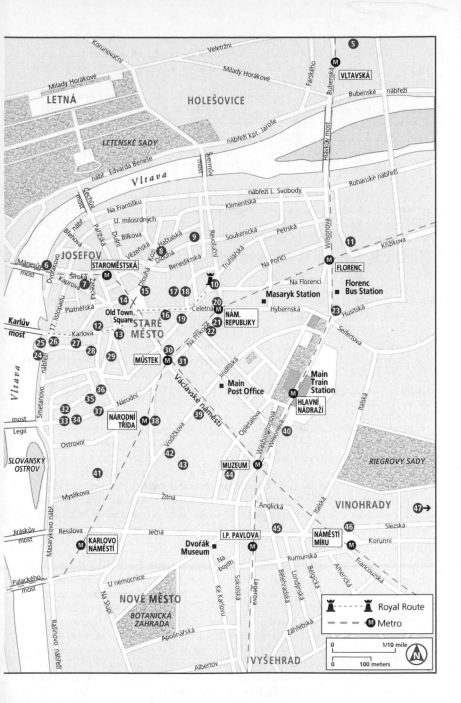

Two solo Czech violinists to look out for when booking your tickets: the veteran virtuoso **Josef Suk,** a grandson of Dvořák, who still plays with crisp, if not exact, precision; and his flashier heir apparent, **Václav Hudeček,** who attacks every stanza with passion and bleeds through his bow.

The city's orchestras all come to life during the international **Prague Spring Festival,** an annual 3-week series of classical music events that runs from mid-May to early June; the events began as a rallying point for Czech culture in the aftermath of World War II. The country's top performers usually participate in the festival, as well as some noted international stars. Tickets for concerts range from 250Kč to 2,000Kč ($10–$83) and are available in advance from Hellichova 18, Praha 1 (© 257-312-547; www.festival.cz).

The newer **Prague Autumn International Music Festival,** in September, hasn't received as much acclaim as the spring event, but the appearances of the world-known Philharmonic Orchestras gave it a much-needed boost. Contact the office (© 222-540-484; www.pragueautumn.cz) or **Ticketpro** (see "Tickets," above) for more information.

CLASSICAL CONCERTS AROUND TOWN

When strolling, you'll undoubtedly pick up or be handed lots of leaflets advertising chamber concerts in churches, museums, and other venues. These recitals and choral arrangements usually have programs featuring a classical and baroque repertoire, with an emphasis on pieces by Czech composers. The quality varies, but the results are usually enjoyable. Tickets range from 100Kč to 350Kč ($4.15–$15) and can be purchased at the churches' entrances or sometimes from hotel concierges.

Because of its extravagant beauty, the **Chapel of Mirrors,** in the Klementinum, Mariánské náměstí, Praha 1 (© 221-663-111), is a favorite chamber concert venue. Almost every evening a classical concert highlights strings, winds, or the organ. The varied programs often rely on popular works by Handel, Bach, Beethoven, and Prague's beloved Mozart.

The Church of St. Nicholas (Kostel sv. Mikuláše), Staroměstské náměstí, Praha 1 (© 224-190-991), is one of the city's finest baroque gems. Chamber concerts and organ recitals are popular here, and the acoustics are terrific. There's also a lot to look at: rich stucco decoration, sculptures of saints, and a crown crystal chandelier.

The **House at the Stone Bell (Dům U kamenného zvonu),** Staroměstské nám. 13, Praha 1 (© 224-827-526), across the square from St. Nicholas, regularly hosts chamber concerts and other small gigs, including operatic arias and duets that are often performed here by soloists of the National Theater and State Opera.

DANCE

Of all the musical arts in Prague, dance is the most accessible. From classical ballet to innovative modern dance, there are several options each week that demonstrate an enjoyable mix of grace, beauty, and athleticism. The **National Theater Ballet** troupe has seen most of its top talent go west since 1989, but it still has a deep roster as the country's premier troupe. Beyond the classical favorites at the venerable National Theater's main stage, the ballet's choreographer, Libor Vaculík, has come up with dance twists on films like *Some Like It Hot* and *Psycho* next door at the modern, comfortable theater in the round, Nová scéna. Vaculík's works are popular, making this one of the most financially secure dance companies in Eastern Europe. Tickets are 200Kč to 550Kč ($8.30–$23); call © 224-933-782 for information.

The **Prague Chamber Ballet** has recently been playing intimate dates at the Estates' Theater, giving the audience the chance to see modern and classical dance in a theater primarily designed for opera. The choreographer's fresh takes on Czech spiritual folk music, Latin or Slavic beats, and provocative religious themes are set to recorded music. But the sound system is adequate and the experience above average. Check the *Prague Post* to see what selections are playing.

LANDMARK THEATERS & CONCERT HALLS

The Czech Philharmonic at Rudolfinum *(Moments*   Named for Prince Rudolf, the beautifully restored Rudolfinum has been one of the city's premier concert venues since it opened in the 19th century. The Rudolfinum's Small Hall mostly presents chamber concerts, while the larger, more celebrated Dvořák Hall is home to the Czech Philharmonic. Though the acoustics aren't faultless, the grandeur of the hall makes a concert experience here worthwhile. Alšovo nábřeží 12, Praha 1. (*C* **227-059-352.** www.rudolfinum.cz. Metro: Staroměstská.

Estates' Theater (Stavovské divadlo) *介介*   In a city full of spectacularly beautiful theaters, the massive pale-green Estates' still ranks as one of the most awesome. Built in 1783, this is the only theater in the world that's still in its original condition. The Estates' was home to the premiere of Mozart's *Don Giovanni*, which was conducted by the composer himself. The building, an example of the late baroque style, was reopened on the 200th anniversary of Mozart's death in 1991, after nearly 9 years of reconstruction. Simultaneous English translation, transmitted via headphone, is available for plays staged here. Ovocný trh 1, Praha 1. (*C* **224-902-322.** www.nd.cz or www. mozart-praha.cz. Metro: Line A or B to Můstek.

National Theater (Národní divadlo) *介介*   This neo-Renaissance building overlooking the Vltava River was completed in 1881. The theater was built to nurture the Czech National Revival—a grass-roots movement to replace the dominant German culture with that of native Czechs. To finance it, small collection boxes with signs promoting "the prosperity of a dignified national theater" were installed in public places. Almost immediately upon its completion, the building was wrecked by fire; it was rebuilt and opened in 1883 with the premiere of Bedřich Smetana's opera *Libuše*. The magnificent interior contains an allegorical sculpture about music and busts of Czech theatrical personalities as well as paintings created by Czech artists of the National Theater generation—Myslbek, Aleš, Hynais. Composer Bedřich Smetana conducted the theater's orchestra here until 1874, when deafness forced him to relinquish his post. Národní 2, Praha 1. (*C* **224-901-448.** www.nd.cz. Metro: Národní třída.

Prague Symphony Orchestra–Smetana Hall (Smetanova síň) *介*   Named for the popular composer and fervent Czech nationalist Bedřich Smetana (1824–84), Smetana Hall is located in one of the world's most distinctive Art Nouveau buildings. Since its 1997 reopening after the building's painstaking reconstruction, the ornate and purely exhilarating Smetana Hall has hosted a series of top-notch events. Such events include a speech by former U.S. Secretary of State Madeleine Albright on her return to her birthplace to invite the Czechs into NATO; and an eclectic evening during a 1997 forum with Gregory Peck, James Earl Jones, and Lynn Redgrave reciting excerpts from Václav Havel plays. In the Municipal House (Obecní dům), náměstí Republiky 5, Praha 1. (*C* **222-002-336.** www.fok.cz. Metro: Náměstí Republiky.

State Opera House (Státní opera) ⚜ First the "New German Theater" and then the "Smetana Theater," the State Opera was built in the 1880s for the purpose of staging Germanic music and drama. Based on a Viennese design, the Renaissance-style theater was rebuilt after suffering serious damage during the bombing of Prague in 1945. Over the years, the auditorium has hosted many great names, including Richard Wagner, Richard Strauss, and Gustav Mahler, whose Seventh Symphony premiered here. In addition to being home to the State Opera, the house stages other music and dance events. Wilsonova 4, Praha 2. ℂ **296-117-111.** www.opera.cz. Metro: Muzeum.

THEATERS

Theater has a long tradition in Czech life. Its enormous influence was reconfirmed during the revolutionary events of 1989, when theaters became the focal points and the strategy rooms for the opposition.

Most of the city's theater offerings are in Czech, but a few English-language expatriate troupes have taken root and stage performances whenever they are ready—or not—at various locations. Check the *Prague Post* (www.praguepost.com) for the latest listings.

Czech productions by local and translated authors are staged almost every night. The most highly respected theaters are the gorgeous **Vinohrady Theater (Divadlo na Vinohradech),** náměstí Míru 7, Praha 2 (ℂ **224-257-601;** www.dnv-praha.cz), the former workplace of ex-president Havel's wife, Dagmar, who made a final performance as Queen Kristina soon after becoming first lady. The **Theater on the Balustrade (Divadlo Na Zábradlí),** Anenské nám. 5, Praha 1 (ℂ **222-868-868;** www.nazabradli.cz), is the place where Havel got his start as a playwright. Tickets, usually costing between 90Kč and 200Kč ($3.75–$8.30), should be bought in advance. Simultaneous translation into English is often offered through earphones provided by the theaters, but the translator reads all parts from a script, usually without much dramatic verve. Ask when booking if translation is offered.

Laterna Magika This performance-art show based in the new wing of the National Theater stages a range of multimedia productions, from a provocative, racy version of *Odysseus* to a choppy, inconsistent version of *Casanova,* but the stunning presence of the lead Linda Rybová lights up the stage. These are adult themes combining unique uses of dance, music, film, and light and can be very entertaining and easy to follow for audiences of any language. Národní třída 4, Praha 1. ℂ **224-931-482.** www.laterna.cz. Tickets 680Kč ($28); should be bought in advance. Metro: Národní třída.

National Marionette Theater (Národní divadlo marionet) This is the best of Prague's small handful of puppet theaters. The company's mainstay has been Mozart's *Don Giovanni.* For adults, the best thing about the show is the soundtrack. Žatecká 1, Praha 1. ℂ **224-819-322.** www.mozart.cz. Tickets 490Kč ($20). Metro: Staroměstská.

<hr>

2 The Club & Music Scene

The Velvet Revolution had its roots in the underground rock clubs that kept the braver Czech sonic youth tuned in to something more than the monotones of the Party during the gray 1970s and 1980s period known as Normalization. The Communists' persecution of the garage band Plastic People of the Universe, named for a Frank Zappa refrain, motivated playwright Václav Havel and his friends to keep the human rights heat on the Politburo. As president, Havel paid homage to rock's part in the revolution and kept company with the likes of Zappa, Springsteen, Dylan, and the Stones—all of whom paid tribute to him as "the rock-'n'-roll president."

Almost universally, the amps in clubs are turned up to absurd distortion. But while most wannabe bands playing Prague today lack the political edge of the prerevolution days, some have kept their unique Slavic passion without being overtaken by the urge to sound like Soundgarden. Throughout the rock clubs on any given night you might run into the acerbic pounding of Psí vojáci (Dog Soldiers), the no-holds-barred horns of Laura a její tygři (Laura and Her Tigers), or bohemian Dan Bárta's Illustratosphere.

ROCK & DANCE CLUBS

Duplex Club & Café 𝒢𝒢 Located right in the heart of Wenceslas Square, this is one of Prague's more exclusive clubs. From the roof terrace, visitors enjoy a magnificent view of the city's very center. Prague's best DJs perform inside the club itself, where cool lighting and high-tech sound set the right atmosphere. Yes, it was here that Mick Jagger had his 60th birthday party in July 2003 during the Stones' fourth concert in Prague. It's no wonder that in 2005, the Duplex was granted a membership in the "World's Finest Clubs" group, which recommends exclusive nightclubs for VIP parties. Prices are reasonable. It's open daily 10:30pm to 3am (Fri and Sat till 5am). Václavské nám. 21, Praha 1. ✆ **224-232-319.** www.duplexduplex.cz. Admission 50Kč ($2), Fri and Sat 150Kč ($6.25). Metro: Můstek.

Karlovy Lázně 𝒢 What used to be a spa house (*lázně* in Czech) now serves as a relaxation center of a different kind. The building consists of four floors of music. On your way up you'll feel and hear all types of tunes at the Paradogs and Kaleidoskop levels. At the third level you can become the dancing queen (or king) at the Discoteque, which will transport you back to the 1970s. Save some energy to climb up

---

⟮Moments⟯ Prague's Mysterious Nights

If you've never been here, the otherwise uninspired film *Kafka* with Jeremy Irons will give you a fine sense of the dark mystery trapped in the shadows cast over the palace walls and cobblestone streets throughout Old Town and Malá Strana. You'll never forget a slow stroll across Charles Bridge, with its dim lampposts (gas flames were used until well into the 20th c.) cutting eerie silhouettes from the attendant statues. The artfully lit facades of Prague Castle hover above as if the whole massive complex is floating in the darkness. The domes and spires of the skyline leading up to Hradčany have more varied textures and contours than a Dutch master could ever have dreamed of painting. Students howling with a guitar, or a single violinist playing his heart out for a few koruny in his hat, create the bridge's ambient sound.

Evenings are also a fine time to walk through the castle courtyards; as the crowds disperse, a quiet solemnity falls over the city. From high atop the castle hill, you can see Prague sparkling below.

Across the river, the brightly lit belfries of Týn Church cast a spine-tingling glow on the rest of Old Town Square, and the mellow lamps around the Estates' Theater provide light for a memorable walk home after a performance.

to the MCM Café for a cup of coffee or a drink. And, who knows, maybe you'll run into Bruce Willis (it's happened to me before) or some other celebrity shooting a film in Prague. The club is open daily 9pm to 5am. Smetanovo nábřeží 198 at Novotného lávka, Praha 1. (C) **222-220-502.** www.karlovylazne.cz. Cover 50Kč ($2) before 10pm and after 4am; 150Kč ($6.25) 10pm–4am. Metro: Staroměstská.

Lávka (★★)   Lávka's black-light and Day-Glo dance area, where techno-dance tunes pound, stands in stark contrast to the terrace, which provides quiet respite. Here you can take advantage of the riverside outdoor seating during warmer months. They also rent boats for 50Kč ($2) per hour. The drink prices help pay what has to be a hefty rent for this location, so bring a fat wallet. The clientele is a mix of well-heeled locals and visitors. Lávka club is open nonstop and music plays from 9:30am to 5am. Novotného lávka 1, Praha 1. (C) **222-222-156.** www.lavka.cz. Cover 50Kč ($2). Metro: Staroměstská.

Lucerna Music Bar   Big and a bit dingy, this Prague landmark in the belly of the downtown palace built by Václav Havel's father provides the best lineup of Czech garage bands, ex-underground acts, and an occasional reggae or blues gig. The drinks are still cheap for the city center, with a pull of beer under 25Kč ($1). The feel of the Lucerna, with its mirrored ball spinning the night away, borrows from disco but is mixed with the funky edginess of the period around the revolution. The crowd is still mostly local. The Lucerna is a frequent stop of the band Laura and Her Tigers. Open daily from 8pm to 3am, with live music usually beginning at 9pm. Vodičkova 36, Praha 1. (C) **224-217-108.** www.musicbar.cz. Cover 50Kč–70Kč ($2–$2.90). Metro: Můstek.

Malostranská beseda   Besides hosting random nights of some good jazz, the *beseda* ("meeting place") on the recently restored baroque main square in Malá Strana once acted as the district's town hall. The mix of bands varies, so check the *Prague Post* to see if the *beseda* is playing your tune. On the second floor, the club consists of little more than two smallish rooms; one holds the bar, the other a stage on which live bands perform most every night. You'll do more sitting than dancing here. The bar is open daily from 5 to 8pm, after 8pm only to ticket holders, and the music usually begins at 8:30pm. Malostranské nám. 21, Praha 1. (C) **257-532-092.** www.mb.muzikus.cz. Cover 80Kč ($3.35). Metro: Malostranská.

Mecca   For those who don't mind trekking into the depths of Praha 7 to be with some of the trendiest people in town, make your way to Mecca. You don't have to pray to the east to get in, but you'd better be one of the beautiful people, dressed well enough to get by the bouncers at the usually packed entrance. This converted warehouse in a northeast Prague industrial area has become the biggest challenge to the Roxy and Radost for Prague's large house parties, with DJ-driven techno, glaring lights, and plenty of sound. Open 11am to 6am daily. U Průhonu 3, Praha 7. (C) **283-870-522.** www.mecca.cz. Cover 100Kč–200Kč ($4.15–$8.30). Metro: Vltavská, then tram no. 1.

Radost FX (★) (*Finds*)   The Radost tries so hard to catch the retro 1960s and 1970s crowd that it has become a cartoon of itself, yet it remains popular with a mixed straight, gay, and model crowd. The rec-room interior of the ground-floor lounge is great for a chat and a drink. The series of downstairs rooms gets filled with rave and techno mixes. The crowd is very attractive and style-obsessed, and the bouncers have been known to boot those who don't look the part. Open daily from 10pm to 5am. A visit to Radost's vegetarian cafe of the same name, upstairs, is usually combined with a trip to the club (see the review in chapter 6). Bělehradská 120, Praha 2. (C) **224-254-776.** www.radostfx.cz. Cover 100Kč–250Kč ($4.15–$10). Metro: I. P. Pavlova or Náměstí Míru.

Roxy   Another reincarnation of a dead cinema, the Roxy pushes the boundaries of bizarre in its dark, stark concrete dance hall down Dlouhá Street near Old Town Square. The balcony allows the art-community crowd to people-watch amid the candlelight. The club is ultra-deconstructionist. Persian rugs and lanterns soften the atmosphere but don't improve the lousy acoustics. Acid jazz, funk, techno, salsa, and reggae are among the tunes on the playlist from the recorded or live acts. The Roxy is the longest late-night romp in town, open from 7pm to 5am. Dlouhá 33, Praha 1. ℂ 224-826-296. www.roxy.cz. Cover 50Kč–250Kč ($2–$10). Metro: Náměstí Republiky.

JAZZ

While Dixieland swing was huge in Prague during the First Republic, urban jazz really made its mark here during the 1960s, when those testing the Communist authority flocked to the smoky caves and wore dark glasses. The chubby Czech songstress Vlasta Průchová grabbed a few hints from Ella Fitzgerald for her throaty voice and set the standard for Czech be-bop wannabes in the postwar period leading up to the Prague Spring. After defecting, her son Jan Hammer made it big in the United States with his computerized scores, among which is the theme for *Miami Vice*.

Luckily, most of Prague's ensembles follow Vlasta's lead and not Jan's. There are several good venues for a cool evening with a traditional upright bass, piano, sax, and drum group or occasional shots of fusion and acid jazz. The most publicized gig was at the Reduta Jazz Club, where Bill Clinton played "Summertime" and "My Funny Valentine" for then-president Havel and Madeleine Albright during a state visit in 1994.

Look for bookings with the venerable Průchová, who's still belting out the blues along with her Swinging Quartet, or her be-bop heiress apparent, Jana Koubková. The Karel Růžička or Štěpán Markovič quartets are also solid, with surprising doses of soul.

U Malého Glena, listed under "Pubs," below, also offers jazz, fusion, and sometimes funk on most nights in its cellar.

AghaRTA Jazz Centrum ℱ   Upscale by Czech standards, the AghaRTA regularly features some of the best music in town, from standard acoustic trios and quartets to Dixieland, funk, and fusion. Hot Line, the house band led by AghaRTA part-owner and drummer Michal Hejna, regularly takes the stage. Bands usually begin at 9pm. Open daily from 7pm to midnight. Železná 16, Praha 1. ℂ 222-211-275. www.agharta.cz. Cover 100Kč ($4.15). Metro: Můstek.

Metropolitan Jazz Club   There never seems to be anyone under 30 in this sophisticated downstairs jazz club, fitted with ceramic-topped tables and red velvet chairs. The small cellar is reached through the courtyard just a few doors down from the McDonald's on Vodičkova. It's home to a house trio that plays several nights a month, and Dixieland and swing bands fill the rest of the calendar. Concerts begin at 9pm. Open Monday to Friday from 11am to 1am and Saturday and Sunday from 7pm to 1am. Jungmannova 14, Praha 1. ℂ 224-347-777. Cover 100Kč ($4.15). Metro: Můstek.

Reduta Jazz Club   Reduta is the most familiar of all of Prague's jazz clubs, and most of the good Czech acts will make an appearance here sometime during the year. This smoky cavern has cramped seating in fixed metallic boxes with veneer-wood tables, forcing everyone to sit in the same position through most of the night. Drinks are usually ordered from the adjacent bar, though a waitress is known to occasionally show up. But the reason people come here is the wide range of solid jazz acts. Music usually starts at 9:30pm. Open daily from 9pm to midnight. Národní 20, Praha 1. ℂ 224-933-487. www.redutajazzclub.cz. Cover 120Kč ($5). Metro: Národní třída.

U staré paní   Some of the best bands perform on a small stage downstairs from an overpriced pension in the middle of Old Town. The jazz is wonderfully close to most every table in this club, which is both visually pleasant and acoustically superior. Karel Růžička and his band play here frequently. Concerts begin at 9pm and usually last until 2am. Michalská 9, Praha 1. ✆ 224-228-090. www.jazzlounge.cz. Cover 150Kč-200Kč ($6.25-$8.30). Metro: Můstek.

3 Pubs

Good pub brews and conversations are Prague's preferred late-evening entertainment. Unlike British, Irish, or German beer halls, a true Czech pub ignores accouterments like cushy chairs and warm wooden paneling, and cuts straight to the chase—beer. While some Czech pubs do serve a hearty plate of food alongside the suds, it's the brew, uncommonly cheap at usually less than 30Kč ($1.25) a pint, that keeps people sitting for hours.

Foreign-theme pubs are popping up all over Prague, offering tastes ranging from Irish to Mexican. Still, it feels a bit like trying to sell Indian tea in China. Below are listed the best of the Czech brew stops followed by choices whose inspirations come from abroad.

CZECH PUBS

U Fleků   One of the original microbreweries dating back to 1459, U Fleků is Prague's most famous beer hall, one of the few pubs that still serves only its own beer. It's a huge place with a maze of timber-lined rooms and a large, loud courtyard where an oompah band performs. The ornate, medieval-style wood ceilings and courtyard columns are charming but not very old. Tourists come here by the busload, but disparaging locals who don't like the German atmosphere avoid the place. The pub's sweet dark beer is excellent and not available anywhere else; however, the sausages and goulash are overcooked and overpriced. For musical entertainment at the Cabaret Hall (daily from 8pm) there is a cover charge of 100Kč ($4.15). Open daily from 9am to 11pm. Křemencova 11, Praha 2. ✆ 224-934-019. www.ufleku.cz. Metro: Národní třída.

U medvídků (At the Little Bears)   This 5-centuries-old pub off Národní třída was the first in town to serve the original Budweiser, Budvar, on tap. It also serves typical Czech pub food, including *cmunda*, potato pancakes topped with sauerkraut and cured meat. It's smoky inside, but it's easier to breathe here than at most local pubs. Be sure to go to the right when you enter; if you don't, you'll head into the darker bar, which serves the same food and a wider range of beer choices at close to twice the price. Open daily from 11:30am to 11pm. Na Perštýně 7, Praha 1. ✆ 224-211-916. www.umedvidku.cz. Metro: Národní třída.

U Vejvodů ✿   In the early years after the 1989 revolution, for many expats, U Vejvodů kept the spirit of a grimy student/workers pub alive in Old Town—dark, smoky, and noisy, with plenty of Pilsner beer flowing for just a couple of crowns. It was only a matter of time that this 15th-century building, "At the Duke's," became the subject of corporate interest for its space, history, and prime location. The brewers of Pilsner have moved in with row upon row of well-tended tables and booths among the alcoves and balconies, along with big-screen TVs showing the latest Czech sports triumph, and a wider range of cuisine beyond the pigs knuckle and pickled eggs of yesteryear. Open Monday to Saturday 10am to 4am and Sunday 11am to 3pm. Jilská 4, Praha 1. ✆ 224-219-999. www.restauraceuvejvodu.cz. Metro: Národní třída.

U zlatěho tygra (At the Golden Tiger)   One of the most Czech of the central city pubs, this was once the favorite watering hole of Václav Havel and one of his mentors, writer Bohumil Hrabal, who died in 1997. Particularly smoky and not especially visitor-friendly, this is a one-stop education in Czech pub culture. Pilsner Urquell is the house brew. Havel and former U.S. president Bill Clinton joined Hrabal for a traditional Czech pub evening here during Clinton's visit in 1994, much to the chagrin of the regulars. Open daily from 3 to 11pm. Husova 17, Praha 1. ✆ **222-221-111.** www.uzlatehotygra.cz. Metro: Staroměstská or Můstek.

INTERNATIONAL PUBS

James Joyce Pub   Guinness and Kilkenny on tap at authentic Irish prices keep locals to a minimum at this real Irish-style pub. Sparsely placed wall hangings make this popular bar closer to the real McCoy than Bennigan's. Juicy burgers and weekend brunches are also available. Open daily from 10:30am to 1am. Liliová 10, Praha 1. ✆ **224-248-793.** Metro: Staroměstská.

John Bull Pub   British and Czech beers are served by the pint in a cozy English pub environment brought to you by the same British corporation that's opening these "neighborhood" pubs around the world. Standard British pub food, including roast beef with Yorkshire pudding, costs just a fraction of the price back home. Open Monday to Saturday from 10:30am to 2am and Sunday from 10:30am to midnight. Senovážná 8, Praha 1. ✆ **224-226-005.** Metro: Náměstí Republiky.

Molly Malone's   This excellent pub evokes the authentic warmth of an old country inn on a rainy Irish night. The farmhouse atmosphere is loaded with old-fashioned sewing-machine tables, green velvet drapes, a roaring fireplace, and turn-of-the-20th-century skivvies hanging on a clothesline. There's plenty of boisterous laughter and Guinness on tap. Pub meals (including huge hamburgers and the best french fries in town) are served daily from 11am to 8pm. Open Sunday to Thursday from 11am to 1am and Friday and Saturday from 11am to 2am. U Obecního dvora 4, Praha 1. ✆ **224-818-851.** www.mollymalones.cz. Metro: Staroměstská.

U Malěho Glena   Guinness is served on draft in this small Malá Strana haunt by the expat American called "Little Glen," who also owns Bohemia Bagel down the street. This place has developed a firm clientele, with jazz nights performed in the small, cozy cellar. Decent food—soups, salads, and focaccias—are served until 1am. Open daily from 7:30pm to 3am. Karmelitská 23, Praha 1. ✆ **257-535-150.** www.malyglen.cz. Metro: Malostranská.

LATE-NIGHT BITES

Of all the restaurants serving past midnight (see chapter 6 for a complete listing), **Radost FX Café** (p. 99) in Vinohrady is the top late-dining choice, offering its fresh vegetarian dishes and stiff espresso daily until 5am.

4 The Bar Scene

The city has acquired a much wider selection of bars in recent years to complement its huge array of beer pubs. The competition has brought out a variety of watering holes—from country to French, from straight to gay to mixed—that match the offerings in most any major European capital.

Tips *Není Pivo Jako Pivo:* **There's No Beer Like Beer**

This seemingly absurd local proverb makes sense when you first taste the cold golden nectar *(pivo)* from its source and realize that you've never really had beer before. While Czechs on the whole aren't religious, *pivo* still elicits a piety unseen in many orthodox countries. The golden Pilsner variety that accounts for most of the beer consumed around the world was born here and has inspired some of the country's most popular fiction, films, poetry, and prayers.

For many Czechs, the corner beer hall *(hospoda* or *pivnice)* is a social and cultural center. Regulars in these smoke-encrusted caves drink beer as lifeblood and seem ill at ease when a foreigner takes their favorite table or disrupts their daily routine. For those wanting to sample the rich, aromatic taste of Czech lagers without ingesting waves of nicotine, dozens of more ventilated pubs and restaurants have emerged since the Velvet Revolution. Alas, the suds in these often cost as much as five times more than those in the standard *hospoda.*

While always informal, Czech pubs observe their own unwritten code of etiquette:

- Large tables are usually shared with strangers.
- When sitting, you should first ask *"Je tu volno?"* ("Is this place taken?"— yeh *two* vohl-no). If it's not, put a cardboard coaster down in front of you to show that you want a beer.
- Don't wave for a waitperson—it'll only delay the process when he or she sees you.
- When the waitperson does finally arrive and sees the coaster in front of you, simply nod or hold up fingers for the number of beers you want for you and your companions.
- If there's a choice, it's usually between size—*malé* (mah-*lay*) is small, *velké* (vel-*kay*) is large—or type—*světlé* (svyet-*lay*) is light, *černé* (cher-*nay*) is dark.
- The waitperson will make pencil marks on a white slip of paper that remains on your table.
- If your waitperson ever comes back for a second round, order enough for the rest of your stay and ask to pay. When he or she returns, say, *"Zaplatíme"* ("We'll pay," zah-plah-*tee*-meh) . . . you might not see him or her again for a long time.

According to brewing industry studies, Czechs drink more beer per capita than any other people. The average Czech downs 320 pints of brew each year; the average American drinks about 190. Of course, a Czech *hospoda* regular will drink the year's average for a family of six. Pub regulars do not wonder why the Czech national anthem is a song that translates as "Where Is My Home?"

Several widely held Czech superstitions are connected with drinking beer. One says that you should never pour a different kind of beer in a mug holding the remnants of another brew. Bad luck is sure to follow. Some believe that the toast—usually *"Na zdraví!"* ("To your health!")—is negated if anyone fails to clink his or her mug with any of the others at your table and then slams the mug on the table before taking the first chug.

Czech beer comes in various degrees of concentration, usually marked on the label or menu. This is not the amount of alcohol, though the higher degree does carry a higher alcohol content. The standard premium 12-degree brew contains about 5% alcohol, though each label varies. If you want something a little lighter on the head, try a 10-degree, with 3.5% to 4% alcohol content.

The never-ending debate over which Czech beer is best rages on, but here are the top contenders, all readily available in Prague. (Each pub or restaurant will usually flaunt its choice on the front of the building.)

- **Pilsner Urquell:** The original Pilsner lager. A bit bitter but with a smooth texture that comes, the locals say, from the softer alkaline waters that flow under Pilsen. Urquell is mostly packaged for export and often seen at beer boutiques across the Atlantic.
- **Budvar:** The original "Budweiser," this semisweet lager hails from České Budějovice, a town also known by its German name, Budweis. The clash with U.S. giant Anheuser Busch over the "Budweiser" trademark kept the American giant from selling Bud in much of Europe for years. There's little similarity in the taste of the two—you decide. Busch wanted a stake in the Budvar brewery, but the Czech government balked at a deal in 1996.
- **Staropramen:** The flagship of Prague's home brewery is a solid choice and is easiest to find in the capital. Now that Britain's Bass owns Staropramen, they're marketing a hybrid called Velvet, a cross between a Czech lager and an Irish ale. It's worth a try.
- **Kozel:** This is a favorite with the American expat community, with a distinctive namesake goat on the label. It has a spicy taste and full body. Light beer it is not.
- **Krušovice:** From a tiny brewery in the cradle of the western hop-growing region, this brew, commissioned by Rudolf II 4 centuries ago, used to be hard to find in Prague, but no longer. Lighter but not fizzy, it has just a hint of bitterness.

Baráčnická rychta (Small Homeowners Association) In the heart of Malá Strana, just off Malostranské náměstí, you can find and taste a little bit of old-fashioned good times. Sample good Czech food with Czech beer. Open daily noon till 1am. Tržiště 23, Praha 1. ✆ 257-532-461. www.baracnickarychta.cz. Metro: Malostranská.

Chateau/Enfer Rouge Hidden on a small Old Town back street, this loud and lively ground-floor place has twin bars, plank floors, and a good sound system playing contemporary rock. It sells four types of beer on tap and features regular drink specials. It's busy and fun—if you avoid the headache-inducing concoctions from the frozen drink machine. Open Monday to Thursday noon to 3am, Friday noon to 4pm, Saturday 4pm to 4am, Sunday 4pm to 2am. Jakubská 2, Praha 1. ✆ 222-316-328. Metro: Náměstí Republiky.

Chez Marcel This very stylish, authentic French cafe looks as though it were plucked straight out of Montmartre. Though casual light meals are served, Chez Marcel is best as a cafe/bar and a great place for café au lait. It attracts a good mix of hipsters and suits around sunset and starts to thin out at about 11pm. Open Monday to Friday from 8am to 1am, and Saturday and Sunday from 9am to 1am. Haštalské nám. 12, Praha 1. ✆ 222-315-676. Metro: Staroměstská.

Jáma (The Hollow) ⊛ This place has been popular for several postrevolutionary years. It feels a lot like an American college pub; Czech and international food is served and Czech beer is on tap. Open daily from 11am to 1am. V Jámě 7, Praha 1. ✆ 224-222-383. www.jamapub.cz. Metro: Můstek.

Marquis de Sade In the same neighborhood as La Provence and Chateau/Enfer Rouge, the Marquis de Sade stands apart from other Czech watering holes because of its huge room with high ornate ceilings that belie the casual wooden furniture and kitschy wall hangings. There's room here to breathe, and the Marquis attracts a solid return business of local expats. Open daily 11pm to 3am. Templová 8, Praha 1. ✆ 224-817-505. Metro: Můstek.

Sport Bar Praha-Zlatá Hvězda ⊛ Prague's original jocks-on-the-tube American bar has moved down the street into a more traditional Czech pub setting. Six kinds of Czech beer still flow freely with the weekly games, and the burgers and chicken fingers have outlasted other contenders for the "Sports Bar" title. You can play a good game of pool if the game on TV bores you. Open Monday 11am to midnight, Tuesday to Thursday 11am to 2am, Friday 11am to 4:30am, Saturday noon to 4:30am, and Sunday noon to midnight. Ve smečkách 12, Praha 1. ✆ 296-222-292. www.sportbar.cz. Metro: Muzeum.

GAY & LESBIAN CLUBS

Prague's small gay and lesbian community is growing in its openness and choices for nightclubs and entertainment. See "Gay & Lesbian Travelers" in chapter 2 for information, or http://prague.gayguide.net. You should also see the review for **Radost FX Café,** in chapter 6.

Aqua Club 2000 This multi-activity venue attracts a mixed gay and lesbian crowd. It has become Prague's transvestite paradise, with weekend shows touted for their precision and authenticity. On the premises are a sauna, a swimming pool, and a disco. Open Monday to Saturday 6pm to 4am (disco 9pm–4am). Husitská 7, Praha 3. ✆ 222-540-241. www.euroshow2000.cz. Metro: Florenc, then bus no. 133 to Husitská.

Friends   Originally situated in Náprstkova Street, Friends moved to its new home at Bartolomějská in 2004. It has the original atmosphere of the old bar, combined with a more comfortable setting, a super sound and video projection system, new dance floor, and private lounge. Free Wi-Fi Internet connection available. Open Sunday to Thursday 6pm to 3am, Friday and Saturday 6pm to 5am. DJ parties start at 10pm Wednesday through Saturday. Bartolomějská 11, Praha 1. ℂ 224-236-772. Metro Narodni třída.

Tingl Tangl   A popular nightclub attracting a mixed gay, straight, foreign, and local crowd near Charles Bridge, Tingl Tangl offers the most extensive cabaret shows in Old Town, with comical drag queens featured during the weekend and Wednesday shows. Open daily from 8pm to 5am. Karolíny Světlé 12, Praha 1. ℂ 224-238-278. Cover charges 250Kč ($10) for show nights. Metro: Národní třída.

5 Casinos & Movie Theaters

CASINOS

Prague has many casinos, and most offer blackjack, roulette, and slot machines. House rules are usually similar to those in Las Vegas, but there are often slight variations.

Casino Palais Savarin, Na Příkopě 10, Praha 1 (ℂ 224-221-636; metro: Můstek), occupying a former rococo palace, is the most beautiful game room in the city. It's open daily from 1pm to 4am. Other recommendable casinos are **Casino Atrium,** in the hotel Hilton Prague, Pobřežní 1, Praha 8 (ℂ 224-810-988; metro: Florenc), open daily from 2pm to 6am; and **Casino U Nováků,** Vodičkova 30, Praha 1 (ℂ 224-222-098; metro: Můstek), open daily from 1pm to 5am.

MOVIE THEATERS

Unlike neighboring Germany, which has made dubbing so commonplace that it has become the scourge of the industry, foreign films are generally screened here in their original language, with Czech subtitles. Now, better Czech films are also being screened for visitors with English subtitles. Unlike the prerevolution days, when hardly a decent Western film could be seen, the cinemas *(kinos)* are filled with most first-run films from Hollywood and the independents within a few weeks after their general release.

Many cinemas are on or near Václavské náměstí (Wenceslas Sq.). Tickets cost 80Kč to 180Kč ($3.35–$7.50). Most screenings have reserved seats, and many popular films sell out in advance, so make your choice early. Check the *Prague Post* for listings, or for a more accurate list, look at the billboards outside **Kino Lucerna,** Vodičkova 36, near Wenceslas Square (ℂ 224-216-972; metro: Můstek).

A new complex of cinemas is at shopping gallery **Palác Flóra,** Vinohradská 149, Praha 3 (ℂ 255-742-021; www.cinemacity.cz). Here, you can visit the virtual world if you get a ticket (160Kč/$6.65) for one of the 3-D movie shows offered on the **IMAX** ℱ screen. On the programs of eight other cinemas are the newest films in English. At the centrally located shopping and cultural center **Slovanský Dům** ℱℱ, Na Příkopě 9/11, Praha 1 (ℂ 221-451-214; www.palacecinemas.cz) you also can enjoy the latest releases at their **Palace Cinemas.** The same chain has newly opened its **Multiplex Palace Cinemas** at the brand-new shopping center **Nový Smíchov,** Plzeňská 8, Praha 5 (ℂ 257-181-212; www.palacecinemas.cz).

11

Day Trips from Prague

Venturing outside of Prague requires much more patience and flexibility than you'll need within the city due to the lack of tourist conveniences and scarcer use of English. For those who possess adventurous qualities, day trips to the surrounding countryside or longer excursions beyond can be surprising and rewarding. While Prague is well into its postrevolution reconstruction, many outlying provinces still groan under the decay of the former regime. But there are still pockets of outstanding beauty, unique history, and eccentric pleasures which you can only experience by exiting the tourist bubble in the capital.

Prague has been blessed with golden spires, but the surrounding area is dotted with some of Europe's most **beautiful castles,** such as the majestic Karlštejn, where you can play a round of golf on a championship course or spend a night in a romantic inn. Also spectacular are the impregnable Český Šternberk, the hunting lodge of Konopiště, and the interior of Křivoklát. I still think the castle in Orlík overlooking the wide expanse of the

Vltava is the nicest of them all. As much as these sites testify to the country's beauty, there are also monuments that reflect its suffering. Witness the remains of **Lidice,** what once was a small, sleepy village before it was leveled by Nazis; and **Terezín** (*Theresienstadt* in German), the "model" Jewish ghetto, the so-called Paradise Ghetto, where a cruel trick duped the world and left thousands to die. Also worth exploring is the medieval mining town of **Kutná Hora** (with the macabre "Bone Church" a mile away in Sedlec).

When you tire of touring castles, you can play a round of golf on a championship course in Karlštejn (or Mariánské Lázně if you have the time for a longer trip), sneak away to a cozy inn, or try the next generation of bungee jumping. You can also enjoy a glass of wine at the Renaissance Lobkovic Château, the center of winemaking in the most unlikely of places, **Mělník.**

Even if you don't have much time, try to spend at least a day or two outside Prague to explore the countryside.

1 Tips for Day Tripping

All the destinations described below are easily accessible from Prague by car, train, or bus. Most do not have accommodations, so they are best visited in a day. Students should always show ID cards and ask for discounts, which are sometimes available.

GETTING THERE
BY CAR A liter of gasoline costs about 30Kč ($1.25), expensive by North American standards but cheaper than in western Europe. Gas stations are plentiful, and most are equipped with small convenience stores.

Except for main highways, which are a seemingly endless parade of construction sites, roads tend to be narrow and in need of repair. Add maniacal Czech drivers in

BMWs and Mercedes fighting for the limited space alongside the Communist-era *Škodas,* and you may think that it's a better option to take the train. Especially at night, you should drive only on major roads. If you must use smaller roads, be careful. For details on car rentals, see chapter 3.

If you experience car trouble, major highways have emergency telephones from which you can call for assistance. There's also the **ÚAMK,** a 24-hour motor assistance club that provides service for a fee. They drive bright-yellow pickup trucks and can be summoned on main highways by using the SOS emergency phones located at the side of the road every kilometer or so. If you are not near one of these phones or are on a road that doesn't have them, you can contact ÚAMK at *© * **1230.** This is a toll-free call.

BY TRAIN   Trains run by České dráhy (Czech Railways) provide a good and less expensive alternative to driving. The fare is determined by how far you travel. 50km (31 miles) cost 64Kč ($2.65) in second class or 96Kč ($4) in first class. First class is not usually available, or needed, on shorter trips.

It's important to find out which Prague station your train departs from, since not all trains leave from the main station, though all major stations are on metro lines. Check when you buy your tickets. Trains heading to destinations in the north, such as Terezín, usually depart from **Nádraží Holešovice,** Vrbenského ulice, Praha 7 (*© * **224-615-865),** above the Nádraží Holešovice metro stop at the end of the Red metro line (line C). Local trains to the southeast are commonly found at **Smíchovské Nádraží,** Nádražní ulice, Praha 5 (© **224-617-686**), on the yellow metro line heading west from the center. Most trains to west and south Bohemia and Moravia leave from **Hlavní Nádraží (Main Station),** Wilsonova 80, Praha 1 (© **224-614-071**), at the metro stop of the same name on the red metro (line C) in the center. Train stations in Prague are now better at providing information, especially in English. There are also timetables for public use that allow you to plan your trips.

BY BUS The Czech Republic operates a pretty decent bus system, and because trains often follow circuitous routes, buses can be a better, though slightly more expensive, option. State-run ČSAD buses are still relatively inexpensive and surprisingly abundant, and they offer terrific coverage of the country. Like train passengers, bus passengers are charged on a kilometer basis, with each kilometer costing about 91 hellers (4¢). Make sure, however, that you buy your tickets early, especially on weekends, and get to the proper boarding area early to ensure you get a seat.

Prague's main bus station, **Central Bus Station—Florenc,** Křižíkova 5, Praha 8 (for bus connections information call © **900-144-444;** www.florenc.cz), is above the Florenc metro stop (line C). Unfortunately, few employees speak English here, making it a bit tricky for non-Czech speakers to obtain schedule information. To find your bus, you can try the large boards just next to the office where all buses are listed. They're in alphabetical order, but sometimes it's tough to find your destination since it may lie in the middle of a route to another place. If you have some time before you depart Prague, your best bet for bus information and tickets is to visit **Čedok,** Na Příkopě 18, Praha 1 (© **800-112-112** or 224-197-111; www.cedok.cz), open Monday to Friday from 9am to 6pm.

ORGANIZED DAY TOURS

Once upon a time, taking a day trip from Prague (or taking any trip in the Czech Republic for that matter) meant dealing with the state monopoly travel agency, Čedok. But as Čedok's stranglehold on tourist services has lessened, dozens of agencies have sprouted up around town offering guided tours both inside and outside Prague. Though most offer more or less the same services, it pays to shop around. Try the following agencies.

Martin Tour, Štěpánská 61, Praha 1 (© **224-212-473;** fax 224-239-752; www. martintour.cz), has been around for several years and offers a couple of worthy tours. The Karlštejn Castle tour is their best. The tour is offered Tuesday to Sunday, departing at 10am. It takes 5 hours and is expedient because you don't wait around for the next general tour at the castle. A traditional Czech lunch at a nearby restaurant is included (diabetics, vegetarians, and babies can be accommodated). The tour with lunch costs 950Kč ($40). The 5-hour trip to the country's Jewish memorial of Terezín costs 1,100Kč ($46). The bus leaves four times a week at 9:30am from Staroměstské náměstí.

Tips **Czech Rail Online**

Czech Rail has a useful though somewhat complicated website in English, German, and Czech at **www.cdrail.cz**. To check the timetable, go to **www.jizdnirady. cz** or **www.idos.cz**.

Tips **A Note on Tours**

Though many good organized tours are offered, for the most part I'd recommend going it alone. This gives you the freedom to change plans at the last minute in order to get a little more of what you want, not just what the tours provide. Besides, you get a greater sense of accomplishment when you navigate Eastern Europe on your own.

Čedok, Na Příkopě 18, Praha 1 (© **800-112-112** or 224-197-111; www.cedok.cz), in the heart of Prague, has its advantages. For one, it offers by far the widest array of tours outside of Prague. Čedok has been doing this so long that it has access to all the important sights as well as guides who speak several languages. Prices are reasonable. A day trip to Karlovy Vary, lunch, a swim at the Hotel Thermal outdoor pool, and a tour of the Moser glass factory costs 1,650Kč ($69), while a journey to Karlštejn Castle and Château Konopiště, lunch and tour included, costs 1,860Kč ($77).

If you're pressed for time, a good tour is offered by **Prague Sightseeing Tours,** Klimentská 52, Praha 1 (© **222-314-655;** www.pstours.cz). The company offers a combination all-day tour of the castles Karlštejn and Konopiště that includes lunch. It's a good way to see both castles without the hassle of negotiating the train and bus stations. However, the price is 1,880Kč ($78) for adults and 1,320Kč ($55) for children.

2 Karlštejn Castle ★★★

29km (18 miles) SW of Prague

By far the most popular destination in the Czech Republic after Prague, Karlštejn Castle is an easy day trip for those interested in getting out of the city. Charles IV built this medieval castle from 1348 to 1357 to safeguard the crown jewels of the Holy Roman Empire. Although the castle had been changed over the years, with such additions as late Gothic staircases and bridges, renovators have removed these additions, restoring the castle to its original medieval state.

As you approach, little can prepare you for your first view: a spectacular Disney-like castle perched on a hill, surrounded by lush forests and vineyards. In its early days, the king's jewels housed within enhanced the castle's importance and reputation. Vandalism having forced several of its finest rooms to close, these days the castle is most spectacular from the outside. Unfortunately, many of the more interesting restored rooms are kept off-limits and open only for special guests.

ESSENTIALS

GETTING THERE   The best way to get to Karlštejn is by **train** (there's no bus service). Most trains leave from Prague's Main Station (at the Hlavní nádraží metro stop) hourly throughout the day and take about 45 minutes to reach Karlštejn. The one-way, second-class fare is 46Kč ($1.90). It's a short, relaxing trip along the Berounka River. On the way you pass through Řevnice, Martina Navrátilová's birthplace. Ondřej Hejma, the lead singer for one of the country's popular rock bands, Žlutý pes (Yellow Dog), also makes his home here. Keep your eyes open for your first glimpse of the majestic castle.

You can also **drive** along one of two routes, both of which take 30 minutes. Here's the more scenic one: Leave Prague from the southwest along Highway 4 in the direction of

Strakonice and take the Karlštejn cutoff, following the signs (and traffic!). The second, much less scenic route follows the main highway leading out of Prague from the west as if you were going to Plzeň. About 20 minutes down the road is the well-marked cutoff for Karlštejn. (You can tell you have missed the cutoff if you get to the town of Beroun. If that happens, take any exit and head back the other way; the signs to Karlštejn are also marked heading toward Prague.)

A trip to Karlštejn can easily be combined with a visit to Křivoklát (see below).

VISITOR INFORMATION   The ticket/castle information booth (⟨ **311-681-370**) can help you, as can any of the restaurants or stores. The castle itself has a website that you can visit at www.hradkarlstejn.cz.

ORGANIZED TOURS   All of the tour operators listed in "Organized Day Tours," above, offer tours of Karlštejn.

EXPLORING THE CASTLE

Since Karlštejn's beauty lies more in its facade and environs than in the castle itself, the 20- to 30-minute walk up the hill is, along with the view, one of the main features that makes the trip spectacular. It's an excursion well worth making if you can't get farther out of Prague to see some of the other castles. Seeing hordes of visitors coming, locals have discovered the value of fixing up the facades of their homes and opening small businesses (even if they have gone a little overboard on the number of outlets selling crystal). Restaurants have improved tremendously. When you finally do reach the top, take some time to look out over the town and down the Well Tower.

To see the interior of the castle, you can choose from two tours. The 50-minute **Tour 1** will take you through the **Imperial Palace, Hall of Knights, Chapel of St. Nicholas, Royal Bedroom,** and **Audience Hall. Tour 2,** which lasts 70 minutes, offers a look at the **Holy Rood Chapel,** famous for the more than 2,000 precious and semiprecious inlaid gems adorning its walls; the **Chapel of St. Catherine,** Karel IV's own private oratory; the **Church of Our Lady;** and the **library.**

Note that you need to make a reservation to visit the Holy Rood Chapel on Tour 2 (⟨ **274-008-154;** fax 274-008-152; www.spusc.cz or www.hradkarlstejn.cz). The shorter Tour 1 costs 200Kč ($8.30) adults, 100Kč ($4.15) students, 20Kč (85¢) children under 6. Tour 2 with the Holy Rood Chapel costs 300Kč ($12) adults, 100Kč ($4.15) students, free for children under 6. The castle is open Tuesday to Sunday: May, June, and September 9am to noon and 12:30 to 5pm; July and August 9am to noon and 12:30 to 6pm; April and October 9am to noon and 1 to 4pm; November, December, and March 9am to noon and 1 to 3pm; closed January and February.

TEE TIME: KARLŠTEJN'S CHAMPIONSHIP GOLF COURSE

Golfers may want to try their luck at the North American–designed **Praha Karlštejn Golf Club,** a course that hosted its first European PGA tour event in 1997. This challenging

---

Tips **A Castle-Viewing Tip**

Karlštejn is probably best seen from a distance, so take time to browse in the stores, enjoy the fresh air, and sit out on one of the restaurant patios or down by the riverside. Buy a bottle of the locally grown Karlštejn wine, a vintage started by King Charles IV, and admire the view.

Moments A Romantic Getaway

If the air and noise of Prague start to grate on your nerves, or if a quiet, romantic, overnight trip to a castle in the country sounds like the perfect getaway, head for the **Romantic Hotel Mlýn (Mill Hotel)** ✻, 267 18 Karlštejn (© **311-744-411;** fax 311-744-444; www.hotelmlynkarlstejn.cz).

On the river's edge on the bank opposite the castle, the Mlýn is exactly what its name says—a mill. Converted into a hotel and recently reconstructed, this reasonably priced country inn takes you away from the hustle and bustle of traveling. Its 28 rooms are a little on the small side, but they're quaint and nicely decorated with rustic furniture. At the outdoor patio bar and very good restaurant, you can relax and enjoy the soothing sounds of the river. Service here is a cut above what it is at the other hotels in the area. If you are here for lunch or dinner when the outdoor grill has been fired up, take advantage of it. Use the hotel also as a base for bike and canoe trips along the river. The staff can help you with local tennis courts and reservations for a round of golf.

Rates are 2,500Kč ($104) for a single and 3,100Kč ($129) for a double. MasterCard and Visa are accepted. To get to the hotel, take the bridge across the river that leads to the train station and turn left at the first street. If you cross the rail tracks, you've gone too far.

6,370m (6,964-yd.), par-72 course on the hill just across the river from the castle offers some pretty views. At the elevated tee on the 2nd hole, you'll hit toward the castle. It's a breathtaking place to lose a ball. If you want a real challenge, see if you can match former Masters winner German Bernhard Langer's four-round total of 264 (24 under par).

Karlštejn is one of the few courses in the Czech Republic that really challenges a golfer's ability—narrow fairways, long rough, and lightning-fast greens. Be prepared to walk uphill between holes. The course is open daily from 8am to sundown, and reservations for weekends should be made a couple of days in advance; call © **311-604-999** or go online to **www.karlstejn-golf.cz**. However, it's a bit expensive, especially equipment like golf balls and club rentals: Greens fees are 2,000Kč ($83) for 18 holes Monday to Friday, and 3,000Kč ($125) Saturday, Sunday, and holidays. Motorized cart rentals are 1,200Kč ($50) per 18 holes, while a pull cart is 200Kč ($8.30) per round. Club rental is 500Kč ($20) per round. There's a driving range to warm up (1.20Kč/5¢ per ball), though you can't actually hit your driver there.

To get here by car from Prague, take Highway 116 south through the castle town of Karlštejn. Once you cross the river and a set of train tracks, stay on the road, which veers right and goes up a hill. You'll see the golf course on the left and an entrance soon after.

If you've taken the train, you can walk to the course through town, but be warned that it's an uphill hike. Take a taxi, which should cost 50Kč to 80Kč ($2–$3.35).

WHERE TO DINE

The **Restaurace Blanky z Valois** (© **608-021-075**), on the main street heading up to the castle, serves pizzas, a far cry from the Provençal feel and cuisine it first set out to serve. It does provide the only alternative to standard Czech fare in the area, however. Pizzas range from 80Kč to 190Kč ($3.35–$7.90); MasterCard and Visa are accepted. The restaurant is open daily from 11am to 10pm. The long wine list includes French and Italian vintages, but sample Karlštejn's own. This light, dry wine is surprisingly good considering it's not from Moravia, and it costs less than half the price of the imports.

Also on the main street, the **Hotel Restaurace Koruna** (☎ **311-681-383**) is usually busy, especially the terrace tables. The restaurant serves large portions of traditional Czech dishes. The real bonus here is the staff: They're used to accommodating families or groups and allow them to spread out at the large tables. Main courses are 59Kč to 219Kč ($2.45–$9.10); MasterCard and Visa are accepted. Open daily 9:30am to 10pm.

At first glance it may appear as though there's not much difference between Koruna and **Restaurace U Janů** (☎ **311-681-210**) across the road, but prices here are a little lower, and the terrace, shaded by trees, is a little nicer on a hot day. The menu is basic Czech. The venison specials make a nice change from the usual meat-and-dumpling meals. Main courses are 47Kč to 199Kč ($1.95–$8.30); MasterCard and Visa are accepted. On weekends, live music adds a nice touch. Open daily 9:30am to 10pm.

If the weather's right for eating outdoors, stock up on goodies at the grocery store before you leave Prague, and have a picnic along the Berounka, where there are plenty of spots to spread a blanket. If you don't want to drag a heavy bag or two from the city, there's a grocery store, which retains its Communist-era name of **Potraviny** (literally, groceries) on the right side of the main street when you're walking up the hill (open Mon–Sat 8am–5pm); here you can buy the essentials, including wine, though selection isn't one of its strong points. Whichever way you go, pick up a bottle of the local Karlštejn vintage with which to wash down your meal.

3 Křivoklát

43km (27 miles) W of Prague

Less crowded and much less touristy than its neighbor upstream at Karlštejn, Křivoklát is the perfect destination for a lazy afternoon of touring. A royal castle mentioned as early as the 11th century, Křivoklát is set in the tranquil Berounka River Valley. The fortress was rebuilt several times over the years but retains its Gothic style. The royal family was among Křivoklát's frequent visitors, and during the Hussite Uprising, King Zigmund of Luxembourg hid his jewels here. The area surrounding the fortress is protected by UNESCO as a biosphere preservation area, making it an interesting place for a nature walk.

ESSENTIALS

GETTING THERE   **Trains** run regularly from Prague's Smíchov station to the town of Beroun, where you must change to go on to Křivoklát. The trip takes 1¼ hours; the one-way, second-class fare is 98Kč ($4.10). This is one of the nicer train

---

⌐Tips A Sightseeing Tip

Křivoklát is near Karlštejn, so consider visiting both in 1 day if you drive or take the train. The contrast between the bustling Karlštejn and the sleepy Křivoklát is startling.

rides in the Czech Republic, even though you have to change trains in Beroun. The train winds its way along the Berounka through some wooded areas near Prague.

If you're **driving,** leave Prague on the E50 expressway heading west toward Plzeň and exit at the Křivoklát cutoff. From there, follow Highway 116 as it snakes along the Berounka and turn left onto Highway 201, which eventually winds its way around to Křivoklát. The trip takes 45 minutes.

VISITOR INFORMATION   There is no tourist information center, but the castle can provide information on the area. There is also an official website for the castle: www.krivoklat.cz.

ORGANIZED TOURS   **Prague Sightseeing Tours** offers a combination tour of Karlštejn and Křivoklát; see "Organized Day Tours," above, for details.

EXPLORING THE CASTLE

Often a castle tour fails to live up to expectations (Karlštejn comes to mind), but this is one of the best castle tours; it's almost a reverse of Karlštejn. Outside, Křivoklát pales in comparison to Karlštejn's beauty. But inside, Křivoklát blows its rival out of the water. Take time to study the intricate carvings at the altar in the **Royal Chapel.** They're not exactly angelic: Actually, the angels are holding instruments of torture; Křivoklát was once a prison for political criminals. The **Kings Hall,** a whopping 24m (79 ft.) long, is the second-longest secular hallway in the country after Prague's Vladislav Hall. In the **Knights Hall** you'll find a collection of fabulous late Gothic art. And the **Furstenberg Picture Gallery** is one of the country's largest castle libraries, with some 53,000 volumes on its shelves. Take that, Karlštejn!

Admission is 150Kč ($6.25) for adults and 80Kč ($3.35) for children. The castle is open to the public in March and November on Saturday and Sunday from 9am to 3pm. In October it's open Tuesday to Sunday from 9am to 3pm. In April, May, June, and September, hours are Tuesday to Sunday from 9am to 4pm. In July and August, hours are daily from 9am to 5pm. It is closed between noon and 1pm. The tour runs about half an hour, and information in English is available.

WHERE TO STAY & DINE

Since Křivoklát is less touristy than Karlštejn, there aren't many restaurants here. Of the few that do exist, **Pension U Jelena,** at the bottom of the hill as you approach the castle, is your best bet. With six rooms, the pension can be used as an overnight stop if you want to spend a leisurely weekend hiking and biking between Křivoklát and Karlštejn. The restaurant specializes in game—try the venison steak with cranberry sauce and cognac at 275Kč ($11) for a sweet twist on a local specialty—and has a great terrace for an afternoon meal or a drink. Main courses are 65Kč to 299Kč ($2.70–$12); American Express, MasterCard, and Visa are accepted.

For reservations at the hotel (you won't need them for the restaurant), call © **313-558-529** or fax 313-558-233. Doubles cost 1,500Kč ($62). If you don't want to stop here, you're better off eating down the road in Karlštejn or back in Prague.

4 Kutná Hora ✸

72km (45 miles) E of Prague

A medieval town that grew fantastically rich from the silver deposits beneath it, Kutná Hora is also a popular day trip from Prague. Small enough to be seen in a single day at a brisk pace, the town's ancient heart has decayed, which makes it hard to believe

---

Tips **Two Warnings**

The Hrádek mine shaft can be a little claustrophobic (what mine isn't?). *Never* take your hard hat off (low, jagged ceilings can quickly bring about premature balding).

---

that this was once the second-most important city in Bohemia. However, the town center is also mercifully free of the ugly, Communist-era buildings that plague many of the country's small towns. The historical center and Kutná Hora's main draw, St. Barbara's Cathedral have been on the UNESCO list for 10 years. Also, the macabre Bone Church (Kostnice), filled with human bones assembled in bizarre sculptures, is worth a visit.

ESSENTIALS

GETTING THERE   The 50-minute **drive** from Prague is relatively easy. Take Vinohradská ulice, which runs due east from behind the National Museum at the top of Wenceslas Square, straight to Kutná Hora. Once out of the city, the road turns into Highway 333.

If you don't have a car, your best bet is to go by **bus,** which departs from Prague's Florenc Bus Station and takes about an hour and 15 minutes. It costs 58Kč ($2.40).

VISITOR INFORMATION   The **Information Center (Informační Středisko;** © 327-512-378; www.kutnahora.cz), on Palackého nám. 377, provides the most comprehensive information service in town. Check to see if anything special such as a recital or an exhibition is showing. The office is open daily 9am to 6pm (Apr–Sept); Monday to Friday from 9am to 6pm and Saturday and Sunday from 10am to 4pm (Oct–Mar). The town has also posted very useful signs just about everywhere to help visitors get where they're going.

SEEING THE SIGHTS

The main attraction is the enormous **St. Barbara's Cathedral (Chrám sv. Barbory)** at the southwestern edge of town. In 1380, Peter Parler began construction of the cathedral. The task was so great that it took several more Gothic masters, including Matthias Rejsek and Benedikt Rejt, close to 200 years to complete the project. From the outside, the cathedral's soaring arches, dozens of spires, and intricate designs raise expectations that the interior will be just as impressive—and you won't be disappointed.

On entering (you have to enter from the side, not the front), you'll see several richly decorated frescoes full of symbols denoting the town's two main industries of mining and minting. The ceiling vaulting, with floral patterns and coats of arms, has made many a jaw drop. Admission is 30Kč ($1.25) for adults and 15Kč (60¢) for children. The cathedral is open October and April, Tuesday to Sunday from 9am to noon and 1 to 4:30pm. May to September, it's open Tuesday to Sunday from 9am to 6pm; November to March, it's open Tuesday to Sunday from 9am to noon and 1 to 4pm.

When you leave the cathedral, head down statue-lined **Barborská Street,** where you'll pass the early baroque **Jesuit College,** built in the late 17th century by Domenico Orsi.

Farther down the road is **Hrádek,** a 15th-century castle that now houses the **Czech Museum of Silver (Muzeum stříbra)** (© 327-512-159; www.cms-kh.cz). If you

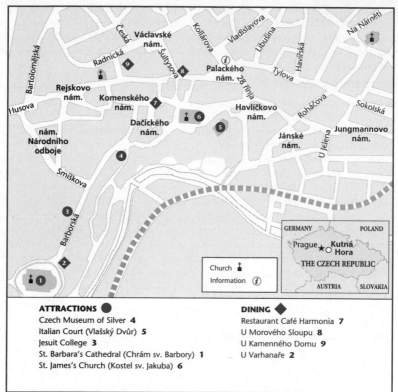

ATTRACTIONS ●
Czech Museum of Silver **4**
Italian Court (Vlašský Dvůr) **5**
Jesuit College **3**
St. Barbara's Cathedral (Chrám sv. Barbory) **1**
St. James's Church (Kostel sv. Jakuba) **6**

DINING ◆
Restaurant Café Harmonia **7**
U Morového Sloupu **8**
U Kamenného Domu **9**
U Varhanaře **2**

take the tour of Hrádek, you'll actually see little of the building. Instead, you'll tour one of the town's mine shafts. The tour begins in a small room filled with artifacts from the town's mining and minting industries. After a brief speech, it's time to don hard hats and work coats to tour the mine shaft. After a hike of about 270m (886 ft.), you'll descend into a narrow corridor of rock and dampness to spend about 15 minutes in the mines. Children like this half-hour tour almost as much as they do the bone church. Admission is 110Kč ($4.55) for adults and 70Kč ($2.90) for children. The museum is open Tuesday to Sunday: April and October from 9am to 5pm; May, June, and September from 9am to 6pm; and July and August from 10am to 6pm.

Once you're back aboveground, go down the hill to **St. James's Church (Kostel sv. Jakuba)** and the **Italian Court (Vlašský Dvůr)** (© **327-512-873**). Even though the door is usually closed at St. James's, it's worth trying to open; perhaps you'll be able to glimpse the baroque paintings on the walls. More likely, though, you'll have to admire the church from the outside and then head on to the Italian Court.

Constructed in 1300 as a royal mint (what better way for a town to become rich than to print money?), the Italian Court derives its name from its original occupants, who were brought in from Florence to mint coins. The building houses a museum of coins made here between the 14th and 18th centuries, including the Czech groschen, the currency of choice in the Middle Ages. Another reason to take the tour is to see the ornate chapels, impressive in their details. Admission is 40Kč ($1.65) for adults and 20Kč (85¢) for children; guided tours 70Kč ($2.90)/50Kč ($2.10). It's open daily: April to September, from 9am to 6pm; October and March, from 10am to 5pm; and November to February, from 10am to 4pm.

WHERE TO DINE

Because of its popularity, Kutná Hora has now developed a better infrastructure, and you can find here several restaurants and local pubs to satisfy the palate.

One of the nice terraces is the **Restaurant Cafe Harmonia** (© 327-512-275), Husova 105 (to the rear of St. James's Church), making it a convenient stop before a visit to the Bone Church. The salads are fresh and the soups are hot and hearty—something that isn't all too common in this town. Main courses are 70Kč to 180Kč ($2.90–$7.50); no credit cards are accepted. It's open daily from 10am to 11pm.

U Morového Sloupu (© 327-513-810), Šultysova 173 (a block west of Palackého nám.), is located in a 15th-century building completely renovated by the owner. This remains one of the few places in town that has tried to lure out-of-towners who aren't part of a tour group through its doors. Try to sit in the first room into which you walk; this is a pleasant dining room with dim lighting. In the second room, a decidedly modern look sterilizes whatever ambience there once was. The food on both sides is the same, however, with large portions of tasty pork steaks, schnitzels, and fish. Main

---

Kids The Bone Church in Sedlec

A visit to Kutná Hora isn't complete without a trip to **Kostnice** *⊛*, the "Bone Church." It's located 1.6km (1 mile) down the road in Sedlec. Those who don't want to walk can board a local bus on Masarykova Street. The fare is 8Kč (35¢), and you have to have a ticket before boarding. Tickets are not sold on the bus but at newspaper stands *(tabák)*.

From the outside, Kostnice looks like most other Gothic churches. But from the moment you enter the front door, you know that this is no ordinary church—all of the decorations are made from human bones. No kidding. František Rint, the church's interior decorator, created crosses of bone, columns of bone, chalices of bone, and even a coat of arms in bone for the Schwarzenberg family, who owned the church.

The obvious questions are: Where did the bones come from, and why were they used for decorations? The first question is easier to answer: The bones came from victims of the 14th-century plague and the 15th-century Hussite wars; both events left thousands dead, who were buried in mass graves on the church's site. As the area developed, the bones were uncovered, and the local monks came up with this idea of how to put the bones to use.

Admission is a bargain at 35Kč ($1.45) for adults and 20Kč (85¢) for children. Note that taking a camera in costs an extra 30Kč ($1.25), and taking a video camera costs 60Kč ($2.50). From April to September, the Bone Church is open daily from 8am to 6pm; October 9am to noon and 1 to 5pm; November to March 9am to noon and 1 to 4pm.

courses are 70Kč to 130Kč ($2.90–$5.40); American Express, MasterCard, and Visa are accepted. It's open daily from 10am to midnight.

U Kamenného Domu (© **327-514-426**), Lierova 147 (2 blocks west of Palackého nám.), is very popular with the locals, serving up hearty Czech specialties at bargain prices. There aren't any English menus, but don't be afraid to point at something you see on another table. The best bet here is the Czech staple meal of roasted pork, potato dumplings, and cabbage (99Kč/$4.10), which will fill you up without the heavy cream sauce that seems to come on a lot of the other dishes. Main courses cost 59Kč to 165Kč ($2.45–$6.85). Credit cards are not accepted. The restaurant is open daily from 11am to 10pm.

U Varhanáře (© **327-512-769**), Barborská 578 (behind the museum), provides possibly the nicest view over the valley from behind the museum, and its garden terrace is one of the few places to get a decent alfresco meal. Standard portions of tasty pork steaks, schnitzels, and fish are served promptly and are better than the pasta dishes. Main courses cost 69Kč to 200Kč ($2.85–$8.30); no credit cards. The restaurant is open daily from 11am to 11pm.

5 Konopiště

48km (30 miles) S of Prague

A 17th-century castle-turned-hunting-lodge built by the Habsburgs, Konopiště was the Club Med of its time. Here emperors and archdukes relaxed amid the well-stocked hunting grounds surrounding the castle. In 1887, the castle became the property of Archduke Franz Ferdinand, who often went hunting, until that fateful day in Sarajevo when he and his wife, Sophie, became the prey.

If you're driving, you can see both Konopiště and Český Šternberk in 1 day (see directions on p. 207).

ESSENTIALS

GETTING THERE   If you're **driving,** leave Prague on the D1 expressway heading south and exit at the Benešov cutoff. From there, turn right at the signs for Konopiště. *Watch out:* The turn sneaks up on you, so start looking for it just after you pass the Benzina gas station on your right. The trip takes 45 minutes. Note that the parking lot just outside the castle is your best bet, at 50Kč ($2). There aren't any closer lots, and police are vigilant about ticketing or booting cars parked at the side of the road. The minimum fine is 1,000Kč ($41).

If you don't have a car, the bus is the next-best option. Several **buses** run daily from Prague's Florenc station and let you off about half a mile from the castle. The 1-hour trip costs 51Kč ($2.10).

It's a little trickier to get here by **train** since the closest station is in nearby Benešov. The trip takes 50 minutes and costs 64Kč ($2.65) for a one-way, second-class fare. From Benešov you'll have to catch a local bus to the castle for 8Kč (35¢).

EXPLORING THE CASTLE & HUNTING GROUNDS

Since hunting on the grounds is no longer an option, Tour 1 at Konopiště will have to suffice. You'll know what I mean as soon as you begin the tour: Hundreds of antlers, bears, wild boars, and birds of prey practically jump off the walls, catching unsuspecting sweaters and dazzling children. The main hall is a testament to the archduke, who reportedly bagged some 300,000 animals—that translates to an incredible 20 animals a day, every day, for 40 years. Only 1% of his total hunting collection is on display, and it still ranks as one of Europe's largest collections. Tour 1 also takes you through the castle's parlors, which have been restored with great attention to detail. Note the handcrafted wooden Italian cabinets with wonderfully detailed inlays and the collection of Meissen porcelain. Tour 1, lasting about 50 minutes, costs 150Kč ($6.25) for adults and 80Kč ($3.35) for children.

Tour 2 (for which you must buy tickets separately) is a little longer at 55 minutes and takes you through the weapons room, the chapel, and the party room, where only men were allowed. This tour is 150Kč ($6.25) for adults and 80Kč ($3.35) for children.

Tour 3 takes you through Ferdinand's private rooms. It lasts only about 10 minutes longer than the other tours and costs 250Kč ($10) for adults and children. While the third tour is interesting, I don't think it's worth the money. Unless you're a die-hard fan of castle rooms, your time is probably better spent roaming the grounds.

After exploring the castle's interior, wander around the manicured gardens where quails, pheasants, and peacocks roam freely. Children enjoy the moat, home to two bears who wander in circles for hours at a time. Down below the castle is a large pond where some people go swimming, though the water quality is questionable; I'd advise against it. Several large, open areas beg for a blanket, some sandwiches, and a nice bottle of red Frankovka wine. Picnicking is allowed, but stock up before coming since there's no place to get groceries near the castle.

The castle is open in April Tuesday to Friday from 9am to noon and 1 to 3pm, Saturday and Sunday 9am to noon and 1 to 4pm; May to August Tuesday to Sunday from 9am to noon and 1 to 5pm; September Tuesday to Friday from 9am to noon and 1 to 4pm, Saturday and Sunday 9am to 5pm; October Tuesday to Friday from 9am to noon and 1 to 3pm, Saturday and Sunday 9am to 4pm; and November Saturday and Sunday from 9am to noon and 1 to 3pm. The castle grounds are open 24 hours year-round. For more information, visit www.zamek-konopiste.cz or call ℂ **317-721-366.**

WHERE TO DINE

On the castle grounds, **Stará Myslivna** (ℂ **317-726-272**) is a straightforward Czech restaurant; its interior resembles a hunting lodge. The soups are first-rate, and the Czech specialty, *svíčková na smetaně* (pork tenderloin in cream sauce), is welcome on a cold day. When the sun is out, sit on the nice terrace around the corner, which usually offers only two meals: pork cutlets and chicken. Both will be cooking on the grill in front of you. Don't bother asking for side orders; they serve only what's on the grill. Main courses are 59Kč to 209Kč ($2.50–$8.70); no credit cards are accepted. Open daily 10:30am to 11pm.

If you're touring late in the afternoon and have a little more time or want a little more formal setting, try **Motel Konopiště** (ℂ **317-722-732**), at the south end of the grounds. The menu is similar to the one at Stará Myslivna, but it offers meals of far better quality and a much nicer (though a little too kitschy) atmosphere. Expect to pay between 89Kč and 359Kč ($3.70 and $15) for hearty meals of grilled meats and traditional Czech specialties like goulash. The restaurant is open daily from 6pm to 1am and accepts American Express, Diners Club, MasterCard, and Visa.

6 Český Šternberk

48km (30 miles) SE of Prague

About 16km (10 miles) east of Benešov lies the menacing Český Šternberk, once one of Bohemia's most powerful fortifications. The structure was built in the Gothic style in the first half of the 13th century, during the reign of Wenceslas I. The Habsburgs put in some baroque additions and improved its defenses, leaving few Gothic elements in their wake.

ESSENTIALS

GETTING THERE If you're **driving,** leave Prague on the D1 expressway heading south and exit at the Český Šternberk cutoff. From there, follow Highway 111. It's a 55-minute drive. From Konopiště, take Highway 112 to Highway 111. It's a 25-minute drive.

Several **buses** run daily to and from the castle but not from Prague's main Florenc station. Instead, you must take the Red metro line (the C line) south to the Roztyly stop. You can buy tickets, costing 62Kč ($2.60) each way, at the Florenc station or from the bus driver at Roztyly. The bus ride takes about 1½ hours.

SEEING THE FORTRESS

This impressive fortress stands atop a hill, rising above the Sázava River. The 1-hour tour of **Český Šternberk** is worth taking. The enormous main hall and several smaller salons with fine baroque detailing, elaborate chandeliers, and period art are testaments to the wealth of the Šternberk family.

After the tour, enjoy the grounds and relax among the trees and babbling streams that surround the fortress before heading out. Admission is 130Kč ($5.40) for adults and 80Kč ($3.35) for children. The fortress is open Tuesday to Sunday: June to August from 9am to 6pm, and May and September from 9am to 5pm. In April and October it's open only on Saturday and Sunday from 9am to 5pm. For information, call © **317-855-101** or go to www.hradceskysternberk.cz.

WHERE TO DINE

Inside the castle, **Vinárna Český Šternberk** (© **317-855-101**) serves standard Czech meat-and-potatoes meals, though the quality of food and service is reflected in the prices. Main courses are 55Kč to 129Kč ($2.30–$5.35); no credit cards are accepted. Since the restaurant's hours are the same as the castle's, you can't stop in for a quick bite to eat before the first tour or after the last one.

7 Mělník

32km (20 miles) N of Prague

Bohemia isn't known as a winemaking region—this is beer country. Except, that is, for the town of Mělník, where the Vltava and Labe (Elbe) rivers meet. While it's not quite the Loire Valley, Mělník has a decidedly French bent, as the vineyards are stocked with vines that originated in the Burgundy region.

Princess Ludmila began the tradition centuries before Bohemia passed through the hands of the Romans and eventually King Charles IV. The center of Mělník winemaking is the **Renaissance Lobkowicz Château,** owned since 1739 by the family of the same name (except for a 40-year Communist-imposed interruption). The confluence of the rivers provides a stunning backdrop to the château, where another French pastime—sitting on a terrace with a glass of Ludmila, Mělník's finest, as the afternoon sun slowly fades—can be an art.

If you get a chance to visit in mid-September, check out the harvest festival, **Mělnické Vinobraní,** for the latest vintages. Even if wine isn't your cup of, well, wine, Mělník's historical center is worth a look, with its Gothic church of St. Peter and St. Paul and its tower that provides a beautiful panorama of the area.

ESSENTIALS

GETTING THERE   If you're **driving** from the north end of Prague, follow Highway 9, which leads straight into Mělník. The trip takes 30 minutes.

Buses leave for Mělník from Holešovice station in Prague every hour or so. The trip takes about 35 minutes and costs 40Kč ($1.65).

Taking a **boat** to Mělník is another option. This romantic and scenic tour on Vltava will take you to your destination in 6 hours (one-way); a round-trip ticket costs 420Kč ($17) adults, 210Kč ($8.75) students. More on www.paroplavba.cz.

VISITOR INFORMATION   The information center is at náměstí Míru 11 (© 315-627-503; www.melnik.cz), and is open from May to September daily 9am to 5pm, October to April Monday to Friday 9am to5pm.

TOURING THE CHATEAU & TASTING THE WINE

Mělník's main attraction is the **Renaissance Lobkowicz Château** (© 315-622-108; www.lobkowicz-melnik.cz). The château is a mélange of styles, from its Renaissance balconies and *sgrafitti* (decoration made by cutting away parts of a surface layer—like plaster or clay—to expose a different-colored layer beneath) to its Gothic touches and baroque southern building. The tour showcases the Lobkowicz's fine taste; in the living quarters, you'll see a barrage of baroque furniture and 17th- and 18th-century paintings. A second tour lets you into the 13th-century wine cellar, where wine tastings regularly occur.

The château tour is 70Kč ($2.90) for adults and 50Kč ($2.10) for students, free for children under 6. The wine cellar tour is 25Kč ($1.05), and wine tastings are 70Kč to 350Kč ($2.90–$15). The château is open daily from 10am to 5pm.

WHERE TO DINE

Inside the château are two restaurants: a pricey wine bar *(vinárna)* and a more realistically priced restaurant, both with stunning views of the river. I prefer the ground-floor **Zámecká Restaurace** (© 315-622-108). The food in the *vinárna* isn't worth the extra money; buy an extra bottle of the house wine with the money you save. Main courses are 105Kč to 350Kč ($4.35–$15); credit cards are not accepted. The restaurant is open daily from 10am to 5pm.

8 Terezín (Theresienstadt) 🖈🖈

48km (30 miles) NW of Prague

Noticing that northwest Bohemia was susceptible to Prussian attacks, Joseph II, the son of Maria Teresa, decided to build **Terezín** to ward off further offensives. Two fortresses were built, but the Prussian army bypassed the area during the last Austro-Prussian conflict and in 1866 attacked Prague anyway. That spelled the end of Terezín's fortress charter, which was repealed in 1888. More than 50 years later, the fortifications were just what occupying Nazi forces needed.

Do You Remember?

You may remember Terezín/Theresienstadt from the TV miniseries of Herman Wouk's *War & Remembrance*—Natalie Henry (Jane Seymour); her son, Louis; and her uncle, Aaron Jastrow (Sir John Gielgud) were interned here near the end of the war and forced to participate in the "beautification" scheme.

When people around the world talk of Nazi atrocities during World War II, the name Terezín (Theresienstadt in German) rarely comes up. At the so-called Paradise Ghetto, there were no gas chambers, no mass machine-gun executions, and no medical testing rooms. Terezín wasn't used to exterminate the Jews, gays, Gypsies, and political prisoners it held. Rather, the occupying Nazi forces used it as a transit camp. About 140,000 people passed though Terezín's gates; more than half ended up at the death camps of Auschwitz and Treblinka.

Instead, Terezín will live in infamy for the cruel trick that SS chief Heinrich Himmler played on the world within its walls. On June 23, 1944, three foreign observers—two from the Red Cross—came to Terezín to find out if the rumors of Nazi atrocities were true. They left with the impression that all was well, duped by a well-planned "beautification" of the camp. The Germans carefully choreographed every detail of the visit. The observers saw children studying at staged schools that didn't exist, and store shelves, which had been specially set up, stocked with goods. So that the observers wouldn't think the camp was overcrowded, the Nazis transported some 7,500 of the camp's sick and elderly prisoners to Auschwitz. Children even ran up to an SS commandant just as the observers passed; the commandant handed the children cans of sardines to shouts of "What? Sardines again?" The trick worked so well that the Nazis made a film of the camp, *A Town Presented to the Jews from the Führer,* while it was still "self-governing."

Russian forces liberated Terezín on May 10, 1945, 8 days after Berlin had fallen to the Allies. Today, the camp stands as a memorial to the dead and a monument to human depravity.

ESSENTIALS

GETTING THERE   If you're **driving,** Terezín lies directly on the main highway leading north out of Prague, which takes you eventually to Berlin via Dresden. It's a 45-minute drive.

Six **buses** leave daily from Florenc bus station (metro line C). The ride takes about an hour and costs 59Kč ($2.45).

VISITOR INFORMATION   The Museum of the Ghetto and the Minor Fortress both have shops that stock reading material in several languages. Before heading out, you can read up on the area at the well-organized website www.pamatnik-terezin.cz.

ORGANIZED TOURS   Through Prague's **Martin Tour,** Štěpánská 61, Praha 1 (© **224-212-473;** fax 224-239-752; www.martintour.cz), you can visit Terezín with their English-speaking guide. Their bus leaves Wednesday, Friday, Saturday, and Sunday at 9:30am from Staroměstské náměstí. The 5-hour trip costs 1,100Kč ($46). The other travel agencies in Prague (listed earlier in this chapter under "Organized Day Tours") arrange their own guided tours to Terezín as well.

Tips **More Flood Damage**

The town of Terezín and its memorial were badly struck by floods in August 2002. After a tremendous effort, the memorial has been reopened and is accessible to the public again.

Wittmann Tours, Mánesova 8, Praha 2 (© **222-252-472;** www.wittmann-tours. com), also offers a bus tour to the Terezín concentration camp costing 1,150Kč ($48) for adults, 1,000Kč ($42) for students, free for children under 10. It leaves from Prague at Pařížská 28 daily at 10am from May to October. March 15 through April and November through December, the tour is available on Tuesday, Thursday, Saturday, and Sunday only. Make an advance reservation online or by calling the office.

If you decide to go on your own and would like to have an English-speaking guide in the Jewish Memorial sites (it is included in the admission anyway), you have to contact the company in writing before your departure. The e-mail address is pamatnik@pamatnik-terezin.cz.

SEEING THE CAMP

Terezín stands as a memorial to the dead and a monument to human depravity. Once inside the **Major Fortress,** you'll immediately be struck by its drab, plain streets. Just off the main square lies the **Museum of the Ghetto,** chronicling the rise of Nazism and life in the camp. English pamphlets describing the exhibits are provided. It's open daily: November to March from 9am to 5:30pm and April to October from 9am to 6pm. Admission is 160Kč ($6.65) adults and 130Kč ($5.40) children. A 10-minute walk from the Major Fortress over the Ohře River gets you to the **Minor Fortress.** In front of the fortress's main entrance is the **National Cemetery (Národní hřbitov),** where the bodies exhumed from the mass graves were buried. As you enter the main gate, the sign above it, ARBEIT MACHT FREI (Work Sets One Free), sets a gloomy tone. You can walk through the prison barracks, execution grounds, workshops, and isolation cells. A ticket to enter both the **Minor Fortress** and the **Museum of the Ghetto** is 180Kč ($7.50) adults and 140Kč ($5.80) children. The Minor Fortress is open daily November to March 8am to 4:30pm and April to October 8am to 6pm. For more information or reservations for guided tours, call © **416-782-225** (fax 416-782-300; www.pamatnik-terezin.cz).

Impressions

The most brutal thing was that they wanted to show a Terezín where there were nice healthy people. Each person was given a specific role to play. It was arranged beforehand down to the last detail, who would sit where and what they would say. Those people looking bad were not to appear at all. They [the Nazis] prepared Terezín so there weren't people looking ill, old, emaciated, or too many of them. They created the illusion of a self-governing normal town where . . . people lived relatively decently.

—Anita Franková, survivor of Terezín

WHERE TO DINE

It's understandable that there are few places to eat in Terezín. Indeed, you may not want to stay here much longer than you have to. However, inside the Major Fortress and the Museum, is a decent inexpensive **buffet** with standard Czech fare.

9 Lidice

32km (20 miles) NW of Prague

More than almost anywhere else in the world, two places in central Europe illustrate the destructive power of revenge: Dresden and Lidice. In 1942, when Czech paratroopers stationed in Britain assassinated SS Obergruppenführer Reinhard Heydrich, the highest-ranking officer in the Czech lands, the Nazis focused their anger on this tiny village. As Hitler's main leader in the newly claimed Nazi protectorate of Bohemia and Moravia, Heydrich had ruthlessly and systematically exterminated Jews and intellectuals, while coddling "ordinary" Czechs. The assassination of such a high-ranking official had to be dealt with severely. Why did Hitler choose Lidice? No one knows for sure, but this town was rumored to have accommodated the assassins, and someone had to pay.

When you get to Lidice, you'll see only a wooden cross and a green field where the town once stood. The Gestapo leveled the town and murdered its men. Women and children were taken to concentration camps, with less than half returning alive. In all, 348 of Lidice's 500 residents were killed. But in 1948, the Czech government, buffeted morally and financially by international outrage at this war crime, created a new town built on neighboring land. Today that town is beginning to get a little run-down, which often makes visitors feel even more melancholy.

ESSENTIALS

GETTING THERE   If you're **driving,** take Highway 7 from the west side of Prague past the airport and head west onto Highway 551. It's a 20-minute drive.

Buses depart for Lidice at the bus stops across the street from the Diplomat Hotel near the Dejvická metro station (last stop on the Green A line). Buses to Kladno don't stop in Lidice, so make sure you're on the right bus by confirming it with the driver. The bus ride takes about 25 minutes; it costs 30Kč ($1.25).

LEARNING ABOUT LIDICE

The **Lidice Memorial Museum** is a sobering monument to the town's martyred residents. In it are pictures of those killed, with descriptions of their fates. You can see a 20-minute English-language documentary on request; otherwise, a Czech version is usually running. There's also a 10-minute cassette that you can listen to as you walk around. Admission is 50Kč ($2), and it's open daily: January to March from 9am to 4pm; April to September from 9am to 6pm; and October to December from 9am to 4pm. Call ✆ **312-253-063** or go to www.lidice-memorial.cz for further information.

You're welcome to wander the field where the village once stood. Memorials in the "old" Lidice include a wooden cross marking the spot where the executed men were buried in a mass grave, and Lidice's old and new cemeteries (the old one was desecrated by the Nazis, who were looking for gold from the teeth of the dead).

Impressions

I am returning, in the name of peace, 82 children to their native place as a warning symbol of the millions of murdered children in the senseless wars of mankind.

—Marie Uchytilová, in dedicating her 82 sculptures of
children ages 1 to 16 who were removed from
Lidice and subsequently executed in Poland in 1942

10 Orlík

70km (43 miles) S of Prague

Castles closer to Prague like Karlštejn and Konopiště get all the attention, but it is worthwhile to take the time to visit **Orlík Castle** ⋇. Set among forests that line the Vltava where it swells from the Orlík Dam, the castle never disappoints. It was built in the 13th century but has burned down several times, only to rise like a phoenix from the ashes with new additions and extensions. Inherited by the Schwarzenberg family in 1719 upon the death of Maria Ernestina, a member of the Habsburg dynasty, the castle was set high up on a hill, overlooking a once-vibrant trade route. It stayed that way until 1962, when water trapped by the Orlík Dam downriver flooded thousands of hectares of land, bringing the water level up to the castle's lower walls.

Returned to the Schwarzenberg family in 1992, the castle retains its splendor, while the surrounding area has become one of the most popular lake resorts in the Czech Republic.

Orlík is also one of the nicest swimming areas in the country and therefore is a very popular holiday destination for camping. It tends to be crowded near the castle, so I recommend taking the **water taxi** (it stops at Orlík throughout the day and costs 30Kč/$1.25) for one or two stops. You don't have to decide to get off until the boat stops, so be choosy.

ESSENTIALS

GETTING THERE   By car, this is an easy 1-hour **drive** from Prague. Take Highway 4 heading southwest out of the city. About halfway there, the highway narrows from four lanes to two. Turn right on Highway 19 and then right again into Orlík.

The **Prague-Orlík bus** leaves from the bus stop Na Knížecí at the Smíchovské nádraží station at 4pm on Monday to Friday. The 80-minute trip costs 80Kč ($3.35) one-way.

VISITOR INFORMATION   There's no real information center in this tiny town, but if you go to the castle gift shop, you can get some basic information.

EXPLORING THE CASTLE

Castle tours explain the history of the Schwarzenberg family and take you through a fine collection of artifacts celebrating the victory over Napoleon at the Battle of Leipzig in 1815. Keep an eye out for the hand-carved wooden ceiling that took over 4 years to complete. Admission is 140Kč ($5.80) for adults and 60Kč ($2.50) for children. Hours are Tuesday to Sunday: June to August, from 9am to 6pm; May and September, from 9am to 5pm; and April and October, from 9am to 4pm. For more information call ℭ **382-275-101** or go to www.schwarzenberg.cz/orlik.

Jumping into the Fourth Dimension

If you're looking for a cheap thrill or a holiday pick-me-up, Orlík could be the place for you. While most visitors come here for a peaceful walk in nature or a day at the beach, this attraction is of a different kind.

From high above the river on the Žďákovský Bridge, near another castle called Zvíkov, fearless men and women, tethered to two cords, jump off of the 50m-high (164-ft.) structure to reach the "fourth dimension." The 4-D jumping is supposed to be better than traditional bungee jumping because it allows you to fall farther before the two cords that tether you start to break your fall.

Many thrill-seekers—an average of 60 people a day—have taken the plunge, from an 11-year-old to a 60-year-old man. Each jump costs 700Kč ($29). Weather permitting, you can try it June to September, from 11am to 5pm on Saturday and Sunday. The bridge is on the main highway leading out of town to the southeast (Hwy. 23). For more information go to www.bungee.cz.

WHERE TO DINE

Behind the castle gift shop, the **Restaurace U Toryka** *, U zámku 112 (© **382-181-777**) surprises you with its quality, though the portions could be bigger. Unfortunately, the restaurant's biggest lure, polka nights in summer, have been scrapped due to the noise. Main courses are 75Kč to 215Kč ($3.10–$8.95); no credit cards are accepted. It's open daily from 10am to 8pm.

12

The Best of Bohemia

Of the two regions which make up the Czech Republic, the most well known is Bohemia. It is the land that gave Europe its favorite moniker for a free spirit: "Bohemian." Despite being beaten into submission by successive Austrian, German, and Soviet hegemony, that spirit has lived on. In the 14th century, the capital, Prague, was the seat of the Holy Roman Empire under Charles IV. So Bohemians maintain their collective historical memory that they too, at least briefly, ruled the world. Even under the domination of the Austrians, Bohemia's industrial base was world-class, and in the peace between the big wars, independent Bohemia, especially Prague, created some of the greatest wealth on earth.

Much was lost in the destruction and decay of World War II and the 4 decades of Communism that followed. But Bohemia is slowly returning to that earlier prominence, leaving behind its reputation as a satellite in the former East Bloc and forging a familiar role as a crossroads at the heart of Europe. When talking to the people (or, even worse, the politicians), note the looks of pain on their faces with every mention of the East. "This is central Europe; we are west of Vienna!" is a common refrain. While the people may wish to put the past 40 or so years away like a pair of worn trousers, the fact is that they can't. Those years only add to the splendor of Bohemia's gentle rolling hills and majestic towns, giving the area a less-polished, more realistic look.

1 Exploring Bohemia

Though Bohemia has historically been undivided, there are clear-cut distinctions in the region's geography that make going from town to town easier if you "divide" it into sections. After exploring Prague and central Bohemia, decide which area you'd like to see first and then plan accordingly.

WEST BOHEMIA

Home to the country's spa towns, west Bohemia is one of the few places where a full-blown tourist infrastructure is already in place. Its main towns—**Karlovy Vary (Carlsbad), Mariánské Lázně (Marienbad)**, and to a lesser extent, **Plzeň**—offer a wide array of accommodations, restaurants, and services to meet every visitor's needs and means.

A relatively inexpensive network of trains and buses covers the region, allowing travel between towns and to and from Prague with a minimum of fuss. West Bohemia is generally rougher terrain, so only serious bikers should consider seeing the area on two wheels.

SOUTH BOHEMIA

Once the religious hotbed of the country, south Bohemia was a focal point of the Hussite wars that eventually ravaged many of its towns and villages. Though the days of

Bohemia

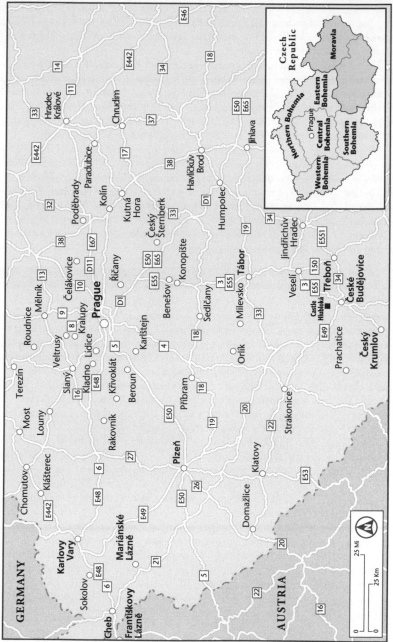

Czech Republic

Moravia

Northern Bohemia

Eastern Bohemia

Prague

Central Bohemia

Western Bohemia

Southern Bohemia

GERMANY

AUSTRIA

Prague

Plzeň

Tábor

Třeboň

České Budějovice

Český Krumlov

Karlovy Vary

Cheb

Mariánské Lázně

Františkovy Lázně

Sokolov

Chomutov

Kláštěrec

Most

Louny

Terezín

Roudnice

Mělník

Veltrusy

Slaný

Kladno

Lidice

Kralupy

Rakovnik

Beroun

Křivoklát

Karlštejn

Příbram

Domažlice

Klatovy

Strakonice

Orlík

Milevsko

Sedlčany

Benešov

Konopiště

Humpolec

Havlíčkův Brod

Jihlava

Chrudim

Hradec Králové

Pardubice

Poděbrady

Kolín

Kutná Hora

Český Šternberk

Čelákovice

Řičany

Jindřichův Hradec

Veselí

Prachatice

Castle Hluboká

E46

14

E442

34

18

11

33

Hradec Králové

E442

32

38

13

10

D11

E67

E50 E65

E55

E55

3

E55

150

34

E551

E49

E53

22

16

20

22

5

E50

E49

21

6

E48

E442

E48

6

E48

16

27

E50

26

19

18

20

22

33

34

19

D1

D1

17

37

33

38

9

8

5

4

18

Castle Hluboká

25 Mi

25 Km

0

0

215

war took their toll, the region still features fine examples of architecture from every era. Southern Bohemia is also home to the Czech Republic's second-largest castle, **Český Krumlov,** a UNESCO-protected site that dazzles with its Disney-like qualities no matter how many times you visit.

There are two good approaches for exploring south Bohemia. If you're traveling by train or bus from Prague, make **Tábor** your first stop. It's on a main route, so the arrangements are easy. Then continue heading south, hooking up with **Třeboň, České Budějovice,** and **Český Krumlov.** If time is of the essence, you may want to set up camp in the area's main city, České Budějovice, and make several day trips, since nothing is that far away (Tábor, the farthest town, is 60km/37 miles away).

For those who have more time, consider a bike tour. These days, with the possibility of attack from Austria far diminished, south Bohemia is a much quieter setting with a less rugged terrain than west Bohemia. Biking here is much more feasible, and you'll find dozens of quaint towns dotting the countryside. **Central European Adventures** ⟨★⟩, Jáchymova 4, Praha 1 (© **222-328-879;** http://cea51.tripod.com), can arrange superb tours that include bike rentals, guides (English-speaking), transportation, and even canoe trips through southern Bohemia at a fraction of what it would cost if you arranged the same trip from home.

2 Karlovy Vary (Carlsbad) ⟨★⟩

120km (74 miles) W of Prague

The discovery of Karlovy Vary (Carlsbad) by Charles IV reads like a 14th-century episode of the TV show *The Beverly Hillbillies.* According to local lore, the king was out huntin' for some food when up from the ground came a-bubblin' water (though discovered by his dogs and not an errant gunshot). Knowing a good thing when he saw it, Charles immediately set to work building a small castle in the area, naming the town that evolved around it Karlovy Vary, which translates as "Charles's Boiling Place." The first spa buildings were built in 1522, and before long, notables like Albrecht of Wallenstein, Peter the Great, and later Bach, Beethoven, Freud, and Marx all came to Karlovy Vary for a holiday retreat.

After World War II, East Bloc travelers (following in the footsteps of Marx, no doubt) discovered the town, and Karlovy Vary became a destination for the proletariat. On doctors' orders, most workers would enjoy regular stays of 2 or 3 weeks, letting the mineral waters ranging from 110°F (43°C) to 162°F (72°C) from the town's 12 springs heal their tired and broken bodies. Even now, a large number of spa guests are here by a doctor's prescription.

Most of the 40-plus years of Communist neglect have been erased as a barrage of renovations continues to restore the spa's former glory. Gone is the statue of Russian cosmonaut Yuri Gagarin. Gone are almost all the fading, crumbling building facades that used to line both sides of the river. In their places stand restored buildings, cherubs, caryatids, and more.

Today, some 150,000 people, both traditional clientele and newer patrons, travel to the spa resort every year to sip, bathe, and frolic, though most enjoy the "13th spring" (actually a hearty herb-and-mineral liqueur called Becherovka) as much as—if not more than—the 12 nonalcoholic versions. Czechs will tell you that all have medical benefits. The Slavic nouveau riche have once again found a comfortable setting after the backlash they faced soon after the iron curtain was drawn. In a throwback to

Karlovy Vary

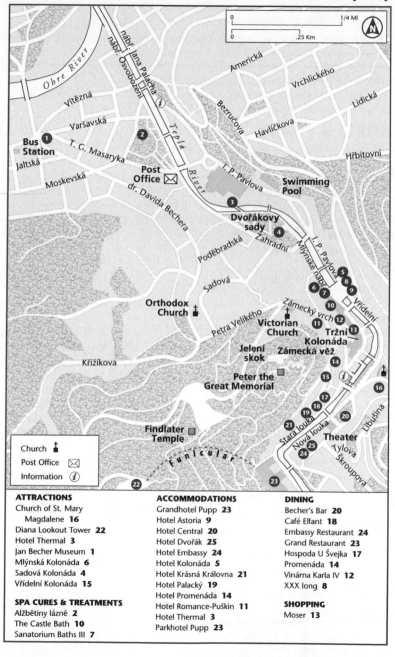

0   1/4 MI

0   .25 Km

ATTRACTIONS

Church of St. Mary
  Magdalene **16**
Diana Lookout Tower **22**
Hotel Thermal **3**
Jan Becher Museum **1**
Mlýnská Kolonáda **6**
Sadová Kolonáda **4**
Vřídelní Kolonáda **15**

SPA CURES & TREATMENTS

Alžbětiny lázně **2**
The Castle Bath **10**
Sanatorium Baths III **7**

ACCOMMODATIONS

Grandhotel Pupp **23**
Hotel Astoria **9**
Hotel Central **20**
Hotel Dvořák **25**
Hotel Embassy **24**
Hotel Kolonáda **5**
Hotel Krásná Královna **21**
Hotel Palacký **19**
Hotel Promenáda **14**
Hotel Romance-Puškin **11**
Hotel Thermal **3**
Parkhotel Pupp **23**

DINING

Becher's Bar **20**
Café Elfant **18**
Embassy Restaurant **24**
Grand Restaurant **23**
Hospoda U Švejka **17**
Promenáda **14**
Vinárna Karla IV **12**
XXX long **8**

SHOPPING

Moser **13**

Tips **A Driving Warning**

Be warned that drivers on Highway E48 between Prague and Karlovy Vary are often reckless. Please take extra care when driving.

Soviet days, many shopkeepers cater to Russian clientele, so don't be surprised if you're nowadays addressed in Russian rather than English or German.

ESSENTIALS

GETTING THERE   At all costs, *avoid the train from Prague,* which takes over 4 hours on a circuitous route. If you're arriving from another direction, Karlovy Vary's main train station is connected to the town center by bus no. 11.

Taking a bus to Karlovy Vary is much more convenient. Frequent express **buses** make it from Prague's Florenc bus station in 2¼ hours at a cost of 130Kč ($5.40). From Karlovy Vary's Dolní nádraží (bus station) take a 10-minute walk or local bus no. 4 into Karlovy Vary's spa center. Note that you must have a ticket to board local transport. You can buy tickets for 10Kč (40¢) at the bus station stop, or from the bus driver, which will then cost you 15Kč (60¢). For timetable information go to www. jizdnirady.cz.

The nearly 2-hour **drive** from Prague to Karlovy Vary can be very busy and dangerous due to undisciplined Czech drivers. If you're going by car, take Highway E48 from the western end of Prague and follow it straight through to Karlovy Vary. This two-lane highway widens in a few spots to let cars pass slow-moving vehicles on hills.

VISITOR INFORMATION   **Infocentrum města Karlovy Vary** is located near the main Mlýnská kolonáda, on Lázeňská 1 (© **353-224-097**). It's open April to October, Monday to Friday from 7am to 5pm and Saturday and Sunday from 9am to 3pm; November to March, Monday to Friday from 7am to 4pm. It has a window at the terminal of the **Dolní (lower) nádraží** bus and train station, Západní ulice (© **353-232-838**). These are the official town's information centers, which will answer your questions and help you with accommodations, getting tickets for entertainment in the city, and so on. Be sure to pick up *Promenáda* magazine, a comprehensive collection of events with a small map of the town center. Alternatively, you'll find information on www.karlovyvary.cz.

SPECIAL EVENTS   The **Karlovy Vary International Film Festival** is the place to see and be seen. Each summer (in early July), the country's film stars, celebrities, and wealthy folks, supported by a cast of international stars like Lauren Bacall, Michael Douglas, Alan Alda, Mia Farrow, Miloš Forman, Jason Robards, Sharon Stone, and Robert Redford, can be spotted taking part in one of Europe's biggest film festivals. Nine venues screen more than 300 films during the 10-day festival. Go to www. iffkv.cz for more information.

Another event that brings out Czech stars, including Karel Gott, the Czech version of Tom Jones and Bert Parks rolled into one, is the **Miss Czech Republic contest,** held annually in April at the Grand Hotel Pupp.

Karlovy Vary plays host to several other events, including a **jazz festival** and **beer Olympiad** in May, a **Dvořák singing contest** in June, a **Summer Music Festival** in August, and a **Dvořák Autumn Music Festival** in September and October.

For details on the festivals, contact the information center listed above.

ORIENTATION   Karlovy Vary is shaped like a T, with the Teplá River running up the stem and the Ohře River at the top of the T. Most of the major streets are pedestrian promenades lining both sides of the Teplá.

EXPLORING KARLOVY VARY

The town's slow pace and pedestrian promenades, lined with turn-of-the-20th-century Art Nouveau buildings, turn strolling into an art form. Nighttime walks take on an even more mystical feel as the sewers, the river, and the many major cracks in the roads emit steam from the hot springs running underneath. It feels like you could meet Vincent Price looming around every corner.

I suggest avoiding the new town, which happens to be conveniently left off most of the small tourist maps. Its only real attractions are a McDonald's and a couple of ATMs (which you can also find in the historic center).

If you're traveling here by train or bus, a good place to start your exploration is the **Hotel Thermal,** I. P. Pavlova 11 (© **359-001-111**), at the north end of the old town's center. Built in the 1970s, it exemplifies how obtrusive Communist architecture can be. Nestled between the town's eastern hills and the Ohře River, the glass, steel, and concrete Thermal sticks out like a sore thumb amid the rest of the town's 19th-century architecture. Nonetheless, you'll find three important places at the Thermal: the only centrally located outdoor public pool; an upper terrace boasting a truly spectacular view of the town; and Karlovy Vary's largest theater, which holds many of the film festival's premier events. Look at it. Take it all in. And after seeing the Thermal, it's best to keep walking before you remember too much of it.

As you enter the heart of the town on the river's west side, you'll see the ornate white wrought-iron gazebo named **Sadová Kolonáda** adorning the beautifully manicured park, **Dvořákovy Sady.** Continue to follow the river, and about 100m (328 ft.) later you'll encounter the **Mlýnská Kolonáda.** This long, covered walkway houses several Karlovy Vary springs, which you can sample free 24 hours a day. Each spring has a plaque beside it describing its mineral elements and temperature. Bring your own cup or buy one just about anywhere (see the box "Spa Cures & Treatments," below) to sip the waters, since most are too hot to drink from with your hands. When you hit the river bend, you'll see the majestic **Church of St. Mary Magdalene** perched atop a hill, overlooking the **Vřídlo,** the hottest spring. Built in 1736, the church is the work of Kilian Ignac Dienzenhofer, who also created two of Prague's more notable churches—both named St. Nicholas.

Housing Vřídlo, which blasts water some 15m (49 ft.) into the air, is the glass building where the statue of Soviet cosmonaut Yuri Gagarin once stood. (Gagarin's statue has since made a safe landing at the Karlovy Vary Airport, where it greets the waves of Russian visitors who flood the town.) Now called the **Vřídelní Kolonáda,** the structure, built in 1974, houses several hot springs that you can sample for free daily from 6am to 7pm. Here are also located public toilets, open daily 6am to 6pm and costing 6Kč (25¢).

Heading away from the Vřídelní Kolonáda are Stará and Nová Louka streets, which line either side of the river. Along **Stará (Old) Louka** are several fine cafes and glass and crystal shops. **Nová (New) Louka** is lined with many hotels and the historic town's main theater, built in 1886, which houses paintings by notable artists like Klimt and has just finished a major renovation project that has restored the theater to its original splendor.

Spa Cures & Treatments

Most visitors to Karlovy Vary come for a spa treatment, a therapy that lasts 1 to 3 weeks. After consulting with a spa physician, you're given a specific regimen of activities that may include mineral baths, massages, waxings, mudpacks, electrotherapy, and pure oxygen inhalation. After spending the morning at a spa or sanatorium, you're usually directed to walk the paths of the town's surrounding forest.

The common denominator of all the cures is an ample daily dose of hot mineral water, which bubbles up from 12 springs. This water definitely has a distinct odor and taste. You'll see people chugging it down, but it doesn't necessarily taste very good. Some thermal springs actually taste and smell like rotten eggs. You may want to take a small sip at first. Do keep in mind that the waters are used to treat internal disorders, so the minerals may cleanse the body thoroughly—in other words, they can cause diarrhea.

You'll also notice that almost everyone in town seems to be carrying "the cup." This funny-looking cup is basically a mug with a built-in straw running through the handle. Young and old alike parade around with their mugs, filling and refilling them at each thermal water tap. You can buy these mugs everywhere for as little as 60Kč ($2.50) or as much as 230Kč ($9.55); they make a quirky souvenir. *But be warned:* None of the mugs can make the warmer hot springs taste any better.

The minimum spa treatment lasts 1 week and must be arranged in advance. A spa treatment package traditionally includes room, full board, and complete therapy regimen; the cost varies from about $40 to $100 per

Both streets lead to the **Grandhotel Pupp,** Mírové nám. 2 (© **353-109-631**). The Pupp's main entrance and building have just come out of extensive renovations that have more or less erased the effects of 40 years of Communism (the hotel's name had been changed to the Moskva-Pupp). Regardless of capitalism or Communism, the Pupp remains what it always was: the grande dame of hotels in central Europe. Once catering to nobility from all over Europe, the Pupp still houses one of the town's finest restaurants, the Grand (see below), while its grounds are a favorite with the hiking crowd.

If you still have the energy, atop the hill behind the Pupp stands the **Diana Lookout Tower** (© **353-222-872**). Footpaths lead to the tower through the forests and eventually spit you out at the base of the tower, as if to say, "Ha, the trip is only half over." The five-story climb up the tower tests your stamina, but the view of the town is more than worth it. For those who aren't up to the climb up the hill, a cable car runs up the hill every 15 minutes daily from 9am to 10pm for 36Kč ($1.50) one-way, 60Kč ($2.50) round-trip.

And if you have some time left at the end of your stay, visit the **Jan Becher Museum,** T. G. Masaryka 57 (© **359-578-156;** www.janbecher.cz), to find out about the history of the town's secret, the formula of Becherovka. This herbal liquor is a person per day, depending on season and facilities. Rates are highest from May to September and lowest from November to February.

For information and reservations in Prague, contact **Čedok**, at Na Příkopě 18, and also at Václavské nám. 53, Praha 1 (© **224-197-632**; fax 224-213-786; www.cedok.cz). Many hotels also provide spa and health treatments, so ask when you book your room. Most will happily arrange a treatment if they don't provide them directly.

If you're coming for just a day or two, you can experience the waters on an "outpatient" basis. The largest balneological complex in town (and in the Czech Republic) is the **Alžbětiny Lázně-Lázně V,** Smetanovy sady 1145/1 (© **353-222-536**; www.spa5.cz). On their menu are all kinds of treatments, including water cures, massages, a hot-air bath, a steam bath, a whirlpool, and a pearl bath, as well as use of their swimming pool. You can choose packages of different procedures between 90Kč and 600Kč ($3.75 and $25). It's open Monday to Friday 8am to 3pm for spa treatments; the pool is open Saturday and Sunday from 10am to 6pm.

The **Sanatorium Baths III,** Mlýnské nábřeží 7 (© **353-225-641**), welcomes day-trippers with mineral baths, massages, saunas, and a cold pool. It's open Monday to Friday 7am to 2pm for spa treatments; the swimming pool and sauna are open Monday to Friday 3 to 6pm and Saturday 1 to 5pm.

The **Castle Bath (Zámecké Lázně),** Zámecký vrch (© **353-222-649**), is a new spa and wellness house located in a reconstructed site at the foot of the Castle Tower (Zámecká věž) in the old city center. Visitors are welcome daily from 7:30am to 7:30pm to enjoy individual spa treatments. A single entry for 2 to 4 hours costs between $21 and $54.

sought-after souvenir, and you will get to taste it here. The museum is open daily 9am to 5pm; admission is 100Kč ($4.15) adults, 50Kč ($2) students, 25Kč ($1) children.

SHOPPING

Crystal and porcelain are Karlovy Vary's other claims to fame. Dozens of shops throughout town sell everything from plates to chandeliers.

Ludvík Moser founded his first glassware shop in 1857 and became one of this country's foremost names in glass. You can visit the **Moser Factory,** kapitána Jaroše 19 (© **353-449-455**; www.moser-glass.com; bus no. 1, 10, or 22), just west of the town center. Its glass museum is open Monday to Friday 8am to 5:30pm and Saturday 9am to 3pm. There's also a **Moser Store,** on Tržiště 7 (© **353-235-303**), right in the heart of new town; it's open daily from 10am to 7pm (Sat–Sun till 6pm). Dozens of other smaller shops also sell the famed glass and are as easy to find in the Old Town as spring water.

WHERE TO STAY

Private rooms used to be the best places to stay in Karlovy Vary with regard to quality and price. But this is changing as more and more hotels renovate and raise standards—as well as prices. Private accommodations can still provide better value, but they take a little extra work. If you want to arrange a room, try the **Infocentrum** (see above). Expect to pay about 1,500Kč ($62) for a double.

Some of the town's major spa hotels accommodate only those who are paying for complete treatment, unless for some reason their occupancy rates are particularly low. The hotels I've listed below accept guests for stays of any length.

EXPENSIVE

Grandhotel Pupp ⚜ Well known as one of Karlovy Vary's best hotels, the Pupp, built in 1701, is also one of Europe's oldest hotels. Its public areas boast the expected splendor and charm, as do the renovated guest rooms. The best ones tend to be those facing the town center and are located on the upper floors; these have good views and sturdy wooden furniture. Some rooms have amenities such as air-conditioning, television, minibar, and safe, though not all do. The Grand has as grand a dining room as you'll find, with the food to match (see "Where to Dine" below). The hotel also has a stylish casino (open midnight–4am).

Mírové nám. 2, 360 91, Karlovy Vary. ✆ **353-109-630.** Fax 353-226-638. www.pupp.cz. 110 units. Note that there are no rates in local currency; hotel charges at a converted rate upon checkout. $362 double deluxe; suite from $437; $1,625 presidential apt. Rates include breakfast. AE, DC, MC, V. Valet parking. **Amenities:** 4 restaurants; bar; cafe; pool; tennis courts; golf course; health club; limousine/taxi service; salon; room service (6am–midnight); same-day laundry; casino.

Parkhotel Pupp ⚜ Part of the Pupp complex, these are basically rooms in the section of the hotel that doesn't quite measure up to the grand standards of its sister. But they are still nice and functional, if not quite as cozy and elegant as the others. Personally, I'd stay in one of these rooms and use the money I save on a nice meal and a couple of Karlovy Vary kisses (Becherovka in a frozen glass).

Mírové nám. 2, 360 91 Karlovy Vary. ✆ **353-109-111.** Fax 353-224-032. 255 units. www.pupp.cz. No rates in local currency; hotel charges at a converted rate upon checkout. $250 double; $437 suite. AE, DC, MC, V. **Amenities:** 4 restaurants (shared w/Grandhotel Pupp); indoor pool; tennis courts; fitness center; sauna; salon; casino. *In room:* TV, minibar, iron, safe.

MODERATE

Hotel Central   Located next to the theater, this hotel certainly is central. A recent face-lift has restored the hotel to its 1920s splendor and yet it still provides good value, with rooms that aren't overly spacious but adequate. Those on the upper floors provide great views of the Vřídelní Kolonáda.

Divadelní nám. 17, 360 01 Karlovy Vary. ✆ **353-182-111.** Fax 353-182-631. www.interhotel-central.cz. 84 units. Note that there are no rates in local currency; hotel charges at a converted rate upon checkout. $100–$155 double; $128–$260 suite. AE, MC, V. **Amenities:** Restaurant; pool; balneo center for treatments. *In room:* TV, minibar, safe.

Hotel Dvořák ⚜ Now part of the Vienna International hotel/resort chain, the Dvořák has improved immensely over the past years, especially in terms of service. This hotel is within sight of the Pupp, but it's less expensive. The Pupp may have the history and elegance, but the Dvořák has the facilities. The rooms are spacious, with elegant decor and medium-size bathrooms with lots of marble. The staff is very attentive. Business travelers will appreciate the hotel's business facilities.

Nová Louka 11, 360 21 Karlovy Vary. ✆ **353-102-111.** Fax 353-102-119. www.hotel-dvorak.cz. 106 units. $146 double. The current exchange rate is used for those who want to pay crowns by cash. AE, DC, MC, V. **Amenities:** Restaurant; indoor pool; tennis courts; fitness center; sauna; salon; casino. *In room:* TV, minibar, iron, safe, pants presser.

Hotel Embassy ⟨⟩   On the riverbank across from the Pupp, the Embassy has well-appointed rooms, many with an early-20th-century motif. Set in a historic house, the rooms are medium-size with medium-size bathrooms. The staff here really helps make this hotel worthy of consideration, as does the proximity to the pub, which serves up some of the best goulash and beer in the city.

Nová Louka 21, 360 01 Karlovy Vary. ⟨⟩ **353-221-161.** Fax 353-223-146. www.embassy.cz. 20 units. 2,595Kč–3,290Kč ($108–$137) double; 3,415Kč–3,830Kč ($142–$159) suite. AE, MC, V. **Amenities:** Pub; lobby bar; indoor golf; pool table. *In room:* TV, minibar, safe.

Hotel Kolonáda   The Kolonáda, with its lovely facade, was formed by a merger of the Otava and Patria hotels. As the name suggests, it's across from the Mlýnská Kolonáda. The hotel's interior is modern and renovated, as are the rooms, the best of which overlook the Kolonáda.

I. P. Pavlova 8, 360 01 Karlovy Vary. ⟨⟩ **353-345-555** or 353-222-010. Fax 353-347-818. www.kolonada.cz. 162 units. Note hotel charges at a converted rate upon checkout. $91–$151 single; $71–$132 double; $102–$163 suite for 2. AE, MC, V. **Amenities:** 2 restaurants; bar; cafe; relaxation center w/pool; mountain-bike rental; laundry. *In room:* TV, safe.

Hotel Krásná Královna (the Beautiful Queen Hotel)   A fresh new property with a familiar face has emerged in the spa zone. The original accents of this 18th-century guesthouse have been revived with fresh colors, classic furniture, and fine accessories. This family-run hotel is again offering comfort and a cozy atmosphere as well as access to spa amenities in the town.

Stará Louka 335/48, Karlovy Vary. ⟨⟩ **353-852-611.** Fax 353-852-612. www.krasnakralovna.cz. 21 units. 3,200Kč ($133) double; 4,100Kč ($170) suite. AE, MC, V. **Amenities:** Restaurant; massage. *In room:* TV, minibar, hair dryer.

Hotel Palacký ⟨*Value*⟩   One of the best deals in town. The hotel is ideally situated on the west side of the river so it gets sun almost all day. The rooms, with their mostly bare walls and low beds, seem huge, especially the ones with a river view. The staff can seem more like furniture than people who help guests, but that's a small price to pay for such inexpensive rooms.

Stará Louka 40, 360 01 Karlovy Vary. ⟨⟩ **353-222-544.** Fax 353-223-561. www.hotelpalacky.cz. 20 units. 1,800Kč–2,700Kč ($75–$112) double. AE, MC, V. *In room:* TV, fridge, hair dryer.

Hotel Promenáda   Next door to the Romance-Puškin, the Promenáda is a recent addition to the Karlovy Vary accommodations scene. The hotel faces the Kolonáda and has a beautiful view of the old center of the town. Rooms on the lower floors are more spacious than those on the upper levels, but all have an elegant decor highlighted with wrought-iron bed frames and large windows.

Tržiště 31, 360 01 Karlovy Vary. ⟨⟩ **363-225-648.** Fax 353-229-708. www.hotel-promenada.cz. 16 units. 2,680Kč–3,380Kč ($111–$140) double. AE, MC, V. **Amenities:** Restaurant; cafe. *In room:* TV, minibar.

Hotel Thermal   What better way to experience what it was like to stay in Karlovy Vary under Communism? Built in the 1970s, Hotel Thermal towers above the town, rising like a steel-and-glass phoenix from the steam of the river's spas. But because of its size—and the cinema on its ground floor—it becomes a hub during the film festival. All kidding aside, the Thermal also qualifies as a possible place to stay because of its location, services, and size. Don't expect anything exciting, but do take a picture of yourself in the *Star Trek* seats in the lobby bar. While the reception area is still very much a throwback to the 1970s, the guest rooms have been tastefully refurbished and the bathrooms refitted in a modern style.

I. P. Pavlova 11, 360 01 Karlovy Vary. ⓒ 359-001-111. Fax 359-002-603. www.thermal.cz. 200 units. 3,400Kč ($141) double; 7,200Kč ($300) suite. AE, MC, V. **Amenities:** 2 restaurants; bar; heated outdoor pool; cinema. *In room:* TV, safe.

INEXPENSIVE

Hotel Astoria   In the heart of the historic town, the restored Astoria mainly caters to spa guests but, unlike many of its competitors, it is big enough to usually have several rooms available for nontreatment visitors. The staff can be a little gruff at times, but the rooms are big, with satellite TV an added bonus. The restaurant serves standard Czech fare, with a lot of vegetable dishes as well, though I'd recommend trying one of the other places in town for a less bland experience.

Vřídelní 92, 360 01 Karlovy Vary. ⓒ 353-335-111. Fax 353-224-368. www.astoria-spa.cz. 100 units. Note that there are no rates in local currency; hotel charges at a converted rate upon checkout. $36–$56 double. AE, MC, V. **Amenities:** Restaurant. *In room:* TV, fridge.

Hotel Romance-Puškin   Recently this place has been renamed, but for years it's carried the name of the great Russian poet we know as Pushkin. The hotel occupies an intricately ornamented 19th-century Art Nouveau building that has just been renovated. It has a terrific location, close to the springs. The rooms are rather basic, but they're comfortable enough. Ask for one that has a balcony facing St. Mary Magdalene Church and enjoy one of the nicest views in the Old Town.

Tržiště 37, 360 90 Karlovy Vary. ⓒ 353-222-646. Fax 353-224-134. www.hotelromance.cz. 37 units. 1,890Kč–2,670Kč ($79–$111) double; 2,640Kč–3,360Kč ($110–$140) suite. AE, MC, V. **Amenities:** Restaurant; room service; massage; laundry. *In room:* TV, minibar, safe, hair dryer.

WHERE TO DINE
EXPENSIVE

Embassy Restaurant CZECH/CONTINENTAL   On the ground floor of the Embassy Hotel, this is one of the oldest restaurants in town. It offers an intimate dining room with historic interior. If you visit in winter, get a table next to the original hearth. Here you'll find many traditional Czech dishes with slight twists that make them interesting. The grilled loin of pork covered with a light, creamy, green-pepper sauce makes a nice change from the regular roast pork served by most Czech restaurants. The spicy goulash is more reminiscent of Hungary's piquant flavors than bland Czech fare.

Nová Louka 21. ⓒ 353-221-161. Reservations recommended. Soups 55Kč–85Kč ($2.30–$3.55); main courses 175Kč–985Kč ($7.30–$41). AE, V. Daily 11am–11pm.

Grand Restaurant ⓕ CONTINENTAL   It's no surprise that the Grandhotel Pupp has the nicest dining room in town: an elegant space with tall ceilings, huge mirrors, and glistening chandeliers. A large menu features equally large portions of salmon, chicken, veal, pork, turkey, and beef in a variety of heavy and heavier sauces. Even the mouthwatering trout with mushrooms is smothered in butter sauce.

In the Grandhotel Pupp, Mírové nám. 2. ⓒ 353-109-646. Reservations recommended. Soups 80Kč ($3.35); main courses 280Kč–590Kč ($12–$25). AE, V. Daily noon–3pm and 6–11pm.

Promenáda CZECH/CONTINENTAL   This cozy, intimate spot may not be as elegant as the Grand Restaurant, but it remains one of the better places to dine and serves creative meals. Across from the Vřídelní Kolonáda, the Promenáda offers a wide menu with generous portions. The daily menu usually includes well-prepared wild game, but the mixed grill for two and the chateaubriand, both flambéed at the table, are the chef's best dishes. The wine list features a large selection of wines from around Europe, but don't neglect the Czech wines, especially the white Ryslink and the red Frankovka. An order of crêpes suzette, big enough to satisfy two, rounds out a wonderful meal.

Tržiště 31. (**C**) **353-225-648**. Reservations highly recommended. Soups 60Kč ($2.50); appetizers 50Kč–320Kč ($2–$13); main courses 240Kč–699Kč ($10–$29). AE, V. Daily noon–11pm.

MODERATE

Becher's Bar CONTINENTAL   A renovation plan in the mid-1990s gave birth to this slightly upscale cocktail lounge—basically the town's one and only cocktail bar— that calls out for Tom Jones (or his Czech equivalent, Karel Gott) to pick up a mic and begin crooning and gyrating. The menu is part roadhouse, part pub, and overall a pleasant change from the regular heavy meals offered around town. Plus, it's the only place around open this late, with live jazz to boot! And despite the potential to gouge, the management has resisted the urge—even the Becher is only 90Kč ($3.75).

In the Grandhotel Pupp, Mírové nám. 2. (**C**) **353-109-483**. Appetizers and light meal 60Kč–190Kč ($2.50–$7.90). AE, MC, V. Daily 7pm–4am.

Vinárna Karla IV. CZECH/CONTINENTAL   Perched high above the Vřídelní Kolonáda, this former hunting lodge of Karel IV, built in the early 1600s, is the perfect place to sit outside on a warm summer night. The menu's a little tough to figure out, but who cares if the lightly baked trout in lemon is listed under the "From the Meat" section or if vegetarian meals come from the "Dungeon"? This is one of the most romantic and satisfying restaurants in Vary. An ample wine list does its best to keep up with the menu and, again, local wines measure up well against their imported, expensive cousins.

Zámecký vrch 3. (**C**) **353-227-255**. Reservations recommended. Soups 45Kč–90Kč ($1.85–$3.75); main courses 119Kč–380Kč ($4.95–$16). AE, MC, V. Wed–Mon noon–11pm.

XXX long ITALIAN/INTERNATIONAL   The interior of this new addition to the list of local restaurants offers an interesting combination of modern decoration and old furniture. On the large menu is a wide assortment of Italian and international meals at reasonable prices. There are several good seafood options to complement the pastas which are not overcooked, as they are in many Czech eateries. Children will appreciate the extensive pizza menu here. Don't forget to get a good Italian cappuccino served here in funky ceramic cups.

Vřídelní 23. (**C**) **353-224-232**. Soups 30Kč ($1.25); main courses 120Kč–350Kč ($5–$15). AE, MC, V. Daily 11am–11pm.

INEXPENSIVE

Cafe Eléfant COFFEE/DESSERT   Who needs to travel all the way to Vienna? Since this is a cafe in the true sense of the word, all you'll find are coffee, tea, alcoholic and nonalcoholic drinks, desserts, and enough ambience to satisfy the hordes of Germans who flock to this landmark. (Be prepared to hear more Russian or German than Czech, as this is a see-and-be-seen haunt for foreigners.) The Eléfant is widely known for its Belle Epoque style and is famous for its freshly baked cakes. Its many outdoor tables overlook the pedestrian promenade.

Stará Louka 32. (**C**) **353-223-406**. Cakes and desserts 20Kč–120Kč (85¢–$5). AE, MC, V. Daily 10am–10pm.

Hospoda U Švejka CZECH   A new addition to the pub scene, U Švejka plays on the tried-and-true touristy *Good Soldier Švejk* theme. Luckily, the tourist trap goes no further, and once inside, you find a refreshingly unsmoky though thoroughly Czech atmosphere. Locals and tourists alike rub elbows while throwing back some fine lager for 55Kč ($2.30) per half liter, and standard pub favorites such as goulash and beef tenderloin in cream sauce.

Stará Louka 10. ⓒ **353-232-276.** Soups 35Kč ($1.45); appetizers 35Kč–109Kč ($1.45–$4.55); main courses 135Kč–319Kč ($5.60–$13). AE, MC, V. Daily 11am–10pm.

3 Mariánské Lázně (Marienbad)

46km (29 miles) SW of Karlovy Vary, 160km (100 miles) W of Prague

When Thomas Alva Edison visited Mariánské Lázně in the late 1800s, he declared, "There is no more beautiful spa in all the world."

Mariánské Lázně now stands in the shadow of the Czech Republic's most famous spa town, Karlovy Vary, but it wasn't always that way. First noted in 1528 by Bohemian historians, the town's mineral waters gained prominence at the end of the 18th and beginning of the 19th centuries. Nestled among forested hills and packed with romantic and elegant pastel hotels and spa houses, the town, commonly known by its German name, Marienbad, has played host to such luminaries as Goethe (this is where his love for Ulrika von Levetzow took root), Mark Twain, Chopin, Strauss, Wagner, Freud, and Kafka. England's Edward VII found the spa resort so enchanting that he visited nine times and even commissioned the building of the country's first golf club.

ESSENTIALS

GETTING THERE   There are four express trains from Prague's main station for 224Kč ($9.30) (trip time: 2 hr. 50 min.). Mariánské Lázně train station, Nádražní nám. 292, is south of the town center; take bus no. 5 into town. If getting here from Karlovy Vary, there are about eight trains daily; the trip takes 1 hour and 40 minutes and the fare is 76Kč ($3.15). For timetables, go to www.jizdnirady.cz.

The **bus** from Prague takes about 3 hours and costs about 150Kč ($6.25). The Mariánské Lázně bus station is adjacent to the train station on Nádražní náměstí; take bus no. 5 into town.

Driving from Prague, take Highway E50 through Plzeň to Stříbro—about 22km (14 miles) past Plzeň—and head northwest on Highway 21. The clearly marked route can take up to 2 hours.

VISITOR INFORMATION   Along the main strip lies the **Infocentrum,** Hlavní 47, 353 01, Mariánské Lázně (ⓒ **354-622-474**). In addition to dispensing advice, the staff sells maps and concert tickets and can arrange accommodations in hotels and private homes. It's open daily 9am to noon and 1pm to 6pm. For information and tips about what's going on, go to www.marianskelazne.cz.

SPECIAL EVENTS   One of the few places in central Europe not to claim Mozart as one of its sons, Mariánské Lázně has instead chosen to honor one of its frequent visitors, Chopin, with a yearly festival devoted entirely to the Polish composer. The **Chopin Festival** usually runs for 8 to 10 days near the end of August. Musicians and directors from all over the world gather to play and listen to concerts and recitals. In addition, several local art galleries hold special exhibits. Tickets range from 150Kč to 1,500Kč ($6.25–$63).

Each June, the town plays host to a **classical music festival** with many of the Czech Republic's finest musicians, as well as those from around the world. For more details or ticket reservations for either event, contact **Infocentrum** (see "Visitor Information," above).

Patriotic Americans can show up on **July 4th** for a little down-home fun, including a parade and other flag-waving special events commemorating the town's liberation by U.S. soldiers in World War II.

Sports-minded travelers can play one of the country's best golf courses and see how you measure up to the likes of Seve Ballesteros, Bernhard Langer, and Sam Torrance, who all played here at the first European PGA tour event, the Czech Open.

ORIENTATION   Mariánské Lázně is laid out around **Hlavní třída**, the main street. A plethora of hotels, restaurants, travel agencies, and stores fronts this street. **Lázeňá ská Kolonáda**, a long, covered block beginning at the northern end of Hlavní třída, contains six of the resort's eight major springs.

TAKING THE WATERS

When you walk through the town, it's almost impossible to miss eye-catching **Lázeňá ská Kolonáda**, just off Skalníkovy sady. From Hlavní třída, walk east on Vrchlického ulice. Recently restored to its former glory, this colonnade of cast iron and glass is adorned with ceiling frescoes and Corinthian columns. It was built in 1889 and connects half a dozen major springs in the town center; this is the focal point of those partaking in the ritual. Bring a cup to fill or, if you want to fit in with the thousands of guests who are serious about their spa water, buy one of the porcelain mugs with a built-in straw that are offered just about everywhere. Keep in mind that the waters are used to treat internal disorders, so the minerals may act to cleanse the body thoroughly by causing diarrhea. You can wander the Kolonáda any time; water is distributed daily from 6am to noon and 4 to 6pm.

Located just next to the colonnade is the modern landmark of the city. A pool surrounding a flower sculpture of stainless steel and stone is known as **"The Singing Fountain"** and contains a set of 250 water jets. At the top of every odd hour, between 7am and 9pm, and at 10pm, these jets spray in syncopation to music by different composers.

LEARNING ABOUT THE CITY'S PAST

There's not much town history, since Mariánské Lázně officially came into existence in 1808. But engaging brevity is what makes the two-story **City Museum (Muzeum Hlavního Města)**, Goetheovo nám. 11 (© **354-622-740**), worth recommending. Chronologically arranged displays include photos and documents of famous visitors.

The Spa Treatment

For a relaxing mineral bubble bath or massage, make reservations through the **Marienbad–Kur&Spa Hotels Information Service,** Masarykova 22, 353 29 (© **354-655-501**; www.marienbad.cz). Also ask at your hotel, as most provide spa treatments and massages or can arrange them. Treatments begin at 350Kč ($15).

Goethe slept here, in the upstairs rooms in 1823, when he was 74 years old. If you ask nicely, the museum guards will play an English-language tape that describes the contents of each room. You can also request to see the museum's English-language film about the town. Admission is 20Kč (85¢), and it's open Wednesday to Sunday from 9am to noon and 1 to 4pm (July–Sept until 5pm).

HIKING OR GOLFING

If the thought of a spa treatment fails to appeal, you can take a relaxing walk through the woods. The surrounding forest, **Slavkovský les (Slavkov Forest)**, has about 70km (43 miles) of marked footpaths and trails through the gentle hills that abound in the area.

If you're a die-hard golfer or just looking for a little exercise, the **Mariánské Lázně Golf Club** (② **354-624-300;** www.golfml.cz), a 6,773-yard, par-72 championship course, lies on the edge of town. The club takes pay-as-you-play golfers, with a fully equipped pro shop that rents clubs. Greens fees are 1,450Kč to 1,650Kč ($60–$68) and club rental is 500Kč ($21). Reservations are recommended on weekends.

WHERE TO STAY

The main strip along Hlavní třída is lined with hotels, many with rooms facing the Kolonáda. If you feel comfortable about doing this, I suggest walking the street and shopping around for a room. Most hotels charge from 2,000Kč to 4,000Kč ($83–$166) for a double from May to September. Off-season prices can fall by as much as half.

For private accommodations, try Palackého ulice, running south of the main spa area.

EXPENSIVE

Hotel Cristal Palace   After a renovation of the building, this hotel has become one of the top establishments on the main strip. Despite the immediate reaction of "Did I just walk onto a set for *Miami Vice?*" upon seeing its pastel colors, you'll enjoy the hotel's enviable location just a few minutes south of the town center. Alas, the guest rooms are outfitted with sterile though decent furniture. The restaurant, cafe, wine room, and brasserie also have been redone, much for the better. All are now bright and cheery, pleasant for a quick coffee or drink.

Hlavní třída 61, 353 44 Mariánské Lázně. ② **354-615-111.** Fax 354-625-012. www.cristalpalace.cz. 94 units. 4,500Kč ($187) double; 6,000Kč ($250) suite. AE, DC, MC, V. Garage parking available for 250Kč ($10) per night. **Amenities:** Restaurant; cafe; pub; spa and health treatments; laundry service. *In room:* A/C, TV, minibar, hair dryer, iron, pants presser.

Hotel Villa Butterfly ⌖   One of the many hotels on the main street to be spruced up and expanded recently, the Butterfly has upgraded its 26 rather ordinary rooms into 94 first-rate bright and spacious ones. In fact, from the front hall to the fitness room and even all the way to its new underground parking, the Butterfly has really taken off. Oddly enough, the renovations, which must have cost a lot, have had a reverse effect on the rates, now a good 15% lower. An English-speaking staff and a good selection of foreign-language newspapers at the reception area are added bonuses. The Fontaine is one of the town's largest restaurants, yet it remains a quiet place to eat top-rate Czech and international cuisine. The hotel offers guests Internet access.

Hlavní třída 655, 353 01 Mariánské Lázně. ② **354-654-111.** Fax 354-654-200. www.marienbad.cz. 96 units. 2,460Kč–3,720Kč ($102–$155) double; 3,660Kč–4,920Kč ($152–$205) suite. Rates include breakfast. AE, DC, MC, V. **Amenities:** 2 restaurants; bar; cafe; wellness center; conference center. *In room:* A/C, TV, minibar, hair dryer.

Parkhotel Golf ⚜ One of the more luxurious hotels in town, the Golf isn't actually in town but across from the golf course about 3km (2 miles) down the road leading to Karlovy Vary. This hotel is busy, so reservations are recommended. The English-speaking staff delivers on their pledge to cater to every wish. The rooms are bright and spacious, and there's an excellent restaurant and terrace on the first floor. Not surprisingly, given the hotel's name, the staff can help arrange a quick 18 holes across the street. The hotel has also recently opened its own spa center to pamper guests a little more.

Zádub 580, 353 01 Mariánské Lázně. ✆ **354-622-651**. Fax 354-622-655. www.parkhotel-golf.cz. 28 units. 2,600Kč–3,800Kč ($108–$158) double; 4,100Kč–4,900Kč ($170–$204) suite. Rates include breakfast. AE, DC, MC, V. **Amenities:** Restaurant; bar; pool; golf course; tennis courts; fitness center; spa center; sauna; room service (6am–11pm); laundry. *In room:* TV, minibar, hair dryer, safe.

MODERATE
Hotel Bohemia In the middle of the action on Hlavní, the Bohemia has several rooms with balconies that overlook the Kolonáda. It has been recently remodeled and improved, rooms tend to be a little larger, and for those looking for location, you can't get more central.

Hlavní třída 100, 353 01 Mariánské Lázně. ✆ **354-610-111**. Fax 354-610-555. www.orea.cz/bohemia. 77 units. 2,200Kč–3,820Kč ($91–$159) double; 2,570Kč–4,980Kč ($107–$207) suite. AE, DC, MC, V. **Amenities:** Restaurant; cafe; balneo center. *In room:* TV, minibar, safe.

Hotel Excelsior Across from the Nové lázně (New Bath), the Excelsior has benefited inside and out from a post-Communist face-lift. Several rooms have ornate balconies overlooking the park that leads up to the Kolonáda. There are two restaurants, including the Churchill, one of the best watering holes on the strip. The hotel staff is also more attentive than those at some other hotels in town.

Hlavní třída 121, 353 01 Mariánské Lázně. ✆ **354-697-111**. Fax 354-697-221. www.hotelexcelsior.cz. 64 units. 2,680Kč–4,190Kč ($111–$174) double. AE, DC, MC, V. **Amenities:** 2 restaurants; spa and health treatments; laundry service. *In room:* TV, minibar, hair dryer.

Hotel Palace ⚜ The 1920s Palace is a beautiful Art Nouveau hotel 90m (295 ft.) from the Kolonáda. The rooms are extremely comfortable, with high ceilings and large bay windows lending an airy effect. In addition to a good Bohemian restaurant with a lovely terrace, the hotel contains a cafe, a wine room, and a snack bar.

Hlavní třída 67, 353 01 Mariánské Lázně. ✆ **354-685-111**. Fax 354-685-151. www.orea.cz. 45 units. 2,630Kč–3,880Kč ($109–$161) double; 3,220Kč–5,220Kč ($134–$217) suite. AE, DC, MC, V. **Amenities:** Restaurant; bar; cafe; wine room; spa and health treatments. *In room:* TV, minibar, hair dryer, iron, safe.

Hotel Zvon Next door to the Palace, the Zvon lacks a bit of the panache of its smaller neighbor, but it still ranks as one of the town's nicer hotels and sits in a prime spot directly across from the Kolonáda. The rooms at the front are brighter and much larger (reflected in the price) than those facing the back, which fail to receive much sun.

Hlavní třída 68, 353 01 Mariánské Lázně. ✆ **354-415-111**. Fax 354-415-222. www.orea.cz. 79 units. 2,510Kč–4,140Kč ($104–$172) double; 3,160Kč–5,500Kč ($131–$229) suite. AE, DC, MC, V. **Amenities:** Restaurant; cafe; bar; balneo center; laundry. *In room:* TV, minibar, safe, iron.

INEXPENSIVE
Grandhotel Pacifik *Value* Facing straight down the main strip, the Pacifik looks like a grand hotel. Well, looks can be deceiving, but it's still not a bad place given its prices. Not as comfortable or nicely appointed as most of the other hotels in the area,

⃝Kids Family Fun

If you're looking for a weekend break with the family and want to have an enjoyable experience outdoors, book a weekend at the **Koliba** ☃, Dusíkova 592 (② **354-625-169**). In the summer, dozens of kilometers of wooded trails are open for hiking and biking—though be careful because many of the paths lead through the golf course, and while golf is becoming more popular in the Czech Republic, the skill level is still such that you need to beware of errant balls. In the winter, try out the mini-ski hill. Two tows at the foot of the hotel take you up a 150m (492-ft.) hill perfect for anyone learning to ski. There are also dozens of kilometers of cross-country ski trails through the local forests that are always in top condition. A 1-day ski-pass costs about 280Kč ($12).

The après-ski atmosphere of the lodge, with its giant fireplace and numerous tables, provides the perfect respite from a hectic week. At night the flames of the open grill roasting all different sorts of game will ease the pain of all those bumps and bruises. In the summer, the trails are ideal for hiking.

the Pacifik is a relatively inexpensive way to stay where the action is. The surly staff will remind you of a bygone era. Ask for a room that faces the street.

Mírové nám. 84, 353 29 Mariánské Lázně. ② **354-651-111**. Fax 354-651-200. www.marienbad.cz. 109 units. 1,020Kč–1,830Kč ($42–$76) double. AE, V. **Amenities:** Restaurant; balneo center. *In room:* TV, minibar, safe, hair dryer.

Hotel Koliba ⓥⓐⓛⓤⓔ   Away from the main strip but still only a 7-minute walk from the Kolonáda, the Koliba is a rustic hunting lodge set in the hills on Dusíkova, the road leading to the golf course and Karlovy Vary. The rooms are warm and inviting, with the wooden furnishings giving the hotel the feel of a country cottage.

Dusíkova 592, 353 01 Mariánské Lázně. ② **354-625-169**. Fax 354-626-310. http://koliba.xercom.cz. 15 units. 1,810Kč ($75) double Sun–Thurs, 1,970Kč ($82) Fri–Sat. AE, MC, V. **Amenities:** Restaurant/bar; ski lift; bike rental. *In room:* TV, minibar.

Residence Omega ⓕⓘⓝⓓⓢ ⓚⓘⓓⓢ   Walk through the passage from the main street and before you know it, you'll be standing at the newest accommodations in town. The Omega is slightly different from the hotels that line the street in that it is several apartments that have been connected to form a hotel. Inside you find very bright, sunny rooms with small living areas and kitchenettes, as well as spotless bathrooms. This is a great find for families, as the hotel is cheap but big enough to allow kids their own living space.

Hlavní třída 36a, 353 01 Mariánské Lázně. ②/fax **354-601-300**. 6 units. 1,600Kč–1,800Kč ($67–$75) double apt. AE, MC, V. *In room:* TV, minibar.

WHERE TO DINE
MODERATE
Churchill Club Restaurant ☃ CZECH   Don't let the name fool you—the food is traditional Czech, not British, with few surprises. A lively bar with a good selection of

local and imported beer makes the Churchill one of the few fun places to be after dark in this quiet town. Try the Winston steak platter if you're really hungry.

Hlavní třída 121. ✆ **354-622-705**. Soups 25Kč ($1); main courses 80Kč–520Kč ($3.35–$21). AE, MC, V. Daily 11am–11pm.

Hotel Koliba Restaurant ✿ CZECH   Every time I'm in town, I make a point of stopping here for a meal. Like the hotel it occupies, the Koliba Restaurant is a shrine to the outdoors. The dining room boasts a hearty, rustic atmosphere that goes perfectly with the restaurant's strength: wild game. Check the daily menu to see what's new, or choose from the wide assortment of specialties *na rožtu* (from the grill), including wild boar and venison. The Koliba also has an excellent selection of Moravian wines that you can order with your meal or at its wine bar. The wine bar has dancing to a Gypsy band from 7pm to midnight Tuesday to Sunday.

Dusíkova 592. ✆ **354-625-169**. Reservations recommended. Soups 25Kč ($1); main courses 99Kč–425Kč ($4.10–$18). V, MC. Daily 11:30am–10pm.

Restaurant Fontaine CZECH/INTERNATIONAL   The Fontaine is one of the more formal gastronomical experiences you will find in town. The dining room is very large but remains quiet, though a little too well lit. Bow-tied waiters serve traditional Bohemian specialties like succulent roast duck, broiled trout, and chateaubriand, as well as some inventive variations. Try the duck in oranges for an interesting mix of sweet and sour.

In the Villa Butterfly, Hlavní třída 655. ✆ **354-654-111**. Soups 45Kč ($1.85); main courses 90Kč–410Kč ($3.75–$17). AE, DC, MC, V. Daily noon–2:30pm and 6:30–10pm.

INEXPENSIVE

Classic Cafe/Restaurant CZECH   A nice place to stop for a light bite, the Classic offers a large assortment of good fresh salads. This open, airy cafe/restaurant has one of the friendliest staffs in town, though a few more tables out front would be welcome. It also brews a mean espresso.

Hlavní třída 131. No phone. Salads 39Kč–137Kč ($1.60–$5.70); main courses 69Kč–219Kč ($2.85–$9.10). AE, MC, DC, V. Daily 9am–11pm cafe, 11am–11pm restaurant.

4 Plzeň (Pilsen)

88km (55 miles) SW of Prague

"Zde se narodilo pivo." The phrase ("the birthplace of beer") greets you at almost every turn. And they aren't kidding. Some 400 years ago, a group of men formed Plzeň's first beer-drinking guild, and today beer is probably the only reason you'll want to stop at this otherwise industrial town. Unfortunately for the town, its prosperity and architecture were ravaged during World War II, and few buildings were left untouched. The main square, náměstí Republiky, is worth a look, but after that there's not much to see.

ESSENTIALS

GETTING THERE   It's more comfortable taking the train to Plzeň than the bus. A fast **train** from Prague whisks travelers to Plzeň in just under 2 hours without you having to witness the mayhem caused by Czech drivers. Trains between the two cities are just as plentiful and fit most every schedule. The train costs 210Kč ($8.75) first class or 140Kč ($5.80) second class. To get from the train station to town, walk out the main entrance and take Americká Street across the river; turn right onto Jungmannova, which leads to the main square.

The **bus** trip from Prague takes 1½ hours, and it tends to be cramped. It costs 80Kč ($3.35) one-way. If you do take the bus, head back into town along Husova to get to the square.

Thanks to the government's highway-building scheme, Plzeň has moved closer to Prague—or at least it seems that way. A once treacherous 2-hour **drive** on a narrow two-lane highway has been replaced by an easy 45-minute cruise on the new Highway D5, which leaves Prague from the west.

VISITOR INFORMATION   Trying to be as visitor-friendly as possible, the **City Information Center Plzeň,** náměstí Republiky 41, 301 16 Plzeň (© **378-035-330;** fax 378-035-332; www.icpilsen.cz or www.plzen-city.cz), is packed with literature to answer your questions. It is open daily April to September 9am to 7pm; October to March Monday to Friday 10am to 5pm, and Saturday and Sunday 10am to 3:30pm.

SPECIAL EVENTS   If you're an American or speak English, being in Plzeň in May is quite an experience. May 8 marks the day when Gen. George S. Patton was forced to halt his advance after liberating the area, thanks to an Allied agreement to stop. The Russians were allowed to free Prague, becoming its successor superpower, as decided at Yalta in 1944. Forty years of Communist oppression, however, means that the town now celebrates **Liberation Day** with a vengeance. You'll be feted and praised into the wee hours, as the city's people give thanks to the forces that ended Nazi occupation.

In mid-August the city hosts a modest music festival called **Jazz on the Streets,** highlighted with several concerts by top-name Czech musicians.

Anxious to capitalize on its beer heritage and always happy to celebrate, Plzeň has started its own Oktoberfest, called **Pivní slavnosti (Beer fest),** which takes place in the end of September and beginning of October.

For more details on festivities for all events, contact the **City Information Center Plzeň** (see above).

ORIENTATION   Plzeň's old core is centered around náměstí Republiky. All of the sights, including the brewery, are no more than a 10-minute walk from here.

TOURING THE BEER SHRINES

Plzeňské Pivovary (Pilsner Breweries), at U Prazdroje 7, will interest anyone who wants to learn more about the brewing process. The brewery actually comprises several breweries, pumping out brands like Pilsner Urquell and Gambrinus, the most widely consumed beer in the Czech Republic. The 1-hour tour of the factory (which has barely changed since its creation) includes a 15-minute film and visits to the fermentation cellars and brewing rooms. The tour starts at 12:30 and 2pm daily. Tours cost 120Kč ($5); the price includes a dozen beer-oriented postcards and a tasting of freshly brewed beer. (For details on other tours, call © **377-062-888,** log onto www.prazdroj.cz, or e-mail visits@pilsner.sabmiller.com.)

If you didn't get your fill of beer facts at the brewery, the **Pivovarské muzeum (Beer Museum;** © **377-235-574;** www.prazdroj.cz) is 1 block away on Veleslavínova 6. Inside this former 15th-century house, you'll learn everything there is to know about beer but were afraid to ask. In the first room, once a 19th-century pub, the guard winds up an old German polyphone music box from 1887 that plays the sweet though scratchy strains of Strauss's *Blue Danube.* Subsequent rooms display a wide collection of pub artifacts, brewing equipment, and mugs. Most displays have English captions, but ask for a more detailed museum description in English when you enter. Admission is 60Kč ($2.50), and hours are daily 10am to 6pm (to 5pm Jan–Mar).

EXPLORING PLZEŇ

Filled with more knowledge than you may want about the brewing process, proceed to the main square to see what's hopping (sorry). Dominating the center of the square is the Gothic **Cathedral of St. Bartholomew,** with the tallest steeple in the Czech Republic at 100m (328 ft.). A beautiful marble Madonna graces the main altar. The church is open daily from about 7am to 8pm.

You'll see Italian flair in the first four floors of the 16th-century **Town Hall** and in the *sgrafitto* (etchings) adorning its facade. Later on, more floors were added, as well as a tower, gables, and brass flags, making the building appear as though another had fallen on top of it. The Town Hall (© **378-032-550**) is open Monday to Friday from 8am to 6pm, Saturday from 9am to 1pm. In front of the Town Hall, a **memorial** built in 1681 commemorates victims of the plague.

Just west of the square on Sady pětatřicátníků lie the shattered dreams of the 2,000 or so Jews who once called Plzeň home. The **Great Synagogue,** the third largest in the world, was built in the late 19th century. A painstaking restoration project has brought back this shrine's beauty and is a must-see to take in some of the history that makes the Czech Republic so fascinating.

WHERE TO STAY

For private rooms that are usually outside the town center but a little cheaper, try **Čedok** at Prešovská 10 (© **377-237-517;** fax 377-236-775), open from Monday to Friday 9am to noon and 1 to 5pm (to 6pm in summer), and Saturday from 9am to noon. Expect to pay about 500Kč to 1,000Kč ($21–$42) for a double.

Hotel Central   As you look around the historically beautiful old town square, one thing stands out: the Hotel Central. This rather sterile building is across from St. Bartholomew's Church. The surly staff notwithstanding, the hotel is good and surprisingly quiet despite its central location. Ask for one of the rooms facing east; they have a nice view of the church as the sun rises.

Náměstí Republiky 33, 301 00 Plzeň. © **377-226-757.** Fax 377-226-064. www.central-hotel.cz. 77 units. 1,550Kč–2,390Kč ($64–$99) double. AE, MC, V. **Amenities:** Restaurant; cafe; bar; exercise room; sauna; solarium. *In room:* TV, minibar, safe.

(Fun Fact   Plzeň's Claim to Fame

Founded in 1295 by Václav II, Plzeň was and remains western Bohemia's administrative center. King Václav's real gift to the town, however, wasn't making it an administrative nerve center but granting it brewing rights. So more than 200 microbreweries popped up, one in almost every street-corner basement. Realizing that the brews they were drinking had become mostly plonk by the late 1830s, rebellious beer drinkers demanded quality, forcing the brewers to try harder. "Give us what we want in Plzeň, good and cheap beer!" became the battle cry. In 1842, the brewers combined their expertise to produce a superior brew through what became known as the Pilsner brewing method. If you don't believe it, look in your refrigerator. Most likely, the best beer in there has written somewhere on its label "Pilsner brewed."

Hotel Slovan   An elegant turn-of-the-20th-century staircase graces the entrance foyer to this venerable hotel. But after that, the rooms descend into the same 1970s-modern decor that, hard as it is to believe, was once in fashion. Nonetheless, it remains one of the few quality hotels in the city with laundry facilities and a lively bar on the main floor. The square is only about 2 blocks north.

Smetanovy sady 1, 301 37 Plzeň. ⓒ **377-227-256.** Fax 377-227-012. http://hotelslovan.pilsen.cz. 96 units. 2,100Kč ($87) double. AE, MC, V. **Amenities:** Restaurant; bar. *In room:* TV.

Interhotel Continental   About a block from the old town square, the modern Continental is considered by locals one of the best hotels in town, though I have to say it's far from the lap of luxury. Still, velvet-covered furniture and blue-tiled bathrooms (in the rooms with facilities, for which you'll pay a higher rate) greet you in units bigger than those in most of the other hotels in the area. Downstairs, the casino stays open late if you're feeling lucky or just thirsty.

Zbrojnická 8, 305 34 Plzeň. ⓒ **377-236-477.** Fax 377-221-746. www.hotelcontinental.cz. 55 units. 2,150Kč–2,450Kč ($89–$102) double; 4,500Kč ($187) suite. AE, MC, V. **Amenities:** Restaurant; bar; casino. *In room:* TV.

Pension K   About a block from the Old Town square, this 18th-century home has been converted into a pension that provides a relaxing atmosphere, though little luxury. All rooms have washroom facilities and satellite TV.

Bezručova 13, 305 34 Plzeň. ⓒ/fax **377-329-683.** 13 units. 1,190Kč ($50) double. No credit cards. *In room:* TV, no phone.

WHERE TO DINE
MODERATE
Grill Restaurant 106.1 CZECH/CONTINENTAL   Near náměstí Republiky, this small restaurant named after a local radio station excels at grilled meats and poultry. Minor remodeling in 2001 made it a little less stuffy. Appetizers like mozzarella slices with tomatoes and olive oil stand out in this city devoted to the beer culture. The fondues are a little pricey but not a bad alternative if you have someone to share with.

Bezručova 20, Plzeň. ⓒ **377-222-371.** Soups 30Kč ($1.25); main courses 80Kč–240Kč ($3.35–$10); fondues 265Kč–450Kč ($11–$18). MC, V. Mon–Sat 11am–midnight.

Pilsner Urquell Restaurant CZECH   In the same building that houses the brewery's management, this pub has remained true to those who supply it with beverages by cooking hearty, basic Czech meals, though it is a little pricier than Na Spilce across the way. Because the brewery workers make up the majority of customers here, don't expect a multilingual menu or staff.

U Prazdroje 1 (just outside the brewery gates). ⓒ **377-235-608.** Soups 25Kč ($1); main courses 65Kč–219Kč ($2.70–$9.10). AE, MC, V. Mon–Sat 10am–10pm.

Restaurace Na Spilce CZECH   The Na Spilce looks like a 600-seat tourist trap, but the food is quite good and reasonably priced. The standard *řízky* (schnitzels), goulash, and *svíčková na smetaně* (pork tenderloin in cream sauce) are hearty and complement the beer that flows from the brewery. If you've got a big appetite or just can't decide, try the *Plzeňská bašta,* with ample servings of roasted pork, smoked pork, sausage, sauerkraut, and two kinds of dumplings.

U Prazdroje 7 (just inside the brewery gates). ⓒ **377-062-754.** Soups 25Kč ($1); main courses 65Kč–235Kč ($2.70–$9.75). AE, MC, V. Mon–Thurs and Sat 11am–10pm; Fri 11am–11pm; Sun 11am–9pm.

INEXPENSIVE

Pivnice Na Parkánu CZECH   There's nothing flashy at this typical Czech pub located next to the Brewery Museum, even though it preys upon the tourist crowd that has built up a thirst looking at all that brewing paraphernalia. Wooden benches and tables provide the setting for large pork schnitzels, hearty goulash, and creamy *svíčková na smetaně*.

Veleslavínova 4. ℂ **377-224-485.** Soups 20Kč (85¢); main courses 55Kč–125Kč ($2.30–$5.20). No credit cards. Daily 10:30am–10pm.

Restaurace Žumbera CZECH   A real pub that attracts mainly Czechs, Žumbera has food that's a cut above that of its competitors (of which there are many). If you can't decide, try the *Žumberská mísa*, which is piled high with roast pork, smoked meat, spinach, cabbage, and several types of dumplings.

Bezručova 14. ℂ **377-322-436.** Soups 20Kč (85¢); main courses 35Kč–135Kč ($1.45–$5.60). MC, V. Mon–Thurs 9am–10pm; Fri–Sat 9am–midnight; Sun 9am–7pm.

Salzmannova Pivnice CZECH   This oldest pub in Plzeň, dating back to 1637, has been renovated to reincarnate a previous *Jugendstil* reconstruction of the building. The beer is fresh, but the food is a little disappointing in its standard appearance and taste—you would expect a little flair, given the edifice. However, if you want to stay near the main square and don't want to make the long walk back across the river and up the hill to the brewery pubs, this pub will fulfill your needs admirably.

Pražská 8. ℂ **377-235-855.** Soups 30Kč ($1.25); main courses 90Kč–195Kč ($3.75–$8.10). AE, MC, V. Daily 10am–11pm.

5 Cheb (Eger) & Františkovy Lázně

168km (104 miles) W of Prague, 40km (25 miles) SW of Karlovy Vary

Few people who travel through Cheb—most on their way across the border to Germany—actually stop and take a look around. From the outside, that's understandable, but it's too bad, since the center of Cheb is one of the more architecturally interesting places in west Bohemia. Its history is fascinating as well.

A former stronghold for the Holy Roman Empire on its eastern flank, Eger, as it was then known, became part of Bohemia in 1322. Cheb stayed under Bohemian rule until it was handed over to Germany as part of the 1938 Munich Pact. Soon after the end of World War II, it was returned to Czech hands, when most of the area's native Germans, known as Sudeten Germans, were expelled for their open encouragement of the invading Nazi army. You can see this bilingual, bicultural heritage in the main square, which could be mistaken for being on either side of the border if it weren't for the Czech writing on windows. These days, the Germans have returned as tourists; many indulge in the town's thriving sex trade and cheap alcohol. Don't be surprised to see women around almost every corner. Still, Cheb is worth exploring for its mélange of architectural styles, the eerie Jewish Quarter Špalíček, and the enormous Romanesque Chebský Hrad (Cheb Castle).

Only about 20 minutes up the road from Cheb is the smallest of the three major Bohemian spa towns, **Františkovy Lázně.** Though it pales in comparison to Karlovy Vary and Mariánské Lázně, Františkovy Lázně has taken great strides in the past few years to erase the decline it experienced under Communism. There's not much to see save for the **Spa Museum,** which holds an interesting display of bathing artifacts, but it's a much quieter and cleaner place to spend the night than Cheb. Listed below are places to stay and dine in both Cheb and Františkovy Lázně.

ESSENTIALS

GETTING THERE   Cheb is located on the E48, one of the main highways leading to Germany. If you're **driving** from Prague, take the same route you would to Karlovy Vary, which eventually brings you to Cheb. The drive takes about 2 hours.

To get to Františkovy Lázně from Cheb by car, take Highway E49. The trip takes about 20 minutes.

Express **trains** from Prague usually stop in Cheb, as do several trains daily from Karlovy Vary. Cheb is on a main train route of the Czech Republic, so it's easy to catch many international connections here. The train takes 3½ hours and costs 375Kč ($16) first class and 250Kč ($10) second class.

Cheb is a long **bus** ride from Prague, and I suggest avoiding it if possible. It's more manageable to take the bus from Karlovy Vary or Mariánské Lázně.

VISITOR INFORMATION   You'll find maps, guidebooks, and lodging at the **Informační Centrum,** náměstí Krále Jiřího z Poděbrad 33 (© **354-422-705;** fax 354-434-385; www.cheb-etc.cz or www.mestocheb.cz).

ORIENTATION   At the center of the old town lies the triangular náměstí Krále Jiřího z Poděbrad. Most of the main sights you'll want to see lie either directly on the square or on one of the many streets leading off it.

EXPLORING CHEB

The main square, **náměstí Krále Jiřího z Poděbrad,** attracts most of the attention and is a good place to begin a stroll of the Old Town. Though it has been overrun with tourist shops and cafes that serve mediocre German fare, the square still shines with Gothic burgher houses and the baroque **Old Town Hall (Stará radnice).** At its south end, the **statue of Kašna Roland,** built in 1591 and a former symbol of capital punishment, reminds people of the strength wielded by justice. At the other end of the square stands the **Kašna Herkules,** a monument to the town's former strength and power. Next to it is a cluster of 11 timber houses, called **Špalíček.** These used to be owned by Jews in the early 14th century, but a fervently anti-Semitic clergy in the area incited such hatred that the Jews were forced up Židská ulice (Jews St.) and into an alleyway called ulička Zavražá děných (Murder Victim's Lane), where they were unceremoniously slaughtered in 1350.

Across from Špalíček is the **Cheb Museum** (© **354-422-246**), where another murder took place almost 300 years later—that of Albrecht von Wallenstein in 1634. On the upper level, a display vividly depicts the assassination. The museum's first floor displays many 20th-century paintings, from which you can trace the town's slow demise. Admission is 50Kč ($2). Hours are March to December, Tuesday to Sunday from 9am to 5pm.

The old town is also packed with churches. The most interesting is **St. Nicholas,** around the corner from the museum. It's a hodgepodge of architectural styles: Its Romanesque heritage is reflected in the tower windows, while a Gothic portal and baroque interior round out the renovations over the years. The church is open daily from 9am to 6pm.

TOURING CHEB CASTLE

An excellent example of Romanesque architecture in the northeast part of the Old Town is **Cheb Castle.** Overlooking the Elbe River, the castle, built in the late 12th century, is one of central Europe's largest Romanesque structures.

The castle's main draws are its **Chapel of Sts. Erhard and Ursala** and the **Černá věž (Black Tower).** The two-tiered, early Gothic chapel has a somber first floor where the proletariat would congregate, while the emperor and his family went to the much cheerier and brighter second floor with its Gothic windows.

Across the courtyard from the chapel stands the **Černá věž (Black Tower).** From its 18m-high (59-ft.) lookout, you'll have the best views of the town. The tower seems dusty and smeared with pollution; its color is black because the blocks from which it is made are lava rocks taken from the nearby Komorní Hůrka volcano (now dormant).

Alas, there are no tours of the castle, and the English text provided at the entrance does little to inform you. Admission is 50Kč ($2.10). It's open Tuesday to Sunday: June to August from 9am to noon and 1 to 6pm, May and September from 9am to noon and 1 to 5pm, and April and October from 9am to noon and 1 to 4pm.

WHERE TO STAY
IN CHEB
Hotel Hvězda (Hotel Star)   Overlooking the rather noisy main square, the Hvězda is a lone star in the Cheb hotel universe. The rooms are small, but most overlook the square, and the staff tries to make your stay comfortable. If you can't stay in Františkovy Lázně and don't want to drive farther, this is really the only recommended hotel in town.

Náměstí Krále Jiřího z Poděbrad 5, 350 02 Cheb. ℂ **354-422-549.** Fax 354-422-546. 40 units. 1,000Kč ($42) double. AE, MC, V. *In room:* TV.

IN FRANTIŠKOVY LÁZNĚ
Hotel Tři Lilie (Three Lilies Hotel)   The Three Lilies is worth the extra money since it's the only luxury hotel in the area. Cheb needs a nice hotel like this. At night, you can relax, blocking out noise in your spotless, spacious room that's outfitted with satellite television. The staff is very attentive and can arrange spa treatments, massages, and other health services.

Národní 3, 351 01 Františkovy Lázně. ℂ **354-208-900.** Fax 354-208-995. www.franzensbad.cz. 32 units. 1,460Kč ($61) double; 1,920Kč ($80) suite. AE, MC, V. **Amenities:** Restaurant/bar; cafe; spa treatments. *In room:* TV, minibar.

WHERE TO DINE
IN CHEB
Kavárna Špalícek CZECH   This is better for a coffee stop than for a full meal. You can enjoy great people-watching from the terrace, but Špalíček's real charm lies inside the building, which sits like an island in the middle of the square. This special place is a piece of living history.

Náměstí Krále Jiřího z Poděbrad. ℂ **354-422-568.** Soups 25Kč ($1); main courses 79Kč–199Kč ($3.30–$8.30). No credit cards. Daily 10am–11pm.

Restaurace Fortuna CZECH   If you're craving a schnitzel, this is as good a place as any. Most Czech specialties are served, and the goulash's slightly piquant sauce is a pleasant surprise. It's one of the only restaurants open late, and a terrace right on the main square lends to its appeal.

Náměstí Krále Jiřího z Poděbrad 28. ℂ **354-422-110.** Soups 25Kč ($1); main courses 79Kč–185Kč ($3.30–$7.70). No credit cards. Daily 10am–2am.

Staročeská–U Koček Restaurace CZECH/CHINESE   This restaurant serves much the same fare as all of the other restaurants on or around the square, but what catches the eye are a few Chinese dishes. The *kuře kung-pao* (kung pao chicken) is a good spicy alternative to the customary sausages and meat with dumplings. The chicken with mushrooms is also a nice light choice if you've had your fill of heavy meals.

Kamenná 1. (C) 354-422-170. Main courses 69Kč–260Kč ($2.85–$11). No credit cards. Daily 10am–10pm.

Zlaté Slunce (Golden Sun) CZECH/CONTINENTAL   Two restaurants in one manage to satisfy almost all tastes in this medieval cellar that calls itself "Goethe's Restaurant" after its most famous patron. On one side, the restaurant serves up Czech specialties, while the grill/bar barbecues steaks, chicken, and pork. If you can't decide, try the grill mix, which puts all three on a plate.

Náměstí Krále Jiráího z Poděbrad 38. (C) 354-422-126. Soups 20Kč (85¢); main courses 80Kč–290Kč ($3.35–$12). MC, V. Restaurant daily 11am–3pm and 5–11pm; grill/bar daily 11am–11pm.

IN FRANTIŠKOVY LÁZNĚ

Hotel Tři Lilie (Three Lilies Hotel) CZECH/CONTINENTAL   Just as its hotel is the cream of the local crop, so too is the Three Lilies restaurant. Though the service fails to keep pace with the upscale appearance, this restaurant does very well with creative game dishes that combine Czech basics and European flair.

Národní třída 3. (C) 354-208-900. Main courses 130Kč–520Kč ($5.40–$22). AE, MC, V. Daily 7am–9pm.

6 České Budějovice

147km (91 miles) S of Prague

This fortress town was born in 1265, when Otakar II decided that the intersection of the Vltava and Malše rivers would be the site of a bastion to protect the approaches to southern Bohemia. Although Otakar was killed at the battle of the Moravian Field in 1278 and the town was subsequently ravaged by the rival Vítkovic family, the construction of České Budějovice continued, eventually taking the shape originally envisaged.

In the 15th century, the Hussite revolution swept across southern Bohemia, with one exception—České Budějovice, which, with its largely Catholic population, remained true to the king. Passing the loyalty test with flying colors, it developed into one of Bohemia's wealthiest and most important towns, reaching its pinnacle in the 16th century. This rise made České Budějovice an architecturally stunning place. As the town prospered, older Gothic buildings took on a Renaissance look. A new town hall was built and the flourishing old market (Masné Krámy) was rebuilt. Towering above it all was a new 72m-tall (236-ft.) turret, the Black Tower. Sadly, the Thirty Years' War (1618–48) and a major fire in 1641 ravaged most of the town, leaving few buildings unscathed. But the Habsburg Empire came to the town's rescue in the 18th century, building baroque-style edifices that stand to this day.

Today, České Budějovice, the hometown of the original Budweiser brand beer, is now more a bastion for the beer drinker than a protector of Bohemia. But its slow pace, relaxed atmosphere, and interesting architecture make it a worthy stop, especially as a base for exploring southern Bohemia or for those heading on to Austria.

ESSENTIALS

GETTING THERE   If you're **driving,** leave Prague to the south via the main D1 expressway and take the cutoff for Highway E55, which runs straight to České Budějovice. The trip takes about 1½ hours.

Daily express **trains** from Prague make the trip to České Budějovice in about 2½ hours. The fare is 306Kč ($13) first class or 204Kč ($8.50) second class. Several express **buses** run from Prague's Florenc station each day and take 2½ hours; tickets cost 120Kč ($5).

VISITOR INFORMATION   Tourist Infocentrum, náměstí Přemysla Otakara II. 2 (© **386-801-414**), provides maps and guidebooks and finds lodging. It is open Monday to Friday 8:30am to 6pm, Saturday till 5pm, and Sunday 10am to noon and 12:30 to 4pm. In winter it is open Monday to Friday 9am to 4pm, and Saturday 9am to noon and 12:30 to 3pm. There is a good website about the city; go to **www.c-budejovice.cz** for information.

SPECIAL EVENTS   Each August, České Budějovice hosts the largest **International Agricultural Show** in the country.

If you're passing through in the late fall or winter and want to see Czechs become emotional, head out to a match of the **Czech Extraliga hockey** league at the Budvar Aréna on ulice F. A. Gerstnera, where the local team does battle. Arguably some of the best hockey in the world is played in the Czech Republic, which you can see for a fraction of the price—from 80Kč to 120Kč ($3.35–$5)—you'd pay to see players of a similar caliber in Western countries. The games are never sold out. The box office (© **386-352-705**) opens 1 hour before the game. The local newspapers, tourist information center, and posters pasted around the town will tell you what time the next match is.

ORIENTATION   České Budějovice's circular Staré Město (Old Town) centers around the Czech Republic's largest cobblestone square, náměstí Přemysla Otakara II.

EXPLORING THE TOWN

You can comfortably see České Budějovice in a day. At its center is one of central Europe's largest squares, the cobblestone **náměstí Přemysla Otakara II**—it may actually be too large, as many of the buildings tend to get lost in all the open space. The square contains the ornate **Fountain of Sampson,** an 18th-century water well that was once the town's principal water supply, plus a mishmash of baroque and Renaissance buildings. On the southwest corner is the **Town Hall,** an elegant baroque structure built by Martinelli between 1727 and 1730. On top of the Town Hall, the larger-than-life statues by Dietrich represent the civic virtues: justice, bravery, wisdom, and diligence.

One block northwest of the square is the **Černá věž (Black Tower),** which you can see from almost every point in the city. Consequently, its 360 steps are worth the climb to get a bird's-eye view in all directions. The most famous symbol of České Budějovice, this 70m-tall (236-ft.) 16th-century tower was built as a belfry for the adjacent **St. Nicholas Church.** This 13th-century church, one of the town's most important sights, was a bastion of Roman Catholicism during the 15th-century Hussite rebellion. You shouldn't miss the church's flamboyant, white-and-cream, 17th-century baroque interior.

The tower is open Tuesday to Sunday from 10am to 6pm; admission is 20Kč (85¢). The church is open daily from 9am to 8pm.

TOURING A BEER SHRINE

On the town's northern edge sits a shrine to those who pray to the gods of the amber nectar. This is where **Budějovický Budvar,** the original brewer of Budweiser beer, has its one and only factory. Established in 1895, Budvar draws on more than 700 years of the area's brewing tradition to produce one of the world's best beers.

One trolleybus—no. 2—and bus no. 8 stop by the brewery; this is how the brewery ensures that its workers and visitors reach the plant safely each day. The trolley ride to the brewery costs 10Kč (40¢). You can also hop a cab from the town square for about 120Kč ($5).

Tours can be arranged by phoning ahead, but only for groups. Contact Budvar n.p., Karolíny Světlé 4, České Budějovice (© 387-705-111; www.budvar.cz). If you're traveling alone or with only one or two other people, ask a hotel concierge at one of the bigger hotels (I suggest the Zvon or Hotel Malý Pivovar) if he or she can put you with an already-scheduled group. Failing that, you may want to take a chance and head up to the brewery where, if a group has arrived, another person or two won't be noticed.

Once you're inside the brewery, the smell may cause flashbacks to some of the wilder frat parties you've attended. This is a traditional brew, and not much has changed at the brewery over the past hundred years or so. The room where everything moves along conveyer belts and goes from dirty old bottles to boxed cartons is fascinating.

WHERE TO STAY

Several agencies can locate reasonably priced private rooms. Expect to pay about 500Kč ($20) per person, in cash. **Tourist Infocentrum,** náměstí Přemysla Otakara II. 2 (© **386-359-480**), can point you toward a wide selection of conveniently located rooms and pensions.

Hotel Bohemia   The Bohemia really isn't a hotel but a small pension in the city center, as you'll discover when you walk into the lobby and think that you've stepped into someone's house. The staff makes you feel like one of the family, with their attentive service, and the rooms are pleasant despite being a little small.

Hradební 20, 370 01 České Budějovice. ©/fax 386-360-691. www.hotel-bohemia-cb.cz. 18 units. 1,790Kč ($74) double. AE, MC, V. **Amenities:** Restaurant. In room: TV, minibar.

Hotel Gomel   Not known for its ambience (even die-hard Communists would find the place drab), the 18-floor Gomel has a straightforward approach and offers comfortable, clean rooms with either a tub or a shower and few other frills. Views from the upper floors can't be beat; ask for one that faces into town. And, if you fancy an air-conditioned room (summer can be really hot), ask for one of the renewed rooms on the 16th floor. Located just off the main road entering the city from the north, the Gomel is hard to miss—it's the tallest building around—and is only a few minutes' walk from the historic Old Town.

Pražská 14, 370 04 České Budějovice. © 389-102-111. Fax 389-102-333. www.gomel.cz. 204 units. 1,990Kč–2,900Kč ($83–$121) double; 3,900Kč ($162) suite. Rates include breakfast. AE, DC, MC, V. **Amenities:** Restaurant; bar; hairdresser; casino. In room: TV, minibar, hair dryer.

Hotel Malý Pivovar (Small Brewery) ⊛   Around the corner from the Zvon, this renovated 16th-century microbrewery combines the charms of a B&B with the amenities of a modern hotel. The kind of management found here is a rarity in the Czech tourism industry: They work hard to help out. The rooms are bright and cheery, with antique-style wooden furniture and exposed wooden ceiling beams providing a farmhouse feeling in the center of town. It's definitely worth consideration if being directly on the square (you're only 30m/98 ft. from it) isn't a problem. This is also one of the best places to arrange a trip to the brewery.

Ulice Karla IV. 8–10, 370 01 České Budějovice. © 386-360-471. Fax 386-360-474. www.malypivovar.cz. 29 units. 2,500Kč–3,100Kč ($104–$129) double; 2,800Kč–3,600Kč ($116–$150) suite. Rates include breakfast. AE, DC, MC, V. **Amenities:** Restaurant/pub; wine bar. In room: TV, minibar.

Keeping Up with the Schwarzenbergs: Visiting a 141-Room English Castle

Only 8km (5 miles) north of České Budějovice lies **Hluboká nad Vltavou** ✦✦ (✆ 387-843-911; www.zamekhluboka.cz). Built in the 13th century, this castle has undergone many face-lifts over the years, but none that left as lasting an impression as those ordered by the Schwarzenberg family. As a sign of the region's growing wealth and importance in the mid–19th century, the Schwarzenbergs remodeled the 141-room castle in the neo-Gothic style of England's Windsor Castle. No expense was spared in the quest for opulence. The Schwarzenbergs removed the impressive wooden ceiling from their residence at Český Krumlov and reinstalled it in the large dining room. Other rooms are equally garish in their appointments, making a guided tour worth the time, even though only about a third of the rooms are open to the public.

The castle is open daily May to August from 9am to 5pm (last tour at 4pm); April, September, and October on Tuesday to Sunday from 9am to 4:30pm (last tour at 3pm). There is a lunch break between noon and 12:30pm. Tours in English cost 160Kč ($6.65) adults, 80Kč ($3.35) students.

To complete the experience, the **Alšova Jihočeská Galerie (Art Gallery of South Bohemia)** (✆ 387-967-041) in the riding school at Hluboká houses the second-largest art collection in Bohemia, including many interesting Gothic sculptures from the area, and Dutch painters from the 16th to 18th centuries. It is open daily May to September from 9am to 6pm.

The castle's distance from České Budějovice is short enough to make it a pleasant bike trip from the city or a quick stop either on the way to or from Prague, Třeboň, or Tábor. The town's information center (see below) can help with bike rentals.

If you're driving to Hluboká from České Budějovice, take Highway E49 north and then Highway 105 just after leaving the outskirts of České Budějovice. For cyclists or drivers who prefer a slower, more scenic route, take the road that runs behind the brewery; it passes through the village of Obora.

The town's new **Information Center** at Masarykova 35 (✆ 387-966-164; www.hluboka.cz) will provide you with maps, souvenirs, and answers to your questions.

Hotel U Solné brány   Another of the growing numbers of conveniently located hotels just off the main square, U Solné brány is one of the products of post-Communism: a bright renovated hotel with friendly management. It almost feels like a pension. Most rooms have balconies, making a cold Budvar from the minibar almost mandatory in the early evening or as a nightcap.

Radniční ul. 11, 370 01 České Budějovice. ✆ 386-354-121. Fax 386-354-120. www.hotelusolnebrany.cz. 11 units. 1,890Kč ($78) double; 2,100Kč ($87) suite. Rates include breakfast. AE, MC, V. **Amenities:** Restaurant. *In room:* TV, minibar.

Hotel Zvon   Location is everything to the city's most elegant hotel, which occupies several historic buildings on the main square. In fact, pretty soon the hotel and its accompanying businesses will occupy nearly a quarter of the addresses in the area. The upper-floor rooms have been renovated and tend to be more expensive, especially those with a view of the square. Others are relatively plain and functional. The views from those in front, however, can't be topped, and since the square is so big, noise is rarely a problem. Try to avoid the smaller rooms, usually reserved for tour groups. There's no elevator, but if you don't mind the climb, stay on the fourth floor. One of the biggest changes here in recent years has been the staff, which appears to be learning that guests deserve respect and quality treatment.

Náměstí Přemysla Otakara II. 28, 370 01 České Budějovice. ℂ 387-311-384. Fax 387-311-385. www.hotel-zvon.cz. 68 units. 1,600Kč–5,600Kč ($66–$233) double. AE, DC, MC, V. **Amenities:** Restaurant; cafe; bar. *In room:* TV, minibar.

WHERE TO DINE

Masné Krámy (Meat Shops) 𝄐 CZECH   If you've pledged not to go to any "tourist traps," rationalize going to this one by reminding yourself that it's also a historical building dating back to the 14th century. Just northwest of náměstí Přemysla Otakara II., labyrinthine Masné Krámy occupies a series of drinking rooms on either side of a long hall and is a must for any serious pub-goer. The inexpensive and filling food is pure Bohemia, including several pork, duck, and trout dishes. Come for the boisterous atmosphere or for what's possibly the best goulash in the Czech Republic. Note that this place was just recently closed for a reconstruction and it hasn't been said when it'll be ready to welcome tourists again.

Krajinská 29. ℂ 387-318-609. Main courses 79Kč–195Kč ($3.30–$8.10). AE, MC, V. Daily 10am–11pm.

Potrefeń husa CZECH/INTERNATIONAL   This new addition to the list of local restaurants is owned by Budvar's competitor, the Prague brewery Staropramen. In its modern interior, which is divided into a bar, restaurant, and large terrace with a pleasant view of the river, there is a good selection of pasta, meat dishes, and salads at reasonable prices. The barbecue ribs are very popular, and so is the Czech potato soup served in a bread bowl.

Česká 66. ℂ 387-420-560. Main courses 69Kč–295Kč ($2.85–$12). AE, MC, V. Mon 11am–midnight; Tues–Thurs 11am–1am; Fri 11am–1:30am; Sat noon–1:30am; Sun noon–midnight.

U královské pečeti (At the Royal Seal) 𝄐 CZECH   This typical Czech-style pub serves up hearty food at reasonable prices. It offers a tasty goulash as well as *svíčková* or game dishes. Located in the popular Hotel Malý pivovar, this is a very good choice for a Czech food experience (especially when Masné Krámy is closed).

In the Hotel Malý Pivovar, ulice Karla IV. 8–10. ℂ 386-360-471. Soups 25Kč ($1); main courses 65Kč–290Kč ($2.70–$12). AE, DC, MC, V. Daily 10am–11pm.

7 Český Krumlov ⋆⋆⋆

19km (12 miles) SW of České Budějovice

If you have time on your visit to the Czech Republic for only one excursion, seriously consider making it **Český Krumlov.** One of Bohemia's prettiest towns, Krumlov is a living gallery of elegant Renaissance-era buildings housing charming cafes, pubs, restaurants, shops, and galleries. In 1992, UNESCO named Český Krumlov a World Heritage Site for its historic importance and physical beauty.

Bustling since medieval times, the town, after centuries of embellishment, is exquisitely beautiful. In 1302, the Rožmberk family inherited the castle and moved in, using

Český Krumlov

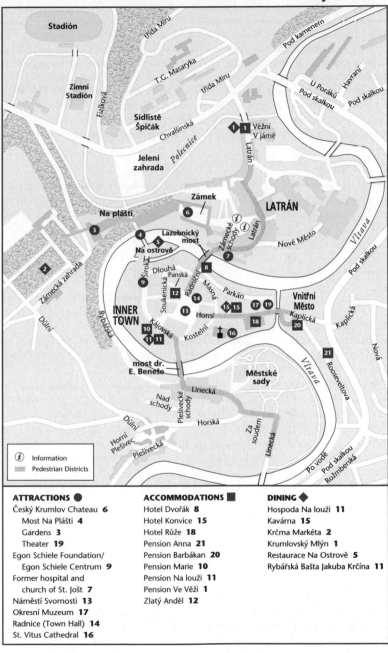

it as their main residence for nearly 300 years. You'll feel that time has stopped as you look from the Lazebnický Bridge and see the waters of the Vltava below snaking past the castle's gray stone. At night, by the castle lights, the view becomes even more dramatic.

Few dared change the appearance of Český Krumlov over the years, not even the Schwarzenbergs, who had a flair for opulence. At the turn of the 19th century, several facades of houses in the town's outer section were built, as were inner courtyards. Thankfully, economic stagnation in the area under Communism meant little money for "development," so no glass-and-steel edifices, like the Hotel Thermal in Karlovy Vary, jut out to spoil the architectural beauty. Instead, a medieval sense reigns supreme, now augmented by the many festivals and renovations that keep the town's spirit alive.

ESSENTIALS

GETTING THERE   From České Budějovice, it's about a 45-minute **drive** to Krumlov, depending on traffic. Take Highway 3 from the south of České Budějovice and turn onto Highway 159. The roads are clearly marked, with several signs directing traffic to the town. From Prague, it's a 2-hour drive down Highway 3 through Tábor.

The only way to reach Český Krumlov by train from Prague is via České Budějovice, a slow ride that deposits you at a station relatively far from the town center (trip time: 3 hr. 50 min.). Six trains leave daily from Prague's Hlavní nádraží; the fare is 336Kč ($14) first class, 224Kč ($9.35) second class. If you are already in České Budějovice and you want to make a trip to Krumlov, several trains connect these two cities throughout the day. The trip takes about 57 minutes and costs 46Kč ($1.90). For timetables, go to **www.jizdnirady.cz**.

The nearly 3-hour **bus** ride from Prague usually involves a transfer in České Budějovice. The fare is 136Kč ($5.65), and the bus station in Český Krumlov is a 15-minute walk from the town's main square.

VISITOR INFORMATION   Right on the main square, the **Information Centrum,** náměstí Svornosti 2, 381 01 Český Krumlov (© **380-704-622;** fax 380-704-619; www.ckrumlov.cz), provides a complete array of services, from booking accommodations to reserving tickets for events, as well as a phone and Internet service. It's open daily in July and August from 9am to 8pm; in June and September from 9am to 7pm; in April, May, and October from 9am to 6pm; and from November to March from 9am to 5pm.

Be warned that the municipal hall is in the same building, and it's crowded with weddings on weekends. If someone holds out a hat, throw some change into it, take a traditional shot of liquor from them, and say *"Blahopřeji!"* ("Congratulations!") to everyone in the room.

SPECIAL EVENTS   After being banned during Communism, the **Slavnost pětilisté růže (Festival of the Five-Petaled Rose)** has made a triumphant comeback. It's held each year during the summer solstice. Residents of Český Krumlov dress up in Renaissance costume and parade through the streets. Afterward, the streets become a stage for chess games with people dressed as pieces, music, plays, and even duels "to the death."

Český Krumlov also plays host to the **International Music Festival** every August, attracting performers from all over the world. Performances are held in nine spectacular venues. For details or ticket reservations, contact the festival organizer, **Auviex,** at Perlitová 1820, 140 00, Praha 4 (© **241-445-404**); or in Český Krumlov at Latrán 37 (© **380-711-453;** www.auviex.cz).

Though much quieter in the winter, the town comes alive on **New Year's Eve** when its spectacular setting is lit up by midnight fireworks shot from a hill next to the center of town. Hotels and pensions fill up quickly, so reservations are recommended. Most restaurants and hotels have a special dinner/dancing deal that is also recommended to ensure you have a place to party when you return from watching the fireworks.

ORIENTATION   Surrounded by a circular sweep of the Vltava River, Český Krumlov is easy to negotiate. The main square, **náměstí Svornosti,** is at the very center of the Inner Town. The bridge that spans the Vltava a few blocks away leads to a rocky hill and the Latrán area, above which is the castle, **Český Krumlov Château.**

STROLLING THROUGH ČESKÝ KRUMLOV

Bring a good pair of walking shoes and be prepared to wear them out. Český Krumlov's hills and alleyways cry out for hours of exploration, but if you push the pace you can see everything in 1 day. No cars, thank goodness, are allowed in the historic town, and the cobblestones keep most other vehicles at bay. The town is split into two parts—the **Inner Town** and **Latrán,** which houses the castle. They're best tackled separately, so you won't have to crisscross the bridges several times.

Begin your walk at the **Okresní Muzeum (Regional Museum;** (380-711-674) at the top of Horní ulice 152. Once a Jesuit seminary, the three-story museum now contains artifacts and displays relating to Český Krumlov's 1,000-year history. The highlight of this mass of folk art, clothing, furniture, and statues is a giant model of the town that offers a bird's-eye view of the buildings. Admission is 50Kč ($2). The museum is open May to September, daily 10am to 5pm (till 6pm in July and Aug); in October to December and March to April, it's open Tuesday to Friday 9am to 4pm, and Saturday and Sunday 1 to 4pm.

Across the street is the **Hotel Růže (Rose),** Horní 154 ((380-772-100), which was once a Jesuit student house. Built in the late 16th century, the hotel and the prelature next to it show the development of architecture—Gothic, Renaissance, and rococo influences are all present. If you're not staying at the hotel, don't be afraid to walk around and even ask questions at the reception desk.

Continue down the street to the impressive late Gothic **St. Vitus Cathedral.** Be sure to climb the church tower, which offers one of the most spectacular views of both the Inner Town and the castle across the river. The church is open daily from 9am to 5pm.

As you continue down the street, you'll come to **náměstí Svornosti.** Few buildings here show any character, making the main square of such an impressive town a little disappointing. The **Radnice (Town Hall),** at náměstí Svornosti 1, is one of the few exceptions. Open daily from 9am to 6pm, its Gothic arcades and Renaissance vault inside are exceptionally beautiful in this otherwise run-down area. From the square, streets fan out in all directions. Take some time to wander through them.

When you get closer to the river, you still can see the high-water marks on some of the quirky bank-side houses, which were devastated by the floods of 2002. Most of the places have taken the opportunity to make a fresh start after massive reconstruction. **Krumlovský Mlýn (The Krumlov Mill),** Široká 80 ((380-712-838; www. krumlovskymlyn.cz), is a combination restaurant, gallery, antiques shop, and exhibition space. For an additional treat, stroll through the exhibition of historical motorcycles. Open daily 10am to 10pm.

One of Český Krumlov's most famous residents was Austrian-born artist Egon Schiele. He was a bit of an eccentric who on more than one occasion raised the ire of the town's residents (many found his use of young women as nude models distressing), and his stay was cut short when residents' patience ran out. But the town readopted the artist in 1993, setting up the **Egon Schiele Foundation and the Egon Schiele Centrum** in Inner Town, Široká 70–72, 381 01, Český Krumlov (© **380-704-011**). It documents his life and work, housing a permanent selection of his paintings as well as exhibitions of other 20th-century artists. Admission depends on the exhibitions being displayed; hours are daily from 10am to 6pm.

After you see the museum, cut down Panenská ulice to Soukenická 39 and stop in at **Galerie u rytíře Kryštofa,** Panenská 6, where you can try on the latest in body armor! This place is like the wardrobe room at a theater, and most everything is for sale. It's open Monday to Saturday from 10am to 6pm, Sunday from 1 to 6pm.

For a different perspective on the town, take the stairs from the **Městské divadlo (Town Theater)** on Horní ulice down to the riverfront and rent a rowboat from **Maleček Boat Rentals** (© **380-712-508;** www.malecek.cz) at 300Kč ($12) for a half-hour trip (400Kč/$16 in July and Aug).

You might want to grab a light lunch at one of the many cafes in Inner Town before crossing the river.

As you cross the bridge and head toward the castle, you'll see immediately to your right the former **hospital and church of St. Jošt.** Founded at the beginning of the 14th century, it has since been turned into apartments. Feel free to snoop around, but don't enter the building.

EXPLORING THE CHATEAU

Reputedly the second-largest castle in Bohemia (after Prague Castle), **Český Krumlov Château** was constructed in the 13th century as part of a private estate. Throughout the ages, it has been passed on to a variety of private owners, including the Rožmberk family, Bohemia's largest landholders, and the Schwarzenbergs, the Bohemian equivalent of the TV show *Dynasty*'s Carrington family.

Perched high atop a rocky hill, the château is open only from April to October, exclusively by guided tours.

Follow the path for the long climb up to the **castle.** Greeting you is a round 12th-century **tower**—painstakingly renovated, with its Renaissance balcony. You'll pass over the moat, now occupied by two brown bears. Next is the **Dolní Hrad (Lower Castle)** and then the **Horní Hrad (Upper Castle).**

Tips **A Crowd Alert**

Consider yourself warned: Word has spread about Český Krumlov. Late spring to early autumn can be unbearable as thousands of visitors blanket its medieval streets. If possible, try to visit in the off season, when the crowds recede, the prices decrease, and the town's charm can really shine. Who knows, you may even hear some Czech!

Also note: The city suffered damage caused by floods in August 2002. Most of its venues along the river have been cleaned and redecorated by now. For more details about the town, go to **www.ckrumlov.cz**.

There are two guided tours. Tour I begins in the rococo **Chapel of St. George,** and continues through the portrait-packed **Renaissance Rooms,** and the **Schwarzenberg Barogue Suite,** outfitted with ornate furnishings that include Flemish wall tapestries, European paintings, and also the extravagant 17th-century **Golden Carriage.** Tour II includes the **Schwarzenberg portrait gallery** as well as their 19th-century suite. Tours last 1 hour and depart frequently. Most are in Czech or German, however. If you want an English-language tour, arrange it ahead of time (© **380-704-721;** www.ckrumlov.cz). The guided tours cost 160Kč ($6.65) adults, 80Kč ($3.35) students (Tour I); 140Kč ($5.85) adults and 70Kč ($2.90) students (Tour II). The tickets are sold separately. The castle hours are from Tuesday to Sunday: June to August 9am to 6pm; April, May, September, and October 9am to 5pm (no Tour II in Apr). The last entrance is 1 hour before closing.

Once past the main castle building, you can see one of the more stunning views of Český Krumlov from **Most Na Plášti,** a walkway that doubles as a belvedere to the Inner Town. Even farther up the hill lie the castle's riding school and gardens.

WHERE TO STAY

With the rise of free enterprise after the fall of Communism, many hotels have sprouted up or are getting a "new" old look. PENSION and ZIMMER FREI signs line Horní and Rooseveltova streets and offer some of the best values in town. For a comprehensive list of area hotels and help with bookings, call or write to the Information Centrum listed above in "Visitor Information."

EXPENSIVE

Hotel Dvořák ⊛   The newest addition to the hotel scene in Krumlov, the Dvořák is a welcome one for those looking for something extra. The views are spectacular and the service is top-notch. Rooms are thoughtfully decorated, bright, and airy. It's a little pricey compared to the rest of the hotels in town, but you'll get a lot more for your money.

Radniční 101, 381 01 Český Krumlov. © **380-711-020.** Fax 380-711-024. www.geneahotels.cz. 22 units. 2,800Kč–3,700Kč ($116–$154) double; 3,300Kč–6,700Kč ($137–$279) suite. Rates include breakfast. AE, MC, V. **Amenities:** Restaurant; bar; sauna. *In room:* TV, minibar, safe.

Hotel Růže (Rose Hotel) ⊛   Once a Jesuit seminary, this stunning Italian Renaissance building has been turned into a well-appointed hotel. Comfortable in a big-city kind of way, it's packed with amenities and is one of the top places to stay in Český Krumlov. But for all of the splendor of the building, you may find the Růže somewhat of a disappointment. The rooms contain no period pieces and look as though they were furnished from a Sears catalog. They're clean and spacious, but the promise of a Renaissance stay dissipates quickly. For families or large groups, the larger suites, which have eight beds, provide good value. For the adventurous or those with the right haircut, try one of the cells, where the Jesuit monks used to stay.

Horní 154, 381 01 Český Krumlov. © **380-772-100.** Fax 380-713-146. www.hotelruze.cz. 71 units. 3,800Kč–7,100Kč ($158–$295) double; 5,300Kč–9,600Kč ($220–$400) suite. Rates include breakfast. AE, MC, V. **Amenities:** Restaurant; bar; pool; health club. *In room:* TV, minibar, hair dryer.

MODERATE

Hotel Konvice   The rooms at the Konvice are on the small side and have rustic furniture. The real lure here is the view. Ask for a room with a view out the back—as you gaze at the river and the castle on the opposite bank, you'll wonder why anyone would stay at the Růže just a few doors up.

Moments A Renaissance Pub Endures

Most visitors don't venture far enough into the castle to experience this place during the day or night. That's their loss, for I've experienced one of my finest dining experiences in the Czech Republic at **Krčma Markéta,** Zámek 62 (© **380-711-453**).

To get here, walk all the way up the hill through the castle, past the Horní Hrad (Upper Castle) and past the Zámecké divadlo (Castle Theater). Walk through the raised walkway and into the Zámecká zahrada (Castle Garden), where you'll eventually find this Renaissance pub.

When you go inside, you'll feel as if you've left this century. Unfortunately, one of the pub's main draws, former owner Robin Kratochvíl, is gone. The new owners have traded in Kratochvíl's big-enough-to-turn-a-Volkswagen tongs for a set of racks where the meat cooks; they brought in sets of plates, as opposed to the original wooden blocks on which food used to be served; and there is even a menu now. But still go up to the fire and see what's roasting; usually there's a wide variety of meats, including succulent pork cutlets, rabbit, chickens, and pork knees, a Czech delicacy. When the plate comes, don't wait for the vegetables. (Vegetarian dishes are available, however.) Before the night is over, you'll probably find yourself talking to someone else at the pub's large wooden tables. Krčma Markéta is open April to October, Tuesday to Sunday from 6 to 11pm and main courses cost 75Kč to 155Kč ($3.10–$6.45).

Horní ul. 144. 381 01 Český Krumlov. © **380-711-611.** Fax 380-711-327. www.boehmerwaldhotels.de. 10 units. 1,500Kč–1,800Kč ($63–$75) double; 1,800Kč–2,700Kč ($75–$112) suite. Rates include breakfast. AE, MC, V. **Amenities:** Restaurant. *In room:* TV.

Pension Barbakán After a change in management, the Barbakán, across from the theater, has spruced itself up, inside and out. The new owners have redone the inside of the pension completely, putting new bathrooms in all the units and generally keeping the premises spotless. Take breakfast out on the back garden's terrace on warm summer mornings and watch the goings-on below at the riverbank.

Horní 26, 381 01 Český Krumlov. ©/fax **380-717-017.** www.barbakan.cz. 8 units. 1,990Kč ($83) double; 2,490Kč ($104) triple. Rates include breakfast. AE, MC, V. **Amenities:** Restaurant; bar. *In room:* TV.

Zlatý Anděl (Golden Angel) The Golden Angel has emerged from a chrysalis with new wings. After a long reconstruction and renovation of its rooms, including new furniture, the Golden Angel has shed its Communist furnishings for more stylish fittings right down to the marble bathrooms. Think about getting a suite rather than a regular room, since a couple of them are loft apartments that are much more open. A piano bar and small pub add to the fact that this is now the best place on the square.

Náměstí Svornosti 10–11, 381 01 Český Krumlov. © **380-712-310.** Fax 380-712-735. www.hotelzlatyandel.cz. 36 units. 2,300Kč–3,400Kč ($95–$141) double; 2,700Kč–4,000Kč ($112–$166) suite. Rates include breakfast. AE, MC, V. **Amenities:** Restaurant; bar; terrace. *In room:* TV, minibar.

INEXPENSIVE

Pension Anna ⚘ *Kids*   Along "pension alley," this is a comfortable and rustic place. What makes the pension a favorite are the friendly management and homey feeling you get as you walk up to your room. Forget hotels—this is the kind of place where you can relax. The owners even let you buy drinks and snacks at the bar downstairs and take them to your room. The suites, with four beds and a living room, are great for families and groups.

Rooseveltova 41, 381 01 Český Krumlov. ©/fax **380-711-692.** www.pensionanna.euweb.cz. 8 units. 1,250Kč ($52) double; 1,550Kč–2,250Kč ($64–$94) suite. Rates include breakfast. No credit cards. **Amenities:** Bar. *In room:* TV.

Pension Marie   Next door to Na louži, the facade of this new pension has been completely restored. Inside, however, the plain furniture fails to rival the charm of its neighbor. On the other hand, the beds are longer.

Kájovská 67, 381 01 Český Krumlov. ©/fax **380-711-138.** www.pensionhotel.cz/marie. 6 units. 1,250Kč ($52) double; 2,400Kč ($100) suite. No credit cards. **Amenities:** Cafe. *In room:* TV.

Pension Na louži ⚘   Smack-dab in the heart of the Inner Town, the small Na louži, decorated with early-20th-century wooden furniture, is a charming change from many of the bigger, bland rooms found in nearby hotels. If the person at reception starts mentioning names without apparent reason, don't worry; it's not a language problem. Management has given the rooms human names instead of numbers. The only drawback is that the beds (maybe the people for whom the rooms were named were all short) can be a little short for those over 2m (6 ft.).

Kájovská 66, 381 01 Český Krumlov. ©/fax **380-711-280.** www.nalouzi.cz. 7 units. 1,350Kč ($56) double; 1,700Kč ($70) triple; 2,300Kč ($95) suite. No credit cards. **Amenities:** Restaurant/bar.

Pension Ve Věži (In the Tower) *Finds*   A private pension in a renovated medieval tower just a 5-minute walk from the castle, Ve Věži is one of the most magnificent places to stay in town, and the only one I would recommend on the Latrán side. It's not the accommodations themselves that are so grand; none has a bathroom and all are sparsely decorated. What's wonderful is the ancient ambience. Reservations are recommended.

Pivovarská 28, 381 01 Český Krumlov. © **380-711-742.** www.ckrumlov.cz/pensionvevezi. 4 units (all with shared bathroom). 1,200Kč ($50) double; 1,800Kč ($75) quad. Rates include breakfast. No credit cards.

WHERE TO DINE
MODERATE

Kavárna CZECH   If weather permits, eat outside overlooking the river at the Kavárna. Try the boned chicken breast smothered in cheese or any of the steaks and salads. Portions are big and the view is spectacular. If this place is full, **U písaře Jana** next door has similarly priced meals with almost the same view.

In the Hotel Konvice, Horní ul. 144. © **380-711-611.** Main courses 115Kč–340Kč ($4.70–$14). AE, MC, V. Daily 8am–10pm.

Krumlovský mlýn CZECH   This newly restored mill house, which history dates back to the 16th century, is a restaurant, antiques shop, and exhibition in one. Large wooden tables and benches are part of the thematic restaurant on the ground floor, where a traditional Czech menu is served. The terrace on the bank of the Vltava River above the water channel here is a super place to sit in the summer.

Široká 80. © **380-712-838.** www.krumlovskymlyn.cz. Main courses 150Kč–425Kč ($6.25–$18). No credit cards. Daily 10am–10pm.

Restaurace Na Ostrově (On the Island) CZECH   In the shadow of the castle and, as the name implies, on an island, this restaurant is best on a sunny day when the terrace overflows with flowers, hearty Czech food (including plenty of chicken and fish), and lots of beer. The staff is very friendly, which helps with your patience since usually only two waiters work each shift, making service on the slow side. A great place to relax and enjoy the view.

Na ostrově 171. © 380-711-326. Main courses 139Kč–399Kč ($5.80–$17). No credit cards. Daily 10am–10pm.

Rybářská Bašta Jakuba Krčína CZECH   One of the town's most celebrated restaurants, this place specializes in freshwater fish from surrounding lakes. Trout, perch, pike, and eel are sautéed, grilled, baked, and fried in a variety of herbs and spices. Venison, rabbit, and other game are also available, along with the requisite roast beef and pork cutlet dinners.

Kájovská 54. © 380-712-692. Reservations recommended. Main courses 85Kč–370Kč ($3.50–$15). AE, MC, V. Daily 11am–10pm.

INEXPENSIVE

Hospoda Na louži CZECH   The large wooden tables encourage you to get to know your neighbors at this Inner Town pub, located in a 15th-century house. The atmosphere is fun and the food above average. If no table is available, stand and have a drink; tables turn over pretty quickly, and the staff is accommodating. In summer, the terrace seats only six, so dash over if a seat empties.

Kájovská 66. © 380-711-280. Main courses 58Kč–158Kč ($2.40–$6.60). No credit cards. Mon–Sat 10am–11pm; Sun 10am–10pm.

8 Třeboň ⟨★

24km (15 miles) E of České Budějovice

Just a 30-minute bus ride east of České Budějovice, Třeboň is a diamond in the rough, a walled city that time, war, and disaster have failed to destroy. Surrounded by forests and ponds, the town slowly grew from the 12th to the mid–14th century, when four of the Rožmberk brothers (also known as the Rosenbergs) took over, making Třeboň a home away from home (their official residence was down the road in Český Krumlov). Třeboň quickly flourished, attaining key brewing and salt customs rights. Adding to the town's coffers were more than 5,000 fishponds built by fish master Štěpánek Netolický and his successor, Mikuláš Rathard.

Though war and fires in the 17th and 18th centuries razed most of the town's historic Renaissance architecture, a slow rebuilding process eventually restored nearly every square meter of the walled town to its original state. Under Communism, Třeboň was awarded spa rights, which kept money flowing in and buildings in good repair.

The town is not as breathtaking as Krumlov, but Třeboň hasn't been completely overrun by tourists who trample everything in their wake. Instead, Třeboň exists with or without visitors. Český Krumlov is great, but if you have time and want to chill out for a day, consider Třeboň. Many of my Czech friends stay here on a regular basis (so does, in the summer, Jaromír Jágr, the hockey player). Třeboň is the best small town in which to overnight when you're traveling in the region or just looking for some peace and quiet.

The 4-day festival "Okolo Třeboně" takes place here in the beginning of July annually. You can experience several street happenings, sport and fun competitions, and listen to

Czech folk music performed on stages in the city center and the nearby park. This multi-genre event always turns out to be a long party with its unforgettable atmosphere. Check the exact dates at the information center and also ask about the historic Knight Tournament, which, if it occurs, can be a lot of fun, too. Unfortunately, there's no set date for it and it isn't an annual event.

ESSENTIALS

GETTING THERE   Buses leave from the České Budějovice bus station every hour or so. The trip lasts 30 to 40 minutes and the fare is about 20Kč (85¢).

By **train,** the town is a stop on the Prague–Tábor–Vienna route. Trains and buses also regularly leave for Třeboň from Jindřichův Hradec and Tábor. From Prague the train takes 2½ hours; the fare is 276Kč ($11) first class or 184Kč ($7.65) second class.

Driving from Prague, take Highway E55 through Tábor and turn left onto Highway 150 just past the town of Veselí nad Lužnicí. The trip takes at least 1½ hours. From České Budějovice, take Highway E551 east to Třeboň.

VISITOR INFORMATION   Informační Středisko is in the heart of the Old Town at Masarykovo nám. 103, 379 01 Třeboň (ℂ **384-721-169;** fax 384-721-356; www.trebon-mesto.cz). The staff members are excellent and speak several languages, notably German. They provide maps, guidebooks, and information on tours and lodging. Open daily from 9am to 6pm.

ORIENTATION   There are only three ways to penetrate Třeboň's Old Town walls, short of pole vaulting. To the east is **Hradecká brána (Castle Gate);** on the southern edge of town lies **Svinenská brána;** and to the west is **Budějovická brána.** Once you're inside any of these gates, the six or so streets that comprise the Old Town can be easily navigated.

EXPLORING TŘEBOŇ

City officials, quick to notice that helping visitors helps them, have placed signs guiding visitors to almost every nook and cranny of the center. Since the walled city is relatively small, there's no wrong place to begin a tour, but I prefer to start at the southern gate by the **Svinenská brána,** the oldest of the town's three gates, for reasons that'll become immediately apparent. Just outside the gate and to the right stands the **Regent Brewery,** founded in 1379. Locals will tell you that their brew is every bit as good as Budvar, and they're not lying. On entering Old Town, continue straight through Žižkovo náměstí and you'll arrive at **Masarykovo náměstí,** where the beautifully colored Renaissance facades look as though they were built yesterday.

To the left lies the entrance to Třeboň's showpiece, **Zámek Třeboň (Třeboň Castle)** (ℂ **384-721-193).** The castle's history is similar to the history of the town. The original Gothic castle was destroyed by fire and reconstructed several times, most recently in 1611. Rather ordinary-looking from the outside, it has splendidly decorated rooms that provide a terrific backdrop to the 16th-century furnishings. An exhibition on pond-building fascinates most children. A large part of the castle now houses regional archives. Admission is 50Kč ($2). April, May, September, and October hours are Tuesday to Sunday from 9am to 11:40am and 12:45pm to 4pm. June through August, it's open from 9am to 11:40am and 12:45 to 5:15pm.

Walk out the castle gate and straight along Březanova Street to the **Augustinian monastery** and the 14th-century **St. Giles Church** next to it. Inside the church are replicas of some of the finest Gothic works in central Europe; the originals have been moved to the National Gallery in Prague. The church and monastery are open Monday to Saturday from 9am to 7pm and Sunday from 9am to 6pm.

To the south of the Old Town lies **Rybník Svět,** a large pond that locals flock to on hot afternoons. Several locations around the pond rent windsurfers, bikes, and other outdoor equipment with which to enjoy the surrounding areas. On the southeast shore of the pond is **Schwarzenberská hrobka (Schwarzenberg Mausoleum).** Built in 1877, this neo-Gothic chapel and crypt is the resting place for most members of the Schwarzenberg family.

WHERE TO STAY

Bílý Koníček (White Horse)   Across from the Zlatá Hvězda, this place has plain but tidy rooms and a friendly staff. However, the rooms tend to be a little noisy because the hotel is on the road that cars take through town. For the most part, though, the streets are pretty quiet, and the restaurant downstairs is a good bet for a quick bite.

Masarykovo nám. 97, 379 01 Třeboň. ⓒ/fax **384-721-213.** 15 units. 1,000Kč ($42) double; 1,400Kč ($58) suite. MC, V. **Amenities:** Restaurant/bar. *In room:* TV.

Hotel Bohemia & Hotel Regent   These two hotels share everything, from a parking lot to a receptionist. If you don't want to stay in the center of town, either one is

---

Finds **A Farm Stay**

With the collapse of Communism and the system of collective farming that went along with it, many farms were returned to their original owners in a state of disrepair. But slowly, some are being restored to the prosperity they enjoyed before World War II. One such farm, **Holenský Dvůr** ⓐ, Ratiboř 52, region Jindřichův Hradec (ⓒ **384-382-376;** fax 384-383-445; www.holensky dvur.cz), is a recently refinished farm offering a comfortable stay surrounded by early European rural charm. Set among the gently rolling hills and fishponds of south Bohemia near Třeboň, this pension is a relaxing alternative to the hustle and bustle of more touristed spots such as Český Krumlov or Karlovy Vary. Rent a mountain bike or go on horseback and tour the countryside, or hike through the meadows and clean your lungs from the days of smog inhalation that come with a trip to Prague.

The pension's 10 rooms and 2 apartments are bright, clean, and refreshingly well appointed, with some of the cleanest and most spacious bathrooms in the country. The owners recently came through on their promise of an indoor pool.

Rooms are rented by the week, from Saturday to Saturday, but management will tailor stays to fit your needs. Doubles (per week, including breakfast) are 3,395Kč to 4,655Kč ($141–$194) per person; apartments are 3,815Kč to 5,355Kč ($158–$223) per person. Mountain bikes rent for 90Kč ($3.75) per day. To get here, take the E55 highway south out of Prague toward České Budějovice. About 19km (12 miles) south of Tábor, head east on Route 23 toward Jindřichův Hradec to Kardašova Řečice.

a good choice. Located down by the "beach" area, their Communist-era functional look sticks out like a sore thumb. However, the rooms are clean and affordable, and the tennis courts and proximity to the pond are a plus.

U Světa 750, 379 01Třeboň. (© **384-721-394**. Fax 384-721-396. www.bohemia-regent.cz. 84 units. 1,590Kč–2,200Kč ($66–$92) double; 1,950Kč–2,900Kč ($81–$120) suite. AE, MC, V. **Amenities:** 2 restaurants; cafe; bar; miniature golf course. *In room:* TV, minibar.

Hotel Zlatá Hvězda Despite having rather spartan rooms, the Zlatá Hvězda is the most upscale hotel in town, and its location on Masarykovo náměstí can't be beat. An added plus is that the friendly staff can help arrange brewery tours, fishing permits, horseback riding, bike rentals, and several other outdoor activities.

Masarykovo nám. 107, 379 01 Třeboň. (© **384-757-100**. Fax 384-757-300. www.zhvezda.cz. 48 units. 1,800Kč ($75) double; 2,200Kč ($91) suite. Rates include buffet breakfast. AE, DC, MC, V. **Amenities:** 2 restaurants; spa; bowling alley; laundry service. *In room:* TV, fridge, hair dryer.

Pension Siesta If all the pensions in the Czech Republic showed up for a contest to see which was friendliest, this one might win. Just outside and to the right of the Hradecká brána, the Siesta is a small but quiet and clean alternative to the hotels on the square. What makes it special are Petr Matějů and his wife, who go out of their way to take care of their guests. The pension also has a pleasant terrace in front by the stream, where you can enjoy an afternoon drink and snack.

Hradební 26, 379 01 Třeboň. (©/fax **384-724-831**. 7 units. 900Kč ($37) per person. No credit cards. *In room:* TV.

WHERE TO DINE

Bílý Koníček CZECH Located in the hotel of the same name, Bílý Koníček has a standard Czech menu of meat, dumplings, and potato dishes that are reasonably priced. In summer, its terrace is a great place to sit and cool off; the building's shadow keeps you out of the direct sunlight. The beer from just down the road is always fresh and cold.

Masarykovo nám. 97. (© **384-721-213**. Main courses 95Kč–210Kč ($3.95–$8.75). V. Sun–Thur 9am–10pm; Fri–Sat 9am–midnight.

Pizzeria Macondo PIZZA If you're tired of fish and can't face another dumpling, Macondo makes decent affordable pizzas that are filling. They seem to have traded the ketchup, which is customary in much of the country, for real tomato sauce, resulting in a definite turn for the better. The salads are also fresh, and the beverage menu features probably the town's widest selection of cocktails.

Zámek 112. (© **384-724-880**. Pizzas 75Kč–140Kč ($3.10–$5.85). No credit cards. Daily 11am–10pm (9pm on Sun).

9 Tábor

88km (55 miles) S of Prague, 59km (37 miles) N of České Budějovice

The center of the Hussite movement following religious leader Jan Hus's execution in Prague, Tábor was officially founded in 1420 and named by the Hussites after the biblical Mount Tábor. Forsaking their property, the Hussites came here to receive Christ on his return to earth. The group of soldiers leading Tábor, some 15,000 in all, felt that they had been commanded by God to break the power of the Catholics at that time.

Legendary warrior Jan Žižka led the Táborites, as this sect of Hussites was known. Time and time again, Žižka rallied his troops to defeat the papal forces, until he was

---

Fun Fact **A-Mazing City**

If you get confused by roads that twist, turn, and then end as you leave the square, the Táborites have caught you exactly as planned—the town was designed to hold off would-be attackers with its maze of streets.

---

struck down in battle in 1424. For 10 more years the Hussites battled on, but their loss at Lipany signaled the end of the uprising, and an agreement was reached with Emperor Sigmund of Luxembourg of the Holy Roman Empire. Later, the town submitted to the leadership of Bohemia's Jiří z Poděbrad (George of Poděbrad) and blossomed economically, creating the wealth needed to construct the Renaissance buildings now found in the historic Old Town.

ESSENTIALS

GETTING THERE   If you're **driving,** leave Prague by Highway D1 and turn off at the E55 exit (signs BENESOV, CESKÉ BUDĚJOVICE). Highway E55 runs straight into the city of Tábor. It's a 1-hour drive.

Tábor is about 90 minutes by express **train** from Prague or close to an hour from České Budějovice. The train station has a baggage check, and you can get to the center of town by taking bus no. 11, 14, or 31. The fare is 130Kč ($5.40) second class.

The **bus** trip to Tábor lasts about 1½ hours from Prague and costs 78Kč ($3.25). To get to the center, it's about a 20-minute walk; go through the park and then bear right at its farthest corner to walk along třída 9. května into town.

VISITOR INFORMATION   Next to the Hussite Museum, **Infocentrum města Tábor,** Žižkovo nám. 2, 390 01, Tábor (© **381-486-230;** fax 381-486-239; www. tabor.cz), is stocked with information of all types: from maps, film, and postcards to advice about lodging, restaurants, and the best place for ice cream. The center's staff has volumes of pamphlets, phone numbers, and good advice. It's open May to September, Monday to Friday from 8:30am to 7pm, Saturday and Sunday from 9am to 4pm; and October to April, Monday to Friday from 9am to 4pm.

SPECIAL EVENTS   In mid-August the **Táborská Setkání (Tábor Meeting)** takes place. Each year, representatives from towns worldwide named after Mount Tábor congregate for some medieval fun—parades, music, and jousting. The 4-day event even reenacts the historic battle of Tábor, with brilliantly clad warriors fighting one another "to the death."

For more details on the Tábor Meeting and summer cultural events, see **www.tabor.cz,** or contact **Infocentrum města Tábor** (see "Visitor Information," above).

ORIENTATION   Outside the historic town, there's little to see in Tábor besides factories and the ubiquitous *paneláky* (apartment buildings) that ring most every big Czech town and city.

Staré město (Old Town) is situated around Žižkovo náměstí, site of the town church and the Hussite Museum. Medieval walls surround the entire Old Town core. The Kotnov Castle, now one of the town's museums, is at the southwest corner.

EXPLORING TÁBOR

Most of the city's sights are on or around **Žižkovo náměstí.** On the square's west side is the **Museum of the Hussite Movement** (© **381-254-286**). The late-Gothic former town hall now chronicles the movement that put Tábor on the map and in the history books. In front of the building lie stone tables where Hussite ministers gave daily communion. Leading from the museum's entrance, twisting and turning 650m (2,132 ft.) underneath the square, is a labyrinth of **tunnels** dating back to the 15th century. After visiting the museum, take one of the guided tours that snakes through the underground maze, which has housed everything from beer kegs to women imprisoned for such dastardly things as quarreling with men. The tunnels also doubled as a way to sneak under enemy guards if the town ever fell, allowing Hussite soldiers to launch an attack from behind. Admission to the Hussite Museum is 80Kč ($3.35), to the tunnels 60Kč ($2.50). They're open April to October daily 8:30am to 5pm, and November to March Monday to Friday 8:30am to 5pm.

When you emerge from the tunnels, you'll be on the opposite side of the square, facing the **Church of Transfiguration of Our Lord** (📞 381-251-226), with its vaulted impressive stained-glass windows and Gothic wooden altar. Climb the tower for one of the best views of the town. Open daily from 10am to 5pm May through August, and Saturday and Sunday 10am to 5pm in September and October. Admission is 20Kč (85¢).

You can pay homage to the Hussite military mastermind Jan Žižka at his **statue** next to the church. For a wondrous avenue of Renaissance buildings, stroll down **Pražská ulice,** off the southeast corner of the square. From here you can turn down Divadelní and head along the Lužnice River toward **Kotnov Castle** (📞 381-252-788). If your feet aren't up to the walk, you can take a more direct route to Kotnov by heading straight down Klokotská ulice, which runs away from the square next to the Hussite Museum.

A 14th-century castle that forms the southwest corner of the town wall, **Kotnov Castle** is most recognizable for its round **tower,** with another great view of the town. Inside the castle is a well-organized collection on the Middle Ages, with old farming tools, armor, weapons, uniforms, and other artifacts. Admission is 60Kč ($2.50), and it's open April to September daily from 8:30am to 5pm.

WHERE TO STAY

Tábor's lack of quality hotels gives you a perfect opportunity to "go local" and stay in a private pension. Expect to pay about 600Kč to 1,000Kč ($25–$42) per person. The information center next to the town hall at Žižkovo nám. 2 can provide a list of recommendations or call and book a room for you.

Amber Hotel Palcát   Since there are few quality hotels in Tábor, the Palcát, a modern but clean place, slips in as one of the town's finest. Though you may be left cold by its Communist-era furnishings, the rooms are spacious if not unforgettable. Try to snag a room on a higher floor, as these have great views of the town.

Třída 9. května 2471, 390 01 Tábor. 📞 381-252-901. Fax 381-252-905. www.legner.cz. 68 units. 1,250Kč–1,450Kč ($52–$60) double; 1,600Kč–1,800Kč ($66–$75) suite. MC, V. **Amenities:** 2 restaurants; bar; nightclub. *In room:* TV.

Hotel Dvořák 🍴   Located in a recently reconstructed historical building of Tábor brewery, which is part of the Kotnov Castle complex, this new addition to the list of hotels in Tábor, is a good choice not only for traveling families. The colorful interior design is inviting, the rooms are good size with comfortable beds.

Hradební 3037, 390 01 Tábor. 📞 381-251-290. Fax 381-251-299. www.dvorakta.genea2000.cz. 72 units. 2,250Kč–2,850Kč ($93–$118) double, 2,950Kč–10,500Kč ($122–$437) suite. AE, MC, V. **Amenities:** Restaurant; bar; pool; sauna, room service. *In room:* TV, minibar.

Hotel Kapitál   Smaller and quieter than the Palcát, the renovated Kapitál has a little more character than its neighbor down the street. The rooms are large, with modern furniture, and the Kapitál has a helpful English-speaking staff.

Třída 9. května 617, 390 01 Tábor. © **381-256-096.** Fax 381-252-411. www.hotel-kapital.cz. 25 units. 1,390Kč ($58) double; 1,590Kč ($66) suite. AE, MC, V. **Amenities:** Restaurant. *In room:* TV.

WHERE TO DINE

Bowling Club CZECH   Yes, really. There's a bowling alley here, too. The pub upstairs serves good Czech food and beer all day, and since there's not too much to do in town at night, you may want to go bowling downstairs. Don't worry—they serve beer downstairs as well—you can't have one without the other.

Třída 9. května 678. © **381-498-308.** Soups 25Kč ($1); main courses 69Kč–269Kč ($2.85–$11). No credit cards. Mon–Thurs 3pm–2am; Fri 3pm–3am; Sat 2pm–3am; Sun 2pm–midnight.

Hotel Palcát CZECH   Reluctantly, I have to admit that the Palcát remains one of the better restaurants in town, though the decor looks as though it hasn't been changed since the 1960s. The soups are first-rate, and the fish and beefsteak are fresh and tasty. Beware of the pizza—I swear Heinz ketchup (or a derivative thereof) is moonlighting as sauce. For a nightcap, the bar/disco is open Tuesday to Saturday until 3am and is one of the few rockin' places in town.

Třída 9. května 2467. © **381-252-999.** Soups 25Kč ($1); main courses 75Kč–220Kč ($3.10–$9.15). MC, V. Daily 11:30am–2:30pm and 4:30–11pm.

Restaurace Beseda CZECH   Beseda is a good place to stop after you slink through the tunnels and climb the tower at the Church of Transfiguration of Our Lord. You've probably seen this menu in just about every town so far, but the food is above average if not new. Their *svíčková* (sirloin in a cream sauce with dumplings) tastes almost as if my mom made it. On hot summer days, the patio is great for people-watching while drinking a cold Budvar.

Žižkovo nám. 8. © **381-253-723.** Main courses 59Kč–249Kč ($2.45–$10). No credit cards. Daily 10am–10pm.

The Best of Moravia

While Bohemia is the traditional home of a beer-favoring populace and the seat of Czech industrial muscle, the less-visited kingdom of Moravia to the south and east has spawned a people more attuned to the farmland and the potent wines it creates. For 1,000 years Moravians have watched as the wealth of their Czech brethren has been put on display in numerous palaces and factories, but Moravians have plenty of their own accomplishments and culture to be proud of. The provincial capital of Brno is the home of modern genetics, the place where a curious monk named Gregor Mendel discovered the building blocks of life in his monastic garden 150 years ago. It is also the birthplace of one of the most famous novelists of the latter half of the 20th century, Milan Kundera. And it is to Brno, the country's second-largest city, that Czech industry comes to show its wares on the national exhibition grounds.

Smaller towns maintain their real Moravian character, with lively song and dance and colorful traditional costumes that seem to have fallen by the wayside in Bohemia. Even the food is a little different: The bland goulash in Prague becomes a little spicier in Moravia, owing to the Hungarian influence that has seeped in from neighboring Slovakia.

Here, winemaking is taken as seriously as it is in most other European grape-growing regions. Many wine bars throughout Moravia serve the village's best straight from the cask, usually alongside traditional smoked meats. While the Bohemians have the sweet taste of Becherovka to sip at meals, Moravians have the sharp taste of *slivovice* (plum spirits) to cleanse the palate (sometimes for hours on end if it's *domácí*—home-brewed).

Having seen its fair share of history, Moravia conjures up a different image than Bohemia: Here, too, castles and picture-perfect town squares exist. But the people and slower lifestyle set Moravia apart.

1 Brno: The Region's Capital

224km (139 miles) SE of Prague, 128km (79 miles) N of Vienna

An industrial city with an industrial-strength image as "boring," Brno suffers a fate that many second cities around the world endure—no respect. Sure, as you approach from the highway, the sight of dozens of concrete apartment buildings may give you second thoughts. But bear with the Communist-inspired urban sprawl—the bad rap is undeserved. In fact, Brno is a vibrant and interesting city with a panache all its own.

Since Brno came of age in the 19th century on the back of its textile industry, the city's architecture, for the most part, lacks the Renaissance facades and meandering alleys of other towns. Indeed, the main square, náměstí Svoboda, bears this out. But spend a day or two here, and the beauty of the old city center will become apparent.

Empire and neoclassical buildings abound. Quirky sights like the Brno Dragon and the Wagon Wheel add character. Špilberk Castle and the Gothic cathedral of Saints Peter and Paul give historical perspective. And lush streets and parks make aimless wandering a pleasure.

ESSENTIALS

GETTING THERE   Driving to Brno is a trade-off. Take the E50—also named the D1—freeway that leads from the south of Prague all the way. The drive shouldn't take more than 2 hours. But the scenery is little more than one roadside stop after another.

Brno is the focal point for **train** travel in Moravia and most points east, making it an easy 2¾-hour trip from Prague. **Trains** leave almost every hour; the majority leave from Hlavní nádraží (Main Station). The fare is 243Kč ($10) first class or 160Kč ($6.65) second class. *Watch out:* If the train is marked EuroCity or Intercity (usually on its way to Vienna or Poland), you'll pay a supplement of 60Kč ($2.50).

Buses leave Prague's Florenc station to Brno every hour. The trip takes 2½ hours and costs 140Kč ($5.80). Reservations are recommended during peak hours. To buy your ticket with reserved seat, go to the AMS booking office at Florenc station, open daily 6am to 8pm, © **222-624-440.**

VISITOR INFORMATION   The new **Turistické Informační Centrum (TIC),** Radnická 8, Brno (© **542-211-090;** www.ticbrno.cz), provides a plethora of information on accommodations, plus what's on in Brno and how to see it. It's open Monday to Friday from 9am to 6pm, Saturday 9am to 5:30pm, Sunday 9am to 3pm October to March; April to September Monday to Friday 8:30am to 6pm, Saturday and Sunday 9am to 5:30pm. A second TIC is across from the train station, at Nádražní 8, Brno (© **542-214-450**), open October to March Monday to Friday 9am to 6pm, April to September Monday to Friday 8:30am to 6pm.

You'll find also the CK Čedok sign across from the train station at Nádražní 10/12, Brno (© **542-211-562;** www.cedok.cz). This office can help arrange accommodations in hotels and private rooms as well as currency exchange. It's open Monday to Friday from 9am to 6pm and Saturday from 9am to noon.

SPECIAL EVENTS   Usually when the words *special events* and Brno are mentioned in the same sentence, the phrase *trade fair* isn't too far behind. Many fairs held at Brno's BVV exhibition grounds are world-class displays of technology, industrial machinery, and even well-groomed pets.

Brno celebrates music as well, hosting the **Janáček Music Festival** each June and the **Brno International Music Festival (Moravský Podzim)** in September and October.

However, probably the most attended event occurs each August when the **Motorcycle Grand Prix** tour rolls into town to tackle the Masaryk Okruh (Masaryk Ring).

For details on all events and a list of fairs at the BVV fairgrounds, contact **Informační Centrum** (see "Visitor Information," above) or go to **www.brno.cz.**

ORIENTATION   Brno is a large rambling city, but most sights are concentrated in its inner core. At the center is **Náměstí Svobody (Freedom Square),** connected to the train station by Masarykova ulice. Just west of Masarykova is **Zelný trh (Cabbage Market),** the largest square in town. Cars can't pass through the Old Town, but tram no. 4 barrels through with little regard for the pedestrians in its way.

The city is small enough for walking. All hotels, restaurants, and sights are close to each other, so you do not have to take public transportation. The only exception is for those staying at the Holiday Inn or Voronež. If you want to take a tram, walk east

Moravia

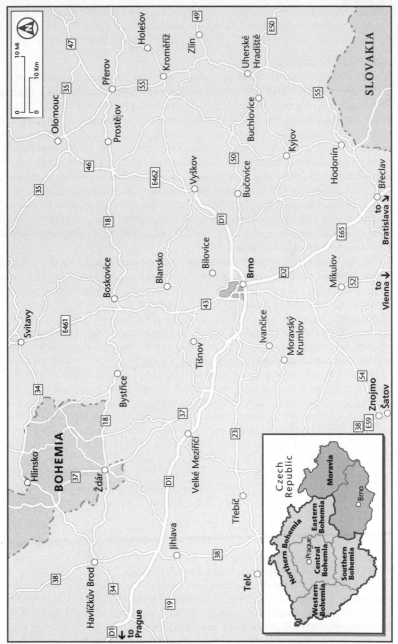

(toward the town center) around the edge of the fairgrounds until you get to the New Gate, where tram nos. 1 and 10 have stops headed to the center. Get off at the stop Hlavní nádraží (train station).

STROLLING AROUND BRNO

The Old Town holds most of the attractions you'll want to see, so it's probably best to start at the former seat of government, the Old Town Hall on Radnická 8. To get there, walk from the train station along Masarykovo and make a left at Orlí Street; if you're coming from náměstí Svobody, head toward the train station and turn right on either Panská or Orlí.

Brno's oldest secular building, from the 13th century, the **Old Town Hall** is a hodgepodge of styles—Gothic, Renaissance, and baroque elements melding together, demonstrating Brno's development through the ages. Almost everything in the building has a story or legend attached to it, beginning with the front door and its crooked Gothic portal. Designed by Anton Pilgram, who lists Vienna's vaunted St. Stephen's Church on his résumé, the door was completed in 1510. Town officials supposedly reneged on their original payment offer, and a furious Pilgram took revenge by bending the turret above the Statue of Justice.

On the second floor, a modest collection of armor, coins, and photos is displayed in the same room where town councilors met from the 13th century right up until 1935. Climb the stairs of the tower for an interesting, if not beautiful, city view; smokestacks and baroque buildings battle for attention.

Before you leave Old Town Hall, examine two of Brno's most beloved attractions— the **Brno Dragon** and the **Wagon Wheel.** The "dragon" hanging from the ceiling is actually not a dragon, but an alligator given to the city by Archprince Matayás in 1608. Here also stands the Wagon Wheel, a testament to Brno's industrious image. Local lore has it that a carpenter named Jiří Birek from nearby Lednice wagered with locals that he could chop down a tree, fashion a wheel from it, and roll it the 40km (25 miles) to Brno all in a single day. Well, he managed to do it, but the townspeople, certain that one man couldn't do so much in 1 day, decided that Birek must have had assistance from the devil. With this mindset, they refused to ever buy his works again.

Just south of the Old Town Hall is **Zelný trh (Cabbage Market),** a farmers' market since the 13th century. You can still buy a head or two of the leafy vegetable at the market today as entrepreneurs sell their wares under the gaze of **Hercules,** depicted in the **Parnas Fountain** in the square's center. The fountain used to be a vital part of the market; quick-thinking fishermen let their carp swim and relax in the fountain until the fish were chosen for someone's dinner.

At the southern corner of **Zelný trh** lies the 17th-century **Reduta Divadlo,** a former home of Mozart. Another block closer to the train station, on Kapucínské náměstí, is the **Kostel Nalezení svatého Kříže (Church of the Sacred Cross)** and the **Kapucínský Klášter (Capuchin Monastery)** (© 542-213-232).

The Capuchin Monastery is famous for its catacombs, which hold many of Brno's most famous citizens. Among those interred here are Moritz Grimm, who was responsible for rebuilding the cathedral in the 18th century, and Austrian army colonel František Trenck, who in the intervening years when the Austro-Hungarian empire ruled the area, lost his head to vandals. A unique ventilation system preserves the bodies, displayed in open coffins. This display is slightly morbid; skin and clothing are slowly decaying. Parents may want to look ahead or get a brochure to make sure children are up to seeing the coffins. Admission is 20Kč (85¢). The monastery is open Monday to

Brno

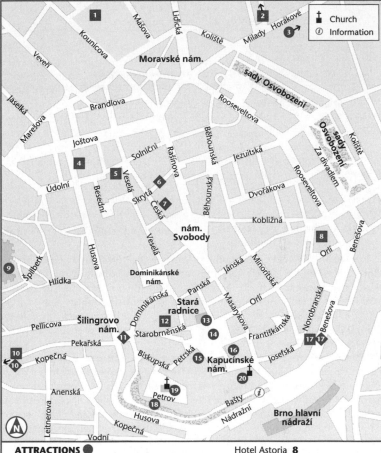

✝ Church
ⓘ Information

ATTRACTIONS ●
Cathedral of Saints Peter and Paul **19**
Denisovy sady **18**
Kapucínský Klášter
   (Capuchin Monastery) **20**
Kostel Nalezení svatého Kříže **20**
Moravian Regional Museum **15**
Old Town Hall **13**
Parnas Fountain **14**
Reduta Divadlo **16**
Špilberk Castle (Brno City Museum) **9**
Villa Tugendhat **3**
Zelný trh (Cabbage Market) **14**

ACCOMMODATIONS ■
Grandhotel Brno **17**
Holiday Inn **10**

Hotel Astoria **8**
Hotel Bobycentrum Brno **2**
Hotel Brno **10**
Hotel Continental **1**
Hotel International **4**
Hotel Royal Ricc **12**
Hotel Slavia **5**
Hotel Voroněž **10**
Penzion na Starém Brně **9**

DINING ◆
La Braseria **10**
Modrá Hvězda **11**
Pivnice Hotel Pegas **6**
Stopkova Plzeňská Pivnice **7**
U Královny Elišky **10**
Zahradní Restaurace **17**

> ### *Tips* What Time Is It?
>
> If you tour the cathedral in the late morning, you may think that you've switched time zones. Don't worry: The cathedral bells strike noon an hour early in remembrance of a quick-thinking bell ringer who, seeing that the city was on the verge of attack by the Swedes during the Thirty Years' War, found out that the army was planning to take the city by noon. If not successful by then, Swedish commander General Torstenson is said to have decided the attack would be called off and the army would beat a hasty retreat. The bell ringer, sensing that the town couldn't repel the Swedes, rang the cathedral bells an hour early at 11am, before the army could attack. True to his word, Torstenson packed up and went home.

Saturday from 9am to noon and 2 to 4:30pm and Sunday from 11 to 11:45am and 2 to 4:30pm.

Dominating **Zelný trh** at its southwest corner is the **Moravian Regional Museum,** Zelný trh 8, Brno (© **542-321-205;** www.mzm.cz), housed in the Dietrichstein Palace. Completed in 1620, the palace was used by Russian Marshal Kutuzov to prepare for the battle of Austerlitz. These days, the museum displays a wide array of stuffed birds and wild game, as well as art, coins, and temporary exhibits. Admission is 50Kč ($2) adults, and 25Kč ($1) students and children. It's open Tuesday to Saturday from 9am to 5pm.

From the museum, head up Petrská Street to the **Cathedral of Saints Peter and Paul.** Perched atop a hill overlooking the city, the cathedral was built in the late 11th and early 13th centuries. In 1743, it was rebuilt in a baroque style, only to be re-Gothicized just before World War I. The resulting melding of styles gives the cathedral a unique character. The cathedral is open Monday to Wednesday and Friday and Saturday from 6:30am to 6pm, Thursday from 6:30am to 7:30pm, and Sunday from 8:30am to 6pm.

Take a break at **Denisovy sady,** the park behind the cathedral, and prepare to climb the hill to get to Špilberk Castle. If you're not up for it, tram nos. 6, 9, 14, and 17 go near the castle, but you'll still have a short but strenuous walk from there. The fare is 13Kč (55¢); tickets are available citywide in yellow automated machines at selected stops or at magazine and tobacco shops. If you want to walk all the way, head along Biskupská, where **interesting houses** provide a nice foreground to the bustling city. Make a left on Starobrněnská to Husova and then left on to Pellicova. At Pellicova 11 is a fine example of František Uherka's cubist architectural vision.

But the real reason for this climb is **Špilberk Castle.** If there's one building in the Czech Republic that's ready to be overrun by visitors, it's Špilberk—and it's had practice. It was built in the 13th century, and the Hussites controlled the castle in the 15th century. The Prussians saw the castle's position as an excellent lookout when they occupied it in the early 17th century. And the Nazis turned it into a torture chamber during their stay, executing some 80,000 people deep inside the dungeons.

At Špilberk's **Brno City Museum** (© **542-123-611;** www.spilberk.cz), you can see several new permanent exhibitions such as "Jail of Nations" or "History of Brno" and others. Admission to all exhibitions, casemates, and the lookout tower is 110Kč ($4.60) adults, 50Kč ($2) students. It's open Tuesday to Sunday from 9am to 6pm May to September, and October and April from 9am to 5pm; and Wednesday to Sunday 10am to 5pm November to March.

MORE TO SEE & DO

MUSEUMS   In 2000, the Ministry of Culture of the Czech Republic approved a plan to present the local **Villa Tugendhat,** Černopolní 45 (© **545-212-118;** www. tugendhat-villa.cz), as a historic monument and museum of the modern movement in architecture of the 1920s. This house, designed by the architect Mies van der Rohe, has been restored to its original form, including the interior decorations. Because of its significant historic value and authenticity it was recently added to UNESCO's World Heritage List. To visit this site, take tram no. 3, 5, or 11 from the center to the Children's Hospital stop. It is open Wednesday to Sunday from 10am to 6pm; admission is 80Kč ($3.35) adults, 40Kč ($1.65) students and children. Guided tours are given every hour; you need to book in advance.

SHOPPING   Once back in the city center, take some time for a quick meal and browse along the **pedestrian shopping zone,** which unfolds between náměstí Svobody and the train station. Prices for goods are often cheaper here than in Prague, so you may find a better deal for the crystal vase or pair of earrings you were thinking of buying.

SOCCER   Sports fans can partake in a Sunday ritual as dear to Czechs as football is to Americans by taking the 20-minute walk north from the main square to Brno stadium, where first league **soccer team 1.FC Brno** plays its home games. Grab a beer and a sausage and cheer along. Tickets—beginning at 60Kč ($2.50)—are always plentiful and can be bought at the stadium on game day.

WHERE TO STAY

Note that prices, even in the high season, often double for major trade fairs and the Motorcycle Grand Prix.

EXPENSIVE

Grandhotel Brno ✦   Ever since it was taken over by the Austrian chain Austrotel in the mid-1990s, the Grandhotel has lived up to its name. Its rooms are spacious and well appointed, though some located at the front get a little noisy due to the major street running past with its never-ending stream of trams; ask for a room that has windows facing north, away from the commotion. The buffet breakfast is an added bonus, with lots of fresh fruit, breads, and Moravian cakes to get you going. The casino is worth a look if only for the chandeliers with their fine cut crystal.

Benešova 18–20, 657 83 Brno. © **542-518-111.** Fax 542-210-345. www.grandhotelbrno.cz. 110 units. 3,300Kč–5,400Kč ($137–$225) double; 6,150Kč ($256) suite. AE, DC, MC, V. Parking 150Kč ($6.25). **Amenities:** 2 restaurants; nightclub; room service (7am–3am); 24-hr. laundry; casino. *In room:* TV, minibar.

MODERATE

Holiday Inn   Yes, that's right. The best surprise is no surprise—even in Brno. The very modern Holiday Inn Brno, on the fairgrounds, caters mainly to the trade-fair crowd, so be warned that prices may jump steeply when events are scheduled. Everything, from the rooms to the restaurant to the bars, looks eerily similar to their counterparts in other Holiday Inns around the world. Still, the beds are more comfortable than most, and the rooms are spotless, with large writing desks and showers that have no problems with water pressure. The staff is very friendly and speaks English.

Křížkovského 20, 603 00 Brno. © 543-122-111. Fax 541-159-081. 205 units. www.hibrno.cz. 3,500Kč ($146) double; 4,600Kč ($191) suite. AE, DC, MC, V. Parking 150Kč ($6.25) per day. **Amenities:** Restaurant; bar; pool; coin-op laundry. In room: TV, minibar, hair dryer, iron, pants presser.

Hotel Bobycentrum Brno
The Bob, as many refer to it, was once one of Brno's newest luxury hotels, just north of the city center. Although the hotel has slowly declined over the past years, it still attracts guests who never leave its grounds. Inside and on the surrounding grounds you'll find, as well as those listed below, a bowling alley, tennis courts, squash courts, a roller-skating rink, and a soccer stadium—even a car wash. The rooms are very comfortable. The walk from the center is a nice 25-minute stroll through long parks. The only drawback can be the bland surroundings and the tackiness of some of the facilities, such as the sex-show bar or the velvety disco in the entertainment complex.

Sportovní 2a, 602 00 Brno. © 541-638-110. Fax 541-638-103. www.bobycentrum.cz. 141 units. 4,400Kč ($183) double; 5,600Kč ($233) suite. Parking in garage 350Kč ($15) per day. AE, MC, V. **Amenities:** 2 restaurants; 3 bars; pool; tennis courts; health club; shopping center. In room: TV, minibar.

Hotel Continental
This is another Communist-era hotel trying to make it in the free market. The rooms still have that Communist trademark of being a little on the small side and a little too modern for those expecting an old-world European experience. The very helpful staff is approachable for advice on how to reach the sights. The Continental is north of the city center, so you'll get some cleaner air and a nice short walk into the center.

Kounicova 20, 662 21 Brno. © 541-519-111. Fax 541-211-203. www.continentalbrno.cz. 228 units. 1,750Kč–2,150Kč ($73–$89) double. AE, DC, MC, V. Parking. **Amenities:** Restaurant; bar; laundry. In room: TV, minibar, hair dryer, iron.

Hotel International
Just on the edge of the city center, the International has joined the Best Western chain of hotels, which has translated into a huge improvement in the quality of service. From the outside, it looks like a dressed-up Communist-era apartment building, and looks are not deceiving. But the rooms have enough space to keep you from feeling claustrophobic. The bar on the main floor is usually crowded with both locals and visitors, making for interesting people-watching.

Husova 16, 659 21 Brno. © 542-122-111. Fax 542-210-843. www.hotelinternational.cz. 262 units. 3,390Kč–4,390Kč ($141–$182) double; 7,100Kč ($295) suite. AE, DC, MC, V. Underground parking 400Kč ($16) per day. **Amenities:** Bar. In room: TV, minibar.

Hotel Royal Ricc ⚑
Brno's newest hotel is one of the nicest. A small, quiet inn set just off the Cabbage Market, the Ricc is part of the Romantic Hotel chain. Though the soft pink facade of the building leaves a little to be desired, the attention to detail inside the building combines the rustic feel of a bed-and-breakfast with the service of a top-quality hotel. Rooms vary in size, but all are decorated with turn-of-the-20th-century—and sometimes older—antiques that give a warm, welcome feeling lacking in most of the competing hotels. Ask to see the rooms first, as each one has its own charms. Make sure to look up, since many have beautifully restored ceilings with intricate artwork. There are sitting rooms, a wine bar, and a restaurant as well that all live up to the surroundings.

Starobrněnská 10, 602 00 Brno. © 542-219-262. Fax 542-219-265. www.romantichotels.cz. 30 units. 3,700Kč ($154) double; 6,000Kč ($250) suite. AE, MC, V. Parking 150Kč ($6.25) per day. **Amenities:** Restaurant; wine bar. In room: TV, minibar.

Hotel Slavia   The Slavia, just on the edge of the pedestrian zone under the castle, falls short of being the upscale hotel it's trying to be, but it is one of the best deals in the center, and the area is a nice one to walk through either day or night. Rooms are spartan, with bland furniture, but clean. The rooms are not uniformly sized, so take a look at a couple before choosing.

Solniční 15, 662 16 Brno. ⓒ 353-232-100. Fax 353-222-999. www.hotel.cz/slavia. 84 units. 2,250Kč–2,850Kč ($93–$119) double. AE, DC, MC, V. *In room:* TV, minibar.

Hotel Voroněž   The Voroněž has added conference rooms and a pool and renovated its restaurants. But for all the new glitz, it still is basically a Czech *panelák* (housing complex) dressed up as a hotel trying hard to shed its Communist-era image—and furniture. It's across from the fairgrounds, making it convenient for those here on business. The hotel is split into two sections: a four-star hotel that is housed in the main building with the conference rooms, and a smaller three-star annex next door. The rooms, however, are similar in each. In many of the medium-size rooms, 1970s Naugahyde furnishings have been replaced with light pastel-and-wood beds, desks, and chairs, and these redone rooms make the grade. Except during the busiest times, you can always find a room here.

Křížkovského 47, 603 73 Brno. ⓒ 543-141-111. Fax 543-212-002. www.voronez.cz. 376 units. 2,190Kč–3,860Kč ($91–$160) double; 4,800Kč ($200) suite. AE, DC, MC, V. Parking 200Kč ($8.30) per day. **Amenities:** Restaurant; bar; pool. *In room:* TV, minibar, iron.

INEXPENSIVE

Hotel Astoria   The Astoria, formerly the Morava, has basic small rooms, but the staff are kinder than staff at most nearby hotels in this class. Ask to see the room first, as some are much brighter and cheerier than others. The hotel is very close to the city center and the train station.

Novobranská 3, 662 21 Brno. ⓒ 542-321-302. Fax 542-211-428. 89 units. 1,150Kč ($48) double. AE, DC, MC, V. *In room:* TV.

Hotel Brno   Once a run-down dive, the Brno has been given a face-lift and a new lease on life. Near the city center, the hotel even has its own tennis courts, but its main attraction is as a quiet place to lay down your head at the right price.

Horní 19, 639 00 Brno. ⓒ 543-214-046. Fax 543-215-308. www.hotelbrno.cz. 90 units. 1,290Kč ($54) double. AE, DC, MC, V. *In room:* TV.

Penzion na Starém Brně   Built into the stables below the castle is a restaurant that has now added a small and very cheap pension. Though a little out of the center, lying halfway between the exhibition grounds and the main square, this spot is very clean and quiet. The rooms are sparsely furnished with rustic pieces and hardwood floors, but since they are relatively small, that's okay.

Mendlovo nám. 1, 639 00 Brno. ⓒ 543-247-872. Fax 541-243-738. www.penzion-brno.com. 7 units. 950Kč ($40) double. MC, V. **Amenities:** Restaurant. *In room:* TV.

WHERE TO DINE
MODERATE

La Braseria 🎯 ITALIAN   They say that when in Rome, do as the Romans do. So when in Brno, follow this saying and do what the Romans do—come here. Their authentic Italian cuisine (sorry, dumpling aficionados) is too zesty to be passed up. Try the chicken in green-peppercorn sauce for a delicate change, or the spicy penne arrabiata to bring some life to your taste buds. If there is a drawback, it is that the seafood can be disappointing. As at most Czech restaurants, much of the fish—except some local varieties—is frozen. The restaurant is located between the fairgrounds and the center, about a 10-minute walk from either.

Pekařská 80. ✆ 543-232-042. Reservations recommended. Soups and antipasti 25Kč–210Kč ($1–$8.75); *primi piatti* 55Kč–215Kč ($2.30–$8.95); *secondi* 85Kč–300Kč ($3.55–$12); pizzas 50Kč–150Kč ($2–$6.25). AE, DC, MC, V. Daily noon–midnight.

Modrá Hvězda (Blue Star) CZECH   The Blue Star is one of the few moderately priced restaurants in Brno where you can get good-quality food well into the night. The pepper steak is the favorite and, as you can tell, anything from the grill is your best bet.

Šilingrovo nám. 7. ✆ 542-215-292. Soups 25Kč–45Kč ($1–$1.85); main courses 99Kč–299Kč ($4.10–$12). MC, V. Daily 11am–1am.

U Královny Elišky CZECH   If you're looking for the quintessential Moravian experience, look no further. Nestled in the back wall of the castle where the stables used to be, this never-ending maze of cellars and alcoves oozes Moravian charm. Browse through a menu loaded with pork, chicken, fish, and beef dishes as a Gypsy band wanders the premises. An extensive wine list complements the wide variety of meals. *One warning:* The appetizers on the tray wheeled to your table can cost anywhere from 30Kč to 350Kč ($1.25–$15), so don't hesitate to ask how much your choice will set you back.

Mendlovo nám. 1. ✆ 543-212-578. Soups 40Kč ($1.65); main courses 90Kč–480Kč ($3.75–$20). AE, MC, V. Tues–Sat 9pm–midnight.

Zahradní Restaurace (Garden Restaurant) CZECH/INTERNATIONAL   When you enter this restaurant, you might expect the prices to be higher than they are. The setting is first-rate, with fountains and lots of plants and nonintrusive background music. This used to be one of Eastern Europe's finest Chinese restaurants, but now the menu features Czech and international dishes. Try the Moravian plate piled with pork, duck, smoked meat, sauerkraut, and two kinds of dumplings.

In the Grandhotel Brno, Benešova 18. ✆ 542-518-111. Reservations recommended. Soups 35Kč–60Kč ($1.45–$2.50); main courses 120Kč–390Kč ($5–$16). AE, DC, MC, V. Daily 3–11pm.

INEXPENSIVE

Pivnice Hotel Pegas CZECH   Set 'em up and knock 'em down. This is a pub and nothing but. Come here for a beer and a quick meal during the day rather than for a formal dinner at night. The Pegas is one of the few pubs in the city center where locals and visitors mix. Hearty goulash and dumplings are always a good choice, as is the fried cheese, though your arteries may not agree.

Jakubská 4. ✆ 542-210-104. Main courses 45Kč–129Kč ($1.85–$5.35). AE, V, MC. Daily 9am–midnight.

Stopkova Plzeňská Pivnice CZECH   Located just off the main square, Stopkova is a classic Czech pub. It has uncomfortable long wooden benches, and little light makes it through the two front windows. Equally classic are the meals—goulash and schnitzels that are filling and tasty. The only thing this place is missing, thank goodness, are the clouds of smoke billowing from table to table. Some traditions are best forgotten.

Česká 5. ✆ 542-211-094. Soups 20Kč (85¢); main courses 60Kč–200Kč ($2.50–$8.30). No credit cards. Mon–Sat 10am–11pm.

BRNO AFTER DARK

While it may lack Prague's energy, Brno still has plenty to offer at night. A strong cultural program dominates, with a local theater and symphony offering world-class entertainment. Go to www.brno.cz to find out what's going on at major venues, or visit the Informační Centrum (see earlier in this chapter) to get tickets.

For the young at heart, the **Boby disco** (open daily 7pm–3am) at the Boby Hotel is the place to dance, dance, and dance. The music is endless, as is the line if you don't get there early enough. Admission is 100Kč ($4.15). Otherwise, be Czech and go to any number of local pubs, which are located on nearly every street corner. Start out at the **Stopkova Pivnice** just off the main square, and from there just wander the streets. You'll go no more than 2 minutes in any direction before another pub tempts you.

2 Telč ⟨★

149km (92 miles) SE of Prague, 86km (53 miles) W of Brno

As you pass through towns on your way here, you may be tempted to pass up Telč, dismissing it as yet another "small town with a nice square." Don't. Those who make the trip to Telč strike gold. Telč is one of the few towns in Europe that can boast of not being reconstructed since its original edifices were built. It now enjoys the honor of being a United Nations (UNESCO) World Heritage Site. Its uniformly built houses and castle give it an almost too-perfect look, as though no one ever really lived here.

Due to its small size, you can explore Telč in a day. Those traveling by car to Brno or Vienna should stop here on the way. I recommend spending the night to admire the **illuminated castle and square,** especially if there's an evening recital or concert at the castle. You can also combine a stop here with a visit to Znojmo (see below).

ESSENTIALS

GETTING THERE   Located about halfway between České Budějovice and Brno, Telč can be reached by taking Highway 23. **Driving** from Prague, take Highway D1 in the direction of Brno and exit at Jihlava, where you pick up Highway 38 after going through the town. Then head west on Highway 23. You can leave your car in the large parking lot near the town's north gate. It's a 2-hour drive from Prague.

Train connections to Telč aren't great, so be patient. A second-class fare from Prague costs 250Kč ($10). The town lies on the Havlíčkův Brod, Kostelec u Jihlavy line, where you'll have to change. Once you get there, you'll find about nine trains departing daily to Telč. The train station offers storage, though its hours aren't the most dependable.

Better than the train is the more direct route by **bus,** costing 124Kč ($5.15). Buses leave from Prague's Florenc bus station daily and take about 3 hours. The castle and town square are a 10-minute walk from the bus station. To get to town, exit through the station's back entrance, turn right on Tyršova, and then turn left on Rudnerova. Follow this street as it bears left, and turn right at the second small alley. This will guide you to the main square.

VISITOR INFORMATION   Since UNESCO gave its backing to Telč in 1992, services for visitors have blossomed, and none more so than the information center on the main square. At the **Informační Středisko,** náměstí Zachariáše z Hradce 10 (② **567-112-407;** www.telc-etc.cz or www.telcsko.cz; info@telc-etc.cz), you'll find a wealth of information concerning accommodations, cultural events, guided tours, and even hunting; brochures are in Czech, German, and English. The staff is eager to arrange reservations. The small white Telč guidebook that costs 75Kč ($3.15) is worth the price; it is filled with minute details about almost every structure in town. Open from May to September Monday to Friday 8am to 5pm, Saturday and Sunday 10am to 5pm; October Monday to Friday 8am to 5pm, Saturday and Sunday 10am to 4pm; November to April Monday and Wednesday 8am to 5pm, Tuesday and Thursday 8am to 4pm, and Friday 8am to 3pm.

SPECIAL EVENTS The **Prázdniny v Telči (Holidays in Telč),** a season of concerts, recitals, and fairs, runs from the end of July to the middle of August. For details, contact the **Informační Středisko** (see "Visitor Information," above) or www.prazdniny vtelci.cz.

ORIENTATION Telč's historic center is shaped like a trapezoid and is surrounded by lakes on three sides. At the center is a very large square named after the town's former owner, Zachariáš z Hradce.

EXPLORING TELČ

Start with a tour of **Telč Château** (© **567-243-943;** www.zamek-telc.cz) at the northwest end of the main square. Zacharias of Neuhaus, whose name now graces the main square, was so enamored of the Renaissance style rampant in Italy that in 1553 he commissioned Antonio Vlach, and later Baldassare Maggi de Ronio, to rebuild the château, originally a 14th-century Gothic structure. This castle's exterior, however, cannot prepare you for its interior—hall after hall of lavish rooms with spectacular ceilings.

Highlights inside the château include the **Africa Hall,** with rhino heads, tiger skins, and other exotica from expeditions accumulated by Karel Podstatky, a relative of the castle's last owner, in the early 1900s. The **Banquet Hall's** *sgrafitti* seems to mock those who overindulge, and the **Marble Hall of Knights** boasts a wood ceiling decorated with bas-reliefs from 1570, plus a fine collection of armor. In the **Golden Hall,** where balls and ceremonies once took place, 30 octagonal coffers with mythological scenes stare down at you from the ceiling.

A 1-hour guided tour of the castle halls is 160Kč ($6.65) adults, 120Kč ($5) students, free for children under 6. To see the apartments, take the additional 45-minute tour, which costs 140Kč ($5.85). The castle is open Tuesday to Sunday: May to September from 9am to noon and 1 to 5pm; October and April from 9am to noon and 1 to 4pm; the castle is closed November to March.

Next to the castle is the **Church of St. James (Kostel sv. Jakuba),** its walls adorned with late-15th-century paintings. Next to St. James is the baroque **Jesuit Church of the Name of Jesus.**

After strolling the castle grounds, head back to the main square, where a sea of soft pastel facades awaits. If you find yourself wondering how the entire square can be so uniform, you're not alone. After rebuilding the castle, Zacharias realized that the rest of the place looked, well, out of place. To rectify the situation, he promptly rebuilt the facade of each building on the square, though Gothic columns belie what once was. Of particular note is the building referred to as **House 15,** where a round oriel and *sgrafitti* portraying the crucifixion, Saul and David, Christopher, and faith and justice jut onto the street corner. And watching over it all are the cherubs on the Marian column, built in 1718.

WHERE TO STAY

If you haven't arranged lodging ahead of time, head straight to the information center in the main square, where the staff has a complete list of what's available. For hotels, expect to pay around 1,250Kč ($52) for a double.

Private accommodations are also available, and for the most part, these rooms are comparable to hotel rooms (if not better and less expensive), though there are far fewer amenities. The information center staff will call and arrange for you to meet the room's owner so you can check out the place. Several rooms located directly on the square are available. Expect to pay about 500Kč ($20) per person. On slow days, owners will usually negotiate a better price.

Hotel Celerin   The most upscale hotel on the square, the Celerin has medium-size rooms; the best ones overlook the square. If you're looking for location, this is the place to stay. Looking out over the square at night when it's bathed in light will remind you why this town is so treasured by the United Nations. Travelers with disabilities will find the staff here helpful, and some rooms are fully accessible.

Náměstí Zachariáše z Hradce 43, 588 56 Telč. ℭ **567-243-477.** Fax 567-213-581. www.hotelcelerin.cz. 12 units. 1,600Kč ($67) double. Rates include continental breakfast. AE, DC, MC, V. **Amenities:** Restaurant; bar. *In room:* TV, fridge.

Hotel Černý Orel (Black Eagle Hotel)   On the main square overlooking the Marian column, the Black Owl is a favorite among visitors. The rooms are spartan but clean. Ask for a view of the square; the staff will usually accommodate this request if a room is available. A lively restaurant downstairs serves good Czech fare.

Náměstí Zachariáše z Hradce 7, 588 56 Telč. ℭ **567-243-222.** Fax 567-243-221. www.cernyorel.cz. 32 units. 1,650Kč ($69) double. AE, MC, V. **Amenities:** Restaurant. *In room:* TV.

Hotel Telč   Just off the main square, the Telč has rooms that feel spacious because of their high ceilings. The park next to it adds to the effect and provides a sense of being out in the country, a good choice if you've had enough of staying in noisy city centers. Rooms facing the street are brighter but louder than those to the rear. The all-wood furnishings add some ambience, but the bathrooms are cramped.

Na Můstku 37, 588 56 Telč. ℭ **567-243-109.** Fax 567-223-887. www.hoteltelc.wz.cz. 10 units. 1,490Kč–1,790Kč ($62–$74) double. AE, DC, MC, V. **Amenities:** Restaurant. *In room:* TV.

WHERE TO DINE

Šenk pod Věží CZECH   This place can get a little loud when the disco in the building starts to crank it up at around 10pm, but in the afternoon the terrace provides a peaceful spot for a quick meal. The food is filling and hearty, even if it's not exciting.

Palackého 116. ℭ **567-243-889.** Soups 25Kč ($1); main courses 75Kč–155Kč ($3.10–$6.45). No credit cards. Daily 10am–midnight.

U Černého Orla (At the Black Eagle) ⊕ CZECH   If it looks as though every visitor in town is trying to get in here, it's because they are. The Black Eagle is worth the effort. This is one of the few restaurants in Telč that can be trusted to serve good food consistently. Crowd in at any free space and enjoy a wide range of Czech meals. The trout is always fresh, and I've never heard a complaint about it or the *řízek* (pork schnitzel). The hearty soups are especially welcome on days when the sun isn't shining. When it is, get a table on the terrace out front—though the service, which is quick if you're inside, usually slows down considerably.

Náměstí Zachariáše z Hradce 7. ℭ **567-243-222.** Reservations recommended. Soups 20Kč (83¢); main courses 50Kč–190Kč ($2–$7.90). AE, MC, V. June–Sept daily 7am–10pm; Oct–May Tues–Sun 7am–10pm.

3 Znojmo

190km (118 miles) SE of Prague, 64km (40 miles) S of Brno

Most travelers blow through Znojmo, the wine and pickle capital of the Czech Republic, at about 97kmph (60 mph), tired of getting caught behind trucks and buses en route to Vienna. But it wasn't always that way.

Znojmo was settled as far back as the 7th century, and the town gained prominence in the 9th century, when the Great Moravian Empire took control. In the 11th and 12th centuries, Prince Břetislav I constructed a fortress here; in 1226, the town was granted rights (including collecting taxes and making wine) by the king—even before the Moravian capital of Brno. Znojmo's position on the border made it a natural location as a trading center, and Czech kings always ensured that the town was taken care of, using it as a lookout over the Austrian frontier. Alas, the original town hall was destroyed during World War II, and the Communist-inspired sprawl that followed has taken away some of Znojmo's character. But the old center remains vibrant, with many religious buildings still intact. The Town Hall's 70m-tall (230-ft.) tower lets you take in a view of the city and surrounding area—both old and new.

And why is Znojmo considered the pickle capital of the Czech Republic? Simply because the **pickles** taste so good. They're made from the best cucumbers the country has to offer. And when put into a spicy sauce, as they are in *Znojemský guláš*, these sweet-and-sour pickles really taste great. You'll get pickle fever, too, I promise. When you do, and want to buy some, you'll notice just how many shops proudly display the Znojmo pickle.

And then there's the **wine.** If you're looking for the region's best vintages, look no farther than **Frankovka** (a smooth, full-bodied red) or **Ryzlink** (a light, dry white), with the Znojemské (from Znojmo) or Mikulov labels. These superb wines are available almost everywhere; a liter costs no more than 75Kč or 125Kč ($3.15 or $5.20). Wine bars often serve the best vintages straight from the cask. You can also fill up—with both wine and fuel—at some gas stations.

To best enjoy the town's wine and pickles, you should spend at least a few hours here, or overnight if you've got some time. Znojmo's location on the Prague–Vienna route makes it a natural place to stop. An added bonus is its proximity to Telč—you can see both in 1 day if you want.

ESSENTIALS

GETTING THERE   Znojmo is most easily reached by **car** and is especially convenient for those heading to or from Vienna or Telč. Take Highway D1 from Prague and exit at Highway 38 in the direction of Jihlava. As you enter the town you're already on the right highway, so just pass by the town center and follow the signs. From Prague, the trip should take about 2½ hours.

Several **trains** to Znojmo leave Brno throughout the day, though some require a quick change in Hrušovany. The ride takes about 2 hours and costs 110Kč ($4.60). From Prague, the complete trip takes 5 hours via Brno and costs 430Kč ($18).

You can also take one of four **bus** trips from Prague's Florenc station, but this more than 3-hour trip via Brno is more cramped and less fun. The one-way fare is 188Kč ($7.85). From Brno, the trip is much quicker and less painful. Almost as many buses run between the two places as do trains.

VISITOR INFORMATION   In the center of the main square in Znojemská Beseda, **Informační Středisko,** Masarykovo nám. 22, Znojmo (© **515-222-552**), can help with accommodations, maps, and directions. Ask what's on in town, and they can book tickets for you on the spot. The office is open April to September, Monday to Saturday from 9am to 1pm and 1:30 to 5pm; and October to March, Monday to Friday from 9am to 1pm and 1:30 to 5pm, Saturday from 8am to 12:30pm. The city has an official website at www.znojmocity.cz.

SPECIAL EVENTS   In late August and early September, residents of Znojmo celebrate their vintages at the **Znojmo Wine Festival.** Taste wine, eat pickles, and listen to traditional Moravian music late into the night, which is normally tranquil on other nights. For details, contact **Informační Středisko** (see "Visitor Information," above).

ORIENTATION   Znojmo's main square is **Masarykovo náměstí,** and pretty much everything you'll want to see is on or near it. **Zelenářská Street,** which runs off the square's northwest corner, leads to the castle and St. Nicholas Church.

STROLLING THROUGH ZNOJMO

A walking tour of Znojmo takes about 2 to 3 hours. Begin at **Masaryk Square,** where the **Art House (Dům umění; ℭ 515-226-529)** holds a small collection of coins, plus temporary exhibitions. It is open Tuesday to Saturday from 9am to 6pm. Admission is 20Kč (85¢). The southern end of the square is one of the few historic areas that hasn't been maintained well; the dilapidated **Capuchin Monastery (Kapucínský klášter)** and **Church of St. John the Baptist** show few signs that they were once focal points of the town.

Impossible to miss is the **Town Hall Tower (ℭ 515-216-297),** the only remaining piece of what was once referred to as Moravia's prettiest town hall. The actual town hall met misfortune during World War II, but the late-Gothic 70m-high (230-ft.) tower still stands guard. For 25Kč ($1), you can climb up to the lookout, which offers a picturesque view of the castle and the Dyje River. Try not to let the nondescript department store that occupies the spot where the town hall once stood wreck the picture. The tower is open May to September, Monday to Friday 9am to 1pm and 2 to 6pm, Saturday and Sunday 9am to 1pm and 2 to 5pm; April, Monday to Friday from 9am to 1pm and 2 to 6pm, Saturday 9am to 1pm; and October to March, Monday to Friday 9am to 6pm, Saturday 9am to noon.

Directly north of the tower on Obroková ulice is the entrance to the **Znojemské podzemí (Znojmo Underground),** where almost 30km (19 miles) of tunnels used to store everything from pickles to munitions are accessed. If there's a tour just leaving or a few people waiting, arrange to join them, since the tours (which are in Czech only, though English-language pamphlets are provided) are given only to groups of more than six. Admission is 40Kč ($1.40). The Underground is open May, June, and September, daily 9am to 4pm; April, Monday to Saturday 10am to 4pm; July and August, daily 9am to 5pm; and October, Saturday only, 10am to 4pm. For reservations call ℭ **515-221-342.**

Head back 1 block west to Zelenářská ulice and follow it away from the square to Malá Mikulášská ulice, which leads to the Gothic **St. Nicholas Church** and behind it the bi-level **St. Wenceslas Chapel.** The church is supposed to be open only for services and the occasional concert, but check the door just in case.

Farther on, you'll come to the 11th-century **Rotunda sv. Kateřiny,** one of the oldest and best examples of Romanesque architecture still standing in the Czech Republic. Inside are painstakingly restored frescoes of the Premyslid rulers dating back to the mid–12th century.

The Painted Cellar of the Šatov Vineyard

Wine, art, and history aficionados unite! The **Painted Cellar of Šatov,** one of the region's most prolific vineyards, awaits. But this isn't an ordinary tour of a vineyard or just a historic place—it's both.

The town of Šatov lies just before the Austrian border, about 10km (6 miles) south of Znojmo. So close is Šatov to the border that it was once part of Austria. The town and its surrounding vineyards have long produced some of the country's finest Moravian wines. The excellent soil conditions and Continental climate make it perfectly suited for grapes.

You'll find several cellars here, and during late autumn Moravian hospitality opens the doors to just about anyone who knocks. Few, however, knock on the door of Josef Kučera, who can give a different sort of tour. Mr. Kučera, who once patrolled the border to ensure that the vices of capitalism didn't breach the country, will happily lead you down a hidden path for about half a mile to a small, unassuming house. Try to keep up, because Kučera sometimes gets so excited about showing newcomers the cellar that he literally talks and walks a mile a minute!

The house's **cellar** ⚔ was most likely carved out in the late 19th century for reasons still a mystery today, but it took on its current form when a one-armed man named Max Appeltauer took to the tunnels and began his work there in 1934. As you enter the cellar and descend about 18m (59 ft.), a musty odor envelops you and you wonder how Appeltauer could have spent so much time here. But as you look around the 20m (66-ft.) tunnel, you'll be thankful he did. Not an artist by trade, Appeltauer set to carving and then painting into the sandstone walls an **eclectic set of scenes** portraying everything from Prague Castle to Snow White and the Seven Dwarfs, as well as the Šatov coat of arms. Running off the main tunnel are five smaller rooms, each depicting a separate theme and carved and painted in painstaking detail.

It's almost as though Appeltauer was expecting to escape one day to his residence inside the cellar, celebrating his departure from life aboveground. Indeed, celebrating had already taken place inside the dark cellar, as the inscription VÍNO, ZENY A ZPĚV, ZAHLADÍ VESKER; HNĚV ("Wine, women, and song will remove all anger") indicates. Kučera will tell you that the cellar was at one time a popular place, where people gathered after Mass, girlfriends and all. Wives searching for their husbands would often enter, sending girlfriends scurrying into the subcellar. Local lore has it that Hitler visited the cellar when inspecting the military bunkers set up to defend his southern flank.

Appeltauer left the cellar for good in 1968 and died 4 years later, never realizing his next dream—to paint farther into the cellar. Some cans of paint and a few jars still sit idly by at the point where he stopped, untouched after 36 years of waiting for his return.

To get to Šatov by car, take Highway 59 out of Znojmo to the south and turn right at the sign for Šatov. Buses and trains also run to the village from Znojmo on a regular basis.

Call ✆ **721-754-548** to book your visit ahead.

At the edge of the embankment lies **Znojmo Castle,** which now houses the **Jihomoravské Muzeum (South Moravian Museum)** exhibition (✆ **515-222-311**). It focuses on the role of Znojmo through the ages, especially as a lookout against the Austro-Hungarian Empire. Admission is 40Kč ($1.65) adults, 20Kč (85¢) students; if you take the tour, note that both sights are included in the tour price. Open May to September Tuesday to Sunday from 9am to 5pm, and in April Saturday and Sunday 9am to 5pm.

WHERE TO STAY

There's not much in the way of quality accommodations in Znojmo, which is probably one reason why so few people spend the night. If you choose to stay, your best option may prove to be the information center, which can arrange a private room. Expect to pay around 500Kč ($20) per person.

Hotel Adler   This former villa, now a hotel with a fitness center and a restaurant with a terrace that overlooks the river valley, is a welcome relief from the dreary Communist-era hotels found throughout Znojmo. The rooms are small and a little sterile, but very bright; several have large bay windows. The "modern" furniture advertised by the hotel is not going to win any awards, but the beds are comfortable.

Na Valech 7, 669 02 Znojmo. ✆ **515-220-307.** 8 units. 1,200Kč ($50) double; 2,400Kč ($100) suite. AE, MC, V. Parking. **Amenities:** Restaurant; exercise room; sauna. *In room:* TV.

Hotel Dukla   In the south part of Znojmo, the Dukla gets its name from the army but is nicer than barracks. The rooms are functional and there is always a vacancy. And don't forget the hotel's discount; every 21st person in a group gets to stay for free!

Holandská 30, 669 02 Znojmo. ✆ **515-227-320.** www.hotel-dukla.cz. 112 units. 700Kč ($29) double; 1,400Kč ($58) suite. AE, DC, MC, V. **Amenities:** Restaurant. *In room:* TV.

Hotel Prestige ✍   Just off the road leading to Prague, this hotel used to be called Družba, and was exactly what a Communist-era hotel was meant to be—adequate but nothing more. Now, after a major makeover, it provides accommodations in cozy rooms with modern furniture and en-suite bathrooms. Bohemian, Moravian, and international food are on the menu in the hotel restaurant, which has a lovely garden terrace and bar. In the Moravian wine cellar, "At King John," you can order excellent wine from this region.

Pražská 100, 669 02 Znojmo. ✆ **515-224-595.** www.hotel-prestige.cz. 89 units. 1,950Kč ($81) double; 2,900Kč ($139) suite. AE, DC, MC, V. **Amenities:** Restaurant; bar; wine cellar; pool; exercise room; sauna; Internet lounge. *In room:* TV, minibar, fridge.

WHERE TO DINE

Morava CZECH/INTERNATIONAL   This small restaurant has a relatively big selection of meals and, not surprisingly, a good choice of Moravian wines. A renovation has contributed a relaxing, homey atmosphere that is far nicer than the Communist-era style of the hotel restaurants. Many items on the menu may look similar to those in other Czech restaurants, but the cooking has a south Moravian accent, lending it a little more spice. In particular, the pork dishes are well prepared with a nice blend of piquant spices.

Horní nám. 17. ✆ **515-224-147.** Soups 25Kč ($1); main courses 69Kč–219Kč ($2.85–$9.10). AE, MC, V. Mon–Sat 9am–10pm.

Appendix A:
Prague in Depth

THE CELTS & THE NEW BOHEMI- ANS A Celtic tribe, the Boii, first set- tled 300 years before Christ in the land around the Vltava River, which forms the heart of the present-day Czech territory. The Latin term Bohemia (Land of the Boii) became etched in history.

The Marcomanni, a Germanic tribe, banished the Boii around 100 B.C., only to be chucked out by the Huns by A.D. 450. The Huns, in turn, were expelled by a Turkic tribe, the Avars, about a century later.

Near the turn of the 6th century, Slavs crossed the Carpathian Mountains into Europe, and the westernmost of the Slavic tribes tried to set up a kingdom in Bohemia. The farming Slavs often fell prey to the nomadic Avars, but in 624 a Franconian merchant named Samo united the Slavs and began expelling the Avars from central Europe.

MORAVIAN EMPIRE Throughout the 9th century, the Slavs around the Morava River consolidated their power. Mojmír I declared his Great Moravian Empire—a kingdom that eventually encompassed Bohemia, Slovakia, and parts of modern Poland and Hungary— into a Christian organization still outside the boundaries of the Holy Roman Empire.

In 863, the Greek brothers Cyril and Methodius arrived in Moravia to preach the Eastern Christian rite to a people who didn't understand them. They created a new language mixing Slavic with a separate

script, which came to be known as Cyrillic. When Methodius died in 885, the Mora- vian rulers reestablished the Latin liturgy, though followers of Cyril and Methodius continued to preach their faith in missions to the east. Ultimately the Slavonic rite took hold in Kiev and Russia, where the Cyrillic alphabet is still used, while western Slavs kept the Latin script and followed Rome.

The Great Moravian Empire lasted about a century—until the Magyar inva- sion of 896—and not until the 20th cen- tury would the Czechs and Slovaks unite under a single government. After the invasion, the Slavs living east of the Morava swore allegiance to the Magyars, while the Czechs, who lived west of the river, fell under the authority of the Holy Roman Empire.

BOHEMIA LOOKS TO THE WEST Bořivoj, the first king of the now-separate Bohemia and Moravia, built Prague's first royal palace at the end of the 9th century on the site of the present Prague Castle on Hradčany Hill. In 973, a bishopric was established in Prague, answering to the archbishopric of Mainz. Thus, before the end of the first millennium, the Ger- man influence in Bohemia was firmly established.

The kings who followed Bořivoj in the Premyslid dynasty ruled over Bohemia for more than 300 years, during which time Prague became a major commercial area along central Europe's trade routes. In the 12th century, two fortified castles were built at Vyšehrad and Hradčany, and a wooden plank bridge stood near where the stone Charles Bridge spans the Vltava today. Václavské náměstí (Wenceslas Sq.) was a horse market, and the city's 3,500 residents rarely lived to the age of 45. In 1234, Staré Město (Old Town), the first of Prague's historic five towns, was founded.

Encouraged by Bohemia's rulers, who guaranteed German civic rights to western settlers, Germans founded entire towns around Prague, including Malá Strana (Lesser Town) in 1257. The Premyslid dynasty of the Czechs ended with the 1306 death of teenage Václav III, who had no heirs. After much debate, the throne was offered to John of Luxembourg, husband of Václav III's younger sister, a foreigner who knew little of Bohemia. It was John's first-born son who left the most lasting marks on Prague.

PRAGUE'S FIRST GOLDEN AGE

Charles IV (Karel IV), christened first as Václav, took the throne when his father died while fighting in France in 1346. Educated among French royalty and fluent in four languages (but not Czech), Charles almost single-handedly ushered in Prague's first golden age (the second occurred in the late 16th c.).

Even before his reign, Charles wanted to make Prague a glorious city (he eventually learned to speak Czech). In 1344,

he won an archbishopric for Prague independent of Mainz. When he became king of Bohemia, Charles also became, by election, Holy Roman emperor.

During the next 30 years of his reign, Charles transformed Prague into the bustling capital of the Holy Roman Empire and one of Europe's most important cities, with some of the most glorious architecture of its day. He commissioned St. Vitus Cathedral's construction at Prague Castle as well as the bridge that would eventually bear his name. He was most proud of founding Prague University in 1348, the first higher-education institution in central Europe, now known as Charles University. In 1378, Charles died of natural causes at age 62.

PROTESTANT REFORMATION

While Charles IV was the most heralded of the Bohemian kings, the short reign of his son Václav IV was marked by social upheaval, a devastating plague, and the advent of turbulent religious dissent.

Reformist priest Jan Hus drew large crowds to Bethlehem Chapel, where he preached against what he considered the corrupt tendencies of Prague's bishopric. Hus became widely popular among Czech nationals who rallied behind his crusade against the German-dominated establishment. Excommunicated in 1412 and charged with heresy 2 years later, Hus was burned at the stake on July 6, 1415,

---

Dateline

- **300 B.C.** Celtic people, the Boii, settle in the area of today's Czech Republic, naming it Bohemia.
- **A.D. 450** Huns and other Eastern peoples arrive in Bohemia.
- **870** Bohemia becomes part of the Holy Roman Empire. Castle constructed in Hradčany.

- **973** Bishopric founded in Prague.
- **1158** First stone bridge spans the Vltava.
- **1234** Staré Město (Old Town) founded, the first of Prague's historic five towns.
- **1257** Malá Strana (Lesser Town) established by German colonists.
- **1306** Premyslid dynasty ends following the death of

teenage Václav III, who leaves no heir.
- **1344** Prague bishopric raised to an archbishopric.
- **1346** Charles IV becomes king and later Holy Roman emperor, as Prague's golden age begins.
- **1403** Jan Hus becomes rector of the University of Prague and launches a crusade for religious reform.

continued

in Konstanz (Constance), Germany, an event that sparked widespread riots and ultimately civil war. Czechs still commemorate the day as a national holiday.

THE HUSSITE WARS　The hostilities began simply enough. Rioting Hussites (followers of Jan Hus) threw several Roman Catholic councilors to their deaths from the windows of Prague's New Town Hall (Novoměstská radnice) in 1419, a deed known as the First Defenestration. It didn't take long for the pope to declare a crusade against the Czech heretics. The conflict widened into class struggle, and by 1420 several major battles were being fought between the peasant Hussites and the Catholic crusaders, who were supported by the nobility. A schism split the Hussites when a more moderate faction, known as the Utraquists, signed a 1433 peace agreement with Rome at the Council of Basel. Still, the more radical Taborites continued to fight, until they were decisively defeated at the Battle of Lipany.

HABSBURG RULE　Following this, the nobility of Bohemia concentrated its power, forming fiefdoms called the Estates. In 1526, the nobles elected Archduke Ferdinand king of Bohemia, marking the beginning of Roman Catholic rule by the Austrian Habsburgs, which continued until World War I. Rudolf II ascended to the throne in 1576, reestablishing Prague as the seat of the Habsburg empire and presiding over what was to be known as Prague's second Ggolden age. He invited the great astronomers Johannes Kepler and Tycho de Brahe to Prague and endowed the city's museums with some of Europe's finest art. The Rudolfinum, which was recently restored and houses the Czech Philharmonic, pays tribute to Rudolf's opulence.

Conflicts between the Catholic Habsburgs and Bohemia's growing Protestant nobility came to a head on May 23, 1618, when two Catholic governors were thrown out of the windows of Prague Castle, in the Second Defenestration. This event marked the start of a series of complex politico-religious conflicts known as the Thirty Years' War. After a Swedish army was defeated on Charles Bridge by a local force that included Prague's Jews and students, the war came to an end with the Peace of Westphalia. The Catholics won a decisive victory, and the empire's focus shifted back to Vienna. Fresh waves of immigrants turned Prague and other towns into Germanic cities. By the end of the 18th century, the Czech language was on the verge of dying out.

INTO THE 20TH CENTURY

THE CZECH REVIVAL　In the 19th century, the Industrial Revolution drew

- **1415** Hus burned at the stake by German Catholics, and decades of religious warfare begin.
- **1419** Roman Catholic councilors thrown from the windows of New Town Hall in the First Defenestration.
- **1434** Radical Hussites, called Taborites, defeated in the Battle of Lipany, ending religious warfare.

- **1526** Roman Catholic Habsburgs gain control of Bohemia.
- **1584** Prague made seat of the imperial court of Rudolf II.
- **1618** Second Defenestration helps ignite Thirty Years' War, entrenching Habsburg rule.
- **1648** Praguers defend the city against invading Swedes—stopping them on

Charles Bridge in the last military action of the Thirty Years' War.
- **1784** Prague's five towns united.
- **1818** National Museum founded.
- **1848** Industrial Revolution begins in Prague, drawing villagers to the city and fueling Czech national revival.
- **1875** Horse-drawn trams operate on Prague's streets.

Czechs from the countryside into Prague, where a Czech national revival began.

As the industrial economy grew, Prague's Czech population increased in number and power, overtaking the Germans. In 1868, the Czech people threw open the doors to the gilded symbol of their revival, the neo-Renaissance National Theater (Národní divadlo), with the bold proclamation NÁROD SOBĚ ("The Nation for Itself") inscribed over the proscenium. Then, in 1890, at the top of Wenceslas Square, the massive National Museum Building (Národní muzeum) opened, packed with exhibits celebrating the rich history and culture of the Czech people.

As the new century emerged, Prague was on the cusp of the Art Nouveau wave sweeping Europe, and Moravian Alfons Mucha's sensuous painting of Sarah Bernhardt wowed Paris.

THE FOUNDING OF THE REPUBLIC OF CZECHOSLOVAKIA
As Czech political parties continued to call for more autonomy from Vienna, Archduke Ferdinand and his wife, Sophie, were assassinated in Sarajevo, setting off World War I. Meanwhile, a 65-year-old philosophy professor named Tomáš Masaryk seized the opportunity to tour Europe and America, speaking in favor of creating a combined democratic Czech and Slovak state. He was supported by a Slovak scientist, Milan Štefánik.

As the German and Austrian armies wore down in 1918, the concept of "Czechoslovakia" gained international support. U.S. President Woodrow Wilson backed Masaryk on October 18, 1918, in Washington, D.C., as the professor proclaimed the independence of the Czechoslovak Republic in the Washington Declaration. On October 28, 1918, the sovereign Republic of Czechoslovakia was founded in Prague. Masaryk returned home in December after being elected (in absentia) Czechoslovakia's first president.

THE FIRST REPUBLIC
The 1920s ushered in an exceptional but brief period of freedom and prosperity in Prague. Czechoslovakia, its industrial strength intact after the war, was one of the 10 strongest economies in the world. Prague's capitalists lived the Jazz Age on a par with New York's industrial barons. Palatial Art Nouveau villas graced the fashionable Bubeneč and Hanspaulka districts, where smart parties were held nonstop.

The Great Depression gradually spread to Prague, however, drawing sharper lines between the classes and nationalities. As ethnic Germans in Czech border regions found a champion in the new German Chancellor Adolf Hitler in 1933, their

---

- **1881** National Theater completed during wave of Czech push for statehood against Austro-Hungarian rule.
- **1883** Franz Kafka born in Staré Město.
- **1918** Czechoslovakia founded at the end of World War I after the fall of the Austro-Hungarian Empire. Independence leader Tomáš G. Masaryk becomes first president.

- **1921** Prague's boundaries expand to encompass neighboring villages and settlements.
- **1938** Leaders of Germany, Great Britain, Italy, and France meet to cede Czech border territories (the Sudetenland) to Hitler in the Munich Agreement.
- **1939** Hitler absorbs the rest of the Czech lands as a German

protectorate; puppet Slovak Republic established.
- **1940s** In World War II, more than 130,000 Czechs murdered, including more than 80,000 Jews.
- **1942** Nazi protectorate leader Reinhard Heydrich assassinated in Prague by soldiers trained in England. Hitler retaliates with the mass murder and destruction

continued

calls to unify under the Third Reich grew louder.

In 1938, Britain's Neville Chamberlain and France's Edouard Daladier, seeking to avoid conflict with the increasingly belligerent Germans, met Hitler and Italy's Benito Mussolini in Munich. Their agreement to cede the Bohemian areas (which Germans called the Sudetenland) to Hitler on September 30 marked one of the darkest days in Czech history.

Chamberlain returned to London to tell a cheering crowd that he'd achieved "peace in our time." But within a year, Hitler absorbed the rest of the Czech lands and installed a puppet government in Slovakia. Soon Europe was again at war.

WORLD WAR II During the next 6 years, more than 130,000 Czechs were systematically murdered, including more than 80,000 Jews. Though Hitler ordered devastation for other cities, he sought to preserve Prague and its Jewish ghetto as part of his planned museum of the extinct race.

The Nazi concentration camp at Terezín, about 48km (30 miles) northwest of Prague, became a way station for many Czech Jews bound for death camps at Auschwitz and Buchenwald. Thousands died of starvation and disease at Terezín even though the Nazis managed to dress it up as a "show" camp for Red Cross investigators.

Meanwhile, the Czechoslovak government in exile, led by Masaryk's successor, Edvard Beneš, tried to organize resistance from friendly territory in London. One initiative was launched in May 1942 when two Czechoslovak paratroopers, in a mission called Anthropoid, attempted to assassinate Hitler's lead man in Prague, Reich Protector Reinhard Heydrich. Setting a charge at an intersection north of Prague, the soldiers stopped Heydrich's limousine and opened fire, fatally wounding him.

Hitler retaliated by ordering the total liquidation of a nearby Czech village, Lidice, where 192 men were shot dead and more than 300 women and children were sent to concentration camps. Every building in the town was bulldozed to the ground.

The soldiers, Jozef Gabčík and Jan Kubiš, were hunted down by Nazi police and trapped in the Cyril and Methodius church on Resslova Street near the Vltava. They reportedly shot themselves to avoid being captured. The debate still rages on whether Anthropoid brought anything but more terror to occupied Bohemia.

THE ADVENT OF COMMUNISM
The final act of World War II in Europe played out where the Nazis started it, in Bohemia. As U.S. troops liberated the western part of the country, Gen. George Patton was told to hold his troops at

---

of the nearby village of Lidice.

- **1945** American army liberates western Bohemia and Soviet army liberates Prague; 2.5 million Germans expelled; their property expropriated under decrees of returning President Edvard Beneš.

- **1946** Communist leader Klement Gottwald appointed prime minister after his party wins 38% of vote.

- **1948** Communists seize power amid Cabinet crisis.

- **1950s** Top Jewish Communists executed in purge as Stalinism reaches its peak. Giant statue of Stalin unveiled on Letná plain overlooking Prague (then destroyed after his death).

- **1968** Alexander Dubček becomes general secretary of the Communist Party and launches "Prague Spring"

reforms; in August, Soviet-led Warsaw Pact troops invade and occupy Czechoslovakia.

- **1977** Czech dissidents form Charter 77 to protest suppression of human rights during Communist "normalization."

- **1989** Student-led antigovernment protests erupt into revolution; Communist government resigns; Parliament nominates playwright Václav Havel for president.

Plzeň and wait for the Soviet army to sweep through Prague because of the Allied Powers agreement made at Yalta months before. Soviet soldiers and Czech civilians liberated Prague in a bloody street battle on May 9, 1945, a day after the Germans had signed their capitulation. Throughout Prague you can see small wall memorials on the spots where Czechs fell that day battling the Germans.

On his return from exile in England, Edvard Beneš ordered the expulsion of 2.5 million Germans from Czechoslovakia and the confiscation of all their property. (An agreement between Prague and Bonn in early 1997 tried to put an end to compensation demands from the families of expropriated Germans and the Czech victims of war crimes by setting up a joint fund, but the demands continue.) Meanwhile, the government, exhausted and bewildered by fascism, nationalized 60% of the country's industries, and many looked to Soviet-style Communism as a new model. Elections were held in 1946, and Communist leader Klement Gottwald became prime minister after his party won about one-third of the vote.

Through a series of Cabinet maneuvers, Communists seized full control of the government in 1948, and Beneš was ousted. Little dissent was tolerated, and a series of show trials began, purging hundreds of perceived threats to Stalinist Communist authority. Another wave of political refugees fled the country. The sterile, centrally planned Communist architecture began seeping into classical Prague.

THE PRAGUE SPRING In January 1968, Alexander Dubček, a career Slovak Communist, became first secretary of the Czechoslovak Communist Party. Long before Mikhail Gorbachev, Dubček tinkered with Communist reforms that he called "socialism with a human face." His program of political, economic, and social reform (while seeking to maintain one-party rule) blossomed into a brief intellectual and artistic renaissance known as the "Prague Spring."

Increasingly nervous about what seemed to them a loss of party control, Communist hard-liners in Prague and other Eastern European capitals conspired with the Soviet Union to remove Dubček and the government. On August 21, 1968, Prague awoke to the rumble of tanks and 200,000 invading Warsaw Pact soldiers claiming "fraternal assistance." Believing that they'd be welcomed as liberators, these soldiers from the Soviet Union, Poland, East Germany, Bulgaria, and Hungary were bewildered when angry Czechs confronted them with rocks and flaming torches. The Communist grip tightened, however, and Prague fell deeper into the Soviet sphere of influence.

- **1990** Free elections held; Havel's loose movement Civic Forum captures 170 of 300 parliamentary seats.
- **1991** Country begins massive program of privatizing shares in thousands of companies by distributing coupons that can be exchanged for stock.
- **1992** Havel resigns, saying he doesn't want to preside over the division of Czechoslovakia.

- **1993** Czechoslovakia splits into independent Czech and Slovak states—the "Velvet Divorce"—by mutual agreement of cabinets. Havel accepts new 5-year term as president of the independent Czech Republic. Country given first investment-grade rating of any post-Communist country by U.S. bond agencies.
- **1995** Czech Republic invited to join the OECD,

an organization of the world's richest countries.
- **1996** Chain-smoking Havel nearly dies after surgery to remove a cancerous lung tumor; he later has two more operations.
- **1997** Prague-born Madeleine Albright, the daughter of a Czechoslovak diplomat, is appointed U.S. secretary of state, becoming

continued

Another wave of refugees fled. The following January, a university student named Jan Palach, in a lonely protest to Soviet occupation, doused himself with gasoline and set himself afire in Wenceslas Square. He died days later, becoming a martyr for the dissident movement. But the Soviet soldiers stayed for more than 2 decades during the gray period the Communists called "normalization."

CHARTER 77   In 1976, during the worst of "normalization," the Communists arrested a popular underground rock band called the Plastic People of the Universe on charges of disturbing the peace. This motivated some of Prague's most prominent artists, writers, and intellectuals, led by playwright Václav Havel, to establish Charter 77, a human-rights advocacy group formed to pressure the government—then Europe's most repressive—into observing the human rights principles of the 1975 Helsinki Accords. In the years that followed, Havel, the group's perceived leader, was constantly monitored by the secret police, the StB. He was put under house arrest and jailed several times for "threatening public order."

THE VELVET REVOLUTION & BEYOND

THE VELVET REVOLUTION   Just after the Berlin Wall fell, and with major change imminent in Eastern Europe, thousands of students set out on a chilly candlelit March on November 17, 1989. As part of their nonviolent campaign, they held signs simply calling for a dialog with the government. Against police warnings, they marched from the southern citadel at Vyšehrad and turned up National Boulevard (Národní třída), where they soon met columns of helmeted riot police. Holding their fingers in peace signs and chanting, "Our hands are free," the bravest 500 sat down at the feet of the police. After an excruciating standoff, the police moved in, squeezing the students against buildings and wildly beating them with clubs.

Although nobody was killed and the official Communist-run media presented the story as the quiet, justified end to the whims of student radicals, clandestine videotapes and accounts of the incident blanketed the country. By the next day, Praguers began organizing their outrage. Havel and his artistic allies seized the moment and called a meeting of intellectuals at the Laterna Magika on Národní, where they planned more nonviolent protests. Students and theaters went on strike, and hundreds of thousands of Praguers began pouring into Wenceslas Square, chanting for the end of Communist rule. Within days, factory workers and citizens in towns throughout the

---

the highest-ranking woman ever in the U.S. government. July floods devastate much of the eastern part of the country.

- **1998** Havel wins another 5-year term, his final allowed under the constitution. Special elections in June result in a center-left government being sworn in by Havel after the center-right cabinet, in power for 6 years, resigns

due to a party financing scandal.
- **1999** The Czech Republic, along with Hungary and Poland, becomes one of the first ex–Soviet Bloc states to join NATO, while talks on joining the European Union drag on.
- **2000** Prague joins eight other cities named by the European Union as "European Cities of Culture 2000,"

with celebrations and events held throughout the city. In September the city hosts International Monetary Fund/World Bank meetings (made famous for their spectacular clashes between police and antiglobalization protestors).
- **2002** Fate tests the city once again in August when record floodwaters from the Vltava River engulf much of Lesser

country joined in a general strike. In Wenceslas Square, the protesters jingled their keys, a signal to the Politburo that it was time to go. On November 24, General Secretary Miloš Jakeš resigned, and by the end of the year, the Communist government fell. By New Year's Eve, Havel, joined by Dubček, gave his first speech as president of a free Czechoslovakia. Because hardly any blood was spilled, the coup d'état was dubbed "the Velvet Revolution."

ECONOMIC & POLITICAL CHANGES

In June 1990, the first free elections in 44 years gave power to the Civic Forum, the movement led by Havel. But it was Václav Klaus who launched the country on its course of economic reform. First as federal finance minister and then as Czech prime minister, Klaus, an economist, helped form a right-wing offshoot of the Civic Forum called the Civic Democratic Party; it won the 1992 elections on a program of massive privatization. First, thousands of small businesses were auctioned off for a song. By the end of 1994, shares in some 1,800 large companies were privatized by giving citizens government coupons they could exchange for stock or fund shares. In less than 5 years, private companies churned out 80% of the Czech economy.

A VELVET DIVORCE GIVES WAY TO A NEW UNION

In 1992, leaders of the Czech and Slovak republics peacefully agreed to split into separate states. The Slovaks wanted to get out of the shadow of Prague (Slovak nationalists had been calling for that since 1918), and the Czech government was happy to get rid of the expected financial burdens of Slovakia's slower reconstruction. The "Velvet Divorce" was final on January 1, 1993, with common property split on a 2-to-1 ratio, without lawyers taking anything—yet. They're still arguing over gold assets and bank accounts, just like any other acrimonious couple.

Privatization, however, did little to bring in new capital or energize management at larger companies. Meanwhile, Czechs bought up Western goods and equipment and ignored domestic suppliers. Speculators pounced on the imbalance to force the central bank to float the Czech crown, causing it to dive in the spring of 1997.

As socioeconomic divisions have widened, voices of discontent have grown louder. Czech reforms hit a wall in 1997, damaged by a series of financial scandals and poor competitiveness. Klaus and his center-right government barely clung to power in the 1996 elections. In November 1997, a fund-raising scandal blew up around Klaus and his party, forcing the

Town and part of Old Town, putting many restaurants and attractions near the riverfront out of business for months. Also, the Czechs have the honor of hosting the western military alliance's annual summit. U.S. President George W. Bush, U.K. Prime Minister Tony Blair, and leaders of all NATO member states join Czech President Václav Havel in Prague Castle.

- **2003** Václav Havel's term as president ends. The new president, Václav Klaus, is elected.
- **2004** The Czech Republic is one of 10 countries to join the European Union.

From Prisoner to President: Václav Havel

*In an atmosphere of decency, creativity, tolerance, and quiet resolution,
we shall bear far more easily the trials we have yet to experience, and
resolve all the large problems we must face.*

—Václav Havel addressing the nation (January 1, 1992)

Václav Havel's often frustrating personal crusade for morality and honesty
in politics made him a most unlikely world leader.

Born in 1936 to a wealthy building developer, he was on the wrong side
of Communism's bourgeois divide and wasn't allowed a top education. His
interest in theater grew from his stint as a set boy and led to the staging of
his first plays at Prague's Theater on the Balustrade (Divadlo Na Zábradlí).
His play *The Garden Party* was widely acclaimed, and he became the playwright from the place he'd later call Absurdistan. After Havel publicly criti-
cized the Soviet invasion and Communist policies, his plays and essays were
banned.

In 1977, he helped draft Charter 77, a manifesto urging the government
to respect human rights and decency; it was condemned by the politburo as
a subversive act. Under almost constant surveillance by the StB (secret
police), Havel was placed under house arrest and imprisoned several times.
His philosophical writings about life under repression during that period—
especially his essay "The Power of the Powerless"—became world-
renowned for their insight into the dark gray world behind the iron curtain.

He was a natural choice for a leader when well-read students and artists
decided that the time was ripe for revolution.

Soon after Havel led the citizen's movement, Civic Forum, that ousted the
Communist government in 1989, he told a joint session of the U.S. Congress
why he accepted the offer to be president: "Intellectuals cannot go on forever avoiding their share of responsibility for the world and hiding their dis-
taste for politics under an alleged need to be independent." Virtually
overnight, he moved from the prison dungeon to the presidential throne,
though he chose to live in his modest apartment on the river even when he
could have lived in Prague Castle. (Havel now lives in a stylish villa in the
smart part of town.)

After the peaceful split of Czechoslovakia into two countries in 1993, he
was elected the first president of the now-independent Czech Republic.

In late 1996, the chain-smoking, 60-year-old Havel was diagnosed with a
small malignant tumor on his lung. The surgery to remove half of one lobe
almost cost him his life less than a year after his wife, Olga, died of cancer.
He has since survived no fewer than three life-threatening illnesses. In the
midst of the first painful and frightening recuperation, Havel shocked the
country by getting married again, this time to a popular (and much
younger) stage and screen actress, Dagmar Veškrnová.

In an interview in mid-1997, the normally reserved Havel railed at the media's negative reaction to his surprise marriage. "I would not hold a referendum on this. I am the one who has to live with my wife, not anyone else," he said to a reporter in an uncommonly terse fashion. Havel also bristles at anyone who suggests that he should become an antismoking advocate after his ordeal, saying that people should have "the right to decide how to kill themselves."

After returning to full duties, the still-popular philosopher won his last 5-year term allowed under the constitution in early 1998. Havel, however, hasn't dirtied his hands much in the rough-and-tumble of postrevolutionary politics, instead using his mostly ceremonial post to act as a moral balancing wheel, warning against possible excesses of the new freedoms.

"From the West we have learned to live in a soulless world of stupid advertisements and even more stupid sitcoms and we are allowing them to drain our lives and our spirits," he told the nation in a speech marking the fifth anniversary of the Velvet Revolution.

Havel has an office full of honors from abroad, including the Roosevelt Four-Freedoms Medal, the Philadelphia Freedom Medal, France's Grande Croix de la Légion d'Honneur, and India's Indira Gandhi Prize. He has been short-listed for the Nobel Peace Prize numerous times, but has never won. An unabashed fan of rock music, Havel kept close company with Frank Zappa until Zappa's death, and he has had friendly meetings with Bruce Springsteen, Lou Reed, Pink Floyd, Bob Dylan, and Joan Baez. He once held up traffic at an Australian airport to have a conversation on the tarmac with Mick Jagger.

The longest reign of any post-Communist president came to an end in February 2003, when Havel was forced by the Constitution to step down. Many Czechs felt he was past his prime as president after 13 years in office, but he remains the most recognizable symbol of the country abroad. Havel returned to his previous life as a philosopher and writer, and spends a lot of his time working in the philanthropic foundation he set up with his wife.

With no apparent successor of Havel's stature available, the contest to replace him turned to farce. On several occasions the parliament could not muster the majority vote needed to elect a new head of state. For weeks, the country was without a president. Finally, some bizarre political gymnastics between the parties led to the election of Havel's archrival Václav Klaus—the former prime minister with whom Havel clashed over social and economic policies throughout the 1990s. Klaus, who frequently scoffed at Havel's idealism and warm acceptance of the European Union, has found many cold shoulders in the palaces of Europe since taking over for his 5-year term.

government to resign. New elections were held in mid-1998, bringing the first left-wing government to power since the revolution, the center-left Social Democrats, not the Communists.

Still, Czech politicians pushed to prove that the country belongs in the big leagues. The Czechs became one of the first former Soviet-bloc states to join NATO in 1999, along with Poland and Hungary (though about half of the country, according to polls, isn't sure it's a good idea).

In May 2004, the Czechs joined nine other countries to become new members of the European Union, completing a quest that the newly elected Democratic leaders started 14 years ago. While the country has promised to eventually change to the E.U.'s common currency, the euro, this won't happen for several years, until there is even more convergence in economic strength. In the meantime, things generally are more expensive as GDP grows. Even though wider access to better-quality suppliers and the competition created by it led to lower prices on some goods, luxurious items and electronics are still more expensive than in western Europe. On the other hand, food and services are cheaper and more affordable.

CRIME & RACISM Throughout Eastern Europe, overt racism appears to be an unwelcome byproduct of revolution. Romanies (Gypsies) and Jews have been the targets of many attacks. The government has stepped up efforts to weed out and crack down on racist groups (most are called Skinheads) after several violent incidents. In 1997, hundreds of Romanies sold their meager possessions to pay for plane tickets to Canada because of a local TV report that said they would find asylum there. They didn't, and most were sent back, penniless and hopeless. Since then, many more have tried to win asylum in Britain, Sweden, and Finland, creating friction in talks on E.U. membership.

With police carrying a smaller stick, crime has risen sharply, as pickpockets and car thieves take advantage of Prague's new prosperity. Violent crime, while rising, is still well under American levels, and Prague's streets and parks are safer than those in most large Western cities.

2 The City Today

Prague was ready for prime time and the First World competitive pressures that full membership of the European Union brought in May 2004. The first decade of a return to capitalism is well past, and the city has taken on the familiar air of a European metropolis that makes a good living from tourism. The most-visited castles and cathedrals are now surrounded by entrepreneurs trying to make back the bucks (or *koruny*) denied to them under Communism—and they're trying to make them back as quickly as possible. For example, a bottle of water that costs just 15Kč (60¢) in most shops can cost 50Kč ($2.05) or more when purchased from a cart in the main tourist areas. Needless to say, vendors have definitely caught on to the theories of supply and demand.

Developers are also making the most of new opportunities. The pounding of jackhammers and the hollow thump of scaffolding being raised and lowered incessantly are the sounds most often blending with the bells and whir of ubiquitous streetcars. There's hardly a corner you'll turn where cobblestones haven't been dug up or sidewalks torn out.

Prague is a city rebuilding its face and its spirit. It's trying to keep up with the massive new flood of cars and visitors and is getting used to the pros and cons of its renewed affluence.

DISASTER IN 2002

The one flood the city could not absorb struck many riverfront areas as well as villages and towns throughout the country in August 2002. It was the worst flooding on record in the historic lands of Bohemia and Moravia. Entire communities were flattened, and much of Prague's ancient districts of Old Town and Malá Strana drowned under flows that reached high above the door frames. A wide swath of the underground metro system was destroyed. Some of the finest restaurants not only lost their alfresco dining areas for months, but were put completely out of business.

But the city responded quickly to its biggest test yet, and returned to its former glory after just a few months of hard work. The metro has been fully restored, cultural landmarks have been cleaned and polished (though not all of them), and most restaurants and shops have reopened and even improved their decor with the insurance money provided, although some had to call it a day.

AT THE CROSSROADS OF EUROPE

Prague lies at the epicenter of Bohemia, which borders Germany to the north and west and Austria to the south. Slovakia to the east (which joined with the Czechs at the end of the Austro-Hungarian Empire in 1918 to form the Republic of Czechoslovakia) split with its Slavic neighbor in 1993 to form the independent Czech and Slovak republics in the "Velvet Divorce."

About 10.3 million people inhabit the Czech lands of Bohemia and Moravia, with about 1.2 million living in the dozen districts comprising the Prague metropolitan area. A small percentage of Praguers live in the city center, which is most frequented by visitors, although that number is dropping as many buildings are bought and remodeled to satisfy the high-paying demand for quality office space.

Most Praguers actually live in the Communist-built housing estates (*paneláky*) ringing the city. In the high summer season, visitors outnumber locals two to one in most main areas in the city, taking away much of Prague's indigenous character.

THE CZECH LANGUAGE

Bohemia, through good times and bad, has been under a strong Germanic influence, and throughout a great deal of its history, German was the preferred language of the power elite. The Czech language, however, stems from the Slavic family, which includes Polish, Russian, Slovak, and others, though German has altered many Czech words. Czech uses a Latin alphabet with some letters topped by a small hat called a háček to denote Slavic phonic combinations like "sh" for š, "ch" for č, and, everyone's favorite, "rzh" for ř. Slovak differs slightly from Czech, but Czechs and Slovaks understand each other's language.

English, however, has become the postrevolutionary foreign tongue of choice for Prague movers and shakers, though German is more abundant in border areas. Outside Prague, it's rare to find someone who speaks English fluently, so be patient, expect to be misunderstood, and cultivate a sense of humor. Many newer words in the Czech vocabulary derive from capitalist English, like *marketink* and *e-byznys,* or from pop culture (*rokenrol*). See appendix B for a basic Czech glossary.

3 The Spoils of Revolution: Capitalism & Culture

Prague has once again become a well-heeled business center in the heart of central Europe. Nostalgic and successful Czechs say it's capitalism, not Communism, that comes most naturally here.

THE FIRST REPUBLIC LIVES ON

If you talk to a Praguer long enough, the conversation will often turn into a lecture about how the country had one of the world's richest economies, per capita, between the world wars. Communism, a Praguer will say, was just a detour. The between-wars period, lovingly called the First Republic, recalls a time when democracy and capitalism thrived, and Prague's bistros and dance halls were filled with dandies and flappers swinging the night away, until the Nazi invasion in 1939 spoiled the party.

The First Republic motif has been revived in many clubs and restaurants, and you can see hints of this style in Czech editions of top Western fashion magazines.

Since the Velvet Revolution, Praguers have been obsessed with style. Many people—especially the *novobohatí* (nouveau riche)—rushed out to buy the flashiest Mercedes or BMW they could find with the quick money gained from the restitution of Communist-seized property.

While the average annual income per person is still just around $9,000, the trappings of conspicuous consumption are evident throughout Prague, from the designer boutiques in the city center to the newly developed luxury suburbs with split-level ranch homes and tailored lawns. Women's fashion has had the most stunning revolution: The blur of loud polyester minidresses that used to dominate the streets has been replaced by the latest looks from Europe's catwalks.

Prague's avant-garde art community used to thrive in secret while mocking Communism, but it now has to face the realities of capitalism, such as rising rents and stiff competition. Many have had to find more mainstream work to survive. But if you look hard enough, you still might find an exhibition, a dance recital, or an experimental performance that's surprising, shocking, and satisfying. The *Prague Post,* the English-language weekly, usually serves as a good source for finding these events.

In the evening, you can find a typical Bohemian playing cards with friends at the neighborhood *hospoda* or *pivnice* (beer hall) or debating at a *kavárna* (cafe). Most likely, though, the typical Czech will be parked in front of the TV, as the country maintains one of the highest per-capita nightly viewing audiences in Europe. TV Nova—launched by the company of New York cosmetics scion Ronald Lauder—attracts around 60% of the population with a nightly mix of dubbed American action films, sitcoms (*M*A*S*H* has been wildly popular), and tabloid news shows. In the most public example of foreign investment gone awry, Lauder's company was thrown out of TV Nova by his Czech partners in 1999, and hundreds of millions of dollars in lawsuits have been batted around in international courts.

Pop literature has also overwhelmed the classics since the Velvet Revolution, with scandal sheets surging in newspaper sales and pulp fiction romances ruling the bookshops.

CZECH POLITICAL & RELIGIOUS BELIEFS

While Praguers tend to look westward and insist that they never belonged in the Soviet Bloc, the average Czech has been ambivalent about the government's push to join the European Union and the NATO security alliance. That's understandable after a long history of living under various foreign spheres of influence.

In contrast to neighboring Poland, Hungary, and former partner Slovakia, the Czech Republic isn't deeply religious. Although Prague was once the seat of the Holy Roman Empire and churches lace the city, less than 20% of the Czech people today say that they believe in God and around 10% say that they're religious.

One opinion poll showed that more Czechs believe in UFOs than believe in God.

Czechs may not be religious, but they're often superstitious. One piece of folk wisdom is similar to the one about Groundhog Day in the United States. If it rains on the day of Medard (June 8), Czechs plan to carry an umbrella another 40 consecutive days. They also believe that having a baby carriage in the house before a child is born is extremely bad luck for your expected child's future.

Each day on the calendar corresponds to one or more of the Czech first names, and it's customary to present a gift to close friends and colleagues on their *svátek* (name day)—it's like having two birthdays a year.

TODAY'S CHALLENGES

The city now faces a host of problems that didn't occur under Communism. Taxi drivers, who were strictly licensed under the old regime and formed a small exclusive club, have become one of the mayor's biggest headaches. Reports that these new entrepreneurs have been gouging tourists have grown exponentially with the number of drivers and visitors. And prostitutes, who were kept behind closed doors in the old days, now solicit business from convent steps.

Leaders have tried to keep a lid on anything that might cast a shadow over the best sights, including a tornado of billboards and the blight of graffiti. They're also searching for a way to curb the traffic rambling through the ancient streets. Though eyesores keep popping up, traffic keeps getting worse, and finicky phones wear you down, Prague is still a magical romp of a city.

THE AMERICAN INVASION

After the Velvet Revolution, Czechs sought the antithesis of Communism—anything that could be called Western.

And Westerners became quite curious about life on the other side of the raised iron curtain.

So postrevolutionary Prague quickly came to know a once-rare species: the American. An estimated 30,000 came to live here, either legally or illegally. Many were 20-somethings postponing the inevitable job hunt in a place where free love, cheap beer, and bad poetry were the order of the day. Some claimed it was a chance to get a taste of the 1960s their parents had always talked about.

But Prague hasn't replicated the rebelliousness of the Left Bank of Paris in the 1920s or San Francisco's Haight-Ashbury in the 1960s. Today's increasingly Western consumer habits make being bohemian in Bohemia somewhat ironic. "There's no bathtub" or "I can't find any iceberg lettuce," complain sandaled masses, yearning to drink cheap beer and write haiku.

With the American invasion came the inevitable array of shops and services for those who really didn't want to wander so far from home. At the spot on Národní třída (National Blvd.) where the Velvet Revolution began, the U.S. discount retailer Kmart bought out an old Communist state department store known as the Máj. It has since been sold to the British chain Tesco, which sells such goods as peanut butter, microwave popcorn, nacho cheese tortilla chips, and fudge brownie mix.

Rising rents and beer prices and a lack of jobs with Western-level pay have pushed many back home. While many Czechs welcomed the "Američany" soon after the Velvet Revolution, they're now using the pejorative moniker "Amíci" more frequently. Perhaps familiarity does breed contempt. And yet, the new presence cannot be denied. At this writing, one general weekly newspaper, the *Prague Post,* dominates the English-language audience, after a flurry of other postrevolutionary attempts failed. Several business magazines and weeklies have popped up, the best of which is the *Prague Business* *Journal.* Sports bars, taco stands, and Chicago-style pizzerias thrive.

4 Famous Czechs

Princess Libuše (pre–9th c.) Fabled mother of Bohemia. Legend holds that the clairvoyant Libuše, the daughter of Bohemian philosopher Krok, stood on a cliff on Vyšehrad Hill looking over the Vltava and foretold that on this land a great city would stand. She and Prince Přemysl Oráč declared the first Bohemian state, launching the Premyslid dynasty, which lasted from the 10th to the 12th century.

St. Wenceslas (Svatý Václav) (ca. 907–935) Patron saint of Bohemia. Prince Wenceslas was executed at the site of the present-day city of Stará Boleslav—on the orders of his younger brother, Boleslav, who took over the Bohemian throne. A popular cult arose proclaiming the affable and learned Prince Wenceslas as the perpetual spiritual ruler of all Czechs. The horse market, Prague's traditional meeting place, was the scene of a brief thrust of Czech nationalism against the Austrian Empire in 1848, when people named the place Wenceslas Square (Václavské nám.). A statue at the top of the square, depicting the horse-mounted warrior, was erected in 1912.

Charles IV (Karel IV) (1316–78) Bohemian king, Holy Roman emperor, and chief patron of Prague. Born to John of Luxembourg and Eliška, the sister of the last Premyslid king, Charles, originally christened Václav, was reared as John's successor; John had taken over the Bohemian crown in 1310. Charles was educated in the royal court in Paris and spent much of his adolescence observing rulers in Luxembourg and Tuscany. Charles ascended the throne in 1346, and during his reign he made Prague the seat of the Holy Roman Empire and one of Europe's most advanced cities. He also inspired several key sites through the country, including Prague's university (Universita Karlova), stone bridge (Karlův most), largest New Town park (Karlovo nám.), and the spa town of Karlovy Vary.

Master Jan Hus (1369 or 1370–1415) Religious reformer, university lecturer, and Czech nationalist symbol. Upset with what he thought was the misuse of power by Rome and the German clergy in Prague, Hus questioned the authority of the pope and called for the formation of a Bohemian National Church. From his stronghold at Bethlehem Chapel in Old Town, he declared that the powerful clergy should cede their property and influence to more of the people. In 1414, he was summoned to explain his views before the Ecclesiastic Council at Konstanz in Germany but was arrested on arrival. He was burned at the stake as a heretic on July 6, 1415, a day considered the precursor to the Hussite Wars and now commemorated as a Czech national holiday. His church lives on today in the faith called the Czech Brethren.

K. I. Dienzenhofer (1689–1751) High baroque architect and builder. He and his son, Kryštof, were responsible for some of the most striking Czech church designs. These include Prague's Church of St. Nicholas in Lesser Town, the Church of St. Nicholas in Old Town, and the Church of St. John of Nepomuk on Hradčany.

Bedřich Smetana (1824–84) Nationalist composer. After studying piano and musical theory in Prague, Smetana became one of Bohemia's most revered composers, famous for his fierce nationalism. His *Vltava* movement in the symphony *Má Vlast (My Country)* is performed on the opening night of the Prague Spring Music

Festival; it's also used as a score in Western movies and TV commercials. His opera *The Bartered Bride* takes a jaunty look at Czech farm life.

Antonín Dvořák (1841–1904) Neo-Romantic composer and head of Prague Conservatory. Dvořák is best known for his symphony *From the New World,* which was inspired by a tour of the United States. His opera about a girl trapped in a water world, *Rusalka,* remains an international favorite; it became a popular film in Europe, starring Slovak actress Magda Vašáryová.

Franz Kafka (1883–1924) Writer. Author of the depressing but universally read novel *The Trial,* Kafka was a German-Jewish Praguer who, for much of his adult life, worked in relative obscurity as a sad Prague insurance clerk. In works like *Metamorphosis, The Castle,* and *Amerika,* Kafka described surreal and suffocating worlds of confusion. Now many use the adjective *Kafkaesque* to mean "living in absurdity." Anyone who tries to apply for anything at a state office here will know that Kafka's world lives on.

Tomáš G. Masaryk (1850–1937) Philosopher, professor, and Czechoslovakia's first president. Educated in Vienna and Leipzig, Masaryk spent decades advocating Czech statehood. In 1915, he made a landmark speech in Geneva calling for the end of the Habsburg monarchy. He traveled to Washington, D.C., and received the backing of President Woodrow Wilson at the end of World War I for a sovereign republic of Czechs and Slovaks, which was founded in October 1918. During his nearly 17 years as president, Masaryk played the stoic grandfather of the new republic. He resigned for health reasons in 1935 and died less than 2 years later.

Klement Gottwald (1896–1953) Communist leader. He was named prime minister after his Communist Party won the highest vote count in the first postwar election in 1946. By February 1948, he had organized the complete Communist takeover of the government and eventually forced out President Edvard Beneš. When he became president in June 1948, the name of his hometown Zlín was changed to Gottwaldov (it changed backed to Zlín after the 1989 revolution). He was abhorred for his role in the 1950s show trials that purged hundreds.

Alexander Dubček (1921–92) Government leader. Though he's not a Czech, Dubček is a key figure in the history of Prague and the country. A Slovak Communist, he became the first secretary of the Communist Party in January 1968, presiding over the Prague Spring Reforms. After he was ousted in the August 1968 Soviet-led invasion, Dubček faded from view, only later to stand with Havel to declare the end of hard-line Communist rule in 1989. He returned to become speaker of Parliament after the Velvet Revolution but was killed in a dubious car accident in 1992.

Václav Havel (b. 1936) Author, dissident, ex-president. Absurdist playwright in the 1960s, Havel became a leading figure in the pro-democracy movement Charter 77 and the first president after leading the Velvet Revolution. See the box "From Prisoner to President: Václav Havel," p. 282.

Among other famous Czech ex-pats are Oscar-winning film director **Miloš Forman** *(Amadeus, The People vs. Larry Flynt)* and **Milan Kundera,** the author of *The Unbearable Lightness of Being* and other controversial works about 20th-century Czech life. Kundera is now a French citizen and bitterly refuses to make a public return to his homeland, after having left during the dark days of Communist "normalization."

Former tennis superstars **Ivan Lendl** and **Martina Navrátilová,** now of Greenwich, Connecticut, and Aspen, Colorado, hail from Ostrava and Řevnice, respectively. Two of the greatest stars in NHL ice hockey, **Jaromír Jágr** and **Dominik "The Dominator" Hašek,** have made millions playing in America, but both say they miss home and will move back. Supermodel and Wonderbra icon **Eva Herzigová** hails from the blue-collar northern Bohemian industrial berg of Litvínov—whose smokestacks are about as far removed as you can get from the catwalks where she works.

Mention should also be made of **Ivana Trump** (pronounced Ee-*vah*-nah), born in Gottwaldov (now known again as Zlín), east of Prague. The woman who first brought meaning to the term "Velvet Divorce" starred as a skier on the Czechoslovak National Team and as a model before going down the slippery slope with billionaire husband "The Donald" and then with her rebound mate Riccardo Mazzucchelli. Her first novel, *For Love Alone,* blatantly autobiographical, took place partly in Bohemia.

5 Prague's Architectural Mix

Look up. That's maybe the best advice we can give you. Prague's majestic mix of medieval, Renaissance, and Art Nouveau architecture shares one fairly universal element—the most elegant and well-appointed facades and fixtures aren't at eye level or even street level, but are on top floors and roofs. Hundreds of buildings are decorated with intricately carved cornices or ornamental balconies and friezes depicting mythical, religious, or heroic figures.

The grime of Prague pollution has been gradually stripped away, and each restored building reveals previously obscured details. What's interesting, though, is how visitors react to the grime. When people visit Paris or Venice and see dirty, crumbling buildings, they consider them quaint. When they see the same old, dirty, crumbling buildings in Prague, however, they point to the failure of Communism—not entirely fair. If you look at photos of Prague taken in 1900, you'll also see dirty, crumbling buildings.

The city's earliest extant forms are Romanesque, dating from 1100 to 1250. The long Gothic period followed from 1250 to 1530. You'll find many Gothic buildings in Staré Město. Plus Prague Castle's most visible superstructure, St. Vitus Cathedral, is a Gothic masterpiece—that

is, its older east-facing half (the cathedral's western sections exemplify Renaissance and neo-Gothic styles). From 1500 to the early 1600s, the Italian Renaissance style prevailed.

Many of the best-known structures are baroque and rococo, sharply tailored in the high Austrian style inspired by the Habsburgs of the 17th and 18th centuries.

Some of the most flamboyant buildings are Art Nouveau, popular from 1900 to 1918. The movement that swept across Europe developed with the Industrial Revolution. Innovative building materials—primarily steel and glass—opened endless possibilities for artistic embellishments. Architects abandoned traditional stone structures, built in a pseudo-historic style. Art Nouveau is characterized by rich, curvaceous ornamentation that seems sadly to have vanished in the push for functionalism later in the 20th century.

Several intriguing cubist designs from that era have also been hailed for their ingenuity. As an architectural style, cubism thrived in Bohemia, and you can find many examples in the neighborhood below Vyšehrad Park.

The late 20th century played havoc with Prague's architecture. Communists were partial to functionalism with virtually no character. Their buildings shed all decorative details. You shouldn't leave Prague before taking the metro out to Prosek to see the thousands of Communist-era flats, called "rabbit huts" even by their occupants. Created partly out of socialist dogma and partly out of economic necessity, these prefabricated a partment buildings *(paneláky)* were named after the concrete slabs used to build them. Cheap and unimaginatively designed, the apartment buildings are surrounded by a featureless world. Exteriors were made of plain, unadorned cement, and halls were lined with linoleum. The same room, balcony, and window design was stamped over and over.

But *panelák* living wasn't always viewed as a scourge. Unlike the larger, older apartments, *paneláks* had modern plumbing and heating and were once considered the politically correct way to live.

Two major post-Communist projects have already triggered a new debate among the progressives and the traditionalists. The Myslbek shopping/office complex on Na Příkopě near Wenceslas Square is the business district's first attempt at blending the new with the old in a functional yet elegant way. And the so-called Dancing Building on the embankment at the Rašínovo nábřeží has conservative tongues wagging. Its design strays from the 19th-century Empire classical houses lining the river, but in a most peculiar way. Controversial U.S. architect Frank Gehry, who designed the American Center in Paris, and New Wave designer Vlado Milunič have created a building that ironically pays tribute to the most classic of film dancing pairs: Fred Astaire and Ginger Rogers. Built as the Prague office of a Dutch insurance company, the building depicts the two intertwined in a spin above the Vltava. See "The Art of Prague's Architecture," in chapter 7, for more.

6 Recommended Films & Books

FILMS

Czech filmmaking has a long tradition. The Prague studios in the Barrandov Hills churned out glossy pre-Communist romantic comedies and period pieces rivaling the output of Paris, Berlin, and even Hollywood at the time.

While Czech literature and music have carved their places in classical culture, the country's films and their directors have collected the widest praise in the mid– to late 20th century. Cunning, melancholy views of Bohemian life (before the Soviets moved in for a few decades) were captured by some of the finest filmmakers in the era known as the "Czech New Wave" of the 1960s.

Directors Jiří Menzel and Miloš Forman were in the vanguard. An easy-to-find example of this period's work (with English subtitles) is Menzel's Oscar-winning *Closely Watched Trains,* a snapshot of the odd routine at a rural Czech train station.

Forman made his splash with a quirky look at a night in the life of a town trying to have fun despite itself. *The Fireman's Ball* shows Forman's true mastery as he captures the essence of being stone-bored in a gray world, yet he still makes it strangely intriguing. Of course, this was made before Forman emigrated to the big budgets of Hollywood and first shocked Americans with *Hair.* He then directed the Oscar-winning *One Flew Over the Cuckoo's Nest.* For *Amadeus,* Forman sought authenticity, so he received special permission from the Communists to return to Prague; while filming, he brought back to life the original Estates' Theater (Stavovské divadlo), where Mozart first performed. Forman also consulted a friend, then-President Václav Havel, before choosing Courtney Love as the pornographer's wife in the Oscar-nominated *The People vs. Larry Flynt.* Havel loved the choice but refused to attend a private 1996 screening in Prague along with Flynt himself.

Czech-based directors after the New Wave mostly disappeared from view, but one stunningly brave film was made in 1970, as the repressive post-invasion period known as "normalization" began its long, cold freeze of talent. In *The Ear (Ucho)*, director Karel Kachyňa presents the anguished story of a man trapped in an apartment wired for sound, subject to the Communist leaders' obsession and paranoia with Moscow. That *The Ear* was made in the political environment of the time was astounding. That it was quickly banned wasn't. Fortunately, local TV has dusted off copies from the archives, and it has begun playing to art-house audiences again.

But maybe a new Czech wave has begun. The father-and-son team of Zdeněk and Jan Svěrák won the Best Foreign Film Oscar in 1997 for *Kolja,* the bittersweet tale of an abandoned Russian boy grudgingly adopted by an aging Czech bachelor on the cusp of the 1989 revolution. After a previous Oscar nomination for the 1992 *Elementary School (Obecná škola),* the 30-something director Jan and his actor father are making an industry out of golden reflections about Czech life.

Prague has become a popular location for major motion pictures, in spite of itself. Producer/actor Tom Cruise and director Brian De Palma chose it for the stunning night shots around Charles Bridge in the early scenes of *Mission: Impossible.* During shooting, a verbal brawl broke out with Czech officials, who jacked up the rent for use of the riverside palace that acts as the American Embassy in the film (the palace is actually claimed by the von Liechtenstein family). *Immortal Beloved,* a story of Beethoven, made use of Prague's timeless streets (shooting around the graffiti).

Finally, *The Beautician and the Beast,* starring "Bond" hunk Timothy Dalton and nasal-siren Fran Drescher, uses Prague as a mythical East European capital invaded by a Brooklyn hairdresser (who makes pretty good use of her Frommer's guidebook while traveling through faux-Prague).

Still, the film about Prague probably most familiar to American audiences is *The Unbearable Lightness of Being,* based on the book by émigré author Milan Kundera. Set in the days surrounding the Soviet invasion, the story draws on the psychology of three Czechs who can't escape their personal obsessions while the political world outside collapses around them. Many Czechs find the film disturbing, some because it hits home, others because they say it portrays a Western stereotype.

BOOKS

Any discussion of Czech literature with visiting foreigners usually begins with Milan Kundera. Reviled among many Czechs who didn't emigrate, Kundera creates a visceral, personal sense of the world he chose to leave in the 1970s for the freedom of Paris. In *The Unbearable Lightness of Being,* the anguish over escaping the Soviet-occupied Prague he loves tears the libidinous protagonist Dr. Tomáš in the same way the love for his wife and the lust for his lover does. More Czech post-normalization angst can be found in *The Book of Laughter and Forgetting* and *Laughable Loves.* Kundera's biting satire of Stalinist purges in the 1950s *The Joke,* however, is regarded by Czech critics as his best work.

Arnošt Lustig, a survivor of the Nazi-era Terezín concentration camp and author of many works, including *Street of Lost Brothers,* shared the 1991 *Publishers Weekly* Award for best literary work with John Updike and Norman Mailer. In

1995, he became the editor of the Czech edition of *Playboy.*

The best work of renowned Ivan Klíma, also a survivor of Terezín, is translated as *Judge on Trial,* a study of justice and the death penalty.

Jaroslav Hašek wrote the Czech harbinger to *Forrest Gump* in *The Good Soldier švejk,* a post–World War I satire about a simpleton soldier who wreaks havoc in the Austro-Hungarian army during the war.

Bohumil Hrabal, noted for writing about the Czech Everyman and maybe the country's all-time favorite author, died in early 1997 when he fell (so they said officially) out of a fifth-story window while trying to feed pigeons. His death was eerily similar to the fate of a character in one of his stories. He had two internationally acclaimed hits: *Closely Watched Trains* (also translated as *Closely Observed Trains,* on which the Menzel film was based), and *I Served the King of England.* When then-President Bill Clinton visited Prague in 1994, he asked to have a beer with Hrabal in the author's favorite Old Town haunt, the pub U Zlatého tygra (At the Golden Tiger). Clinton may have gotten more than he bargained for, as the gruff but lovable Hrabal, who turned 80 that year, lectured the president on his views of the world.

No reading list would be complete without reference to Franz Kafka, Prague's most famous novelist, who wrote his originals in his native German. *The Collected Novels of Franz Kafka,* which includes *The Castle* and *The Trial,* binds his most claustrophobic works into a single volume.

If it's contemporary philosophy you want, there is, of course, the philosopher ex-president. Václav Havel's heralded dissident essay, "The Power of the Powerless," explained how the lethargic masses were allowing their complacency with Communism to sap their souls. His "Letters to Olga," written to his wife while in prison in the 1980s, takes you into his cell and his view of a moral world. Available are two solid English-translated compilations of his dissident writings: *Living in Truth* and *Open Letters. Disturbing the Peace* is an autobiographical meditation on childhood, the events of 1968, and Havel's involvement with Charter 77. His first recollections about entering politics are in "Summer Meditations," a long essay written during a vacation.

While he hasn't had much time to write since his presidency, Havel says that his speeches given around the world each continue a dialogue about morality in politics. If you read the anthology of his presidential speeches, *Toward a Civil Society,* you'll find it clear that Havel hasn't stopped being the dissident. However, now his target is incompetence and corruption in politics and society, including in democracies.

Madeleine Albright's father, diplomat Dr. Josef Koerbel, wrote a definitive contemporary history of his homeland in his final book, *Twentieth Century Czechoslovakia,* before his death in 1977. More than an academic study, it reads as a personal memoir of Prague's chaotic events, many of which he witnessed.

Finally, for an epic intellectual tour of the long, colorful, and often tragic history of the city, try the 1997 release of *Prague in Black and Gold* by native son and Yale literature professor Peter Demetz.

Appendix B:
Useful Terms & Phrases

Although Czech is a very difficult language to master, you should at least make an attempt to learn a few phrases. Czechs will appreciate the effort and will be more willing to help you out.

1 Basic Phrases & Vocabulary

CZECH ALPHABET
There are 32 vowels and consonants in the Czech alphabet, and most of the consonants are pronounced about as they are in English. Accent marks over vowels lengthen the sound of the vowel, as does the *kroužek,* or little circle "8," which appears only over "o" and "u."

A, a f*a*ther
B, b *b*oy
C, c ge*ts*
Č, č *ch*oice
D, d *d*ay
Ď, ď *Di*or
E, e n*e*ver
F, f *f*ood
G, g *g*oal
H, h un*h*and
Ch, ch Lo*ch* Lomond
I, i n*ee*d
J, j *y*es
K, k *k*ey
L, l *l*ord
M, m *m*ama

N, n *n*o
Ň, ň Ta*ny*a
O, o *aw*ful
P, p *p*en
R, r slightly trilled *r*
Ř, ř slightly trilled *r* + *zh* as in P*er*sian
S, s *s*eat
Š, š cru*sh*
T, t *t*oo
Ť, ť no*t y*et
U, u r*oo*m
V, v *v*ery
W, w *v*ague
Y, y funn*y*
Z, z *z*ebra
Ž, ž a*z*ure, plea*s*ure

CZECH VOCABULARY
EVERYDAY EXPRESSIONS

English	Czech	Pronunciation
Hello	**Dobrý den**	*doh*-bree den
Good morning	**Dobré jitro**	*doh*-breh *yee*-troh
Good evening	**Dobrý večer**	*doh*-bree *veh*-chair
How are you?	**Jak se máte?**	*yahk* seh *mah*-teh
Very well	**Velmi dobře**	*vel*-mee *doh*-brsheh
Thank you	**Děkuji vám**	*dyek*-ooee vahm
You're welcome	**Prosím**	*proh*-seem
Please	**Prosím**	*proh*-seem
Yes	**Ano**	*ah*-no

English	Czech	Pronunciation
No	**Ne**	*neh*
Excuse me	**Promiňte**	*proh*-min-teh
How much does it cost?	**Kolik to stojí?**	*koh*-leek taw *stoh*-ee
I don't understand.	**Nerozumím.**	*neh*-roh-zoo-meem
Just a moment.	**Moment, prosím.**	*moh*-ment, *proh*-seem
Good-bye	**Na shledanou**	*nah* skleh-dah-noh-oo

Traveling

Where is the . . . ?	**Kde je . . . ?**	*gde* yeh . . .
bus station	**autobusové nádraží**	*au*-toh-boos-oh-veh *nah*-drah-zhee
train station	**nádraží**	*nah*-drah-zhee
airport	**letiště**	*leh*-tyish-tyeh
baggage check	**úschovna zavazadel**	*oo*-skohv-nah *zah*-vahz-ah-del
Where can I find a taxi?	**Kde najdu taxi?**	*gde nai*-doo *tahks*-eh
Where can I find a gas station?	**Kde najdu benzínovou pumpu?**	*gde nai*-doo *ben*-zeen-oh-voh *poomp*-oo
How much is gas?	**Kolik stojí benzín?**	*koh*-leek *stoh*-yee *ben*-zeen
Please fill the tank.	**Naplňte mi nádrž, prosím.**	*nah*-puln-teh mee *nah*-durzh, *proh*-seem
How much is the fare?	**Kolik je jízdné?**	*koh*-leek yeh yeesd-neh
I am going to . . .	**Pojedu do . . .**	*poh*-yeh-doo doh . . .
One-way ticket	**Jízdenka**	*yeez*-den-kah
Round-trip ticket	**Zpáteční jízdenka**	*zpah*-tech-nee *jeez*-den-kah
Car-rental office	**Půjčovna aut**	*poo*-eech-awv-nah ah-oot

Accommodations

I'm looking for . . .	**Hledám . . .**	*hleh*-dahm . . .
a hotel	**hotel**	*hoh*-tel
a youth hostel	**studentskou ubytovnu**	*stoo*-dent-skoh *oo*-beet-ohv-noo
I am staying . . .	**Zůstanu . . .**	*zoo*-stah-noo . . .
a few days	**několik dnů**	*nyeh*-koh-leek dnoo
2 weeks	**dva týdny**	dvah tid-*neh*
a month	**jeden měsíc**	*yeh*-den *myeh*-seets
I have a reservation.	**Mám zamluvený nocleh.**	mahm *zah*-mloo-veh-ni *nohts*-leh
My name is . . .	**Jmenuji se . . .**	*meh*-noo-yee seh . . .
Do you have a room . . . ?	**Máte pokoj . . . ?**	*mah*-teh *poh*-koy . . .
for tonight	**na dnešek**	*nah* dneh-sheck

English	Czech	Pronunciation
for 3 nights	na tři dny	*nah* trshee dnee
for a week	na týden	*nah* tee-den
I would like . . .	Chci . . .	khtsee . . .
a single	jednolůžkový pokoj	*jed*-noh-loosh-koh-vee *poh*-koy
a double	dvojlůžkový pokoj	*dvoy*-loosh-koh-vee *poh*-koy
I want a room . . .	Chci pokoj . . .	khtsee *poh*-koy . . .
with a bathroom	s koupelnou	*skoh*-pehl-noh
without a bathroom	bez koupelny	*behz* koh-pehl-nee
with a shower	se sprchou	*seh* spur-choh
without a shower	bez sprchy	*bez* sprech-eh
with a view	s pohledem	*spoh*-hlehd-ehm
How much is the room?	Kolik stojí pokoj?	*koh*-leek *stoh*-yee *paw*-koy
with breakfast?	se snídaní?	*seh* snee-dan-nyee
May I see the room?	Mohu vidět ten pokoj?	*moh*-hoo *vee*-dyet ten *paw*-koy
The key	Klíč	kleech
The bill, please.	Dejte mi účet, prosím.	*day*-teh mee *oo*-cheht, *praw*-seem

GETTING AROUND

I'm looking for . . .	Hledám . . .	*hleh*-dahm . . .
a bank	banku	*bahnk*-oo
the church	kostel	*kohs*-tell
the city center	centrum	*tsent*-room
the museum	muzeum	*moo*-zeh-oom
a pharmacy	lékárnu	*lek*-ahr-noo
the park	park	pahrk
the theater	divadlo	*dee*-vahd-loh
the tourist office	cestovní kancelář	*tses*-tohv-nee *kahn*-tseh-larsh
the embassy	velvyslanectví	*vehl*-vee-slahn-ets-tvee
Where is the nearest telephone?	Kde je nejbližší telefon?	gde yeh *nay*-bleesh-ee *tel*-oh-fohn
I would like to buy . . .	Chci koupit . . .	khtsee *koh*-peet . . .
a stamp	známku	*znahm*-koo
a postcard	pohlednici	*poh*-hlehd-nit-seh
a map	mapu	*mahp*-oo

Signs

No Trespassing	Cizím vstup zakázán	No Smoking	Kouření zakázáno
No Parking	Neparkovat	Arrivals	Příjezd/Přílet
Entrance	Vchod	Departures	Odjezd/Odlet
Exit	Východ	Toilets	Toalety

| Information **Informace** | | Danger **Pozor, nebezpečí** |

Numbers

1	**jeden** (*yeh*-den)	16	**šestnáct** (*shest*-nahtst)
2	**dva** (dvah)	17	**sedmnáct** (*seh*-doom-nahtst)
3	**tři** (trzhee)	18	**osmnáct** (*aw*-soom-nahtst)
4	**čtyři** (*chtee*-rshee)	19	**devatenáct** (*deh*-vah-teh-nahtst)
5	**pět** (pyet)	20	**dvacet** (*dvah*-tset)
6	**šest** (shest)	30	**třicet** (*trshee*-tset)
7	**sedm** (*seh*-duhm)	40	**čtyřicet** (*chti*-rshee-tset)
8	**osm** (*aw*-suhm)	50	**padesát** (*pah*-deh-saht)
9	**devět** (*deh*-vyet)	60	**šedesát** (*she*-deh-saht)
10	**deset** (*deh*-set)	70	**sedmdesát** (*seh*-duhm-deh-saht)
11	**jedenáct** (*yeh*-deh-nahtst)	80	**osmdesát** (*aw*-suhm-deh-saht)
12	**dvanáct** (*dvah*-nahtst)	90	**devadesát** (*deh*-vah-deh-saht)
13	**třináct** (*trshee*-nahtst)	100	**sto** (staw)
14	**čtrnáct** (*chtur*-nahtst)	500	**pět set** (*pyet* set)
15	**patnáct** (*paht*-nahtst)	1,000	**tisíc** (tyee-seets)

Dining

Restaurant	**Restaurace**	*rehs*-tow-rah-tseh
Breakfast	**Snídaně**	*snee*-dah-nyeh
Lunch	**Oběd**	*oh*-byed
Dinner	**Večeře**	*veh*-chair-sheh
A table for two, please. (Lit.: There are two of us.)	**Jsme dva.**	*ees*-meh dvah
Waiter	**Číšník**	*cheess*-neek
Waitress	**Servírka**	ser-*veer*-ka
I would like . . .	**Chci . . .**	khtsee . . .
a menu	**jídelní lístek**	*yee*-del-nee *lees*-teck
a fork	**vidličku**	*veed*-leech-koo
a knife	**nůž**	noosh
a spoon	**lžičku**	lu-*shich*-koo
a napkin	**ubrousek**	*oo*-broh-seck
a glass (of water)	**skleničku (vody)**	*sklehn*-ich-koo (vod-*dee*)
the check, please	**účet, prosím**	*oo*-cheht, *proh*-seem
Is the tip included?	**Je v tom zahrnuto spropitné?**	yeh *ftohm*-zah *hur*-noo-toh *sproh*-peet-neh

2 Menu Terms

GENERAL

Soup	**Polévka**	*poh*-lehv-kah
Eggs	**Vejce**	*vayts*-eh

Meat	**Maso**	*mahs*-oh
Fish	**Ryba**	*ree*-bah
Vegetables	**Zelenina**	*zehl*-eh-nee-nah
Fruit	**Ovoce**	*oh*-voh-tseh
Desserts	**Moučníky**	*mohch*-nee-kee
Beverages	**Nápoje**	*nah*-poy-yeh
Salt	**Sůl**	sool
Pepper	**Pepř**	*peh*-psh
Mayonnaise	**Majonéza**	*mai*-o-neza
Mustard	**Hořčice**	*hohrsh*-chee-tseh
Vinegar	**Ocet**	*oh*-tseht
Oil	**Olej**	*oh*-lay
Sugar	**Cukr**	*tsoo*-ker
Tea	**Čaj**	chye
Coffee	**Káva**	*kah*-vah
Bread	**Chléb**	khlehb
Butter	**Máslo**	*mahs*-loh
Wine	**Víno**	*vee*-noh
Fried	**Smažený**	*smah*-sheh-nee
Roasted	**Pečený**	*pech*-eh-nee
Boiled	**Vařený**	*vah*-rsheh-nee
Grilled	**Grilovaný**	*gree*-loh-vah-nee

SOUP

Potato	**Bramborová**	Tomato	**Rajská**
Lentil	**Čočková**	Chicken	**Slepičí**
Goulash	**Gulášová**	Vegetable	**Zeleninová**

MEAT

Steak	**Biftek**	Sausage	**Klobása**
Goulash	**Guláš**	Rabbit	**Králík**
Beef	**Hovězí**	Mutton	**Skopové**
Liver	**Játra**	Veal	**Telecí**
Lamb	**Jehněčí**	Veal Cutlet	**Telecí kotleta**
Duck	**Kachna**	Pork	**Vepřové**

FISH

Carp	**Kapr**	Pike	**Štika**
Caviar	**Kaviár**	Cod	**Treska**
Fish Filet	**Rybí filé**	Eel	**Úhoř**
Herring	**Sleď**	Oysters	**ústřice**

EGGS

Scrambled Eggs   **Míchaná vejce**

Fried Eggs   **Smažená vejce**

Boiled Eggs   **Vařená vejce**

Soft-boiled Eggs   **Vejce naměkko**

Bacon and Eggs   **Vejce se slaninou**

Ham and Eggs   **Vejce se šunkou**

SALAD

Bean Salad   **Fazolový salát**

Mixed Green Salad   **Hlávkový salát**

Cucumber Salad   **Okurkový salát**

Beet Salad   **Salát z červené řepy**

VEGETABLES

Potatoes   **Brambory**

Celery   **Celer**

Asparagus   **Chřest**

Onions   **Cibule**

Mushrooms   **Houby**

Cauliflower   **Květák**

Carrots   **Mrkev**

Peppers   **Paprika**

Tomatoes   **Rajská jablíčka**

Cabbage   **Zelí**

DESSERT

Cake   **Koláč**

Cookies   **Cukroví**

Chocolate Ice Cream   **Čokoládová zmrzlina**

Apple Strudel   **Jablkový závin**

Pancakes   **Palačinky**

Vanilla Ice Cream   **Vanilková zmrzlina**

FRUIT

Lemon   **Citrón**

Pear   **Hruška**

Apple   **Jablko**

Plum   **Švestka**

BEVERAGES

Tea   **Čaj**

Coffee   **Káva**

Milk   **Mléko**

Wine   **Víno**

Red   **Červené**

White   **Bílé**

Water   **Voda**

Index

See also Accommodations and Restaurant indexes, below.

it's better on the train!

Europe Your Way

For over 50 years, we've been putting people like you on the right track. From railpasses to simple point-to-point tickets, experience the real Europe with Rail Europe.

It's easy getting around Europe

Relaxing, convenient and an outstanding value, no other form of transportation offers you so much of Europe for so little. It's how Europeans travel!

Get on track before you go

Designed exclusively for North American travelers, our passes and tickets must be purchased before you leave home (they're not available in Europe). So buy before you go.

Make Tracks with Frommer's...
a great tool for planning your European rail trip!

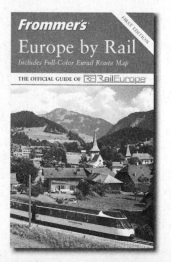

Contact your travel agent or RailEurope.

1-877-272-RAIL
www.raileurope.com

A Division of Rail Europe Group

THE NEW TRAVELOCITY GUARANTEE

EVERYTHING YOU BOOK WILL BE RIGHT, OR WE'LL WORK WITH OUR TRAVEL PARTNERS TO MAKE IT RIGHT, RIGHT AWAY.

*To drive home the point,
we're going to use the word "right" in every single sentence.*

Let's get right to it. Right to the meat! Only Travelocity guarantees everything about your booking will be right, or we'll work with our travel partners to make it right, right away. Right on!

Here's a picture taken smack dab right in the middle of Antigua, where the guarantee also covers you.

The guarantee covers all but one of the items pictured to the right.

Now, you may be thinking, "Yeah, right, I'm so sure." That's OK; you have the right to remain skeptical. That is until we mention help is always right around the corner. Call us right off the bat, knowing that our customer service reps are there for you 24/7. Righting wrongs. Left and right.

For example, what if the ocean view you booked actually looks out at a downright ugly parking lot? You'd be right to call – we're there for you. And no one in their right mind would be pleased to learn the rental car place has closed and left them stranded. Call Travelocity and we'll help get you back on the right track.

Now if you're guessing there are some things we can't control, like the weather, well you're right. But we can help you with most things – to get all the details in righting,* visit **travelocity.com/guarantee**.

*Sorry, spelling things right is one of the few things not covered under the guarantee.

I'd give my right arm for a guarantee like this, although I'm glad I don't have to.

travelocity
You'll never roam alone.

©2005 Travelocity.com LP. LST # 2065327-50